COPLAND

Aaron Copland, 1972.
Drawing by Marcos Blahove.

COPLAND

SINCE 1943

by AARON COPLAND

and VIVIAN PERLIS

St. Martin's Griffin

NEW YORK

•

Library of Congress Cataloging-in-Publication Data

Copland, Aaron, 1900-1990.
  Copland: since 1943 / Aaron Copland and Vivian Perlis.
    p. cm.
  ISBN 0-312-05066-6
  1. Copland, Aaron. 1900-1990. 2. Composers—United States—
Biography.   I. Perlis, Vivian. II. Title.
ML410.C756A3 1990
780'.92—dc20
[B]   90-36888
                                                                              CIP
                                                                              MN

First St. Martin's Griffin Edition: May 1999

10 9 8 7 6 5 4 3 2 1

To Serge Koussevitzky

For his devotion to American music.

Contents

CONTENTS

Acknowledgments

Those who were "first and foremost" in *Copland: 1900 Through 1942* continue to be so in *Copland: Since 1943*. They deserve an extra hearty round of thanks, not only for all they have done in practical and supportive ways, but for the duration of their devotion: Sanford Perlis, Janice Fournier, and David Walker. As previously, we salute Minna Daniel, Ellis J. Freedman, and William Schuman for their friendship and valued advice. We express gratitude to Robert Lantz and Joy Harris of the Lantz Office, who have been associated with the Copland book project from its inception.

A book project goes through many stages. Although the traditional method of gathering (and shuffling) information on three-by-five cards has all but disappeared thanks to the wonders of the computer, the transformation of research materials into a book manuscript is still a major challenge. That metamorphosis was made possible by a Guggenheim Fellowship in 1987–1988 for Vivian Perlis. Therefore, we acknowledge with gratitude the John Simon Guggenheim Foundation.

Readers and researchers who helped shape the manuscript through its revisions are Ann Browning, Leonard Burkat, Ron Caltabiano, Walter Chmielewski, Janice Fournier, Cynthia Schmidt, and David Walker. Our editors at St. Martin's Press, Jesse Cohen and Jared Kieling, gave invaluable editorial advice. Jesse Cohen guided the material with great care and expertise through the next stage—from manuscript to published book. In the fast-changing world of publishing, working again with Amelie Littell at St. Martin's Press has been a special pleasure. She and design director Glen Edelstein have been responsible for the complex visual aspects of this volume's production.

Visits to the Library of Congress for research were enjoyable as well as necessary, due to the cooperation and assistance of scholars Gillian Anderson, Geraldine Ostrove, Samuel Brylawski, and Wynn Mathias. Wayne

Shirley, Specialist in American Music at the Music Division, deserves particular mention for the generous sharing of his extraordinary knowledge and talents. In addition to the Library of Congress, we thank the Yale Music Library and Sterling Memorial Library, and the Music and Dance Divisions of the Lincoln Center Library for the Performing Arts.

Many queries were answered patiently by Sylvia Goldstein and David Huntley of Boosey & Hawkes, Inc. We recall with appreciation the hospitality of Daniel R. Gustin, Richard Ortner, and others at the Tanglewood Music Center. Other organizations that offered assistance are The American Academy and Institute of Arts and Letters, Brown University, the Cleveland Orchestra Library, the Lincoln Center Archives, Fisk University (Carl Van Vechten Archive), and the Whiteman Archive, Williams College.

Interviews of Copland's friends and colleagues in *Copland: Since 1943* have, in some cases, been shortened for publication, and some interviewees included in the first volume are occasionally quoted in volume two. All interviews will be preserved in their entirety to become an extensive oral history on Copland for the use of scholars and historians in the future. We are grateful to those who gave of their time, thoughts, and memories to *Copland: Since 1943:* Carroll Baker, Arthur Berger, Arvin Brown, Leonard Burkat, William Conroy, Merce Cunningham, Phyllis Curtin, Mario Davidovsky, David Del Tredici, Jacob Druckman, Verna Fine, Lukas Foss, Jack Garfein, Alberto Ginastera, Sylvia Goldstein, Benny Goodman, Martha Graham, Erick Hawkins, Alice Howland, Erik Johns, Harry Kraut, Pearl Lang, Roger Levey, William Masselos, Paul Moor, May O'Donnell, Julián Orbón, Tod Perry, Stuart Pope, Mel Powell, Phillip Ramey, Ned Rorem, Howard Shanet, Murry Sidlin, Leo Smit, Stanley Sussman, David Walker, and William Warfield.

Many individuals were helpful in many and individual ways. Among them are William Austin, Leonard Bernstein, Victor Basso, Helen and Elliott Carter, Robert Cornell, David Diamond, Charles Harmon, Lucille J. (Mrs. Gurney) Kennedy, John Kirkpatrick, Cynthia Krupat, Lawrence Morton, Petey Neyland, Michael O'Connor, Vincent Plush, Marta Robertson, Julia Smith, John Solum, Virgil Thomson, Eldridge Walker, and Keith Wilson.

The continuing encouragement and support of so many friends and colleagues in the world of music has sustained the authors and made it possible for them to see this project through to its conclusion.

Aaron Copland and Vivian Perlis

Preface

The second volume of Copland's autobiography begins in 1943, at a time when America was deeply involved in the war. Anxious to do his part, but too old for active service, Copland was serving on music committees for the State Department and composing patriotic music. *Fanfare for the Common Man* and *Lincoln Portrait* had been written and performed in 1942, and a contract was accepted to compose a score for a pro-Russian film. However, by 1943, Copland was yearning for both the end of the war and new musical experiences. One such opportunity was a commission already in hand: music for a ballet by Martha Graham, destined to become the composer's best known and most popular work, *Appalachian Spring*. Little did Copland know that this was only the beginning of even greater success and recognition. Some of his most significant works were to follow, as well as a rewarding new career as a conductor. *Copland: Since 1943* chronicles these rich and exciting decades.

In *Copland: 1900 Through 1942*, the reader was introduced to the young man from Brooklyn who became an aspiring composer, studying in Paris in the twenties with Nadia Boulanger and returning to the States as the protégé of Serge Koussevitzky. Volume one told the story of Copland's early years and followed his increasing success as the most promising young American composer on the scene. The reader came to know Copland's family, friends, and colleagues. In volume two, these people continue to be the core of Copland's life. They include: Nadia Boulanger in France; Serge Koussevitzky in Boston and Tanglewood; Harold Clurman, Copland's roommate in Paris and his lifelong friend; Claire Reis, executive director of the League of Composers; Minna Lederman, editor of *Modern Music* in New York; Carlos Chávez in Mexico; colleagues William Schuman, David Diamond, Arthur Berger, and Marc Blitzstein; and the young Leonard Bernstein, Lukas Foss, and Irving Fine, with whom friendships were strengthened during the opening years of the Music Center at Tanglewood, 1940–1942.

Copland: Since 1943 follows the format established in the first volume. The reader can readily distinguish between Copland's text in the first person and my interludes, which are in the third. Copland's material is drawn from interviews made for the Yale project, Oral History, American Music in 1975 and 1976, and from an extensive collection of earlier writings and lectures. Interviews with colleagues and friends appear at appropriate places in the text.

In a "Note to the Reader" at the beginning of the first volume, Copland stated his aim in writing an autobiography: "My idea was not to present a personal memoir so much as to tell the story of American music as I experienced it in my lifetime." Perhaps it is significant that Copland's life began with the birth of the century in 1900; it has moved through dramatic change and been witness to violent wars and times of peace, amazing scientific and technological achievements, and extraordinary creations in the arts. Copland's music holds the sounds of twentieth-century America within it; his autobiography tells the story of how it all came to be.

Vivian Perlis

COPLAND

Introduction
Music in Wartime
America

When President Franklin D. Roosevelt changed from The New Deal to a wartime economy, the Great Depression was over. People moved off the bread lines into the factories. World War II was a war of just causes, and patriotism ran high: It was not long before patriotism and prosperity went hand in hand. A feeling of exhilaration and excitement filled the air as the country began to have a new look. Suddenly, all sorts of people were in uniform, feeling special: young men in active service (the few *not* in uniform lived in a state of shame); older men in the Civil Defense to conduct air raids and blackouts; women in the WACS or Nurses Corps; and even the youngest "Victory Girls," who baked cookies with rationed sugar for servicemen—all were in uniform.

From 1941 to 1945, war was a national preoccupation and a unifying force stronger than any the country had ever experienced. Everyone wanted to do his share for the war effort; the result was a communal solidarity that has been compared to the days of the American frontier.[1] The Depression and the war have been viewed by social scientists and educators as "rich opportunities to help create a true collective democracy in the United States."[2] Across the nation, families grew Victory Gardens and bought war bonds, and in the evenings, everyone gathered around the radio for the latest war news. When President Roosevelt's Fireside Chats were broadcast from the White House, the sound of his voice was so inspiring that it is still recalled by those who heard it so many years ago.

At first, there was an air of unreality about the war, given the fact that the economy was booming and the country itself seemed in no physical danger. Many Americans felt guilty to be living so well while there was killing and destruction abroad, their natural humane impulses in conflict with feelings of satisfaction in punishing the Germans and Japanese. In his excellent book *Culture as History*, Warren I. Susman describes the change experienced in the psyche of the American people after the "Age of Insecurity" of the Depression: "An age of shame and fear had passed into history; it was somehow to be followed by an age that frankly thought of itself as an age of anxiety. . . ."[3] As the war dragged on, and the bloodshed and killing escalated, patriotic activity was the most effective means of dealing with the rising waves of uncertainty that threatened to destroy morale. Recognizing this, the Office of War Information devised radio programs, posters, and slogans ("The War Against Fascism"; "Loose Lips Sink Ships") to make the people feel that what they did or said really counted.

The sudden production boost that catapulted farmers, factory workers, and businessmen into prosperity did nothing to help creative artists: Art galleries, subsidized concerts, theaters, and publications devoted to the arts folded, and recording companies and instrument makers struggled to survive. Some did so by adapting to war-related needs: The Steinway Company, for example, kept their factory open by making coffins for the State Department.[4] The public had little appetite for productions of ballet, opera, and symphonic music. Literary critic and historian Edmund Wilson wrote in his memoirs:

> I felt pleasant when I went to the opera, and sat in my excellent seat down front before the performance began. I thought, this is probably all wrong—is there an element of sadism in my satisfaction: to sit peaceful, well fed, and secure . . . when the performance began, I realized that it was impossible to enjoy the masterpieces of musical art in the teeth of what was happening in Europe.[5]

If the immediate effect of the war on the arts was little short of disastrous, in the long run, the displacement of European artists would result in profound changes. Within a few years in the late thirties and early forties, the best of Europe's creative talent landed on American shores, causing a dramatic shift in the focus of world culture. Many of the greatest artistic figures of the century left Europe, their lives totally disrupted in mid-career. Those who came early were able to bring families and belongings along; others stayed in Europe too long and had to flee quickly, leaving everything behind. Conductors, opera singers, performers, and composers—Paul Hindemith, Stefan Wolpe, Darius Milhaud, Kurt Weill—all came. Some were Jewish, others were married to Jews, and still others were connected with activities considered subversive by the Nazis. Many chose to wait out the war in Pacific Palisades, California, an area reminiscent of the Riviera. There one could find Stravinsky, Schoenberg, Otto Klemperer, Nadia Boulanger, Heinrich Mann, and Bertolt Brecht. When the war

2

was over, leaving much of Europe in ruin, most of these artists stayed on. Whether America gained or lost from such a strong dose of Europeanization, and what the effects were on individual creative figures, are matters yet to be fully explored by historians.[6]

Few artists, whether native or émigré, were able to pursue their chosen careers as they had prior to the war. Literature and drama took a backseat to *Life* magazine, the fine arts to Bill Mauldin's "Up Front" cartoons, and concert music to Kate Smith's ubiquitous "God Bless America." The contemporary arts, struggling in the best of times, barely survived. It was particularly difficult for those concerned with so esoteric an activity as modern music to find a connection to the war effort. Composers competed vigorously for the few commissions offered for patriotic works, and promoters tried to convince the public that contemporary music could stimulate free debate, thereby promoting democracy.

One series of concerts, the Town Hall Music Forum, declared in its brochure: "It becomes more important than ever before to encourage the writing, the hearing, and the discussion of new music, for a major part of our battle is to prove that the democracies are *not* decadent. We believe this can best be shown through a display of the vitality of that all important segment of democratic society—the free artist." A major event of the 1943 season was "An Aaron Copland Evening," featuring a concert followed by a forum, in which the audience was encouraged to "fire away with bouquets or brickbats" at the composer.[7]

Other musical organizations adapted themselves to the war as best they could. The League of Composers offered to make a survey of the abilities and skills of composers of draft age for the Army and Navy Recreation Commission in Washington, and they sponsored a program by composers already in the service. Claire Reis, the indomitable executive director of the League, formed a committee to produce two seasons of "Wartime Concerts for Soldiers and Sailors" on the mall in New York's Central Park and in Prospect Park in Brooklyn. A benefit for Russian War Relief was organized, and, at Mrs. Reis' urging, Copland wrote to Prokofiev requesting new works by Russian composers (a response was not received). The League commissioned a series of eighteen short works on wartime subjects, which Artur Rodzinski, conductor of the New York Philharmonic, agreed to play as a patriotic gesture at the opening of each program. Many of the commissioned composers derived their pieces from personal experiences; for example, *The Anxious Bugler* by John Alden Carpenter and *In Memoriam—The Colored Soldiers Who Died for Democracy* by William Grant

Still. One of the most poignant was Bohuslav Martinů's *Memorial to Lidice,* in honor of the Czechoslovakian town destroyed by the Germans. Even Charles Ives, who had not composed for many years, made his contribution by arranging his World War I song "He Is There" for chorus as "War Song March: They Are There."[8]

The League's publication, *Modern Music,* featured war-related articles, such as Sessions' "Artists and This War" (1942) and Milhaud's "Music and Politics" (1944). One column, "By Cable to *Modern Music* from Moscow," included information about Russian composers and activities, with a great deal of space devoted to Kabalevsky, Miaskovsky, Shostakovich, and Prokofiev. Editor Minna Lederman printed correspondence from servicemen regularly. Most reviews were of patriotic music, such as William Schuman's "A Free Song," Copland's *Lincoln Portrait,* and Roy Harris' *Fifth Symphony* (dedicated to the U.S.S.R.). Minna Lederman wrote to Copland (22 September 1944), "News from Europe is all people want right now. It makes all the difference between being successful or just visibly fading out."

Popular culture, always a barometer of the mood of a people, followed the usual pattern in wartime, adding patriotic songs to the ubiquitous love ballads and nonsense tunes. Irving Berlin's "This Is the Army" came closest in popularity to World War I's "Over There." The airwaves reverberated with the Andrews Sisters' renditions of "The Boogie Woogie Bugle Boy of Company B," "Don't Give Up the Ship," and "The White Cliffs of Dover." Performers were enormously popular and very much in demand. Many were sponsored by the U.S.O. and often went to the camps and hospitals under dangerous and uncomfortable conditions. Some, such as bandleader Glenn Miller, never returned.

Movies were a tremendous influence on the lives of Americans at home and a major source of entertainment for the armed forces. As in other fields, the rise of Hitler brought some of the best talent in films to America. It is interesting to note that none of the refugee filmmakers made films opposing Nazism. In a book about Hollywood in the forties, Otto Friedrich cites fear of retaliation as one reason. He explains further:

> Hollywood as a whole made movies for profit and it earned about one-third of its income from abroad. The studios did not want to offend anyone, neither Fascists or anti-Fascists. . . . Hollywood's political timidity toward Naziism was also a consequence, however, of its feelings about Jewishness and anti-Semitism. . . . Anti-Semitism in America in 1940 was widespread and strong.[9]

Hollywood continued along its glamorous way, convinced that the film studios were doing their patriotic duty by boosting the spirits of the American people. Producers looked for material with a patriotic or uplifting message, such as *Commandos Strike at Dawn,* featuring Paul Muni (music by Louis Gruenberg), or *Mission to Moscow* (music by Max Steiner). Semidocumentaries, such as *Siege of Leningrad* and *Moscow Strikes Back,* exploited pro-Russian sentiments by using films shot by Soviet cameramen and with music by Russian composers. The Office of War Information, responsible for authorizing scripts, was effective in spreading propaganda for the New Deal. When Russia was an ally, liberal writers such as Lillian Hellman were wooed and encouraged as avidly as they were castigated when Russia became the enemy. According to film critic Pauline Kael:

> A lot of movies were very condescending to Europeans and Asiatics. There were films like *Bataan* with Robert Taylor screaming epithets about the Japs. . . . We had stereotypes of a shocking nature. . . . In contrast, there was *The Grand Illusion,* one of the great war films of all times. . . . In *The White Cliffs of Dover* the people know that the war is coming home because two little German children are already warlike. *The Clock* was a popular movie. It featured Judy Garland and Robert Walker as two kids who meet in New York. He's a soldier who has to leave in a couple of days. They meet, fall in love and are separated. . . . That was the kind of thing people could love. . . .[10]

Hollywood is an example of America's schizophrenia in the 1930s and 1940s: While the country was struggling to survive the Great Depression, followed by a life-threatening war, Hollywood was in its halcyon days.[11] For musicians, it was the one place "real" money could be made, sometimes for doing very little. As for composers, they were paid whether they were working or not. For example, composer (former jazz pianist) Mel Powell went to Hollywood after studying at Yale University with Paul Hindemith and trying to eke out a living as a "serious" composer. Powell was astounded to spend his first six weeks waiting to be called to the studio, while checks of five hundred dollars arrived regularly each week. According to Powell, "I thought at the time—boy, this is it—the way for the composer in America!"[12] Before Powell could go to Hollywood, he had to get a film credit, and as Copland had done before him with *The City,* Powell accepted Willard Van Dyke's offer to compose music for documentaries. Not knowing anything about film scoring, Powell went to see Copland. "I remember Aaron telling me, 'Never write a woodwind solo for film—it sounds as though it is crawling on the top of the screen. The warm body of strings will get in nobody's way.' "

Some of the finest performers from Europe could be found playing all kinds of things in the movie studios. Powell was hired by the most powerful studio, MGM (Metro-Goldwyn-Mayer). On the payroll were twenty full-time composers, among them André Previn and Adolph Weiss, and many virtuoso performers. Powell's first experience was typical of music in the Hollywood studios at the time. As pianist for a "Tom and Jerry" cartoon, he was to play a glissando after counting sixty-eight measures of rest:

> I had never been on a sound stage before. I arrived at the studio a little nervous. I was handed earphones, and over the earphones a voice counted the measures for me. You might say I was over-informed about that glissando! When we got to measure fifty the earphones warned me to get ready, and at sixty reminded me that we had eight measures to go. I played the finest white-note gliss you'd ever want to hear just as Tom the Cat ran up the clock to catch Jerry the mouse—and I finished just right. The conductor beamed at me as though I had just played a remarkable performance of the *Emperor Concerto!* And that was it for a few weeks. When André [Previn] came in and heard what I had done, he said, "You don't mean you use your *fingers* to play a glissando?" And he handed me a rubber comb saying, "From now on, use this. You don't want to hurt your fingers." (André always had a perfectly balanced outlook and sense of humor about what was going on.) I wondered about all the magazines around the studios and learned that they were for the musicians, who spent lots of time sitting around. You could be accompanying Judy Garland in "Over the Rainbow" for a while, and then wait an hour or two before having anything else to do. These same musicians also played in the splendid Monday "Evenings on the Roof" concerts. Often one heard passages from *Pierrot Lunaire* or some other serious work being practiced over in the corner. Cushy as it was, after a few months, I became disenchanted and returned east.

Copland knew very well the price paid by those who chose to work in Hollywood: In exchange for financial security, they endured almost complete isolation from the established concert-music circles. Once a musician became part of the entertainment business, it was virtually impossible to change the image. Mel Powell and André Previn are rare exceptions. Previn has described the situation as "a peculiarly American attitude. Here, one is not allowed to have worked in the commercial media. In Europe everybody does, and nobody even blinks. The irony now is there's a whole generation that doesn't know I've ever done anything except stand in front of a symphony orchestra!"[13]

Copland and Virgil Thomson had reputations for composing excellent film scores, but they were saved from being labeled "film composers" by not staying in Hollywood too long. In retaliation for the patronizing attitudes of concert composers, film composers became a tight group, a "closed shop," as Copland described them. They were convinced that their highly developed craft was understood only by colleagues in the film community, with few exceptions—Copland among them, probably because he did not patronize film composition. Some highly admired film composers (Bernard Herrmann, Alex North, David Raksin, Miklos Rozsa, Bronislaw Kaper, Elmer Bernstein, and Leonard Rosenman) also wrote concert music, but they were rarely encountered on concert programs, and almost never on the East Coast. Nevertheless, Copland believed that the best film composers were those who had gone through traditional channels of study, those who, like Rosenman and North, had yearned to compose symphonies, chamber music, and opera.

When Alex North asked Copland for advice about his music in 1945, Copland responded (11 October 1945), "Sounds to me as if you have a case of 'stage fright.' I'd be glad to see the Clar. work and offer friendly advice, however. Maybe all you need is to face the Muse squarely, look her in the eye, and conquer." Later, North wrote to Copland (10 November 1957), "Someday I will tell you why I have worked like mad out here these past five years, writing scores in three weeks, sacrificing my yen to write 'absolute'—I never knew when the axe would fall." In 1956, Copland included North, along with Herrmann, Rosenman, and Gail Kubik, on a list of composers he most admired in Hollywood. Copland knew what it took to compose a successful score for a major film. He thought that a composer such as North, who had a special talent for film composition and could write a score like *Death of a Salesman*, had little reason to be apologetic.

The estrangement between film composers and concert composers is part of a larger picture in American music. A division has separated concert and popular music since Colonial times. These attitudes, strengthened in the nineteenth century and continued in the twentieth, include a suspicion of money-making in connection with the arts and the belief that in order to create, an artist must suffer. Film composers were not suffering. Films were part of the world of entertainment, a world that had little to do with what the public viewed as art music.

Copland had deplored the narrow views of some of his colleagues from the time of his first Hollywood film, *Of Mice and Men.* He recommended that the *Composers News-Record* of the League of Composers carry a report in each issue, "Film Scores in Progress," and he devoted entire sessions to film music in his lectures at home and abroad. Copland praised the work of Herrmann and Rozsa, comparing them with the "old-fashioned" Hollywood writers Tiomkin, Newman, and Steiner:

> Take his [Herrmann] orchestral approach. *The Magnificent Ambersons* had a sleigh ride accompanied by eight celestas only—an unheard of combination, unobtainable outside Hollywood. The title music for *Hangover Square* was scored for piano solo instead of the usual full orchestra, and *Anna and the King of Siam* called for winds and brass without strings. The other composers in Hollywood watch what Herrmann does—and with reason, for he is one of the few men who has been able to introduce a few new ideas in the Hollywood musical scene. Miklos Rozsa is generally considered to be in a class with Newman and Steiner—that is, much sought-after by producers. His film scores for *The Lost Weekend* and *The Killers* were much appreciated. He has made liberal use of the so-called echo-chamber, which gives a macabre, unearthly effect. But such effects are quickly overdone. . . . I like more the music he wrote for the beginning of *The Killers*—stark and dramatic, in an idiom which takes full advantage of modern musical resources.[14]

Copland was in his forties during the war, too old for the draft. He accepted commissions for patriotic works and continued to serve on the Advisory Committee on Music and the Pan-American Union in Washington. He corresponded with Harold Spivacke (chief of the music division of the Library of Congress and music chairman of the joint Army and Navy Committee on Welfare and Recreation), requesting more active war service.[15] The War Department occasionally sent Copland to army camps and colleges to present lectures, such as "Music in America at War."[16] But for the most part, he felt disconnected from the war effort. When Abe Meyer, Copland's Hollywood agent, wrote about Samuel Goldwyn's plan to produce a lavish and costly pro-Russian film, Copland was immediately interested. Patriotism was not Copland's sole motivation; it had been three years since *Our Town,* and he needed the money. He had rejected several scripts, judging them too frivolous for the times, but when he heard that the intellectual and liberal-minded playwright Lillian Hellman was responsible for writing Goldwyn's new film, *The North Star,* and that the Office of War Information had reviewed the script, pronouncing it "a magnificent job of humanizing the plain people of Russia," Copland was convinced that this was what he had been waiting for. A contract was negotiated, and he left for Hollywood in February 1943.

There was something about Los Angeles that seemed closer to the war than New York. It had become a big metropolis filled with defense plants and shipyards, and it was very much alive and thronging with people, many in uniform, at all hours of the day and night. Bands of young Mexicans wearing zoot suits roamed the city. During the time Copland was in Los Angeles, the atmosphere became increasingly uneasy, culminating in the zoot suit riots of June 1943. The large Japanese population in Los Angeles contributed to the tension, and Copland would find that Hollywood had become clannish with the arrival of the Europeans: The German-Jewish group stayed to themselves; the British formed their own émigré colony; and the American moviemakers viewed them all as outsiders. But when Copland first arrived in Los Angeles, it was so different from New York that it was exhilarating. Copland rented a piano, a small house to put it in (on Hollowell Plaza Drive), and got down to work on the score for *The North Star.*

SAMUEL GOLDWYN'S

Brilliant Production

★ THE ★ NORTH ★ STAR ★

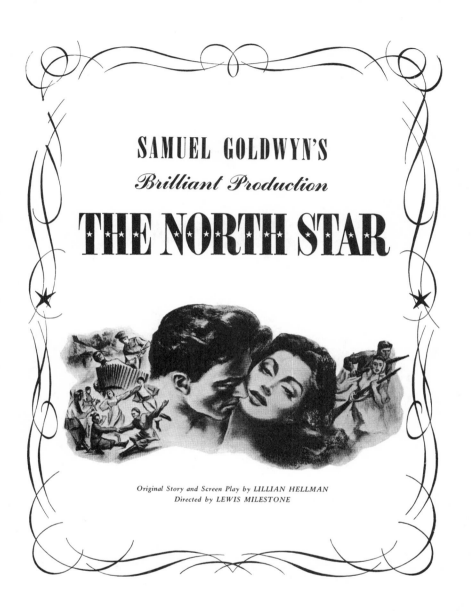

Original Story and Screen Play by LILLIAN HELLMAN
Directed by LEWIS MILESTONE

The War Years

1943-1945

Verso: Publicity release for *The North Star.*
Opposite: Copland, 1943.

The North Star was a Samuel Goldwyn production that cost more than 3 million dollars and was more than a year in preparation. It had an original screenplay by Lillian Hellman, author of *The Little Foxes* and *Watch on the Rhine,* plays I had seen and admired. *The North Star* was about a Russian agricultural community before and after the Nazi invasions. Goldwyn assembled an impressive cast and staff for what was the most costly production of his career. Lewis Milestone, with whom I had worked on *Of Mice and Men,* was chosen as director. Ira Gershwin was to write lyrics for several songs and choruses, and a noted Russian, David Lichine, was engaged as choreographer. The cast included Anne Baxter, Dana Andrews, Walter Huston, Ann Harding, Walter Brennan, Jane Withers, Erich von Stroheim, Farley Granger, and Dean Jagger, and the publicity releases boasted "A Company of One Thousand."

An exact replica of a Russian airplane cockpit was constructed, and a complete Russian village of twenty buildings was built on the back lot of the studio where once had stood an English village for *Wuthering Heights,* and at another time, the tropical town for *Hurricane.* The buildings included thatched-roof cottages, a school, a hospital, an assembly hall, a radio station, and a railroad station, complete with a freight train and ten cars built from specifications of a Russian railroad system. These were not mere shells of buildings but ones with interiors and hundreds of authentic props. Irving Sindler, a veteran property man on the staff, was famous for having his name appear on a prop in every picture he ever worked on: In *The North Star* it was etched on the side of a sewing machine that was shown being rescued from a burning village by a peasant housewife.

Everyone on the set kidded about the livestock—pigs, horses, cattle, chicken, and sheep increased in quantity as the picture progressed. Sixty pigs were born on the village set. The dogs came from the Los Angeles pound. They had never had it so good! Later they were adopted by

AROUND
THE STUDIO

Lewis Milestone, Samuel Goldwyn, Anne Baxter

James Wong Howe, Perry Ferguson, Mr. Goldwyn, Mr. Milestone and William Cameron Menzies

Ann Harding, Dean Jagger, Ann Carter, Miss Baxter, Mr. Milestone and Mr. Goldwyn

Messrs. Goldwyn, Milestone and Jagger, and Misses Carter and Harding

Messrs. Goldwyn, Milestone, Howe and Aaron Copland

Photographs made on the set during production of *The North Star* for use in a publicity release.

employees and members of the cast. One mongrel became famous for disappearing. When Mr. Goldwyn offered a large reward of five hundred dollars, the public interpreted it as the kindhearted gesture of an animal lover; in fact, Goldwyn would have faced a large loss if retakes had had to be made with a different dog (I was told that the dog, "Dada," had cost Goldwyn four dollars at the local pound).

I was brought out to Hollywood quite early for this film and saw some of it being shot. It was a soft life with nothing much to do, yet I was on salary the whole time. I remember being present at the shooting of a scene when the "evil" Germans—it was action during the war and the Russians were the good guys and the Germans the bad ones—were burning the village, which was portrayed much like an American town with people at work, women at home, and children at play. The peasants were all brilliant, and the kids were all beautiful and very smart. On that particular day when I was watching the shooting, the Germans were burning down the whole village. It was fascinating to watch because the soldiers would run in carrying their torches on fire and would touch the straw roofs of these simple peasant houses, producing lots of flames. But hidden behind the cameras, right behind me, was the fire department, ready to put out the flames the instant they stopped turning the cameras! It looked so very realistic in the film, and you said to yourself, O my Lord, those awful Germans are burning down a whole village!

The North Star provided unusual scope for the musical score. I wrote to Nadia Boulanger (23 April 1943), "The film I am doing calls for a great variety of music—songs, choruses, orchestral interludes, etc. It is like having a new toy to play with. But in Hollywood, one never can foretell the result. In my case I am learning a lot—excellent preparation for operatic writing!" There were decisions to make, principally questions of style. Since the picture took place in Russia, how authentically "Russian" ought the music to be? (Shostakovich might have faced the same problem had he been asked to supply a score for a movie set in the United States.) When I saw that the actors were Americans performing without even attempting Russian accents, I decided to use a musical style that would suggest, rather than emphasize, the Russian flavor. This was not an unfamiliar challenge: I had adapted Mexican folk material in *El Salón Méx-ico,* and American cowboy tunes for *Billy the Kid* and *Rodeo.* By using the same technique with Russian folk songs, I developed fragments of a few carefully chosen tunes until they became very much my own, while still retaining a sense of their Russian derivation. (I had found a book of

First page of the sheet music for "Song of the Guerrillas" from *The North Star.*

old Russian folk songs in the library before leaving New York.) Several sequences called for Russian-sounding music, but only in four instances did I make direct use of actual Soviet material.[1] To my mind, the most effective was "Song of the Fatherland," sung by the children at the end of the school term, a kind of Russian "My Country 'Tis of Thee." I also made use of the "Internationale," but the orchestral setting was my own. During the advance screenings of the film, some of the Russians brought over by Goldwyn told him that my music wasn't Russian enough. After the film was released, I was amused to hear from Lillian Hellman that the

Russians liked the film and the score, but some of them complained that the "Ukrainian" tunes came from the wrong part of the U.S.S.R.!

I composed three songs with lyrics by Ira Gershwin: "No Village Like Mine," sung by the young people who are interrupted by the falling of Nazi bombs on the village; "Younger Generation"; and "Song of the Guerrillas."[2] Lillian Hellman wrote to me after a quick trip to the West Coast when we did not get to see each other: "What music I heard and what Ira sang for me, seemed fine, and I am grateful to you." Ira Gershwin also wrote lyrics for a choral piece I composed (it was played on a "March of Time" broadcast dedicated to Russia). I made arrangements for balalaikas, worked on a ballet interpolation for Lichine, and had my first chance at a bang-up battle sequence. Finally, the time came to compose music for the titles and credits. I wrote to my friend Victor Kraft back in New York (9 September 1943), "The title music is pastoral-like, with a heavy middle part when the Foreword comes on about those awful Germans. Everyone is shocked because there is no fanfare for Goldwyn's credit, but even I couldn't solve the problem of a fanfare in a pastorale."

Except for the title music, which was conducted by a musician from Warner Brothers, I conducted the score myself. It gave me more control of the results. It stands to reason that the composer who has already worked through the material has a better chance of accuracy than someone who comes in to conduct the music cold. I heard the recorded dialogue through earphones while the picture flashed before my eyes. Timings are inserted throughout film scores to help with the synchronizing, and important musical cues are indicated in the rough cut so the conductor can know exactly where he is.[3] We recorded for four days, and the musicians in the orchestra seemed unusually pleased with the material they were given to play. I wrote again to Victor: "Now I spend most of my time in the Purgatory Room—dubbing to you. They are doing all they can for me but oh what a heartpain it gives one to hear the music played at those inhuman levels. Well, the fact is a movie is not a concert with pictures, but pictures with some offstage noises. Still I come off pretty well."

I spent very little time in my small house in L.A., until I got a traffic summons and could not drive. I have never learned my way around a kitchen, so I found a fellow who was serving lunch at the studio to make my dinner every evening I stayed home. I was much relieved not to have to go out to restaurants. Once in a while, I had dinner with friends—Jerry Moross, Ingolf Dahl, and even Stravinsky invited me to their places. I saw quite a lot of Lawrence Morton, instigator of the Monday Evening

Concerts, and of the Group Theatre people. Bobby Lewis took me to the movies and kidded me about "watching" with my eyes closed (I had to admit that I really went to hear the music).[4] I got a kick out of seeing some movie stars off the set: Farley Granger was friendly; Ruth Ford invited me to a cocktail party; and I met Groucho Marx at a modern music concert one evening. Groucho heard my *Piano Sonata* played at the concert, and at intermission, he expressed surprise at the advanced idiom of the piece. "Well," I said, "you see, I have a split personality." And Groucho shot back, "It's okay, Copland—as long as you split it with Sam Goldwyn."

Many distinguished personalities were living in Hollywood at the time of *The North Star*—Schoenberg, Stravinsky, Toch, and others—but, strangely enough, they didn't make a culture. The musical life seemed provincial, with no signs of improvement on the horizon. I depended a great deal on letters from friends at home to keep in touch with what was going on in the music world and for news about performances of my compositions: *Fanfare for the Common Man* was premiered in New York by George Szell and the Cincinnati Symphony (14 March 1943) while I was in Los Angeles, and *Four Dance Episodes from Rodeo* by Alexander Smallens with the New York Philharmonic (22 June); Artur Rodzinski conducted the Suite from *Billy the Kid* for a radio broadcast; and Lenny Bernstein played my *Piano Sonata* at the Composers Laboratory-Forum in New York. I was to have been on the panel, and virtually everyone I knew commented about my absence and about Lenny's performance. Lenny wrote about it himself, adding that he had just finished composing a piece, *Dedication to Aaron Copland.*[5] Also, he had attended the premiere of my choral piece *Lark* (13 April 1943), and commented, "It has a lovely sound, and it was fairly well sung, except that Bob Shaw missed the whole point—the 'spurtive ascension' in the music. You know what I mean. But as good as a piece without its essential quality can sound, that sounded good. It's kind of foolproof, you know."

Otto Luening reported about the founding of the American Music Center (21 March 1943): ". . . missed your judgment, strength and wisdom. . . . I suppose your particular brand of nuthouse equals this in its own way." David Diamond filled me in on what was going on with the New York crowd:

Janie [Bowles] was very peculiar the other night. Nothing pleased her. Paul [Bowles] was very obtuse and Arthur [Berger] was all musicology and proverbs. Esther [Berger] was cagey. Everyone keeps saying, why doesn't Aaron write a symphony when he's capable of getting such wonderful ideas down . . . make

18

lots of money, come back and write a wonderful large orchestra work and show people that you can pull it off.

David was not the only colleague concerned about my possible defection to Hollywood. I could read the relief behind Elliott Carter's lines: "It is good news that you are writing a violin sonata. . . ." Even Lenny expressed it: "I had a long fight with Kirk and Constance Askew about whether you could hold out to the Hollywood glamour. They were skeptical. I was, of course, loyally adamant." I responded (6 March 1943): "Of course you were right . . . Hollywood glamour couldn't get me in a million years." I knew that William Faulkner had written his best work, *Light in August,* after a stretch in Hollywood. I knew what my friends did not—that I was composing during the waiting-around periods on the film production, that I was collecting ideas for a ballet for Martha Graham and for a large work, either a piano concerto or a symphony. I mentioned the concerto idea to Hans Heinsheimer, who was then with my publishers, Boosey & Hawkes in New York. Heinsheimer mentioned it to Rodzinski, who wrote to me immediately (3 March 1943):

> Here is my offer: I never heard you play the piano, but I guess if your concerto will be difficult, then you certainly must be a good pianist to do justice to it. If you are a pianist only for domestic use, then your concerto wouldn't be technically too difficult. In both cases, I will be more than delighted to present you with the New York Philharmonic next season, providing this will be the American premiere.

Rodzinski then jumped the gun by announcing to the newspapers that I would premiere a new piano concerto with him, thus creating some misunderstandings when I gave up the idea of composing another piano concerto after all.[6]

With Lenny's urging, Victor Kraft decided to join me in Hollywood. "He'd be so much happier there," wrote Lenny, "and you would be so much happier. So why not?" It's true that Victor was not happy in the loft we used for work space on Sixty-third Street. Victor complained: "The Femininos are a fire hazard. The street gets more and more slummy and full of wayward kids." Victor was working with photographer Margaret Bourke-White, and when she came to Hollywood to do publicity photos for *The North Star,* Victor went along and stayed from April to June. Later that summer, Lenny Bernstein was appointed assistant conductor of the New York Philharmonic, and he wrote this amazing news to me immediately on Philharmonic stationery, adding, "I have so much news for you—

19

Lillian Hellman

May 30, 1943

Mr. Aaron Copland
c/o Samuel Goldwyn ·
1041 N. Formosa Avenue
Hollywood, Calif.

Dear Aaron:

I am sorry not to have seen
you when I was on the coast. I had a
miserable week, and people who didn't
see me are lucky.

I only wanted to say here that
what music I heard, and what Ira sang
for me, seemed fine and I am grateful to
you.

My warm regards,

Lillian
Lillian

won't you please hurry home? The score must be done by now. . . . Come back!"

The recording of the film score was finished during the first week of September. I was pleased at the prospect of going on to different things. I wrote to Bill [William] Schuman (22 September 1943):

I feel like a general exiled to Syria, and any news from headquarters is manna to the expatriate. I hope you like the picture when you see it. There is more than an hour's worth of music and you can actually hear about half of it, which

20

is pretty good as pictures go. After seven and a half months on it, I am in a mood to doubt whether any picture is worth that much time. On the way home, I am stopping off in Harris country—Denver and Colorado Springs to make lectures on the South Americans. Never been in that part of the USA. Unfortunately the patriarch Himself [Roy Harris] will be in the east just as I get there.

I left Los Angeles for Denver to deliver lectures at two army camps, at the Phipps Museum, then the Art Institute in Colorado Springs, and at the University of Colorado at Boulder. Victor had gone to Mexico and was urging me to join him, but the Hollywood job had taken longer than expected and I was anxious to get back to New York. After I returned, I wrote to Ira Gershwin about our songs from *The North Star*, and he responded (22 November 1943): "I'm sorry to hear the songs aren't being played on the air. . . . It may be as in the case of Harburg and Kern's *And Russia Is Her Name* that songs from *North Star* would be considered controversial by the advertising agencies, which, frequently, control the policy of music on their programs." He promised to write to the publishers, however, and signed the letter "Your lyric writer, Ira."

The North Star was released in October 1943, just before Russia became an enemy instead of an ally. Except for *The Daily Worker*, most of the reviews were unfavorable. For the most part, it was taken as propaganda, and as *The Journal American* reviewer commented, "not even good propaganda." It must have been a great disappointment to Goldwyn. Some reviewers cited the fact that the familiar stars constituted a barrier to acceptance of the film as Russian; and it was inevitable that comparisons were made with the great Russian films. Lillian told me that when she visited the U.S.S.R., she found that Soviet officials viewed *The North Star* "as a great joke." She wrote, "But outside of Moscow there were simple peasants glad to find themselves so noble on the U.S. screen." I was somewhat surprised to receive an Academy Award nomination for the musical score, and *Variety* carried a favorable notice (5 January 1944):

> Further indication of the advancing maturity of film music can be seen in Aaron Copeland's [sic] score for the recently released Sam Goldwyn-RKO story of the Russian people, *North Star*. In this score, Copland duplicated his successes in *Of Mice and Men* and *Our Town*. The music based on Russian themes is so authentic as to be capable of deceiving even the experts into thinking them genuine.

Some years later, Lillian wrote to tell me that *The North Star* was being released for television: "It has been butchered, with any favorable remarks

IRA GERSHWIN
1021 NORTH ROXBURY DRIVE
BEVERLY HILLS, CALIFORNIA

Nov. 22, 1943

Dear Aaron,

thanks for the clipping (Alton Cook's article). Yes, I have seen the New York notices on "North Star". Leonore, who is in New York at the moment, sent them to me. I thought, on the whole, they were very good. I haven't, as yet, seen the picture as it hasn't opened here but I'm sure I'll get a kick out your contribution.

I'm sorry to hear the songs aren't being played on the air. I believe I once told you I never bothered the publishers about performances but in this case I'll write Wolfin and see if we can't get some sort of break. It may be, of course, as in the case of Harburg and Kern's "And Russia Is Her Name" that songs from "North Star" would be considered "controversial" by the advertising agencies, which, frequently, control the policy of music on their programs. Anyway, I will write.

How are you otherwise and what are you working on? Me, I finally finished with "Cover Girl" and am on a Twentieth Century-Fox opus with Kurt Weill. It's too early to know how we're coming along but I do like the little we've done

All the best and in the meantime you ought to run up to Chappell's and say hello to Dreyfus and Simay. You have a perfect right to protest in a mild way that when Chappell publishes you expect some kind of results. In any event, when I get a response from Wolfin I'll let you know.

Your lyric writer,
Ira

about the Russians deleted and turning them from the heroes to the villains of the movie. This travesty now goes by the name *Armored Attack.*"

I had carried sketches for a violin and piano piece with me to California. During the frequent periods when I had to wait for the studio to move ahead on *The North Star,* I played through the piano parts of violin sonatas from various periods. My idea was for the piano to complement the violin rather than merely accompany it; thus the title: *Sonata for Violin and Piano.* But the piece is usually referred to as *Violin Sonata.* I had just completed it when I heard that a friend had died while on active duty in the South Pacific. The *Sonata for Violin and Piano* is dedicated to Lt. Larry H. Dunham (1910–1943).[7]

For whatever reasons, at that time I had little desire to compose a dissonant or virtuosic work, or one that incorporated folk materials. Nevertheless, certain qualities of the American folk tune had become part of my natural style of composing, and they are echoed in the *Sonata.* It is composed in the usual three movements, with the last two to be played without pause. The first movement, based on an eight-note phrase with the interval of a fourth prominent, alternates in mood between a tender lyricism and a more rapidly paced section. Changes in the timing occur throughout; in fact, the strong feeling of contrasting moods in the composition is achieved mainly through rhythmic changes. The second movement, in a simple ABA form with two-part counterpoint between the instruments, is calm and bare in outline. The scherzo-like third movement is characterized by irregular rhythms and a strong penetrating melody. The *Sonata* ends with a short coda that refers back to the theme of the opening movement.[8]

I asked Louis Kaufman, a violinist friend in Hollywood, to check the violin part and to play through the piece with me, and from Hollywood I sent the *Sonata* to David Diamond (a violinist himself). David responded (29 October 1943):

> Got back from Rochester last night and found the violin part to your *Sonata.* Thanks, and I'm already practicing and refingering. Kaufman's fingering is certainly very special . . . I'm doing it my way—as all violinists should: individual ways.

David and I played through the *Sonata* for friends at my loft, before the first public performance, which took place at a concert of contemporary

American and English music presented by Boosey & Hawkes at Times Hall (17 January 1944). Ruth Posselt was the violinist, I the pianist. The music critic of *The New York Times,* Olin Downes, called my piece "poor and characterless." The rest of the concert, with works by Quincy Porter, Benjamin Britten, and Eugene Goossens, fared little better. Downes wrote of ". . . one dismaying thing, namely the persistence of its rearward vision, and the absence, as it impressed the writer, of any consciousness of a new age or a changing order." Virgil Thomson's review in the *Herald Tribune* was more favorable about my *Sonata:* "I suspect it is one of its author's most satisfying pieces. . . . It has a quality at once of calm elevation and of buoyancy that is characteristic of Copland and irresistibly touching."

Louis Kaufman sent me some very nice reviews after the West Coast premiere of the *Violin Sonata* (May 1944). I wrote (2 June): "I was delighted to know that it had gone over so well. I feel certain your fiddling had a lot to do with it." We played the *Sonata* together at Kaufman's Town Hall recital in New York (14 March 1945), and in 1948 we recorded it for the Concert Hall Label. (I turned to Kaufman later when I needed help with bowings and fingering for the violin and piano arrangements of "Hoe-Down" from *Rodeo* and "Waltz" from *Billy the Kid.*) The *Sonata* has made an occasional appearance on violin and piano programs, and more recently, it has been heard in arrangements for other instruments. Almost forty years after I composed the *Violin Sonata,* a young clarinetist, Timothy Paradise, came to see me in order to play an arrangement of the *Violin Sonata* for his instrument. I never would have believed that such an arrangement would be so successful! I particularly admired the way the grace notes at the end of the piece sounded. Another young clarinet player, Michael Webster (son of my old friend, pianist Beveridge Webster) helped prepare the clarinet version for publication. Paradise had set the *Sonata* a whole step lower; Webster took it down another full step (the published clarinet arrangement is a major third below the original). In the late seventies, bassist Gary Karr paid me a visit to play a version of the *Violin Sonata* for double bass. Gary took the violin part down a whole octave in appropriate places, and in the second movement, he used harmonics that worked like a charm for his instrument.

Harold Clurman left for Hollywood just as I returned to New York in the fall of 1943, to my room at the Empire Hotel and to my loft, which Clurman described as "that dismal sanctuary on Sixty-third Street." Clurman wrote: "My apartment is pretty and theatrical in Stella's taste [actress

Stella Adler, Clurman's wife]—not monastic in yours. Why, my beloved friend of all time, must every one of your permanent residences have a hangover of Washington Ave. in Brooklyn?" My rent at the Empire Hotel had gone up from $8.50 a month to $3.25 a week, and although I usually rented the loft to a friend (Leo Smit or Edwin Denby) when I went away, I was beginning to yearn for a place of my own in the country. I even began to look with the help of my friends Mary and Bill Lescaze (Bill was an architect and knew his way around the real estate scene). But I put it off and answered Clurman: "If I continue to live simply, I can get by with the money from *The North Star* plus fees for a few lectures, leaving me free to spend most of my time composing."

My teaching assignments included five lectures as the Horatio Appleton Lamb lecturer at Harvard in the spring of 1944.[9] I enjoyed Cambridge and returned to New York only for a meeting at the Blue Ribbon restaurant, called by Margaret Grant, secretary of the Koussevitzky Music Foundation, to discuss arrangements for a testimonial dinner to honor Koussevitzky's twentieth year as conductor of the Boston Symphony. What began as a gesture by composers to show appreciation for Koussevitzky's devotion to American music grew to include organizations and institutions, performers, critics, patrons, and friends—even the Russian Embassy! The event took place at the Plaza Hotel (16 May 1944). I acted as host, and there were many tributes and toasts. The original purpose of the evening was kept in mind—the program listed all of the American works performed under Koussevitzky's leadership. It was a reminder that he had championed not only recognized talents but many lesser-known composers.[10]

Victor Kraft had returned to the States while I was teaching at Harvard, and since he knew his way around Mexico, we drove down there together for the summer and early fall of 1944. I had read a book by an American who had spent eight months in the tiny town of Tepoztlán in 1927 and did an anthropological study of the place. No American had lived there since. Although only a few hours from Mexico City, Tepoztlán was definitely off the main road and pretty much the way it had been in Cortez' time. It is 5,500 feet up amidst extraordinary mountains. The Indians there are full-blooded Aztecs, and the older folks still spoke the Aztec language in preference to Spanish. They were not friendly to strangers. I

Copland in Tepoztlán, Mexico, 1944.

wrote to Bill Schuman, "Being the only *gringo* makes one feel very conspicuous—a simple walk through town turns one into a symbol and puts the whole civilized structure on trial. I try to be a worthy representative—but it's a strain." There were no newspapers, radios, or telephones, and no traffic because the streets were unpaved. Victor and I had the only livable house in the village. It was charming in the simple Mexican patio style. It had a separate studio with a piano of sorts (borrowed from a wealthy American who lived in Cuernavaca, the nearest city), and the whole place came complete with cook and gardener. Nights were dark, since there was no electricity. I wrote to Arthur Berger (8 September 1944):

> Twice a week a kind of public dance takes place in the open-air market. Instead of doing *jarabes* and *huapangos*, I am amazed to see the people attempting a kind of Tepoztlán version of a fox trot. The nearest movie house is fifteen miles away, but obviously its effect has been felt. The whole thing is hardly conducive to inspiring a "Salón Tepozteco."

Nothing ever happened in Tepoztlán, so when a special messenger arrived with a letter for the *gringo*, it caused a lot of excitement. The letter, mailed

26

from Brooklyn a week earlier, was from my sister Laurine, telling me of our mother's death. It was upsetting being so far from home at a time like that! I wrote to Lenny (26 July): "The trip turned out to be a sad one. Five days after I left, my mother died suddenly, and I didn't get the news in time to attend the funeral. I was relieved to know that the end came so painlessly—but I've been left with a depressed feeling nonetheless." I wrote to Koussevitzky (7 September): "The first part of the summer left me distressed because of the news of my mother's death in July. It is an experience that time alone can help to adjust. . . . I am hard at work on the symphony I plan to do for you." Eventually, letters were delivered to me in Tepoztlán from my friends. Harold Clurman advised, "Read *Sholem Aleichem* to understand yourself better, your Mom and Pop or at least my Mom and Pop." I heard from Nadia: "My thoughts are all going to your Mother, who must have been so proud of her son—and in her memory, I kiss you tenderly . . . as when you were a little boy." And Lenny wrote (16 August), "I wish I could be with you now that your Mother has died. . . . I wonder what really goes on in your insides now. And what of your Father? You must be very worried about him." I *was* worried about Pop. His memory was going, and after Mother died, he became much worse. Lillian Coombs—the same Lil who had been with the family all these many years—was taking care of Pop, and she and Laurine kept me informed. Lil wrote (30 August):

> He was in pretty bad shape on the 21st so he had to be sent away. I am home all tired out. . . . I know how you feel—we all feel the same way. So you all have to be brave and take the situation as it comes . . . the Missus would want you all to keep in touch with each other just as before she kept you all together. The boss may be here for quite a while. Yours always, Lilly.

The reality of Mother's death came home to me sharply only after I returned to New York. As Nadia wrote in her annual birthday letter, "This year, for the first time, your Mother will not be there." Pop's health continued to deteriorate, and when I returned home, I met with my family to make arrangements for his care. Pop never recovered and died six months after Mother (2 February 1945). (My brother Leon stayed on in the house on President Street in Brooklyn and Ralph managed the property.)

While in Tepoztlán, I felt so far away from everything and everybody that I suddenly wished I was sitting in the middle of Times Square! However, working conditions were good and I was determined to make headway on the commission I had been given by the Koussevitzky Music Foundation. But first, I had to take a few weeks to compose a radio piece promised to Paul Whiteman, Director of Music for the Blue Network (a division of the American Broadcasting System). The commission would help pay for the summer.

The "Blue" had a newly established "creative music fund" from which it paid commissions for "streamlined works, or symphonettes," to be performed by the Whiteman Orchestra on the Philco Radio Hour. Commissions went to Stravinsky, Bernstein, Roy Harris, Richard Rodgers, Morton Gould, Peter De Rose, Erich Korngold, Victor Young, Ferde Grofé, and myself. The agreement was for the network to retain first broadcast rights and exclusive performance rights for a year; accrued royalties would go to the "Blue" until the sum originally advanced was returned to the fund. The works were to be performed one each week, beginning July 1944.

My piece, *Letter From Home,* had been sketched in Cambridge the previous spring. While completing it in Mexico, I wrote to Arthur Berger, "It's very sentimental, with five saxophones that are sometimes five clarinets and sometimes four flutes—but it *modulates!*" (The original version for radio orchestra included alternatives to the saxophone, since I knew that five sax players would not always be available.)[11] The title of my seven-minute piece was not meant to be taken too literally—I meant only to convey the emotion that might naturally be awakened in the recipient by reading a letter from home. I sent the score off to Paul Whiteman and a copy to my publishers. Hans Heinsheimer responded, "Whiteman intends to conduct your piece himself (is that a threat or a promise?)." After the broadcast (18 October 1944), Heinsheimer wrote:

> Despite the shortcomings of the performance, it is a lovely piece. Poor Whiteman was over his head. . . . He said in *The New York Times* that in order not to bother anyone with these pieces, he plays them at midnight when nobody listens in. . . . He never removed his cigar during rehearsals and never took his nose out of the score for an instant.

Whiteman made a recording, which I heard when I got home. It was much too fast from beginning to end. Nevertheless, I was grateful to Whiteman for commissioning the piece.

Letter From Home was given its first public performance by the Cleveland Orchestra under George Szell (27 February and 1 March 1947) with an expanded and revised orchestration.[12] I was not able to attend, so

The Blue Network

BLUE NETWORK COMPANY, INC.

30 ROCKEFELLER PLAZA · TELEPHONE CIRCLE 7-5700

NEW YORK 20, N.Y.

May 9 1944

Mr Aaron Copland
c/o H W Heinsheimer
Boosey and Hawkes, Inc
119 West 57th Street
New York City

Dear Mr Copland:

Enclosed you will find the instrumentation. Would
you please send me the title of your composition
just as soon as possible? I should like to have it
just as soon as you decide on it since there is the
possibility that someone else may pick the same
title and the one that comes in first will naturally
be the one accepted.

Also, would you kindly send me biographical data
about yourself. I would appreciate having this at
the earliest opportunity.

Sincerely

Paul Whiteman
Director of Music

A M E R I C A N   B R O A D C A S T I N G   S Y S T E M   I N C.

Heinsheimer again reported: "It seemed a little hurried—more the letter
of a German PW to mutter." In 1962, I revised the instrumentation again,
providing a slightly shortened version, with an orchestral setting suitable
for about twenty-five instruments.[13]

I had long been an admirer of Martha Graham's work. She, in turn, must have felt a certain affinity for my music, since as early as 1931 she had used my *Piano Variations* for a solo dance composition—*Dithyrambic.* Surely only an artist with an understanding of my work could have visualized dance material in so rhythmically complex and thematically abstruse a composition.[14] From then on, we hoped to collaborate on a stage work. In 1941, Martha asked whether I would compose music for a ballet on a Medea subject, but the script seemed rather severe to me, so I declined the offer.[15] Then, in 1942, Martha's partner, Erick Hawkins, introduced Elizabeth Sprague Coolidge to Martha's work. Aware of Mrs. Coolidge's interest in contemporary music, Hawkins suggested she commission original scores for three new Graham ballets.[16] The commissioning of new music for modern dance was most unusual at that time, but Mrs. Coolidge, with typical energy, translated her enthusiasm into action by inviting Martha to create the ballets for the 1943 program of the fall festival sponsored annually by the Coolidge Foundation. Each commission was for five hundred dollars, an amount Mrs. Coolidge thought appropriate for little-known composers. Erick Hawkins (backed up by Harold Spivacke) convinced Mrs. Coolidge that Martha's dances ought to have music by established composers. They suggested that commissions be offered to Heitor Villa-Lobos and myself. Ostensibly because Villa-Lobos was so far away, Mrs. Coolidge suggested Paul Hindemith; Martha countered with Carlos Chávez, and the decision was made for Chávez.[17] Mrs. Coolidge need not have been concerned about the amount of the commission—as far as I was concerned, five hundred dollars was not a small amount in those days.

Since I had met Mrs. Coolidge in Mexico in 1938, she wrote to me directly (23 July 1942): "Although I may be a little premature in writing to you before Dr. Spivacke addresses you officially, I am allowing myself the pleasure of asking you . . ." and I responded (31 July), "I have been an admirer of Miss Graham's work for many years and I have more than once hoped that we might collaborate. It particularly pleases me that you should make this possible."[18] I heard from Martha (7 November): "I think I am the most fortunate dancer anywhere to have you and Chávez. I cannot believe it as yet . . ." Mrs. Coolidge told Martha that the working out of the ballet could be in our hands. She asked only that the score be about one-half hour long and ". . . for an ensemble of not more than ten or twelve instruments at the outside . . . a small orchestra with one instrument of each kind, both wind and strings with piano."

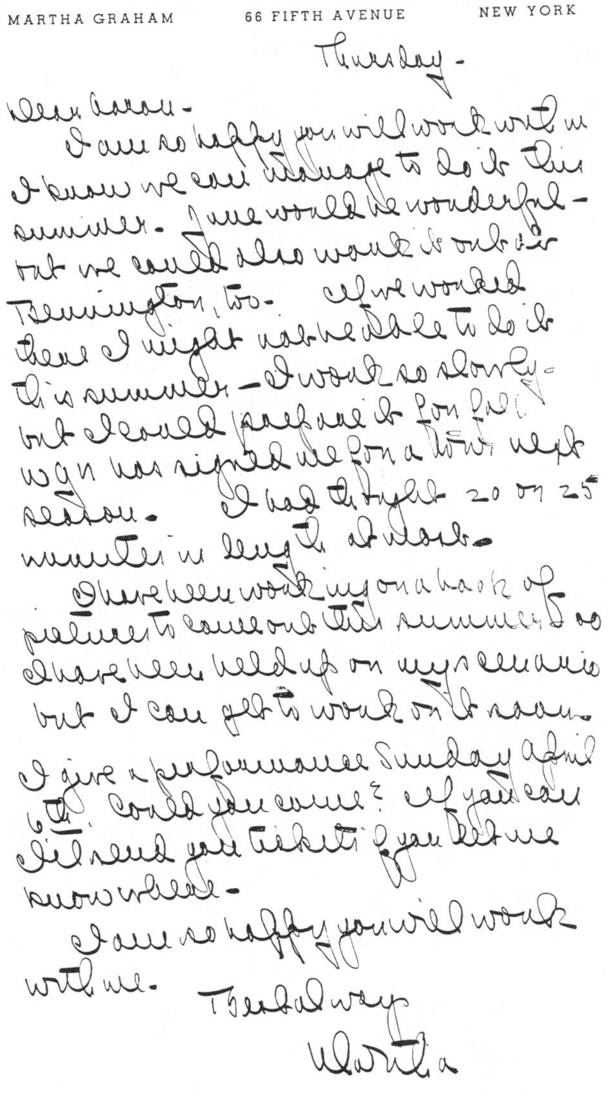

MARTHA GRAHAM   66 FIFTH AVENUE   NEW YORK

[Handwritten letter reproduced]

Letter from Martha Graham to Copland, c. February 1943.

Martha hoped that I could complete the score by July 1943 so she could create the dance during the summer for performance in October. But when I left for Hollywood in February to work on *The North Star,* the script Martha had promised by Christmas had not yet arrived. She wrote

31

(7 October 1943): "The ballet has to do with roots in so far as people can express them, without telling an actual story."

The first script arrived in the early spring with a working title, *House of Victory*. It included biblical quotations, an Indian girl, and references to the Civil War.[19] The script began: "This is a legend of American living. It is like the bone structure, the inner frame that holds together a people." Although the script was to change considerably as the ballet developed, it was already possible to recognize the essence of Martha's ideas. I had misgivings about the spoken words and the Civil War episode, but only when Martha asked my opinion did I say so. I liked the idea in general, and I told Harold Spivacke, "I think I have my first theme."

When composing for the dance, I found it best not to know the choreography in advance. Finding the musical ideas to suit the feeling and the spirit comes first. Then, when the composer has a general idea of what the dance is about and approximate timings for the sequences, it becomes possible to set the musical ideas on paper. I was pleased to hear from Martha (22 July): "Once the music comes I never look at the script. It is only to make a working base for the composer and myself. Now it exists in words, in literary terms only and it has to come alive in a more plastic medium which music is to me. So please feel free to let the music take its own life and urge." Martha's ballet (eventually to be called *Appalachian Spring*) concerned a pioneer celebration in spring around a newly built farmhouse in the Pennsylvania hills in the early part of the last century. The principal characters are a bride and her young farmer husband. After Martha gave me this bare outline, I knew certain crucial things—that it had to do with the pioneer American spirit, with youth and spring, with optimism and hope. I thought about that in combination with the special quality of Martha's own personality, her talents as a dancer, what she gave off, and the basic simplicity of her art. Nobody else seems anything like Martha, and she's unquestionably very American. There's something prim and restrained, a strong quality about her, that one tends to think of as American. Her dance style is seemingly, but only seemingly, simple and extremely direct. Martha carries a certain theatrical atmosphere around with her always, and she communicates that to her dancers.

I found the Shaker song "Simple Gifts" in a collection of Shaker tunes published in 1940.[20] The song had previously been unknown to the general public. It is sometimes known as "The Gift to Be Simple" or by the first line of text, " 'Tis the Gift to Be Simple." I no longer recall who led me to this songbook, but I felt that "Simple Gifts," which expressed the

32

unity of the Shaker spirit, was ideal for Martha's scenario and for the kind of austere movements associated with her choreography.[21] "Simple Gifts" was originally meant to be used for dancing. I read that the dance would have been in "a lively tempo, with single files of brethren and sisters two or three abreast proceeding with utmost precision around the meeting room. In the center of the room would be a small group singing the dance song over and over until everyone was both exhilarated and exhausted." Lest this seem very scholarly, my research evidently was not very thorough, since I did not realize that there never have been Shaker settlements in rural Pennsylvania![22]

For practical reasons, Harold Spivacke was urging me to stay close to the instrumentation Chávez was using for his commissioned ballet: string quartet, four woodwinds, and double bass. My original plan called for double string quartet and piano, but I decided to add a double bass and three woodwinds. I wrote to Spivacke, "That adds up to thirteen men, which is one more than your original letter called for."

I had only about one-third of the music written by midsummer for what was to be an October premiere, and Chávez' situation was even worse than mine. By the end of August, after many frantic letters, telephone calls, and telegrams between all concerned, there was no choice but to postpone the program for a full year, until the fall of 1944. I went to see Martha and played her what I had written so far, and she was enthusiastic. Chávez continued to delay during the winter months: When he finally sent some music to Martha, it was so far from what she had expected that she wrote to Spivacke in concern over how to proceed.[23] Victor Kraft, who had stayed in Mexico, had seen Chávez and wrote: "It would be a great loss to Martha and Spivacke to lose his score. Chávez feels good music can't be done the way shoes are made to order." But Spivacke thought he had no choice but to suspend the commission. It was then given to Paul Hindemith.

Martha and I continued to correspond about various aspects of the ballet (she was either on tour or teaching at Bennington College). By the beginning of 1944, I wrote, "It is quite safe to go ahead; set the date, and I will send completed piano sketch. The orchestration is a mere detail. With me it always comes last." I completed the piano score in the spring of 1944 while teaching at Harvard, and the orchestration during a very hot July in my New York loft and at Helen and Elliott Carter's Fire Island dining room table. I asked a young pianist friend, Leo Smit, to help me make some piano records so Martha would know my tempi. I played through the score on a rather doubtful-looking (and sounding) instrument at the Nola Studios. It cost twenty-six dollars for two sets of records: one for Martha and one for the Library of Congress.[24] When I left for Mexico, I asked Leo to make sure the recordings were sent out.

I have often thought about what a wild chance a choreographer takes by agreeing to work with music not heard in advance. Martha once described it to me as "that dreadful moment when you hear the music for the first time." So I waited anxiously while at Tepoztlán to hear her reactions and I was immensely relieved when she wrote (5 August):

> The music is so knit and of a completeness that it takes you in very strong hands and leads you into its own world. . . . I also know that the gift to be simple will stay with people and give them great joy. I hope I can do well with it, Aaron. I hope you will be here before the performance so that we can check with you. I do not have any idea as yet so we must get together on that.

My plan was to fly to Washington directly from Mexico, arriving 26 October. I wrote to Spivacke (26 September 1944), "My budget will stand $4 or $5 a day for a room—but the main thing is to put me where 'everybody' will be. Half the fun of going to festivals is bumping into people in your hotel lobby." I stayed at the Hotel Raleigh for $4.50 per night. I no longer recall whether I met anyone in the lobby. What I *do* remember is the pleasure of seeing my music actually danced to—I had seen nothing at all before the dress rehearsal! To my initial surprise, some music composed for one kind of action had been used to accompany something else. For example, music originally conceived for children at play was used for the Revivalist's dance. But that kind of decision is the choreographer's, and it doesn't bother me a bit, especially when it works.

The first thing I said to Martha when I saw her in Washington was, "What have you called the ballet?" She replied, *"Appalachian Spring."* "What a pretty title. Where did you get it?" I asked, and Martha said, "Well, actually it's from a line in a poem by Hart Crane." I asked, "Does the poem itself have anything to do with your ballet?" "No," said Martha, "I just liked the title and used it."[25] *My* title had always been *Ballet for Martha,* and it became the subtitle of *Appalachian Spring.* The music had always been connected in my mind with Martha's extraordinary stature as an artist and as a human being, and with the American quality of her personality.

Manuscript, the first page of the short score of the "Ballet," later called *Ballet for Martha* by Copland, that was finally titled *Appalachian Spring, Ballet for Martha*.

Martha Graham[26]

The first time I met Aaron Copland was at a concert in which I heard Aaron's Piano Variations. *After the performance when I was introduced to Aaron, I asked might I choreograph to it. He threw his head back and laughed that wonderful laugh of his and said, "Very well, but I don't know what on earth you'll be able to do with it." Years later when I commissioned a work from Aaron, I drove him to near desperation: I could not decide on a title and the day of the first rehearsal I noticed he had written on the title page, "Ballet for Martha." Finally I shared with Aaron the title,* Appalachian Spring, *and he laughed that wonderful laugh and sighed, "At last!"* Appalachian Spring *has been one of the pleasures of my life—a kind of keystone and I treasure every note of it and the experience I had to be able to choreograph to it.*

I have been amused that people so often have come up to me to say, "When I listen to that ballet of yours, I can just *feel* spring and *see* the Appalachians." But when I wrote the music, I had no idea what Martha was going to call it! Even after people learn that I didn't know the ballet title when I wrote the music, they still tell me they see the Appalachians and feel spring. Well, I'm willing, if they are! The only problem I have ever had with the title is the pronunciation. After always saying Appa*la*chian with the third syllable accented, I was told, when traveling in West Virginia in 1972, that it's supposed to be pronounced with a flat *a*. So, I'd been pronouncing it wrong all those years!

At the time of the Washington premiere, no one thought of me as a conductor, least of all myself! Louis Horst, Martha's music director, conducted, and I sat in the audience close to Mrs. Coolidge. Nothing quite matches the excitement of a first performance for a composer. The audience reaction to *Appalachian Spring* was terrific and so was mine. Martha was extraordinary. I have seen (and conducted) performances with other fine dancers in the leading roles, but I just don't think of *Appalachian Spring* without Martha as the Bride and Erick Hawkins as the Husband.

The original cast of *Appalachian Spring* (left to right): May O'Donnell, Martha Graham, the Followers, and Erick Hawkins.

Photographs by Arnold Eagle.

The entire original cast (left to right): Martha Graham, Erick Hawkins, May O'Donnell, Merce Cunningham, and the Four Followers.

Erick Hawkins[27]

Something in my bones said if you are going to try to invent any new aspect of dance movement you have to have contemporaneous new expression in the music. Lincoln Kirstein was deeply committed to getting some American feeling into ballet. When he got Aaron to do the music for Billy the Kid, *I recognized its virtues right away (I was born in Colorado, and so the idea of using a cowboy as a subject seemed perfectly natural). I danced in Aaron's* Billy the Kid *in 1938 with Lincoln Kirstein's Ballet Caravan. Lincoln took Ballet Caravan to Bennington College School of the Dance, headed by Martha Graham. I was already an admirer of Graham's work. I knew that Balanchine was never going to get into the American swim and that I would never find my way with him, so I went to take Martha Graham's course at her Fifth Avenue studio. Her group was working on* American Document. *To my surprise, Martha put me into the dance, making changes in the choreography. Within one month, I became Martha Graham's partner and the group's first male dancer (the following year Merce Cunningham became the second). I was also one of the few ballet dancers ever to work with Martha.*

American Document heralded a narrative dance style, one that led the group in a new direction. After appearing with Martha and Merce in El Penitente *and* Every Soul Is a Circus, *I did less and less with Ballet Caravan. I loved what Martha was doing. She had become convinced that it was important to relate more directly to her audiences. For the next twelve years, I worked as Martha's principal dancer, and also as teacher, manager, publicist, and fundraiser.*

I approached people for money for the Martha Graham Company, not because I liked doing so but because without it, the Company could not afford sets and costumes. I felt that Martha's art deserved better scores than her musical director Louis Horst could regularly supply, and ones that used instruments other than two pianos. When I heard that Elizabeth Sprague Coolidge had a foundation at the Library of Congress, I wrote and encouraged her to see Martha dance, and then asked her to commission composers for new works, Copland among them.[28] Once Mrs. Coolidge decided to do the Copland-Hindemith-Chávez dances at the Library on her music series, she agreed to give Isamu [Noguchi] five thousand dollars to do a whole new proscenium for the stage and for the designs. I was responsible

Photograph by Arnold Eagle.

Martha Graham and Erick Hawkins in the premiere performance of *Appalachian Spring,* 30 October 1944.

for all the financial reports right down to the fifty dollars for the rocking chair!

I feel responsible for Isamu's work with Martha on Appalachian Spring. *Having such a great artist as Noguchi was a real breakthrough and satisfied three terribly important elements of the dance—the movement, the music, and the scenery. Dancing in Noguchi sets, you felt you were in a world that the great sculptor had created, a whole new world, one that was not on a stage.*

There's no question that one reason Appalachian Spring *took hold was the charm of Aaron's music. It has a simplicity of texture; there are no highly contrapuntal sections to divert the listener from the dance. In Martha's earliest works, she chose either a completed musical score or had a new work in hand before creating the dance. With* Appalachian Spring, *she wrote the scenario and worked out some of the dance without the music, sending Aaron the timings for the sections and general ideas for each segment. But it all really came together after Aaron sent the music. Fortunately for all of us, it was wonderful.*

One day when Aaron was working on the score, I went up to see him at the Empire Hotel. He mentioned possibly using a second piano as well as the strings, woodwinds, and the single piano. I was appalled and said, "Aaron, you simply can't get two pianos in that pit!" And I remember when we danced the piece at the National Theatre in New York, you could barely get by the one piano. When we went on tour, we had a terrible time because we took with us the four strings, the woodwinds, and the pianist but had to pick up four additional strings on the road and rehearse them every afternoon. Sol Hurok lost money, and we lost money.

The original people in Appalachian Spring *were very special, and some of the movement in the dance was naturally ours. Martha, as a beautiful creator, could take things we would try out and suggest and make them into her own choreography. I did everything with Martha in those days—from renaming the group "The Martha Graham Company" to projecting a scheme for a nonprofit corporation to sponsors. I wrote to Koussevitzky and others for support of that idea. I believed in it. We all had such wonderful hope. It was a time when we all thought that American art was going to blossom and continue to blossom.*

The premiere of *Appalachian Spring* was the climax of a festival to honor Elizabeth Sprague Coolidge on her eightieth birthday. As it turned out, the delay that had caused everyone so much difficulty gave time for Mrs. Coolidge to recover from a serious illness. The evening of dance followed three days of The Tenth Festival of Chamber Music at the Library of Congress (30 October 1944). There in the front row of the Coolidge Auditorium was Mrs. Coolidge in her customary seat, an unusually interested spectator. The program opened with *Imagined Wing,* music by Milhaud[29]; followed by *Mirror Before Me* (later called *Herodiade*), music by Hindemith; and after intermission, the small stage was transformed with a set by Isamu Noguchi for *Appalachian Spring.*[30] The farmyard was suggested by a simple fence rail and the house by a peaked entrance and one wall. The Revivalist's pulpit was a stump and his acolytes sat on a bare bench. The rocking chair for the Pioneer Woman was only a suggestion of a chair. Even when the script was in its early stages, Martha had envisioned "a new town, someplace where the first fence has just gone up . . . the framework of a doorway, the platform of a porch, a Shaker rocking chair with its exquisite bonelike simplicity, and a small fence that should signify what a fence means in a new country."

The program was repeated the following evening and recorded.[31] In addition to Martha and Erick Hawkins, the original cast of *Appalachian Spring* included Merce Cunningham, who describes how the role of the Preacher came into being:

> Graham said, as I remember it, "I don't know whether you are a preacher, a farmer or the devil" (I think there were four categories and don't remember the last). She shortly said, "Why don't you work on it?" She left the room and I began to try out movements with the pianist obligingly playing short sequences over and over. I worked that afternoon and part of the next, and later on the second afternoon asked Graham to come and see what I had made. "I don't know if this is what you want," I said. I did the dance, and afterward Graham said, "Oh, it's fine. Now I know what to do with the rest of the piece."[32]

May O'Donnell took the part of the Pioneer Woman; and Nina Fonaroff, Marjorie Mazia, Yuriko [Kikuchi], and Pearl Lang were the Followers. Yuriko, at a rehearsal of a performance I conducted, said (June 1982): "This was my first artistic role. I had not heard of the Shakers, and Martha told me who they were and described the austerity of their lives." Pearl Lang and May O'Donnell also described their experiences with *Appalachian Spring* in interviews.

Pearl Lang [33]

I first danced in Appalachian Spring *as one of the four Followers. The dancers were not involved in the early stages of a work—that was Martha's time with the composer and with Louis Horst. In the process of choreographing a work like* Appalachian Spring, *Martha would say things that would enhance the imagination of the dancer and that were important to hear—not only* what *she said but* how *she said it—not only what is danced but how it's danced at the time of the creation of the work. In the midst of rehearsals, Martha would say, "You know there was an innocent kind of religion there, and they had a kind of ecstatic wildness—that Shaker bursting out to the point where something issues out of the body, and it's a movement." I remember in one section, Martha saying, "Do it as though you're shouting 'I've got Jesus by the foot!' "—it had to have that kind of ecstatic religious commitment. Aaron's music fired us to do so much more than we had ever anticipated. That's the great thing about Aaron's music for dance—it drives the choreographer. It drives the dancer.*

41

I was dancing in Agnes de Mille's Carousel *during rehearsals for* Appalachian Spring. *(De Mille had borrowed me from Martha, and that enabled me to pay rent and eat. Before that, Merce Cunningham and I were working at Schrafft's—he was behind the soda fountain and I was carrying trays.) I would get on a sleeper after the evening performance of* Carousel *in New York and at 9 A.M. be on the floor at the Library of Congress in Washington for rehearsal until four. Then I would catch The Senator back to New York and do a performance. And this went on for two solid weeks!*

It was extremely painful for Martha to turn over roles she had created for herself to someone else. The first role of hers I danced was El Penitente: *and then I learned the Bride in* Appalachian Spring. *I danced the role on and off for several years. (In 1955 I left the company officially but have come back every other year as a guest soloist.) How does one perform a very famous role after a famous dancer has done it? As one of the Followers, I had been onstage all through the work, and I had been able to see exactly what Martha did every night. I was there when she was creating the work, so I knew the style of the piece—where the energies were, and the punctuations. When* Appalachian Spring *is done now, it is different. The difficulty is that people who are dancing it have never seen Martha do it, and films just about tell you which foot you start on, and where you are on the stage and not always that, because the element of space, the third dimension, and the attacks are distorted.*

One evening when Aaron was conducting in 1975, I found myself onstage with Rudolf Nureyev—I didn't even know he was going to dance the Preacher! Appalachian Spring *is choreographed almost like an opera—the soloists all have arias. The Husband and the Bride, of course, have to dance a great deal together; the Followers and the Preacher have to dance together, but the Bride has nothing to do with the Preacher (except there's a little Sunday walk where we shake hands, but you don't need to rehearse to do that). Between Nureyev and Cunningham there's a world of difference. The Preacher is an enchanting role and most male dancers want to do it. I think Nureyev heard the rhythm as very Russian. Neither in the choreography or in the manner of dancing is it Russian—it was only Russian when Nureyev did it. When Merce did it, or Bertram Ross, or Mark Ryder, who was the second dancer in the Preacher role, it was very American in style. It has humor, and Nureyev, always cast as a tragic figure in Martha's other pieces, wanted to do this as a lark—and it is a lark, but it's very difficult technically.*

Appalachian Spring is a joyous piece and that's unusual for Martha's repertory. Without a tragic moment in it—there is only the hint of one—in the allegro toward the end of the Bride's solo where she rolls down the stairs, there is an anticipation of a storm, of something dissonant in her life. The Preacher's part had much more darkness in it originally the way Merce did it—a lot of the movement—the arm stretched down from on high directly following the square dance. I always thought it meant you would roast in hell if you continued to dance!

I don't think there is another dance that has sustained year after year after year as Appalachian Spring *has. It's a classic—a national treasure. I was there from the very beginning, so it is half a lifetime that I have lived with this work, and I am still always moved by it. Aaron's music seems to peel away all extraneous sounds that might interfere with the spine of the thing— which Noguchi did with the sets and Martha with the choreography. But then to keep the spine glistening takes a tremendous amount of work.*

I was born in Illinois outside of Chicago and the feeling of space there was and still is a very important thing to me. Since coming to New York, I had never gotten over not being able to see the horizon—the inner person can't move out. The idea of space is like fuel to a dancer. Aaron has given sound to this space. There's a reason why Russian dancers and American dancers are the best in the world—because we have the concept of space in the land. American dancers trained in the west know space differently, jump higher, than dancers who are trained in urban areas. Not too many dancers who were trained in New York City become soloists. Isadora Duncan was a westerner; Martha grew up on the West Coast, as did Merce and May [O'Donnell]. Erick and I are midwesterners.

It may seem to people who are not dancers that it's easier to dance to the rhythmic sections in Appalachian Spring, *but perhaps the more creative movement comes in the sustained and quiet sections. The movement then takes on its own focus. You are not dancing concomitantly to a beat. This is particularly true in* Appalachian Spring.

At the time of Aaron's seventy-fifth birthday, I was privileged to be invited to choreograph one of his works for a concert at Alice Tully Hall,[34] and when he had his eightieth, one of the celebrations was a "Wall-to-Wall Copland" day at Symphony Space. I read a letter to him from the stage. Here's a part of it that I did not get to say:

> *I am very grateful for the opportunity to at last say something to Aaron Copland, because dancers are usually seen and not heard. What are dancers' tools? Essentially, a usually obstinate and resistant body, a restless soul, and time, of which there is never enough, energy less than enough, and space that is so increasingly being annihilated and for which the dancer has an insatiable need. Aaron seems*

to supply what dancers don't have. We thank Aaron for the wide use of time that his music provides, for the energy his music ignites in us, and for the limitless space that we hear in his sound. With Aaron's music, one leaps not across the stage, but across the land. And above all, we thank him for the wonder of that defiant innocence and affirmation that sings in his music about America.

May O'Donnell [35]

I was a good strong American western girl studying dance in Los Angeles, and someone watching the class said, "You should go to New York City and work with a person called Martha Graham." So I came to New York, looked in the telephone book and found Martha's name and the address on Ninth Street. Martha taught where she lived—it was the Depression and nobody had any money. She took me in her class in the spring of 1932.

My first adventure in dance with Martha was Primitive Mysteries, *which is one of the most difficult dances imaginable. I survived that and I stayed with Martha until 1938. When Erick first came into the group and he and Martha got together, I had been with Martha six years and wanted to try some things of my own. I loved Martha and worked well with her, but she was beginning to get some younger dancers in, and it was a practical time for me to leave. After five years in San Francisco, the war came along, and all activity stopped, so I came back to New York. One day when I was getting settled, the phone rang, and it was Erick asking me to come back to dance with the Graham Company. I agreed, but as a guest artist, because I had started to develop my own dance vocabulary and needed to continue with my own work. I stayed as guest artist from 1944 to 1950. I had a sense of what Martha's style was and she seemed to need me as a foil—being larger and taller and as a sustaining power against her exuberance.*

At the studio, there was tension growing between Erick and Merce, and Martha was getting more involved with Erick—she was very much in love with him—and he used that sometimes to obtain the authority to run things. I didn't like getting into their personal situations, but I liked the work. The next thing I knew I was at Bennington. Martha had started Appalachian Spring *during the winter, so the rest of the cast knew their parts before I did. The stylization was already set when I went into it. My part, the Pioneer Woman, was like an integral thread that held the whole thing together in a delicate way. I was the prevailing spirit, and it was a right part for me. I could work with Martha and try different things, asking her if it worked.*

I tried to do my part like an early American primitive—an archaic quality actually. Martha could trust me to feel the style of it.

Appalachian Spring opens with a sense of horizon. We each take our places almost like characters in a play. My first movement was to sit. I could just take time to sit quietly, but I could never turn to see where that seat was! I didn't have a solo, but I might run through the others, blessing each of the girls, or stand behind Martha, or look out over the bright future as though watching the generations, or send Erick on his way with a kind of maternal gesture—always that kind of benign, hopeful, devotional thing. The transitions would be filled out with me reminding everybody that there was hope, there was a new land, fresh possibilities. It was a free part in a peculiar kind of a way. Martha never said, "May, make your arm go this way or that." She would instill me with that kind of brightness and devotion that comes out of a land you love and out of a culture you love—Martha never talked quite like that, but if you felt it and you did it, and it was convincing, she would love it too, and then she didn't mind what you did. She worked in a more definite way with the rest of the group, because they were a stylized whole and had to have a precision and a concentrated kind of control.

Martha didn't talk to me about the music. She never, as far as I know, worked with her dancers and composers together. And I never saw Aaron during the time we were working things out. It was one of the most success- ful of collaborations between Aaron and Martha, and a turning point for Martha, coming between her symbolic works and her Greek pieces. It was the peak of Erick and Martha's feelings for each other, and while Merce was still with the group. Appalachian Spring has a gentleness and sweetness about it that you don't expect from Martha. It was not easy for Martha to be that simple. It was a one-of-a-kind dance for her. The audience was so surprised to see Martha doing that kind of a piece, and they loved it. Appalachian Spring is a dance people can relate to—most people cannot imagine being Clytemnestra, but everyone can imagine being a bride!

Appalachian Spring came in for the highest praise from reviewers. The dance critic of *The New York Times* concluded (5 November 1944), "It is, as the saying goes, a natural." I was quite amazed when my music won so many awards and became so popular. I must admit I'm influenced by public opinion! When you are working on a piece, you don't think it might have use past the immediate purpose for its composition, and you certainly

Announcement of the 1944 Pulitzer Prize winners on the front page of *The New York Times* the day war ended (Copland's name appeared on page 16).

don't consider its lasting power: You are so relieved just to have it finished for the premiere! Of course, I was delighted to receive a Pulitzer Prize for *Appalachian Spring*. It was announced on the front page of *The New York Times* (8 May 1945), under the big news: THE WAR IN EUROPE IS ENDED! A happy day all around. Louis Biancolli from the *New York World-Telegram* viewed the prize as a sign that American ballet had come of age. He wrote: ". . . the Brooklyn boy who made top concert billing is one of America's most versatile writers. The man's mark is as much on the dance as on the symphony, not to mention the screen. . . . Ballet is giving rise to a whole new school of serious American music."

Martha took *Appalachian Spring* on a tour sponsored by Sol Hurok during the winter months. It included Boston, Cincinnati, and Cleveland, before the New York premiere (14 May 1945).[36] The National Theatre run was for seven performances. Martha wrote to me (1 May 1945):

46

It is a beautiful piece, Aaron. I have reworked it, particularly the points you spoke about, the variations, principally the last one of Erick's, the solo, certain points of my solo and May O'Donnell's. . . . I've also worked on the costumes. It's been a joy to do so.

Edwin Denby, dance critic of the New York *Herald Tribune,* wrote (15 May 1945):

> *Appalachian Spring* has a mysterious coolness and freshness, and it is no glorification by condescending cityfolk of our rude and simple past; it is, despite occasional awkwardness, a credible and astonishing evocation of that real time and place. To show us our country ancestors and our inherited mores as real is a feat of genius no one else who has touched the pioneer subject in ballet has been able to accomplish. The company, and quite particularly Mr. Cunningham in a thrilling passage, were excellent. . . . Mr. Copland's score is a marvel of lyricism, of freshness and strength; and with thirteen instruments he seemed to have a full orchestra playing.

A few weeks after the Pulitzer was announced, The Music Critics Circle of New York voted its annual awards: to Walter Piston's *Symphony No. 2* for symphonic music, and to *Appalachian Spring* in the category of dramatic composition. Winning an award from the music critics was the biggest surprise of all—after having been lambasted by those gentlemen so frequently through the years! Virgil wrote in the *Tribune* (2 June 1945):

> Aaron Copland's *Appalachian Spring* received the award for dramatic music with only two dissenting votes. One of these went to Jerome Moross' ballet, *Frankie and Johnnie,* the other to Arnold Schoenberg's *Ode to Napoleon.* Personally I have no quarrel with the outcome. I voted for the Copland piece myself because, though the *Ode to Napoleon* contains musical writing of far higher methodological sophistication, I consider Copland's ballet to have a greater degree of specific expressivity.

Appalachian Spring was hailed as a breakthrough for Martha, who had been recognized as one of the most gifted of modern dancers and choreographers, but with appeal only to those "in the know," and who, until this ballet, had not had a popular success. Its enormous popularity was partially due to the lyric and joyous quality of the dance. *Appalachian Spring* was Martha's last work about America and the American spirit, and it came at a time when she was at the height of her artistic powers. We composers respected not only her achievements as a dancer and choreographer but the fact that since 1934 she had used nothing but original music, most of it American. As Virgil pointed out, Martha had reached a place musically toward which she had been heading for some time:

Miss Graham has given us in the past music by reputable living composers . . . but none of this has ever been strong or memorable. . . . The Copland and Hindemith scores are another line of musical country, I assure you, higher and more commanding and incredibly more adequate both to the support of a choreographic line and to the evocation of their stated subjects. . . . Miss Graham's work has long leaned toward the introspective and the psychologically lurid. Copland, in *Appalachian Spring*, has, by the inflexibility of his pastoral landscape mood, kept her away from the violence of solitary meditation and drawn her toward awareness of persons and the sweetness of manners . . . she turns out to be, as one has long suspected, not only an expressive dancer but a great actress, one of the very great among living actresses, in fact.[37]

Appalachian Spring had a great deal to do with bringing my name before a larger public, particularly after the Pulitzer Prize. However, it was Martha's admiration for the music that held the most meaning for me. She wrote (14 September 1945): "You are quite the sensation of the music world and other worlds, too. I am happy over your acclaim. It is certainly your year, Aaron. If I could sing, I would sing. With deep gratitude for working with me and letting me dance your piece."

When I told Martha I wanted to arrange an orchestral suite from the ballet score, she readily agreed. The *Appalachian Spring Suite* is a condensed version of the ballet, retaining all essential features but omitting those sections in which the interest is primarily choreographic (the largest cut was the Minister's dance). The *Suite* follows a sectional arrangement of eight sequences and is scored for an orchestra of modest proportions. I wrote to Harold Spivacke (May 1945): "I recently finished a version of the ballet for normal-sized orchestra (about twenty minutes long) and it will be premiered next October by Rodzinski and the Philharmonic. . . . I think we can all congratulate ourselves on a happy ending."

In addition to the New York Philharmonic's premiere, the *Suite* was performed in the first Boston Symphony Orchestra concerts of the season conducted by Koussevitzky (6 October 1945). After Lenny conducted it in London in 1946, he wrote (23 June 1946), ". . . my one comfort these days is studying it. I manage somehow to borrow some of that fantastic stability of yours, that deep serenity. It is really amazing how the clouds lift with that last page." Lenny made his Italian debut conducting *Appalachian Spring* (16 May 1948) and wrote about the audience: "It was a wild success. . . . I love the one that wonders what a *Bolletto per Marta* is, and the one that says it reminds him of American movies." Even Virgil Thomson, who did not conduct very often, conducted *Appalachian Spring* in Barcelona in 1954. In June 1946, I had a letter from Mrs. Coolidge: "I am so pleased to read that the Tanglewood program of July 27th includes an orchestral version of 'our' ballet. I am glad to say that I expect to be present at this performance and it would give me a great deal of pleasure if you could use one of my tickets and sit with me during this program as you did during the original performance in Washington two years ago."

The first recording of *Appalachian Spring* was made under Koussevitzky's direction for Victor in 1945. Evidently, I felt uneasy about cuts that had to be made to suit the demands for a broadcast in 1946 (less than for Victor's set of six 78 rpm records), for I wrote to Koussevitzky (26 February 1946), "I am a little nervous. Cutting is always a dangerous business"; and again (27 October), "The cuts are made . . . the big cut is slightly different than the one we discussed." In 1954, Eugene Ormandy invited Martha Graham and the dance company to perform the ballet in Philadelphia, accompanied by the Philadelphia Symphony Orchestra, for which I orchestrated the sections previously excluded from the *Suite*. Ormandy promised to record the complete ballet for Columbia, and I felt something had to be done to make the seventh recorded version of *Appalachian Spring* different from the others. I knew that the Philadelphia's legendary strings would not hurt such a recording! Another top conductor who performed *Appalachian Spring* was Pierre Monteux with the San Francisco Symphony, but he made an unauthorized cut and did what seemed to me an uneven interpretation.[38]

For some time in the late sixties, my friend Lawrence Morton in Los Angeles had been urging me to prepare a concert version using the original scoring. I thought that once the listening public had become used to the large version, the thirteen-instrument one would sound "skinny," so I was hesitant about making it available. Lawrence said, "You are wrong, you are wrong! The thirteen-instrument version has a different atmosphere, it's more personal, it's more modest, more tender, closer to what the ballet was originally about." And he added, "You come out to California and conduct it and you will see for yourself if I am right or not." So I went and conducted it at a concert in honor of my seventieth birthday at the Los Angeles County Museum of Art, and as everybody seemed very enthusiastic,[39] I decided to publish it and am very glad I did. Often people (particularly the English) tell me they like the thirteen-instrument version better than the full orchestra because it seems more intimate and more touching. I, myself, am glad to have both arrangements available. In time, I have come to think that the original instrumentation has a clarity and is closer to my original conception than the more opulent orchestrated version.

Appalachian Spring in the original orchestration is recorded by Dennis Russell Davies and the St. Paul Chamber Orchestra.

I have conducted several recordings of *Appalachian Spring* myself: with the BSO for R.C.A., about the time of my sixtieth birthday; with the London Symphony Orchestra for Columbia Records; and with the St. Paul Chamber Orchestra for Columbia's "Meet the Composer" series (the thirteen-instrument version for which I reinstated the episode that had originally preceded the final variations of "Simple Gifts"; it added a variety necessary when omitting the full orchestra dynamics).[40] I have conducted all of my own compositions as well as works by other composers, but *Appalachian Spring* is the one I know best from a conducting point of view. I have often admonished orchestras, professional and otherwise, not to get too sweet or too sentimental with it, and I have reminded performers that *Appalachian Spring* should be played cooler than Tchaikovsky and lighter and happier than Stravinsky's *Sacre du Printemps.* My own favorite place in the whole piece is toward the end, where I have marked a *misterioso.* I would tell string players that we don't want to know where the up and down bows are.[41] They must have a special sustained quality there—kind of organlike in sound, with each entry like an Amen.

Interlude I

Forty-one years after the historic premiere of *Appalachian Spring*, Martha Graham and Aaron Copland attended a performance of their ballet together: Graham was ninety-one, Copland eighty-four. It was 21 April 1985. Composer and choreographer sat quietly in the wings at the New York City Center as dancers from the Martha Graham Dance Company in various costumes milled about, stretching or rehearsing a few steps. Occasionally, dancers leaped on or offstage on either side of the elderly pair. Graham and Copland hardly spoke, yet each seemed intensely aware of the other's presence. As the familiar opening music of *Appalachian Spring* was heard and the dancers took their places one by one onstage, everyone backstage—dancers, guests, stagehands—felt the significance of the moment.[1]

Difficult as the birth of *Appalachian Spring* had been, it was blessed with success from the premiere on. Those connected with the original production went on to extraordinarily successful careers: Erick Hawkins, Merce Cunningham, May O'Donnell, and Pearl Lang as solo dancers and choreographers with their own companies; Isamu Noguchi as one of the most celebrated visual artists of the century; and Copland as a great American composer.[2] Some ballets take time to work into the repertory, others disappear soon after the first season, yet others are vehicles for one dancer only. *Appalachian Spring* is the rare example of a dance that has continued to speak to performers and audiences through the decades.

In 1944, with World War II at its grimmest and the world in turmoil, people yearned for the kind of pastoral landscape and innocent love that Martha Graham's most lyrical ballet offered. *Appalachian Spring* affirmed traditional American values that were being dramatically challenged by Nazism. Audiences knew immediately what the country was fighting for when they saw *Appalachian Spring*, even though it had no explicit patriotic theme. However, the real test of this ballet's success has been in its

Photograph by Diana Walker.

Martha Graham and Copland at the Kennedy Center Honors, December 1979.

power to reaffirm established ideals through so many years of chaotic change and rapidly shifting mores. Even in today's turbulent, confused, and unloving age, *Appalachian Spring*'s sensitivity and integrity reach out to audiences. It has gone beyond the world of dance, where it is considered a classic, to become an American symbol: Mention Aaron Copland, Martha Graham, or *Appalachian Spring* anywhere in the world, and America comes immediately to mind.

Every work of art derives from a complex set of circumstances. In addition to the patriotic climate in the contemporary arts that was engendered by the war, the determinants for *Appalachian Spring* included Erick Hawkins' desire to promote Martha Graham and her company; Harold Spivacke's determination to expand performing arts at the Library of Congress; and the personal and professional lives of those involved at the time of the ballet's creation.

Appalachian Spring was the culmination of Martha Graham's "Americana" period, one which began with *American Frontier* and continued with *American Document* and *Letter to the World.* Graham's desire to create an American "look" in dance paralleled other activities in the arts in the thirties and forties: photographer Alfred Steiglitz and the "affirm

America" movement; Harold Clurman and the Group Theatre; Lincoln Kirstein and Ballet Caravan; and Copland's own patriotic works.[3] Sculptor Noguchi said, *"Appalachian Spring* was in a sense influenced by Shaker furniture, but it is also the culmination of Martha's interest in American themes and in the puritan American tradition."[4] American writers William Carlos Williams and Emily Dickinson were sources for Graham's creative ideas. One poet admired by both Graham and Copland was Hart Crane (Copland had known Crane in the twenties; when the poet died, Copland sketched a page in his notebook with the heading "Elegy for Hart Crane," 1932). It was Crane's American epic *The Bridge*[5] with its mixture of nationalism, pantheism, and symbolism that was the basis for the script Graham devised for the Coolidge commission. Graham was drawn to a section of *The Bridge* called "The Dance." There she found the line "O Appalachian Spring!" The stanza of Crane's poem ending with this line does not refer to springtime in the Appalachian Mountains, but to the uninhibited joyful leap of a mountain spring:

I took the portage climb, then chose
A further valley-shed; I could not stop.
Feet nozzled wat'ry webs of upper flows;
One white veil gusted from the very top.
O Appalachian Spring! . . .

Martha Graham did not correct the impression that the title of her ballet *Appalachian Spring* refers to the Appalachians in springtime. Perhaps she interpreted Crane's "O Appalachian Spring!" as a general salute to springtime. In any case, in 1975 she gave this description to dance critic Anna Kisselgoff of *The New York Times:*

> It's spring. There is a house that has not been completed. The bare posts are up. The fence has not been completed. Only a marriage has been celebrated. It is essentially the coming of new life. It has to do with growing things. Spring is the loveliest and the saddest time of the year.

An evocative title can become inextricably connected with a work in the public mind, although it may mean far less to a composer or choreographer, who frequently decide on titles after works are created. Difficult as it is today to think of *Appalachian Spring* as anything *but* that, the piece had earlier working titles: Graham's *House of Victory* and *Eden Valley;* and Copland's *Ballet for Martha* (or *Martha's Ballet* as on the first rough sketches of the score).[6] He has often stated: "I was fully aware of her very special personality and it affected my writing of the piece. In my own mind it was a 'Ballet for Martha.' Very much so."

While the influences on the creation of *Appalachian Spring* included Graham's interests in American roots and identity, the ballet's enduring qualities stem more from a kind of poetic universality than from specifics of a time and place. Although American in spirit, the ballet is first and foremost a love story, and audiences relate to it, as they tend to with a beautifully told love story. Martha Graham and Erick Hawkins' personal relationship was at its most passionate during the time *Appalachian Spring* was created; their love affair strongly affected the subject and form of the ballet. Martha Graham created the Bride for herself, and the role of the Husband for Hawkins. The energy of the dance is concentrated on these two, and the lovers' scenes hold a kind of stillness, a fragility, that separates them from the action going on around them. It was Graham's great genius to retain the intensity of the relationship while idealizing and abstracting the Bride and Husband just enough so that they reach beyond themselves to express the springtime of the nation as well as the springtime in their own lives.

It was Copland's good fortune to find himself with key people at important junctures in his career—Boulanger when he went to study abroad, Koussevitzky just as he returned to the States, and then Martha Graham. Perhaps it was partly luck (as Copland frequently claimed) that brought these two creative figures together to create one single gem of a dance, but what Copland modestly credits to happenstance had a great deal to do with his highly developed sense of selectivity. Copland recognized Graham's genius and knew he wanted to work with her (other dance commissions had been discreetly refused). Typical of Copland was his confidence once a decision was made: No matter how many convoluted letters and complex scripts Martha Graham sent (and there were many), Copland never doubted for a moment what she was doing or worried about changes and delays.

Aaron Copland's temperament was a perfect foil for Martha Graham and the ballet she created in 1944. Although warm, witty, and sociable, Copland is also detached, wry, and objective. Essentially a very private person, he does not make overt gestures, either in person or in his music. He does not intrude on others, nor does his music intrude or impose itself on the scene in collaborative works. The result for *Appalachian Spring* was music with a quiet glow, a Puritan restraint, and the tenderness of young love.

Copland seemed to intuit the vocabulary of dancers as he did filmmakers—not their words but their gestures. There is a similarity between the sequence of actions and their formalization in dance and film that match the cumulative effect of musical phrases in composition. Copland understood precisely what Graham meant when she told him that the written script would have little resemblance to the final product; he knew very well that a collaboration between dance and music was not tied to verbal language.

It is interesting to note how closely some of the dance movements in *Appalachian Spring* match the music. One example is when the four Followers mimic the staccato pattern of sixteenth notes in Copland's score. Graham has them do so unconventionally—by squatting on their toes—and she has them do so for dramatic reasons—to project the idea that they *are*, in fact, Followers, not free agents. A choreographic analysis of *Appalachian Spring* shows similar instances where Graham chose specific steps and phrases that connect closely to the rhythmic elements in Copland's score,[7] and other segments where the dance has a great deal of freedom from the music. The choices for Graham had to do with a combination of visual image and dramatic integrity.

One of Copland's great accomplishments is that much of his music, so perfectly matched to dance and film, can exist independent of its original purpose. After all, *Appalachian Spring* is known best as a symphonic suite. Because Copland's work, no matter how specific the purpose, was stimulated by musical ideas, it would be possible for his *Appalachian Spring* music to be used for one scenario or another, or to stand on its own as a purely musical composition. The "illusion of space," described by dancers such as Pearl Lang, was accomplished in specific musical ways: wide-open intervals and octaves; light instrumentation (primarily winds and strings) to achieve the "transparent" texture; and a minimizing of intricate chromaticism, difficult polyrhythms, and complicated polymeters.

Graham and Copland were not to collaborate on a dance again after *Appalachian Spring*. The choreographer went on to work with other outstanding American composers, among them Samuel Barber and William Schuman, with whom she had more direct contact than she had had with Copland (he had been in either California or Mexico while Graham was choreographing *Appalachian Spring*). When in 1974 Martha Graham asked Copland to provide a score for a ballet based on Hawthorne's *The Scarlet Letter*, Copland had virtually stopped composing, and he had no choice but to refuse. The score for *The Scarlet Letter* was composed by Hunter Johnson, and the dance was premiered in 1975 during the fiftieth anniversary of the Martha Graham Dance Company, a year that also

Martha Graham and
Copland at the New
York City Center, 1965.

Photograph by Martha Swope.

marked Graham's sixtieth anniversary as a performer, the beginning of the Bicentennial celebrations, and Copland's seventy-fifth birthday.

If Copland could not compose a new piece for that landmark season, he *could* accept Martha Graham's invitation to conduct *Appalachian Spring* for the Company's "Gala," which featured works on American themes (16 December 1975). Although Copland's conducting career had become very active, this was the first time he conducted the ballet version of *Appalachian Spring;* in fact, it was his first conducting of any dance since Ruth Page's *Hear Ye! Hear Ye!* of 1934. Copland shared the 1975 program with Stanley Sussman, a "regular" Graham conductor.[8] Copland told Anna Kisselgoff of *The New York Times,* when asked how he felt about conducting his own Pulitzer Prize score—"Nervous!" The great Russian star Rudolf Nureyev had requested the Preacher role in *Appalachian Spring.* On the afternoon of the performance, Copland arrived for rehearsal at the Mark Hellinger Theater. All went smoothly until the

56

moment arrived for the Preacher's dance. Nureyev had taken his position on a small platform at the rear of the stage. At the appropriate time in the score, Copland launched into the music and Nureyev came forward, but instead of beginning the dance as expected, he stopped the performance and continued walking forward, not halting until he was directly in front of the conductor. Copland looked up in surprise—he had no idea what would come next. "Maestro," said the great Russian dancer, "may I ask for four beats in order to position myself before I begin the dance?" Copland, visibly relieved, said, "Why, of course," and he wrote the cue in his score so that Nureyev would have time to come center stage and position himself—Russian ballet style.[9]

In the spring of 1982, Copland conducted *Appalachian Spring* for the Graham Company for the last time. When he arrived at the New York City Center for dress rehearsal, he was greeted by Pearl Lang, ballet mistress for the season's performances of *Appalachian Spring*. As conductor Stanley Sussman turned the podium over to Copland, the orchestra members welcomed the composer warmly, and the dancers stood poised to begin. Copland opened his score and picked up his baton. Soon it was clear something was amiss: Copland had conducted the *Suite* so often that some of his tempi were too slow for the dancers. Copland conferred with Sussman, who advised that certain tempi, such as in the duet, go faster, and similarly, in the theme and variations.[10] Another difficulty was that the placement of instruments in the ballet orchestra is different from the concert orchestra, with basses and cellos separated instead of on the same side. But there was a more serious problem: Some of Copland's conducting score did not match the orchestra parts or the action onstage.

After rehearsal, Copland stepped down to confer with Sussman. Sussman said to Copland, "I hope you don't mind my telling Aaron Copland how to conduct certain tempi in *Appalachian Spring!*" And Copland replied kindly, "I have been conducting it a certain way for twenty-five years, and I'm sure I can make some changes for this performance."

If the ballet conveys the impression of simplicity, it is deceiving. The work is not easy for the dancers or the musicians. Several versions exist, each with a different score.[11] At the 1982 rehearsal, only Sussman's score matched the current Graham Company production,[12] and it contained eighteen years of markings reflecting cast changes and other variables. Conducting scores in general can become highly personalized; Sussman's for *Appalachian Spring*, with its overlaying of cues, tempo markings, and assorted directions, would have been difficult for Copland to use at any time, no less the afternoon of the performance! The solution was for David Walker (Copland's assistant), who was present at the rehearsal, to mark changes in red pencil into Copland's score during the few hours between rehearsal and performance. None of this was in any way apparent to the audience, who applauded the composer at the beginning and end of the ballet. To the amazement of those at the rehearsal, all went smoothly.

In October 1987, Martha Graham invited two great Russian stars to dance in *Appalachian Spring* for her Company's "Gala": Rudolf Nureyev in the Revivalist role; Mikhail Baryshnikov in that of the Husband (Teresa Capucilli was the Bride). After rehearsal, Nureyev said, "Please don't ask me about Copland's music. I can say only I definitely love it."[13] And Baryshnikov said, "*Appalachian Spring* is about passion and possession."[14] In the evening, the audience, having waited patiently for the stars to appear, broke into cheers as each of the great Russian dancers came onstage, drowning out some of Copland's most tender music. Nevertheless, by any measure, this performance conducted by Stanley Sussman must be considered a dramatic moment in the rich history of *Appalachian Spring.* For those present who knew that Copland was seriously ill, it was a moving, if bittersweet, experience[15] as they recalled the many times Copland had taken his bows onstage with Martha Graham or greeted her backstage after a performance of *Appalachian Spring.* The last time he had done so was in the spring of 1986. Martha Graham took her old friend's hand and said, "Aaron, life has been wonderful to us, hasn't it?" Copland responded simply, "Martha, it certainly has." Some things never change.

Photograph by Sara Krulwich.

Across the Americas

1945-1949

A commission for a major work to be played by the Boston Symphony had been offered by Koussevitzky in March 1944. It would be my major concern for two years following *Appalachian Spring*. But it was still wartime, and one could not in good conscience refuse requests of a patriotic nature. I *tried* to refuse when Eugene Goossens asked me to contribute to an unusual project he cooked up for the Golden Jubilee of the Cincinnati Symphony in 1945, but Goossens would not take no for an answer. His idea was for ten composers to each write a variation on a theme by Goossens. He pointed out that the entire work would be dedicated to the men in the armed services. Goossens ignored my refusal, sent his theme along, and wrote, "I hope when you see the theme and realize that I don't need your minute-and-a-quarter variation until the beginning of October, you may perhaps find a free minute here and there to relax and pen something in your inimitable fashion. It is unthinkable that you should not be in our ultra-select group of composers." (The contributors in the order of performance were Paul Creston, myself, Deems Taylor, Howard Hanson, William Schuman, Walter Piston, Roy Harris, Anis Fuleihan, Bernard Rogers, and Ernest Bloch.) Along with his sixteen-measure "Jubilee" theme, Goossens sent instructions that my variation be "spirited in feeling and in A major."

Variations on a Theme by Goossens was performed in its entirety by the Cincinnati Symphony on 23 and 24 March 1945. Then it disappeared from the scene. Recently, someone in Cincinnati got the idea of performing my variation again. My publishers searched out the score, and the thirteen-page variation was performed and recorded by the current conductor of the Cincinnati Pops Orchestra, Erich Kunzel (14 September 1986).[1] *Jubilee* is about three minutes in duration and similar in style to *Fanfare for the Common Man*.

Another war-related commission came from the Office of War Information. I had been in touch with them because Lenny Bernstein wanted me to help plan two concerts of American music in Paris, and he needed help in contacting officials in France. Understandably, the French had other matters on their minds in the spring of 1945. The plan fell through, but the OWI put their Overseas Motion Picture Bureau in touch with me about composing a score for a film concerning life in a small New England town. It would be for distribution abroad and to the armed services. Instead of Paris in the spring, I went to Bernardsville, New Jersey, where I rented a small cottage, "Claremont," on the estate of a wealthy gentleman concert pianist who was away. Victor Kraft returned from Mexico and came along with me. I told very few people where I was going, with the idea of having some uninterrupted composing time. The cottage was ideal for my needs. I could get into New York easily by train to work on the film score, and use the rest of my time to meet various deadlines. I arranged the *Appalachian Spring Suite,* made an arrangement for violin and piano of "Hoe-Down" from *Rodeo,* and completed the slow movement of the symphony for Koussevitzky.

The film score, *The Cummington Story,* was composed during one week in June, with the orchestration and recording finished a month later.[2] A piano was moved into the projection room at the OWI office in New York, and I was given a print of the film with the narration. The fifteen-minute documentary, one of a series called "The American Scene," was for distribution to servicemen and twenty-two foreign countries during the war. It was essentially a plea against intolerance. The story concerns a group of refugees from Eastern European countries, their arrival at a hostel in the town of Cummington, Massachusetts, the difficulties they encountered with the townspeople, and the final acceptance by both sides. The closing words by the minister of the church sum up the message: "Strangeness between people breaks down when they live and work and meet together with people as neighbors."

The Cummington Story was shot in Cummington (not far from Pittsfield) because the town actually had a program for refugees, with a house on Main Street that was available for ten or twelve refugees at a time. The townspeople were pleased to cooperate in what was considered "psychological warfare." Included are scenes of the town hall, the church, the Cummington Press, the former home of poet William Cullen Bryant, and the surrounding countryside. I have seen the film recently and still find it straightforward and rather touching. Having been made on a very limited budget, it has a simplicity that is appealing.[3]

The narrator in *The Cummington Story* takes the part of the minister of the town. Except for his voice, there is no sound but the musical score, which is continuous but for one silent segment—when the town's "old stove league at the general store" gives the silent treatment to Joseph, the newcomer. For the segment that shows Anna, the refugee woman, singing her child to sleep on their first night in Cummington, I used an unaccompanied Polish lullaby. In another section, the refugees perform part of a Mozart trio. During most of the film, the music, scored for full orchestra, takes over as the camera shows outdoor scenes. The main theme is related to the Polish lullaby, and a second theme consists of an ascending and descending figure. For the country fair scene, with horseracing and ox-cart-pulling contests, I used a phrase with offbeat rhythms that repeats over and over again.

After the film score was recorded, I retrieved my music and placed it in my files. (In 1962, while looking for something to satisfy a commission for a short piano piece, I salvaged the main theme of *The Cummington Story* and arranged it as a short piano piece, *In Evening Air.*[4])

The OWI liked the film score and asked whether I would cooperate on another matter. Could they put the Radio Program Bureau in touch with me? I agreed, and to my surprise, I heard from Roy Harris, who had just become chief of the music section. Roy wrote, "The OWI is making a democratic survey of the opinions of our leading musicians concerning American music. That means you! Send me a list of ten composers you consider most worthy to represent American culture to European nations." I explained that it was a difficult task because such a list would vary according to the purposes for which works were chosen. But finally, I sent the following:

> For a broad radio audience I would prescribe RR Bennett or M. Gould rather than a R. Sessions, altho from a purely cultural standpoint I think the latter more significant. But the significance would only be apparent to an elite public. Well, anyhow, for the purposes of a poll, here are ten names: Barber, Diamond, Gershwin, Harris, Ives, Piston, Schuman, Sessions, V. Thomson, R. Thompson.

While in Bernardsville in the summer of 1945, I felt my *Third Symphony* finally taking shape. I had been working on various sections whenever I could find time during the past few years. My colleagues had been urging me to compose a major orchestral work (especially when I went to

Hollywood). Elliott Carter, David Diamond, and Arthur Berger reminded me about it whenever they had the opportunity. A note from Sam Barber sent from Italy was typical (16 September 1944): "I hope you will knuckle down to a good symphony. We deserve it of you, and your career is all set for it. *Forza!*" They had no way of knowing that I had been working on such a composition for some time. I did not want to announce my intentions until I was clear in my own mind what the piece would become (at one time, it looked more like a piano concerto than a symphony). The commission from Koussevitzky stimulated me to focus my ideas and arrange the material I had collected into some semblance of order.

A forty-minute symphony is very different from a short work for a specific purpose. It has to be planned very carefully and be given enough time to evolve. I had put the first movement of my *Third Symphony* together in Mexico during the summer of 1944, and the second in the summer of 1945. David Diamond came out to Bernardsville for a few days in July, and we showed each other what we had of our symphonies. David was composing a great deal, and his work was becoming more and more classical in style. He was working on his *Fourth Symphony* at that time, and I kidded him, saying if he was not careful he'd turn into the Glazunov of American music. David was horrified. After he returned home, he wrote about my symphony: "Can't tell you how impressed I am by the two mvts. . . . As elusive as the opening theme is, it sticks pretty easily with me." A few other friends came out to visit—Marc Blitzstein, Leo Smit, and Lenny, who was full of plans for his New York City Symphony Orchestra. For the most part, I kept to myself and left the cottage only when I had to work on *The Cummington Story* in New York, and once to see Sam Barber and Gian Carlo Menotti at their home, "Capricorn," in Mt. Kisco. By September, I was able to announce to Irving Fine, "I'm the proud father—or mother—or both—of a second movement. Lots of notes—and only eight minutes of music—such are scherzi! It's not very original—*mais ça marche du commencement jusqu'au fin*—which is a help." Having two movements finished gave me the courage to continue, but the completion seemed years off.

When I had to give up the Bernardsville cottage in the fall of 1945, Victor found another rental on Limestone Road in Ridgefield, Connecticut. Again, I told almost no one where I could be found. I felt in self-exile, but it was essential if I was to finish the symphony. By April I had a third movement to show for it. With Tanglewood reopening in the summer of 1946, and an October date set for the premiere, I headed to the Mac-

Photograph by Victor Kraft.

Samuel Barber (middle) and Gian Carlo Menotti (right) visiting Copland in Bernardsville, New Jersey, summer 1945.

Dowell Colony for the month of June to work on the last movement.

It was my first visit to the Colony since 1938. I found a nice studio with
a fireplace waiting for me (the studio David Diamond had occupied in
1935). Musicians in residence were Esther and Harold Shapero and Mabel
Daniels. "Sonny" Shapero played jazz in the evenings, and I loved listening to him improvise. When I showed him the completed movements of
my *Third Symphony,* he thought I should make some changes (I didn't).[5]
Sonny was a severe critic—he listed only about thirty objections, so I
figured it must be a marvel of a piece! While I was at the Colony, Victor
returned to New York and wrote that he hated the job he had just taken
with *Harper's Bazaar.* I responded, "Your letters always sound as if they
were written while seated on a volcano. . . . Why not give yourself two
years of apprenticeship and if nothing happens by then to make you
happier, you can start to complain and I'll listen." I urged Victor to be
in touch with a psychoanalyst—someone I had heard recommended
highly—and eventually he took my advice.

I left the Colony reluctantly, knowing how limited my composing time
would be once I got to Tanglewood. I received a letter from my agent, Abe
Meyer, who said that Sam Goldwyn was willing to pay twelve thousand
dollars for a picture if I would go right out to Hollywood. Of course, I had

Copland with Marc
Blitzstein in Bernardsville,
New Jersey, 1945.

to turn it down, along with an offer to teach at UCLA—or no symphony!
I worked whenever I could during the summer, and I played parts of
various movements for everyone who came to visit. Paul Moor has reminded me, "You played the *Third Symphony* and explained that it was
the first time you had used thirty-second notes. I was flabbergasted when
you turned to me and said, 'React!' I didn't know *how* to react, but you
were tactful and went on to explain various things in the score."[6]

To get a piece finished, it helps to have a definite date by which time
you *must* be finished. In the case of the *Third Symphony,* I knew from
the start that the original 1945 date might be unrealistic, but now, it *had*
to be completed for the opening of the 1946 BSO season. After Tanglewood, I stayed on in the Berkshires to work on the orchestration. It was
a mad dash! The finishing touches were put on the score just before
rehearsals were to start for the premiere, 18 October 1946. It was two years
since I had started working on the piece in Mexico.

This commission meant a great deal to me, over and beyond the money:
The work would receive its world premiere by Koussevitzky with the BSO,
an organization I greatly admired, and the score was to be dedicated to
Madame Natalie Koussevitzky, who had died in 1942. I knew the kind of
thing Koussevitzky liked to conduct and what he wanted from me for the
occasion. I was determined that this piece be a major work. To be sure,

66

Photograph by Victor Kraft.

Copland taking a break from composing, Ridgefield, Connecticut, fall 1946.

I was influenced by the circumstances of the commission, but the conditions for the writing of such a piece had been in place for some time. The Koussevitzky Foundation made no demands of me, other than to suggest that the premiere take place in 1945, and that the manuscript eventually be deposited with the archive of the Koussevitzky Music Foundation at the Library of Congress.[7]

In the program book for the first performance, I pointed out that the writing of a symphony inevitably brings with it the question of what it is meant to express. As I wrote at the time, if I forced myself, I could invent an ideological basis for the *Third Symphony*. But if I did, I'd be bluffing—or at any rate, adding something ex post facto, something that might or might not be true but that played no role at the moment of creation.[8]

The *Third Symphony*, my longest orchestral work (about forty minutes in duration), is scored for a big orchestra. It was composed in the general form of an arch, in which the central portion, that is the second-movement scherzo, is the most animated, and the final movement is an extended coda, presenting a broadened version of the opening material. Both the first and third themes in the first movement are referred to again in later movements. The second movement stays close to the normal symphonic procedure of a usual scherzo, while the third is freest of all in formal

67

structure, built up sectionally with its various sections intended to emerge one from the other in continuous flow, somewhat in the manner of a closely knit series of variations. Some of the writing in the third movement is for very high strings and piccolo, with no brass except single horn and trumpet. It leads directly into the final and longest of the movements: The fourth is closest to a customary sonata-allegro form, although the recapitulation is replaced by an extended coda, presenting many ideas from the work, including the opening theme.[9]

One aspect of the *Third Symphony* ought to be pointed out: It contains no folk or popular material. Any reference to either folk material or jazz in this work was purely unconscious.[10] However, I do borrow from myself by using *Fanfare for the Common Man* in an expanded and reshaped form in the final movement. I used this opportunity to carry the *Fanfare* material further and to satisfy my desire to give the *Third Symphony* an affirmative tone. After all, it was a wartime piece—or more accurately, an end-of-war piece—intended to reflect the euphoric spirit of the country at the time. It is an ambitious score, often compared to Mahler and to Shostakovich and sometimes Prokofiev, particularly the second movement. As a longtime admirer of Mahler, some of my music may show his influence in a general way, but I was not aware of being directly influenced by other composers when writing the work.

I went up to Boston before the premiere and played the score for Koussevitzky in the evenings on the piano at his home. I never had the feeling that this was necessary, only helpful in familiarizing him with the rhythms. Koussevitzky had a Russian point of view; he would feel things in a different way from that of a native American. Some of the parts that I thought were expressive of a certain American simplicity, Koussevitzky would tend to "lean on." But he certainly could whip up a storm! I always remember that he gave a very effective version of the final movement.

The premiere was set for the Friday afternoon subscription audience. The reception and reviews were generally favorable. *The Third Symphony* was hailed as a major American symphony along the lines of Roy Harris' *Third Symphony*. A few weeks after the Boston premiere, Koussevitzky conducted my *Third Symphony* at the Brooklyn Academy of Music and at Carnegie Hall in New York, and the critics agreed that it was a "big" work. *Time* magazine quoted Koussevitzky as he came offstage: "There is no doubt about it—this is the greatest American symphony. It goes from the heart to the heart."[11] The review was mixed, however, accusing me of stealing from others as well as myself, and of being "too popular to be a great composer." Virgil Thomson wrote a long and thoughtful piece for the *Herald Tribune*, which was essentially laudatory but not devoid of negative criticism. In part, here is what Virgil wrote:

> What is a mature artist? It is any free-lance worker who has practiced his profession long enough to know on inspecting his finished work whether it really says most of what he has meant to say and who is willing for his work to mean forever what it does in plain language really say. Any composer who crawls thus naked out on a limb has written great music. Shooting him down will not wipe out that fact. It will merely prevent his doing it again. I should like Copland to do it again.[12]

It took some time for my friends and colleagues to decide how they felt about the *Third Symphony*. Arthur Berger wrote an article about it in an all-Copland issue of *Tempo* magazine in 1948[13] and included a lengthy section dealing with the *Third Symphony* in his book about my music (1953).[14] Arthur's view was that it represented both a summing up and a step forward in terms of the technical demands of a large orchestral work. Irving Fine wrote, "I am not entirely in sympathy with the symphony's popularist tendencies, but you would not expect otherwise from me." Later on, Irving admitted, "It does get better on hearing it a third time, and I think it will make its way surely. It has some of the noblest music you have ever written, which means some of the most inspired music of our generation." When I complained to Lawrence Morton that some of my colleagues were calling the *Third Symphony* "too triumphant" and were urging cuts, Lawrence responded in his typically laconic fashion, "Since most of the persuaders have themselves never known any triumph as composers, how would they have any way of knowing whether a compositional statement was 'too triumphant'?"[15]

The *Third Symphony* has come to be viewed as something of an anomaly, standing between my abstract works and the more accessible ballet and film music. The fourth-movement finale is perhaps the clearest example of this fusion of styles. I, myself, have thought of this piece as being closest in feeling to the *Symphonic Ode,* at least in intention: a full orchestral work for the concert hall that makes a serious statement. Personally, I am satisfied that my *Third Symphony* stands for what I wanted to say at the time. The musical ideas that came to me (or that I chose) were appropriate for the particular purpose of the work.

The conductor who has always understood my music almost intuitively is Leonard Bernstein: His conducting of the *Third Symphony* is closest to what I had in mind when composing the piece. Despite misgivings about

Hotel Castiglione
Paris
27. v. 47

Old charmer!

It's done. Fait. The Symphony's been heard. Two days ago in Prague.

First I must say it's a wonderful work. Coming to know it so much better I find in it new lights & shades —— and new faults. Sweetie, the end is a sin. You've got to change. Stop the presses! We must talk — about the whole last movement, in fact.

The reactions were mixed. Too long, said some; Too eclectic, said Shostakovich (he should talk!). It lacks a real Adagio, said Kubelik. And everyone found Tchaikovsky's Fifth in it, which only proves their inanity. I haven't seen the press yet, but I think it will be good. It just wasn't a wow, that's all; it was, I said, it was serious. The orchestra was exhausted (end of the festival), and the

Not up my street, said Wee Willie Walton

Letter from
Leonard Bernstein
to Copland,
27 May 1947.

rehearsals were nightmares. (We had six!) But at the concerts they played marvelously. Even to catching our private rubatos in the third movement

which, by the way, is my favorite part. That's the real inspiration — the real Aaronchen. I could make out fine anti-cases for Mov'ts. I & II (and of course IV) but not III. That's my personal wow.

By the way, I did it awfully well, and I'd love to do it in the states. Maybe Tangle— well, maybe the City Center.

There's much to say. Letters are impossible. But won't you write me and tell about May and Harvard & the Virgil Opera and where you are and Koussie and Victor and everyone? And DD?

If you write me to Holland I'll be sure to get it. I'm there June 8–13. Write now, and they'll hold it for me.
c/o G. de Koos
Noordeinde 60?-A
Den Haag, Holland

Palestine was a real thrill. More later. Will you be in NYC for my Stadium week? Love, love, L.

some passages, particularly the ending, Lenny conducted the *Third Symphony* in Prague only seven months after the world premiere. In 1948, after conducting it in Israel, Lenny seemed more positive about the piece (8 November): "The *Symphony* seems to be a success! . . . After the fourth performance it has begun to sound, and quite magnificent at that. It's really a fantastic piece! I must confess I have made a sizable cut near the end and believe me it makes a whale of a difference."[16] At the time, I thought it was pretty nervy of Lenny to take it on himself to make a cut. Being a careful and slow worker, I rarely felt it necessary to revise a composition after it was finished, and even more rarely after it was published. In the case of the *Third Symphony,* however, I came to agree with Lenny and several others about the advisability of shortening the ending. It's interesting to note that with a cut of eight measures, the difference was apparent and was commented on when Lenny conducted this new version with the BSO at Tanglewood in 1952.[17] When he conducted the New York Philharmonic for a television broadcast of my *Symphony's* fourth movement, I said jokingly from the stage to The Young People's Concerts audience, "Maestro Bernstein conducts the music as if he wrote it. But I just want to make one thing clear. He didn't write it, *I* did!"

When Chávez invited me to Mexico to conduct the *Symphony* in June 1947, Koussevitzky advised against it. I decided to try it out, however, since at least it would be across the border! (I was also scheduled to conduct *Appalachian Spring Suite* and *Two Pieces for String Orchestra.*) For weeks before leaving for Mexico, I stood in front of a mirror in my studio and flailed my arms around and snapped my fingers. I really got cold feet when I arrived in Mexico City and saw my name staring at me from posters all over town! I was revived by telegrams announcing that I had won the BSO Merit Award and the Music Critic's Circle Award of 1946–1947 for the *Third Symphony.* As rehearsals proceeded, I gained confidence. I was not sure the orchestra would learn the work, but I certainly did! I wrote to Lenny (4 June 1947): "My main trouble is giving cues for entrances. Kouss said to me before I left, 'If you ruin MY Symphony I vill keel you.' "

As much as I enjoyed working with the Sinfonica musicians, I found the Mexican audiences icy toward modern music, and I had very little idea of what, if anything, they got from the *Third Symphony.* Helen and Elliott Carter happened to be in Mexico at the time. They remember going with me to rent my tuxedo. The jackets were all several sizes too big for me, with the sleeves hanging down over my hands! After the concert, I had some fun showing them the "Salón México" dance hall. Helen Carter still

Manuscript page from the fourth movement of Copland's conducting score for the
Third Symphony showing the beginning of cut suggested by Bernstein.
© Copyright 1946 by Aaron Copland; copyright renewed. Boosey & Hawkes, Inc., Sole Publishers and Licensees.

recalls how they frisked Elliott and me before allowing us into the hall, to make sure we had no guns![18]

The *Third Symphony* has been performed and recorded by many different orchestras and conductors. George Szell wrote to me while I was on the State Department tour of Latin America in 1947 (16 September 1947): "I have studied the work during the summer and got rather close to it and hope to be able to give a satisfactory performance. Needless to say, I shall be glad to have you sit in at the rehearsals and help me with your suggestions and criticisms." So I went to Cleveland, and later Szell conducted the *Third Symphony* in New York and for a radio broadcast (21 December 1947). Antal Dorati made the first recording with the Minneapolis Symphony, and I have conducted two recordings myself, both with English orchestras.[19] Lenny continues to program the *Third Symphony*, particularly for special birthdays.[20] His conducting of it in 1985 left me marveling at how he had that tough New York Philharmonic playing like angels—well, there's only one Lenny Bernstein![21]

It was brave of me to accept a commission for a choral work to be premiered at a Symposium on Music Criticism at Harvard in May 1947, never having composed anything of length for chorus. If I was going to have the work ready in time, I had to get away from New York. Verna and Irving Fine lived in Cambridge, and Verna's mother, Florence Rudnick, had a comfortable apartment in Boston, which she left in the winter months. Verna arranged for me to use Mrs. Rudnick's place while she was in Florida from February through April 1946, and they agreed "not to tell a soul." I wrote to Verna, "I plan to use the BSO as an address, and to be mysterious about my real whereabouts. It's come to this! A nice simple guy like me."

The Department of Music at Harvard had suggested that I use a Hebrew text for the choral piece, but I opted for part of the King James Version of the Bible (Genesis 1:1; 2:7) concerned with the seven days of creation. My plan was to use a mezzo-soprano soloist and mixed chorus a capella to tell the oft-told story in a gentle narrative style using the biblical phrase "And the next day . . ." to round off each section. I was uncertain about how it would proceed until I got to the third day of creation—only then did I feel that my idea would work.

In The Beginning is dedicated to Nadia Boulanger. I have been told that its duration of thirteen and one-half minutes is long for an a capella work. It does not incorporate folk music or jazz materials, but jazz rhythms are

Manuscript, first page of the pre-final score of *In The Beginning*.

used in various sections, particularly for the verse "And let there be light in the firmament of the heavens. . . ." A cadenza-like passage for the singer and a final coda force all the voices to the top of their range, bringing the work to a climax that I hoped would depict the text—"And man became living soul"—in musical terms. Because the solo part is difficult and exacting and there are some quick harmonic changes for the chorus, when the piece was published, I included an optional piano part as an aid to the singers. Organ has occasionally been substituted for piano.

I finished the score just in time for the rehearsals at the end of April 1947.[22] A prestigious group gathered in Sanders Theatre for the Harvard Symposium[23] to hear commissioned chamber music works on the first day; the three new choral works the second day (Hindemith, Malipiero, and Copland); and new dances by Martha Graham on the third.[24] The choral concert took place in Memorial Hall, Robert Shaw conducting, Nell Tangemen soloist (Shaw also conducted the New York premiere at Carnegie Hall). All agreed Shaw had done an expert job, and *In The Beginning* was given a cordial reception by the critics.

Of all the times I, myself, conducted *In The Beginning,* one stands out as most memorable: in Israel during the Passover week concerts at the Ein Gev Music Festival, with the Tel-Aviv vocal ensemble and soprano Naomi Zurin (21 April 1951). A stage had been built for the performers, but the audience, comprised of outstanding artists as well as members of the surrounding kibbutzim, sat in the open air. It was not that the performance itself was so much better than others, but the setting and the experience of conducting my work in Israel gave the occasion a special quality.

The last time I conducted *In The Beginning* was at Brown University as part of the 1980 commencement proceedings, at which I received an honorary degree. The students put on a concert of my vocal music, and I was moved by their dedication and enthusiasm. They were not musicians, but their obvious excitement and pleasure at having me in their midst heightened my enjoyment, although at first they were tense and afraid to look at me. I realized that these young people might never again have the experience of working with a living composer. The Brown University chorus was made up of a varied group—from delicate young girls to the captain of the football team, who happened to be the head of the chorus. I found myself telling *him* to "get tough" and "don't be sentimental!" Conducting a student group is a very different experience from conducting a top-flight professional chorus. You feel as though you are all in something special together. The Brown group was well trained, yet I could enjoy hearing their sound change as I worked with them. I try never to be patronizing to nonprofessionals, and I like to make them feel more comfortable by getting a laugh once in a while. On this particular occasion, I told the Brown students, "Creation was quite a stunt, so make it *grand*— don't be pathetic about it. What happened *after* creation is an entirely different story!"

A catalogue of a composer's published works gives only part of the picture. In addition, there are projects that are abandoned and others that are considered but not accepted for one reason or another. A production that took time and effort without coming to fruition was *Tragic Ground,* a musical planned by choreographer Agnes de Mille and stage designer Oliver Smith. Their idea was a musical play based on Erskine Caldwell's novel *Tobacco Road;* when the rights could not be secured, Caldwell's *Tragic Ground* was substituted. Lynn Riggs was to write the script, I the music. We did several songs together, among them "I Bought Me a Cat" (an arrangement of an Arkansas folk song) and an original ballad, "Alone at Night."[25] The script for *Tragic Ground* was turned down by various producers, until finally, Agnes wrote (22 November 1946): "Dear Fellow Grounders, There is not enough humor in the story. We are at a deadlock. The project is abandoned."[26]

Various film scripts had been carefully considered before turning them down: a feature film with John Wayne; an MGM adaptation of Ketti Fring's book *God's Front Porch;* and Samuel Goldwyn's *Earth and High Heaven,*[27] which was to feature Koussevitzky and the BSO playing music composed by me. An offer I had considered was from the famous Billy Rose, who invited Stravinsky, Schuman, and myself to compose pieces for a big show he was putting on in 1945. I figured I could ask Billy Rose for $2,500 plus $1,000 advance against royalties. But Billy wrote (18 April 1944):

> Frankly, I didn't know that modern composing came so high. The terms you outline are several times as expensive as they would be had I asked Kern, Rodgers or Cole Porter . . . if the theatre is that fat I haven't discovered it.

Another "might-have-been" in 1946 was an offer from Woody Herman, made through Goddard Lieberson (Goddard was a representative of CBS then, before becoming president of Columbia Records). Goddard wrote (5 August 1946), "Woody wants a piece. Something Copland, not Woody Herman, for his band. Woody does *not* want any strings. He suggests a contract along the exact lines of our deal with Stravinsky." At about the same time, I was approached to compose a clarinet concerto. It would have to be one or the other. The request for the concerto was from Benny Goodman, and I accepted it.

I asked Benny whether he could send some of his recordings, and he responded, "I'm looking forward in anticipation to the piece. I do think it would be easier for you to get the two sextet albums from your record dealer or even a phone call to Goddard Lieberson may get quick results as they are recorded for Columbia. . . ." I listened to the recordings, made some notes and took them with me on a four-month tour of Latin America. I hoped to compose some of the concerto during that time.

I did a brash thing in the summer of 1947: I fell in love with a house in the Palisades area and rented it for three years, just before leaving for Latin America. I had been wanting a place of my own for so long that I was afraid to let this one go. I rationalized that at least I would have a proper home to return to from my travels. My loft in New York had been robbed again: Victor lost expensive photographic equipment and his violin, while I lost only some clothes and a few days in leaving for Mexico. We did as the police advised—put bars on the windows, padlocks on the door, and riveted the skylight down, but the time had come for a change.

In 1946, I had visited friends, the pianists Robert Fizdale and Arthur Gold, in a house they had rented in Sneden's Landing.[28] I had been impressed with the fact that it was close to the city but gave the feeling of being way out in the country—the tiny village on the Hudson with one general store was a pocket between Palisades State Park and the next state park. I started looking in that area, never dreaming I would find something right away! The house at Sneden's Landing was a rambling white Colonial, rather unusual in that it had been built in three installments. The earliest part dated from pre-Revolutionary times and had been a one-room house belonging to Molly and William Sneden, whose ferryboat crossed from Sneden's Landing to Dobbs Ferry. In fact, the story goes that George Washington used the boat during the Revolutionary War. The original house had been added to twice. Wide lawns led down to the Hudson River, and lovely old trees, a grapevine, and flower beds added to the natural setting. My studio was to be situated on the side of the house where there were no neighbors to be concerned about (I was always sensitive about that—it was one of the reasons I wanted to be out of the city). For some reason, perhaps to do with the ferryboat, the Sneden's Landing house was called the "Ding Dong House." I wrote to Victor from South America: "That name will have to go!"

Victor was in charge of moving our things from the loft while I was away (Leo Smit was moving in), and getting the house in order. He wrote to me in Rio to say, "I have hired us a housekeeper, and we have a kitten named 'Quetzel.' Truman Capote drove out to Sneden's Landing with me one day—Truman really loved it." I responded in a more practical vein: "Have you bought dishes? What will we have to eat out of?"

My 1947 tour of South America stemmed from the belief many of us in the arts had in those days—that the history of twentieth-century music was going to be written from both North and South America. In hindsight, perhaps we were naïve. I was chairman of a committee called The U.S. Group for Latin American Music, which sponsored cooperative programs between this country and three Latin American countries—Argentina, Brazil, and Uruguay. The committee included two experts on Latin American culture, Gilbert Chase and Carleton Sprague Smith, and composers Paul Bowles and Henry Cowell. The executive director, Erminie Kahn, somehow convinced a tractor company to sponsor a competition to select young composers for scholarships to the Berkshire Music Center. Considering that I was about to leave on a four-month tour of Latin America sponsored by the State Department, the committee asked me to keep an eye out for talented young composers and to make recommendations for the Tanglewood scholarships.

The tour was to include not only the big cities of Montevideo, Buenos Aires, Rio de Janeiro, São Paulo, and Pôrto Alegre but smaller places where no one had ever seen an American composer and where any composer of symphonic music was a rare bird. In all these places, our government had cooperated with local persons to maintain cultural centers for the teaching of English and the spreading of comprehensive ideas about our civilization, in order to expand the picture of the United States beyond what could be obtained from the Hollywood movies that were seen everywhere. I was to deliver twenty-eight lectures before sixteen different organizations, nineteen radio talks, and five concerts at which I either played and/or conducted.

I landed in Rio de Janeiro on 19 August 1947. It was quite a jump from Tanglewood—in space, in language, in musical atmosphere. The only thing in common with the Berkshires was the housing shortage. Nothing had been arranged in advance. I had to stay in a dingy airport hotel until the beginning of September when Eleazar de Carvalho found me an apartment. I prepared lectures and made the usual dull rounds of embassy receptions. Finally settled into the apartment on top of a mountain overlooking the Rio harbor, I wrote to Verna and Irving Fine: "The view is superb but the piano stinks! Well, you can't have everything! I feel as though I am living in the country but can walk down to the city in ten minutes. The streets are always full of people—no one ever seemed to want to go home!" The city was as beautiful as I remembered. A friendly, democratic feeling was in the air and this came across because of the lack of color lines. It was endlessly amusing to sit at a sidewalk café and watch the passing scene.

With Carvalho back in Rio, the Berkshire Music Center and American composers were not entirely unknown. His first concert with the Orquestra Sinfonica Brasileira after his return was devoted to an all-American program—my *Third Symphony*, Bill Schuman's *Symphony for Strings*, and Peter Mennin's *Folk Overture*. This was a brave gesture, since the public had heard comparatively little contemporary music of any kind. Musical conditions reminded me of what we had had at home some thirty or forty years earlier. Opera was the big social event in Rio, and the mere carrying through of a full symphonic season was quite an achievement. I was somewhat disappointed in the Orquestra. My *Third Symphony* was performed three times, but it didn't improve much.

I stayed eight weeks in Rio de Janeiro, which gave time for me to deliver a series of twelve lectures, "Panorama of American Composers." This was essentially the course I had presented at Tanglewood during the summer: The first two were delivered in English before the Ministry of Education and the Brazilian Press Association; and the others were translated and read in Spanish at the Instituto Brazil-Estados Unidos. I took part in a chamber-music concert (15 October), playing in *Vitebsk* and the *Violin Sonata*. The audience was small but sympathetic. In general, there was a very restricted group interested in new music—only the opera stars seemed to draw the crowds.

A German composer named [Hans Joachim] Koellreutter had all the talented young pupils in Rio. Somewhat like Ardévol in Cuba, he was the leader of the new generation, which published a magazine, *Musica Viva*, had radio programs, and held seminars. It was a curious situation, in which Brazilians were being brought up by a typical German twelve-toner. I attended a concert of works by his pupils, and both master and pupils made a singularly humorless impression. I knew that Koellreutter could not harm

Copland in front of the State Department in Washington before his 1947 tour of Latin America.

gifted young people, but he certainly encouraged a lot of dullards to imagine they were composers! Along with the *Musica Viva* tenets went many pious pronouncements about the "Muse of Music" and the social role of music. It was all very German and rather jejune.

Before my arrival, I had received very lively letters from Villa-Lobos, which would begin with "I've got atomic news!" or some equally colorful phrase. Villa-Lobos was only slightly less ebullient in Brazil. I was relieved to see him so friendly, because I had not seen him since a concert of his music I had organized for the League of Composers a few years earlier, which had not been a success. Not having had access to many of his printed scores, I had settled for music that was not the best Villa-Lobos, and after the program at the Museum of Modern Art (February 1945), I was conscience-stricken. I had often scolded the League's board about programs I thought were not carefully chosen, but no one scolded me, not even Villa-Lobos when he heard about it. In Rio, Villa-Lobos took me to visit his school, which trained music teachers, and he showed me his

80

studio, where copyists and engravers were all working on his manuscripts. We searched for local music up in the hills together, but it was difficult to find a real samba—the Broadway version had exerted a baleful influence on Rio's samba composers. Camargo Guarnieri suddenly turned up from São Paulo, and we made plans for my São Paulo visit. Guarnieri seemed against most things Brazilian.

One very embarrassing thing happened in Rio: The critics put on a lunch inviting twenty of the most important people, but they had neglected to tell me where it was to be, so I missed the whole thing! Pictures were taken, with my chair empty. I felt as though I had to explain myself to all of Rio. However, I then left in a blaze of glory when the Academy of Music, headed by Villa-Lobos, gave an *homenaje* with speeches and music in my honor.

I arrived in São Paulo for a four-day visit (16 October). They were organized to the hilt for my arrival. It began with a reception at the airport with representatives of the governor, the Ministry of Culture, the Musicians Sindicato, the Uniao Cultural, the consul general and, of course, Guarnieri. I was informed by the U.S. consul that I must leave my card for the governor and that caused a moment of consternation—I didn't have a printed card (I never have had one). More receptions and lunches than I could count took place. I gave a lecture on film music in Spanish for an audience of four hundred, made radio appearances, and played the *Piano Variations* at a morning concert in the opera house, which was full at 10 A.M.! Also on the program was Guarnieri's *Second String Quartet*, which struck me as a good playable work, if nothing surprising. The middle movement has definite Gershwin touches, which Guarnieri assured me were "pure Brazilian." Before leaving town, I made an official visit to the local conservatory, and it was like walking into the middle of the nineteenth century. An all-girl chorus sang, and somebody played my *Cat and Mouse.*

My next stop was Pôrto Alegre in the south of the country, a clean and compact little city that seemed to be peopled mostly by blond Germans. It reminded me of Guatemala City or Baden-Baden. I visited the local Belas Artes school and met the composers. My lecture in the Teatro São Pedro with 169 in the audience was rather lost in a place seating 1,000. I flew to Buenos Aires for a few days preparatory to returning for two weeks in November. The city looked larger and more imposing than in 1941. Switching from the little Portuguese I knew to proper Spanish was very confusing. I had dinner with the Ginasteras and afterward we all went to

José María Castro's bookshop, where I found composers I had met in 1941—everyone seemed genuinely glad to see me again. I was impressed all over again with how sweet a person Ginastera was.

By the end of October, I was in Montevideo, Uruguay, an overnight boat ride from Buenos Aires. I conducted the Sodre Orchestra, considered the best in South America next to the Colon in Buenos Aires. The concert included my *Lincoln Portrait*. It was odd hearing Lincoln's words in Spanish! I also conducted *Appalachian Spring* and *Outdoor Overture*, and Hector Tosar played his *Piano Concertino* (led by a local conductor). The concert was obviously a huge success, for the audience reacted with screams and bravos after *Lincoln* (Juana Sujo narrated in Spanish), and everyone seemed to think I was a good conductor.[29] Tosar said I was influenced by Lenny Bernstein and that my left hand was like Bruno Walter! The second *homenaje* of the trip was made by composers who looked much older than I had remembered them.

The two weeks in Buenos Aires were the busiest of all: Ginastera had planned several activities with the Liga de Compositores, including an entire concert of my music by Argentine musicians. Ginastera made a simple, sincere, and touching introductory speech to a packed house—I apparently had a "public" there. The Sociedad Hebraica gave a reception followed by a lecture on film music, also to a full auditorium. I was surprised to see my 1945 documentary, *The Cummington Story*, shown there in a Spanish version. I enjoyed meeting young composers at a series of lectures on American music at the Instituto Cultural Argentino Norteamericano. Arrangements had been made for me to conduct an all-Copland program with the Colon Orchestra, which in Buenos Aires terms is like the Philharmonic at Carnegie Hall. I suggested including something by Ginastera but was informed that, for political reasons, it would not be possible. The Colon was a first-rate orchestra, and I felt that it would be a real testing ground as to whether I could venture the same kind of program in the States. At rehearsal, however, the orchestra seemed rather less good than I expected. They were not very smart about rhythms. I conducted the entire concert in their enormous opera house—the same program as in Montevideo, with the addition after intermission of the *Third Symphony.* The house, as large as the Metropolitan Opera, was full. The ambassador and his wife attended, and at the reception afterward, I was afraid I might have to shake hands with Mrs. Perón, but it seemed she never went to musical affairs. I wrote to Verna and Irving Fine, saying,

"With Mexico that makes three orchestras I've handled since June. Bernstein better look out."

Publicity had been distributed about the Tanglewood scholarships, but the only composer I felt deserved one was Sergio de Castro. He played works for me that showed a clear logical mind, and at times, real inspiration. He reminded me of Israel Citkowitz—the same type of childlike innocence and purity of spirit. I also spent some time with Julián Bautista, a Spanish refugee composer whose music was expertly done but with no originality whatever. I always felt like commiserating with composers such as Bautista; they come so close to having everything it takes, and then their music adds up to nothing.

On my forty-seventh birthday, some of the composers suddenly produced a birthday cake after supper; the Fines sent a wire; and Victor called from New York. When he told me that "The house on the Hudson looks swell," it made me want to go right home. I still had to travel up the north coast of Brazil, however. It was in those smaller places that I met and heard some real Brazilian samba composers. Bahia, one of the oldest towns in Brazil, is charming and colorful, and claimed to have preserved the real samba. I discovered that it is not the rhythmic element that gives the samba interest. The bottom rhythm is always the same; it is the freshness of melodic line, plus the cross accents, plus the highly amusing sound of the carioca words that make them indigenous and very hard to sing, copy, or remember. I was told they must be simplified for ordinary Carnaval use, and I don't wonder. In Bahia, I heard an instrument called the birimbau. No one seemed able to tell me its origins. I'd never heard anything like the sound that several birimbau players make—a sweetly jangled tinkle.

I flew to Recife (21 November) and was taken directly to the radio station for a broadcast. People there seemed in awe of me, even the newspapermen! I was honored by a full evening's demonstration of Recifian popular arts. Most interesting was a dance, the frevo, which is no cinch: You dance it alone in a deliberately restricted space to music deriving from street marches, similar to our New Orleans jazz. For my benefit, an army band of twenty-eight men was rounded up to play frevos on an exceedingly hot night, and they played with deadpan faces—on army rations and army pay. I thought how easy it would be to make an orchestral piece out of the frevo—or easier still—a band piece. Recife at Carnaval time is said to outrival Rio, and from my brief twelve-hour visit there, I could well believe it. I heard some drumming that was phenomenal.

Copland in Recife with Brazilian musicians, November 1947.

Gradually, I was able to distinguish a basic 4/4 rhythm, but what they packed into it!

My next stops were Fortaleza and Belém. I gave lectures to full auditoriums but felt that the reactions were provincial. I was getting anxious to return home, and I wrote to Victor from Belém, which is almost at the equator and very hot: "*Please!!* Hang out my overcoat at the loft so it won't smell of mothballs. Bring it with you to Washington." (After returning to Rio, flying to Puerto Rico, and landing in Miami, a State Department employee escorted me to Washington to report on the trip.)

I had received a great deal of attention as a cultural ambassador. The South Americans really went for that kind of thing in a big way. I had more receptions in my honor in those few months than in years at home, but I did not meet as many new composers this trip as in 1941. I was hard put to make recommendations of Brazilian and Uruguayan artists for Tanglewood, but Argentina was developing more rapidly. The daily diary I kept helped me in making my reports to the State Department,[30] and was

84

useful for an article I sent to *The New York Times*,[31] for lectures at Tanglewood the following summer,[32] and in retelling the adventure for this book.

Once back in the States, what I really wanted to do was stay put and enjoy my new home, but I had only one week before going to Cleveland, because I had promised Szell I would attend the rehearsals of the *Third Symphony*, and then on to Boston for an MTNA (Music Teachers National Association) conference to make a report to the Committee for Latin American Music. Nevertheless, I marveled at all the space in the house at Sneden's Landing. What a wonderful feeling it was to be roosted at last! Victor caught me up on things: Lenny had conducted *Statements* while I was away; *Billy the Kid* had been danced several times; and my book *What to Listen for in Music* had been published in German. I was amused no end to imagine *me* telling the Germans anything about what to listen for in music!

Soon after my return, I met with my publishers. Hans Heinsheimer, whom I had known since 1928, had been in charge of my music at Boosey & Hawkes for several years.[33] He had an assistant who was also familiar with my catalogue—Arnold Broido. Sylvia Goldstein began working for Boosey in 1940. Soon she knew all about my music, and for many years she has been in charge of contracts, permissions, and many other matters.[34] In the changing world of music publishing, Sylvia has been the steady and indispensable link with my publishers. In the early days, publishers took on more management and publicity duties for their composers: new scores were distributed to performers, conductors, and colleagues; and the Boosey & Hawkes publication *Tempo* reached a wide audience in the music world. Ralph Hawkes, who had become my friend as well as my publisher, recommended a "cutting service" in England, and since 1946, the pale-green clippings from Durrant's Press Cuttings have arrived at my house continuously (they still do). In 1948, when Heinsheimer left Boosey (I believe he once told me they let him go because he was writing a book), a young lady named Betty Bean, who had been working with Koussevitzky's encouragement on a library of American music for the Soviet-American committee, took Heinsheimer's place as director of serious music. I had seen Betty Bean briefly in Rio in September; once home, there was a great deal of work to do to catch her up with my affairs.

I was involved with several organizations that now required my time and attention, among them the Composers' Forum, the Soviet-American Music Council, and the League of Composers. I always went to see Claire

Reis after a trip. She caught me up on the news in the music world, particularly the League of Composers. Most unfortunately, *Modern Music* finally was forced to cease publication. The National Composers' Committee of the League, of which I was chairman, agreed on the need for a newsletter. In February 1947, the first issue of *The Composers News-Record* was distributed, with Everett Helm as editor. This was in no way intended as a replacement for *Modern Music.* As I explained in a front-page note, "We want to establish contact with composers in our own country and between ourselves and composers living in the rest of the world. Europe is gradually coming to life again, musical centers in South America are stirring."

The loss of *Modern Music* was a serious blow to the League's prestige, and by 1947–1948 the board was rife with internal friction and personal differences. During the war, Claire had done her best to keep the League alive, but the freshness of spirit and enthusiasm that had characterized the organization's early years had faded. At one time, I even suggested to Claire that we change the League's name to give it a new start, but that idea was voted down by the board. Claire had been the strength of the League of Composers since its inception in 1923. After her husband's sudden death in 1947, she felt the need to resign and she wrote this to me in confidence with the hope that we might find some new direction before her resignation became known. I wondered how the League could exist without Claire! We composers owed her an enormous debt of gratitude.

On a personal level, Claire and Arthur Reis' friendship had meant a great deal to me. I was away when Arthur died, but when I returned, I was determined to do as much as I could to help Claire during the difficult period following Arthur's death. When Claire's resignation became official (1948), I accepted the position of director of the League of Composers with the idea of supervising a restructuring of the organization (I held the position until 1951). It was important to act quickly so as not to lose our membership and past support: A notice went out announcing the changes and the events planned for the 1948–1949 season, the League's twenty-fifth anniversary.[35]

Sacks of mail had accumulated while I was away! I have always answered correspondence myself. At times, Victor helped me (as David Walker did later), but even so, I always dictated responses. The most important mail had been coming from Hollywood: Abe Meyer, my agent at MCA, kept

BENNY GOODMAN
654 MADISON AVENUE
NEW YORK 21, N.Y.
RHINELANDER 4-1715

*1123 Cashmere St
LA 24*

Feb 5th, 47

Dear Aaron

I'm sorry about the delay, but if I'm not mistaken You were late getting to Sidney, then he late getting to me, and I'm the latest offender.

Anyway, I'm looking forward in great anticipation for the piece. I do think it would be easier for you to get the two septet albums from your record dealer or even a phone call to Goddard Lieberson may get quicker results as they are recorded for Columbia *(over)*

Letter from Benny Goodman to Copland,
5 February 1947.

I expect to be here at least till April 15th so would appreciate hearing from you about the piece and where you will be located.

My best to you
Benny.

me informed about film projects, and now he had a "hot" prospect. I was willing to listen. The house at Sneden's Landing was a big expense compared to the Empire Hotel and the loft, and if I wanted to eventually build or buy a place, I would have to increase my income.[36] Hollywood was the only way for me to do that.

I had composed the first movement of the *Clarinet Concerto* for Benny Goodman while traveling in Latin America, and from Rio, I had written to Victor (4 October 1947), saying, "I badly need a fast theme for part 2. The usual thing. I used the 'pas de deux' theme for part 1, and I think it will make everyone weep." I had hoped to finish the piece soon after returning to Sneden's Landing, but what Abe Meyer was offering in Hollywood was too good to turn down: a film script adapted from John

Steinbeck's 1938 novel *The Red Pony.* I admired Steinbeck, and after reading the book, I knew this was a film for me. A contract was negotiated with Republic Pictures, which called for ten weeks of work at $1,500 a week for less than one hour of music, which I was to compose, orchestrate, and conduct. I rationalized about the *Clarinet Concerto:* Since I had not been able to find a theme for the second movement, it would be a good idea to put it aside temporarily.

I left for the San Fernando Valley at the beginning of February 1948 to work on *The Red Pony.* Lewis Milestone (with whom I had worked on *Of Mice and Men* and *The North Star*) was producer and director for *The Red Pony.* The cast included Myrna Loy, Robert Mitchum, Louis Calhern, Shepperd Strudwick, and Peter Miles. Steinbeck's well-known tale is a series of vignettes concerning a ten-year-old boy and his life on a California ranch. It is not a typical Western with gunmen and Indians. There is a minimum of action of a dramatic or startling kind. The story gets its warmth and sensitive quality from the character studies of the boy Tom, his grandfather, the cowhand Billy Buck, and Tom's parents, the Tiflins. The kind of emotions that Steinbeck evokes in his story are basically musical ones, since they deal with the unexpressed feelings of daily living.

In directing *The Red Pony,* Milestone left plenty of room for musical treatment, which made the writing of the score a gratifying task. The principal restriction of most movie scores is having to write in small two- or three-minute forms. *The Red Pony* offered larger opportunities, such as a six-minute sequence describing a fight with a vulture, for which I composed dissonant music with complicated rhythms. This was more readily accepted for enhancing a dramatic situation in a film than it would have been in the concert hall. Much of the story called for simple harmonies and clear melodies and, of course, some of the inevitable steady rhythmic accompaniment to simulate cowboys on horseback. Searching through my notebooks of musical ideas, I came across "kids' music" written for the unproduced musical *Tragic Ground.* It was ideal for *The Red Pony.*

I always found that relating music to a picture was a stimulus rather than a restriction. It set the imagination going. But I had to be moved by what I saw on the screen, and I was never moved when a film had too much sheen or when the style was overly dramatic. *The Red Pony* had none of that. It was not a pathbreaker or an epic type of film, but it was moving in a quiet way. My aim was to compose music that would not obtrude and

Publicity release for *The Red Pony;* Copland on the set of *The Red Pony* with Peter Miles in the role of Tom.

that would reflect what I saw. It was a challenge to think up instrumental colors to suit a particular situation: When the pony is being operated on and the little boy winces painfully, I used three bass clarinets to match the dramatic situation; and for Tom and his school friends, I came up with the instrumentation of toy trumpet and tuba. The only problem I had with *The Red Pony* was that it was shot on the same ranch that was used for *Of Mice and Men.* Now I ask you: If you had to look at the same landscape every day, could you think up different music?

I did not like what I heard from Harold Clurman about the political situation building up in Hollywood as a result of the Cold War, but I was totally removed from all that in the San Fernando Valley, and my schedule was very concentrated and demanding. I had to come up with fifty-two minutes of orchestrated music in eight weeks and be ready to record it during the last two weeks of my contract. All of my efforts were directed toward that purpose, so I had no direct contact with any of the Red-baiting that Clurman had written me about before I went out to California (25 October 1947):

> Of course none of this is funny, but how can one not laugh? On the Hanns E. [Eisler] case—please let me use your name for a protest from musicians.[37] Even Stravinsky says he will sign a protest if it goes to the authorities . . . but not to the press. Lenny says he will sign every protest—public and private—and says all the composers, conductors, etc. will follow suit—especially if Aaron signs.

I agreed to lend my name for the Eisler benefit. While I was working on *The Red Pony*, I heard from Harold again (17 February 1948): "How do you like Hollywood in these sour days?" Later (March), he wrote, "I'm glad that you're for Wallace . . . the [Eisler] benefit 'tho too long, went off well. Good reviews by D. D. [Diamond] and V. T. [Thomson] but poor Eisler is still in a jam. Olin Downes is trying to get Toscanini to get Eisler a visa."

The Red Pony was not a commercially successful film. The critics admired certain aspects, one being the musical score, but since the film was not widely distributed, the music was rarely heard. When Efrem Kurtz, newly appointed conductor of the Houston Symphony Orchestra, asked whether I would accept a commission for a work to be premiered by his orchestra, I suggested a suite to be drawn from the film. In reshaping the score, I recast much of the musical material to achieve continuity for concert purposes, although all the music in the twenty-four-minute suite may be heard in the film.[38] It breaks down into six sections: "Morning on the Ranch"; "The Gift"; "Dream March and Circus Music"; "Walk to the Bunkhouse"; "Grandfather's Story"; and "Happy Ending." Although some of the melodies in *The Red Pony* may sound rather folklike, except for a tinge of "So long, Old Paint," they are actually mine. *The Red Pony Suite* is dedicated to my friend Erik Johns, and was premiered by Kurtz with the Houston Symphony (30 October 1948).[39]

When *The Red Pony Suite* was about to be recorded, I wrote to John Steinbeck asking for a commentary to be used with the music. He responded (17 July 1964):

> The music for the Red Pony is very beautiful. I wish the picture could have been as good. Except for the music, I am not unpleased that this film, to the best of my knowledge, is still held as hostage in a bank vault. I am glad that the suite is not a captive—your suggestion that I write some kind of commen-

tary for the music also pleases me very much and I would like very much to do it. I would also be happy to narrate it on tape, at least for you to decide whether I can do it well enough. However, you are holding the baton on this.

However, when I suggested that the version with his commentary be for children, Steinbeck balked. He explained (September 22):

> This is an old theme with me. The reason I have never written books for children is not because of the children but because of the so-called adults who choose what books may be printed for children. Children have nearly always understood my work—and yours. It is only critics and sophisticates who do not. . . . Children have always understood the little book *The Red Pony*. They have been saddened by it, as I was when it happened to me, but they have not been destroyed by it. . . . When you wrote this suite, being an artist and therefore automatically truthful, you let the sombre come into your music to balance the gaiety and to give it proportion and significance. And children surely understand that as they understand form, being instructed by heartbeat and morning and night. In your original music, I remember that you had a passage which covered an owl's sweep down on a rabbit and you had a fantastic passage during the fight of Jody with the buzzard, which was of course man's defiance of death. Children think a great deal about death, much more than adults do, for to the idcentric child his own death is the death of the world. . . . What I am trying to say, I guess, is that if you want a children's version, you must get someone else to write it for you. Surely you may use my notes as you wish, but sometime I would hope that you will let a group of children hear a "children's version" and soon after hear mine, and judge for yourself, their reaction. . . . Sorry to be so vehement, but this is one of my strong feelings.

After Steinbeck's letter, I gave up the idea of a narration, but I did call *The Red Pony* "a suite for children," since the music and action were intended to come from a child's point of view.[40]

My first spring at Sneden's Landing was glorious. Instead of getting back to work on the *Clarinet Concerto*, I relaxed and used the remaining time before Tanglewood to put together *Four Piano Blues*. I composed one new "Blues," which, when put together with three others written at various times, formed the suite.[41] None of the pieces is very difficult. Each is dedicated to a pianist with some special connection to my piano music: Leo Smit, Andor Foldes, William Kapell, and John Kirkpatrick. The order of *Four Blues* does not follow the order of composition.[42] The first performance was by Leo Smit in a League of Composers concert in New York (13 March 1950).

I finally finished the *Clarinet Concerto* after the 1948 Tanglewood season. It is about sixteen and one-half minutes long and dedicated to Benny

Manuscript page of the original coda of the *Clarinet Concerto;* changes suggested by Goodman written in pencil. The memo on top reads: "1st version—later revised—of Coda of *Clarinet Concerto* (too difficult for Benny Goodman)."

Goodman. Goodman had commissioned a work by Bartók in 1938 and from Hindemith in 1947, the same year he approached me. I never would have thought of composing a clarinet concerto if Benny had not asked me for one. I can't play a single note on the instrument! Other than my arrangement of the *Short Symphony* as the *Sextet,* in which clarinet is one of the featured instruments, the only experience I had with clarinet writing was orchestral parts. I had long been an admirer of Benny Goodman, and I thought that writing a concerto with him in mind would give me a fresh point of view. We did not work together while I was composing the piece, but after it was finished and sent off, Benny wrote to thank me and to say: "With a little editing, I know we will have a good piece." When we played it through together, he had clarinetist David Oppenheim around for moral support. I had written the last page too high, so it had to come down a step. Benny made a few other suggestions—one concerned a high note in the cadenza (I knew Benny could reach that high because I had listened to his recordings). He explained that although he could comfortably reach that high when playing jazz for an audience, he might not be able to if he had to read it from a score or for a recording. Therefore, we changed it.[43]

The first movement of the *Clarinet Concerto* is a languid song form composed in 3/4 time, rather unusual for me, but the theme seemed to call for it. The second movement, a free rondo form, is a contrast in style—stark, severe, and jazzy. The movements are connected by a cadenza, which gives the soloist considerable opportunity to demonstrate his prowess, while at the same time introduces fragments of the melodic material to be heard in the second movement. The cadenza is written fairly close to the way I wanted it, but it is free within reason—after all, it and the movement that follows are in the jazz idiom. It is not ad lib as in cadenzas of many traditional concertos; I always felt that there was enough room for interpretation even when everything is written out. Some of the second movement material represents an unconscious fusion of elements obviously related to North and South American popular music: Charleston rhythms, boogie woogie, and Brazilian folk tunes. The instrumentation being clarinet with strings, harp, and piano, I did not have a large battery of percussion to achieve jazzy effects, so I used slapping basses and whacking harp sounds to simulate them. The *Clarinet Concerto* ends with a fairly elaborate coda in C major that finishes off with a clarinet glissando—or "smear" in jazz lingo.

I assumed that Benny would schedule a performance soon after the work was finished, but almost a year later, he wrote (14 February 1949), "I'm terribly disappointed about not being able to perform the concerto May 10th but obviously with my present state of affairs I would be silly to take on such an important job at this time. [Goodman had a virus infection and was also changing management.] I am anxious to play the concerto in public and I will put in a lot of hard work with Ingolf Dahl in L.A. and meanwhile keep in touch with you until we find the next opportune time to perform it." I made a tape recording of the score for two pianos and sent it off to Benny. The premiere of the *Clarinet Concerto* finally took place 6 November 1950, Fritz Reiner conducting the NBC Symphony of the Air from the NBC studios.

Benny Goodman[44]

I made no demands on what Copland should write. He had completely free rein, except that I should have a two-year exclusivity on playing the work. I paid two thousand dollars and that's real money. At that time, there were not too many American composers to pick from—people of such terrific status—as Hindemith and Bartók. I recall that Aaron came to listen when I was recording with Bartók. Copland had a great reputation also. I didn't choose him because some of his works were jazz-inspired. In my mind, the Clarinet Concerto *was related to the ballet because of the ¾ time in the first movement. We never had much trouble except for a little fracas about the spot before the cadenza where he had written a repetition of some phrase. I was a little sticky about leaving it out—it was when the viola was the echo to give the clarinet a cue. But I think Aaron finally did leave it out. The work is difficult for the players, especially the rhythms. We were fortunate to get Fritz Reiner to do the premiere. Aaron and I played the concerto quite a few times with him conducting, and we made two recordings.*

Our first recording was for Columbia with the Columbia String Orchestra, but it's the second recording we made in the sixties that's the best. Once when I was in Rome at the American Academy in the fifties, I played Aaron's concerto with a friend of his at the piano. The kid surprised me by knowing how to play jazz! [Harold Shapero].[45] A lot of clarinetists have played Copland's Clarinet Concerto *by now, all the best ones, and all over the world. Of the concertos I commissioned, the Copland is performed*

94

Benny Goodman and Copland at rehearsal of the *Clarinet Concerto* with the Los Angeles Philharmonic, c. 1970.

most. It's a very popular piece. Aaron and I did it out of town, but not in New York until 1960 at Carnegie Hall [17 November]. That was something! We played it with the Cleveland Orchestra [1968], and in L.A. in the seventies. I've always felt good about that commission and about playing the Clarinet Concerto *with Aaron conducting.*

Lenny Bernstein had wanted to conduct the premiere of the *Clarinet Concerto* at Tanglewood, and he wrote from Israel, where he was conducting the Israel Philharmonic (21 May 1951): "I fought with Kouss valiantly over the *Clarinet Concerto*, to no avail. Benny and Tanglevood don't mix in his mind. By the way, here in Israel, BG means Ben-Gurion." At about the same time, Koussevitzky telephoned me to suggest I arrange the first movement for full orchestra and call it "Elegy." And he told me he wanted it for BSO performances in December 1950. I agreed at first, but then after sober reflection, I had to write my feelings to him (29 August):

Dear Sergei Alexandrovitch: Ever since our telephone conversation about the *Clarinet Concerto* arrangement the thought has been growing in my mind that

I made a mistake. You can understand how easy it would be for me to make such a mistake: my natural desire to please you and the thought of the wonderful interpretation you could give such a piece and the suddenness of your definite proposal and your persuasiveness on the telephone. . . . I am convinced that it takes away from the integrity of the concerto as I originally conceived it, and I am basically unwilling to do that—at least until the work has had a chance through several seasons to make its own way as a complete concerto. . . . I know this decision will not make you happy, but try to see it from my point of view, and you will realize that it makes me even less happy.

The public premiere of the *Clarinet Concerto* (Reiner's was a radio broadcast) was by the Philadelphia Orchestra, Ormandy conducting, Ralph McLane as soloist (28 November 1950). Early reviews were not overwhelmingly enthusiastic; in fact, one might call them lukewarm. The piece was described as "lightweight." Virgil wrote in the *Herald Tribune,* "It sounds as if some essential explanation were lacking, as if a ballet or a film belonging to it had been left out." The fate of a piece of music is a curious thing—so much depends on the first reception. But with the *Clarinet Concerto,* after a somewhat inauspicious send-off, it has become one of my most frequently performed works and a standard for clarinetists. Gervase de Peyer has performed and recorded it, as well as other outstanding soloists, among them Harold Wright, Stanley Drucker, Richard Stoltzman, and David Glazer. I always thought that it would help if a player had some feeling and knowledge of jazz, yet when jazz clarinetist Johnny Dankworth attempted the *Clarinet Concerto* in concert, he ran into difficulty. It was the recordings Benny and I made that garnered the good notices and really launched the *Clarinet Concerto.* I was pleased when we had the chance to do a second recording—the first had been one of my earliest as conductor, and I was concerned that I had conducted the first movement too slowly.

During a year abroad in 1951, I conducted the *Clarinet Concerto* in London, Rome, and Trieste. European orchestras seemed to enjoy the novelty and audiences appeared genuinely welcoming. Gradually, the piece grew in popularity, so that when Lenny Bernstein took the New York Philharmonic to Japan for eleven concerts as part of Expo 70, it was the only American composition on the schedule. The Philharmonic received an overwhelming reception in Japan—in Osaka and Tokyo—where, according to *The New York Times* (10 Sept 1970):

Leonard Bernstein tossed his baton to the crowd in exultation. The audience of 2,400 brought the orchestra's first-chair clarinetist Stanley Drucker back for four curtain calls. . . . After eight minutes of applause, he [Bernstein] motioned for silence and declared in Japanese: "We are delighted, very happy."

When we were planning the second recording, Benny played the *Clarinet Concerto* for Yale clarinetist Keith Wilson and asked his advice. Years later, I was in New Haven to conduct, and Vivian Perlis took me to Wilson's master class at Yale (1980).[46] They had all studied my piece and had no trouble "swinging," where swinging was called for. The students asked questions and took my picture, while I put on my "Mt. Rushmore" look. One young clarinetist asked whether I would compose another clarinet concerto for them, and I answered laughingly, "I wish I could!"

I had made a clarinet and piano version for rehearsals with Benny, which has been used occasionally for concerts, something I had not foreseen. When I heard it, I thought it stood up well, so the clarinet and piano arrangement was published. I am told that the clarinet glissando at the end is much more difficult without the orchestra to back up the soloist.

My friend, pianist Bob Fizdale, told Jerome Robbins that the recording of the *Clarinet Concerto* was out, and when Jerry heard it, he asked me whether he could use it for a ballet. I admired Jerry's work and told him to go ahead. The ballet is called *The Pied Piper,* and Jerry said he did in the dance what he heard in my music.[47] The Piper is the clarinetist and his part calls for wandering around on stage, and then parking himself on a high stool. At the end of the ballet, a large group of dancers participate in a kind of conga line behind the Piper. I am told that once, when the ballet was performed on tour, a clarinetist simply refused to be onstage, and George Balanchine had to go up and pantomime the part while the clarinetist played it from the pit!

The Pied Piper had its world premiere at the New York City Center (4 December 1951).[48] It was well received in New York, Washington, and even in Paris in 1952. Genêt's (Janet Flanner) "Letter from Paris" in *The New Yorker* included the following in her review of a dance program (31 May 1952):

> In the end, it was *Pied Piper,* here titled *Le Joueur de Flute,* with Jerome Robbins' choreography and dancing and Aaron Copland's brilliant, lyric, jazzed music, that really took the cake. After the final curtain, the packed house broke into a rare pandemonium of laughter, applause, and bravos.

I had not intended to return to Hollywood soon after *The Red Pony,* but when I heard through my agent, Abe Meyer, that producer-director William Wyler of Paramount Pictures was looking for a composer for *The Heiress*, I could not help but be interested. The film script was based on a stage play by Ruth and Augustus Goetz, which had been derived from the nineteenth-century novel *Washington Square* by Henry James. I had read the novel and seen the play on Broadway, starring Wendy Hiller in the principal role. The cast of the film included Olivia de Havilland, Sir Ralph Richardson, Montgomery Clift, and Miriam Hopkins. The plot is about a plain young heiress who, after falling in love with a handsome and ambitious young man, agrees to marry him against the wishes of her father, who suspects that the gentleman is after his daughter's inheritance.

Since the drama is more concerned with the psychological relationships between the characters than with external action, I felt that the music might be an important element. Abe Meyer sent me the film script with a note (14 May 1948):

> After you have read the script, Wyler would like you to write him your ideas about the treatment of the music. While I believe that he has great confidence and respect for your musical judgment, I got the feeling that there was a slight question in his mind as to how your music, which is predominantly modern, could be fit into a period picture.

After giving considerable thought to the type of musical score I envisioned for *The Heiress*, I wrote to Wyler:

> In my opinion, the picture does not call for a great deal of music, but what it includes, ought to really count. It should contribute to the tone and style of the picture. My fear is that a conventionally written score would bathe the work in the usual romantic atmosphere. What I would try for would be the recreation in musical terms of the special atmosphere inherent in the James original. That atmosphere—as I see it—would produce a music of a certain discretion and refinement in the expression of sentiments.[49]

I saw certain similarities in *The Heiress* to what I had encountered when composing the score for *Our Town*, where it was necessary to recreate the feeling of life in a typical New Hampshire town around 1900. My method then had been not merely to confine myself to the harmonies and melodies of the period but to make use of every resource in order to suggest the essence of a particular time and place. I hoped to do the same for *The Heiress*.

Wyler responded favorably to my ideas and comments (19 June 1948):

> Naturally, I would not be so mechanical in my thinking as to throw out any music which postdates the technique and development of music up to 1850. I, too, want to take advantage of the growth in music during the past hundred

PARAMOUNT PICTURES INC.
WEST COAST STUDIOS

5451 MARATHON STREET   HOLLYWOOD 38. CALIF.

TELEPHONE   CABLE ADDRESS
HOLLYWOOD 2411   "FAMFILM"

June 19, 1948

Dear Mr. Copland:

Thank you for your letter of May 29th. Of course, I am "still interested" in having you compose the score for THE HEIRESS. Please do not let the fact of my not having answered more promptly mislead you as to that. I start shooting Monday, June 21st, and as you can imagine, the past few weeks have been very rushed for me.

Our present schedule indicates that we will finish shooting by Labor Day, and allowing a reasonable time for editing, I should say the picture should be ready for scoring by the last week in September. Once I know definitely, I shall let you know.

I agree with what you say abou the "conventionally written score" and feel that a special Jamesian tone of discretion and refinement is necessary for THE HEIRESS. Naturally, I would not be so mechanical in my thinking as to throw out any music which postdates the technique and development of music up to 1850. I, too, want to take advantage of the growth in music during the past hundred years and create the feeling and emotion of the past through proper use of modern musical resources.

As for the arrangements between you and Paramount, I have spoken to Mr. Louis Lipstone, the head of the Music Department here at the Studio, and he informs me that he will contact your agent at MCA. As you know, I do not have any hand in settling the terms, or drawing up the contract, but the proper people will, I am sure, get to work on that immediately.

Meanwhile, I am enclosing a copy of the final screenplay for your use. Please let me know if you have specific suggestions for any scenes regarding music. You may have some thoughts which I ought to bear in mind while shooting, such as allowing enough time for music, etc.

I really am looking forward to our association in the Fall, and I hope that if you have any questions or suggestions you will keep in touch with me.

Kindest regards.

Sincerely,

William Wyler

WW:es

Mr. Aaron Copland
Palisades
Rockland County, New York

Copland and William
Wyler, Hollywood, 1948.

years and create the feeling and emotion of the past through proper use of modern musical resources.

By mid-July 1948, a contract had been signed, and the final script arrived while I was teaching at Tanglewood. Along with it, Wyler sent along a song, "Plaisir d'Amour," by the eighteenth-century composer Giovanni Martini,[50] which was to be sung by the male lead character, Morris Townsend. Wyler wrote (24 July):

> I feel that it is a charming song and comes off very well in the scene as shot. I believe you can use this song to advantage in the score, not literally, but possibly as thematic material for the scoring of the love scenes, the scene of the jilt, and the final sequence between Catherine and Morris.

Before turning a film over to the music department, Wyler liked to hold sneak previews without music. Depending on the reactions, he made changes and did retakes. *The Heiress* fell behind schedule, and therefore, I did not have to leave for Hollywood until mid-November. The first thing I did, of course, was see the picture. The initial viewing by the composer is a solemn moment—after all, he will have to live with the film for at least several weeks. The solemnity is emphasized by the exclusive audience that usually views the picture with the composer: producer, director, musical director of the studio, picture editor, music cutter; in fact, everyone involved. It is difficult for the composer to view the photoplay coldly, and there is an understandable compulsion to like everything. What a relief it was to see that *The Heiress* was really very good!

The film was still not finished, which meant that I could collect ideas and start composing without feeling rushed. After a few weeks, I was given half the picture to score. I wrote Victor, who was taking care of my affairs back in Sneden's Landing (14 November 1948), "I am to try for a Dec. 26th recording date if possible—looks like a hectic Christmas for me." I worked from a script with timings and cues for the musical sequences. These were indicated by titles derived from the plot ("Cherry Red Dress," "Early Morning Visitor," "Morris Suggests Love," and so forth.)[51] I saw no reason not to use whatever period music I could to strengthen the score (mazurkas, polkas, and waltzes), with the idea of weaving them into original music composed in nineteenth-century style.[52] My plan was to give each principal character a musical motive, leitmotiv style, to be developed as the drama unfolds; these themes were to be introduced in a "Prelude" during the opening titles.

I was not finding composing for *The Heiress* as easy as I had hoped. For one thing, there were no outdoor scenes, which would have given me the opportunity to compose music with a wide instrumental range, as in *The Red Pony*. Also, I'd never before written a really grown-up love scene (*Our Town* had a boy and girl affair and *The North Star* a young kind of kiss), but in *The Heiress*, I had to figure out what to do when the lovers embrace à la Tristan and Isolde. It seems that nobody has invented a new way to compose love music! I was surrounded by popular songwriters at the studio who were turning the tune "Plaisir d'Amour" into a pop song for general propaganda. I saw very little of William Wyler, but more of his assistant, Lester Konig. The secretaries at the studio tended to address me as "Dr. Copland," in spite of my protests. Everyone on the set said that, although *The Heiress* was a wonderful film, it would make no money because it was a serious and mature drama.

By mid-December, I had only about eight minutes of music ready to record. It was a mad scramble to finish by the end of the month. I could not judge the finished product because I'd never heard the music played in sequence from start to finish, but I sensed that the score had some good spots along with the ones that sounded movie-like. Wyler seemed very pleased with what he heard on the recording stage, but he wanted to try the film at one of those little neighborhood theaters where people don't know they are going to see a new picture.

There is a scene in the film where the young lovers, who are disapproved of by the girl's father, decide to go off and get married right there and then. It's close to midnight and the young man leaves to get ready and promises to return soon. A carriage is heard approaching and she goes out to greet it. To her disappointment, it passes. After this happens several times, and it is getting quite late, she finally has to admit to herself that he is not going to return—she's been jilted. The situation was ideal for a composer because nobody is saying much, so there is little conversation to get in your way. She is all excited—"he is coming, he is coming!"—and I had written a very romantic kind of music, expressing her emotions. Well, when they took the film out for the sneak preview and that scene was played, at the moment Olivia de Havilland realizes that her bridegroom is not in the passing carriage, the audience burst into laughter! Wyler came up to me after the film ended and said, "Copland, you've *got* to do something about that scene, because if the audience laughs at her then, they'll never take her seriously, and we won't have a picture! We might as well go home and forget the whole thing." I protested, "But how can *I* stop an audience from

Copland working on the film score for *The Heiress.*

laughing?" He said, "I don't care how you do it, but do *something* to stop them from laughing."

I began to wonder whether I *could* stop an audience from laughing. It was certainly worth a try. So I threw out the music I had written and substituted a completely different kind, much more dissonant than you normally hear in a motion-picture theater. Fortunately, I had taken my notebook with musical ideas along to Hollywood, and I found something I thought I could use for that crucial scene when Catherine is jilted by her lover. (It was, of all things, a variation originally composed for my *Piano Variations* of 1929. It had not fit into the *Variations* at the time, but it worked well when adapted for the film.) They brought in an entire orchestra—at considerable expense—to record about three minutes of the new music. Then they took the film out for another showing, played the same scene, and there wasn't a sound in the house! I'm sure the audience didn't even know they were listening to music, except for the few musical ones who were there, but it worked on them anyway. It created the kind of tension Wyler had intended for that scene. Clearly nothing could be

Copland conducting the studio orchestra during a recording session of music for *The Heiress.* William Wyler is seated at the left.

considered funny with that dissonant, rather unpleasant-sounding music going on!

Wyler had relied on the camera and the music to take over in several segments where dialogue was abandoned altogether. During those silent close-ups, I found that the use of a ground or passacaglia bass could generate a feeling of continuity and inevitability, as well as provide the necessary dissonance when combined with other music. For example, when Catherine realizes her fiancé has abandoned her, she cries out to her aunt, "Morris must love me for all those who have not." The dialogue stops, the two women sit silently, and the music takes over. I used a theme heard during Catherine and Morris' love scene over a pedal in the basses. Late in the film, when the embittered Catherine confronts her ailing father, I made use of the instrumentation of three bass clarinets, which had worked well in *The Red Pony.*

When recording *The Heiress,* I saw no reason not to make use of "Hollywood tricks." In fact, I was interested in trying out techniques that were not customarily used on the concert stage. One was called

The first page of Copland's original version of the title music for *The Heiress,* with suggested instrumentation penciled in by Copland.

The first page of the title music as changed by the studio (after forty-one measures, the film score returns to bar twenty-six of Copland's original version).

105

"sweetening"—a technique Benny Herrmann had used in several films. The music is recorded first with full orchestra, and then it is recorded again using only the strings. When both are used together, the string sound is considerably altered. I found this effective for the end of *The Heiress* when the dramatic situation called for an intense sound.

I had not objected to using the song "Plaisir d'Amour" in the film, and I even adapted it in my own style after it was heard in its original form.[53] I balked, however, when I was asked to ditch my title music and make an arrangement of the tune instead. I had the right to refuse, but it seems that the producers had the right to ask someone else to arrange the title music. After the score had been completely finished and recorded and I had returned to New York, I learned that "Plaisir d'Amour" had been inserted into my title music![54] All I could do was to issue a statement to the press disclaiming responsibility for that part of the score. It was a disagreeable incident that marred an otherwise satisfying collaboration. I had invited Lawrence Morton to be present at the recording sessions, and after he heard what happened, he wrote to me about my original title music: "It is not pretty, perhaps, as is its substitute, but it is certainly much more relevant to the film that Wyler produced."

The world premiere of *The Heiress* took place at Radio City Music Hall in New York City (6 October 1949). Dimitri Tiomkin, Max Steiner, and I were nominated for an Academy Award in 1950. When I won, I was told that it was the only instance of a score winning an Oscar after having been shorn of its overture, the part of a score that usually makes the strongest impact. I heard from Ingolf Dahl from Los Angeles (24 March 1950):

At last Oscar has found a worthy home—congratulations! We are terribly happy about the fact that sometimes (all too rarely) Hollywood shows good sense. Etta and I were fully determined to walk down Hollywood Boulevard with picket signs in case Tiomkin had received the award! This gives me also an opportunity to tell you how deeply impressed I was with *The Heiress* music. The main title, of which I was forewarned, was a scandal.

While in Hollywood for *The Heiress,* I rented a small house in Los Angeles. I saw Lawrence Morton and Ingolf Dahl frequently, and other colleagues occasionally: Poulenc, when he came to visit in December; Roy Harris, who was on the scene part of the time; and Stravinsky, who invited me to his home for dinner one evening. I did a few lectures at UCLA. Alfred Wallenstein asked me to attend rehearsals and the performance of my *Third Symphony* by the Los Angeles Philharmonic, and I even did some conducting myself. The studio musicians were so bored playing movie scores, they had formed an orchestra for their playing pleasure and invited me to conduct *Appalachian Spring* and *Statements.*

When I needed some secretarial assistance, I asked a young dancer, Erik Johns, whom I had first met in New York, to help me out. We became friends and enjoyed exploring California together when I was not working on the picture. Between finishing the recording, the dubbing, and the next preview, we drove to San Diego, where we spent New Year's Eve and had a few days' vacation in Ensenada, Mexico. Erik traveled back east with me on The Super Chief at the beginning of 1949.

I never worked in Hollywood after *The Heiress*—perhaps they gave me the cold shoulder because of my critical statement to the press after my title music was changed. Also, I may have been on the boycott lists as the Cold War escalated. I did have a few offers, among them one from William Wyler, who was very anxious to have me do the score for *The Big Country,* but I was not able to fit it into my schedule. In the fifties and sixties, Hollywood productions became more commercial and less artistic, and I was outspoken about the movie studios not bringing in fresh blood from the outside.

I have often been questioned about whether I liked writing movie music, the implication being that it was possibly degrading for a composer of symphonies to trifle with a commercial product. "Would you do it anyhow, even if it paid less well?" asked one interviewer. My answer was that I would, and moreover, that I thought most composers would, principally because film music constitutes a musical medium with a fascination all its own. At the time I was composing for films, I believed that it was a new form of dramatic music, related to opera, ballet, and theater music, and that it should be explored for its own unique possibilities. From Hollywood, when I was working on *The Heiress,* I wrote an article for *The New York Times* stating my position: "Someday the term 'movie music' will clearly define a specific musical genre and will not have, as it does nowadays, a pejorative meaning."[55]

Interlude II

The summers at Tanglewood from 1946 to Koussevitzky's death in 1951 made a lasting impression on those fortunate enough to have been there. Many people have had the experience of a brief period of time (perhaps college or the war) of such intensity and concentration as to affect an entire lifetime. The Koussevitzky years at Tanglewood held that quality—from the youngest musician to the most senior faculty, everyone had the sense of something wonderful happening all the time. Koussevitzky's vitality, idealism, and dedication were contagious. Composer Jacob Druckman has said about his student years at Tanglewood: "It was exciting, exhilarating, glamorous to be in the same place every day with the likes of Koussevitzky, Aaron, Lenny, Lukas—everyone you saw was someone you had heard about and admired. It was a young musician's dream come true."[1]

For Copland, it was the three years he spent in Paris as a young man in the twenties that proved to have the most powerful influence on his life; after Paris, the Koussevitzky summers at Tanglewood were most memorable. In Paris, Copland had come into contact with the two major influences on his musical life—Boulanger and Koussevitzky. At Tanglewood, Copland's relationship with Koussevitzky had the opportunity to mature. Other of Copland's close friendships, as well as many contacts in the music world, were made and strengthened at Tanglewood in the forties. Moreover, it was the only place Koussevitzky, Copland, and Bernstein had the opportunity to be together over an extended time.

The Berkshire Music Center, which had opened in 1940, was officially closed after the 1942 season because of the war, but Serge Koussevitzky, its founder and director, had been determined to keep Tanglewood alive.[2] When the Boston Symphony Orchestra board voted not to allocate funds, Koussevitzky arranged for "minifestivals" to be supported by the Koussevitzky Music Foundation, which had been established in 1942 in memory of Koussevitzky's wife, Natalie.[3] The reopening of Tanglewood in 1946

Photograph by Ruth Orkin

Left to right: Copland, Bernstein, and Koussevitzy, summer 1947.

signaled the rebirth of the arts in America. A summer festival of such magnitude as Tanglewood was unique outside of Europe. For several years, until other organizations followed suit, Tanglewood had little competition for the best students and players.[4]

Koussevitzky welcomed students and faculty, and Randall Thompson's "Alleluia" rang out again in the Theater–Concert Hall: Tanglewood was back in full swing. Four hundred students were enrolled, many on the newly enacted GI Bill of Rights.[5] Koussevitzky invited musicians he considered most talented in his or her field to become part of the Tanglewood "family." Many had been on the faculty in 1942; most would return in future years.[6] Copland's popularity and his stature as the leader of American composers made him the perfect choice as Koussevitzky's assistant. With Copland in charge, Koussevitzky knew he could count on things running smoothly.

When Copland saw the cottage near Pittsfield that had been chosen for him before the summer of 1946, he decided to stay at Heaton Hall, a hotel

Copland in front of his summer home, the barn studio in Richmond, Massachusetts, 1949 or 1950.

in Stockbridge, where he worried about not having a piano, and about paying for his room by the day, with extra for visitors (Victor Kraft and Paul Moor both visited that summer). In August, Copland moved into a charming converted stable and arranged for a piano to be delivered. At the end of the following season, Copland found the barn in Richmond that would become his Tanglewood home. It belonged to Mrs. Ralph Hooker (later, the Gettys family, then the Birts). The barn had an artistic history: Alexander Calder had lived there and built some of his sculptures and mobiles in that space. It was still very "barny" and informal, and the surrounding meadows assured Copland the privacy he needed for composing.

In 1946, members of the student orchestra played Copland's *Sextet,* and the BSO performed *Appalachian Spring* under Koussevitzky. The big event of the season, however, was the American premiere of Benjamin Britten's *Peter Grimes.* [7] Copland invited Britten to come from England, and then worried about what he would think of a student performance. With Bernstein conducting and several professionals to bolster the students, *Peter Grimes* was such a success that the following season Koussevitzky gave Boris Goldovsky a free hand to build a special opera program. Many leaders in the operatic world started their careers during the sixteen years Goldovsky led the opera program at Tanglewood, among them Sarah Caldwell.

Leonard Bernstein and Eleazar de Carvalho were Koussevitzky's conducting assistants (Carvalho was a thirty-two-year-old Brazilian recommended by Villa-Lobos). Bernstein was conducting in London and did not arrive in Lenox until a week into the season. He wrote to Copland (23 June 1946):

> Don't let Kouss think bad thinks about me because I'm staying. He must know how much I want to get back to the Boiks. And I'm scared Kouss will take away some of the summer chores I really want to do—like the Festival concerts. Don't let him. It's on your head! Keep Tanglewood safe for Bernstein!

Copland was to share the composition program with the European composer Bohuslav Martinů, but soon after Martinů's arrival, he fell off the porch of a Tanglewood building in Great Barrington. Irving Fine taught Martinů's students until Copland found a replacement in Nikolai Lopatnikoff. [8] Copland's students were Jacob Avshalomov, James Beale, Edmund Haines, Ned Rorem, Leonard Meyer, and several South Americans Copland had met during his 1941 Latin American tour. [9] The presence of many foreign students added an international flavor to the atmosphere. Among the Latin Americans were Julián Orbón and Alberto Ginastera. Orbón, who had met Copland earlier in Cuba, described how the Latin American composers would get together to play their music at Tanglewood:[10]

> We would invite Aaron, who was like a father figure of Latin American composers, and he would comment, "Oh, you Latin people—you are something!" One day I was riding in Copland's car together with Hector Tosar and Ginastera. Copland said, "My God, I have to drive very carefully, because I have with me the hope of Latin American music!" And Ginastera said, "Well—and the reality of North American music!"

Alberto Ginastera[11]

When I first became aware of modern music, I heard Copland's Music for the Theatre. *I was a very good friend of an Argentine conductor who knew Copland, Juan José Castro, and he introduced the work to me. After that, Copland came several times to Argentina. The first date was 1941, at the time of the world premiere of his* Piano Sonata *in Buenos Aires. I was writing the ballet* Estancia *and I played it for him. I was sending for the Guggenheim Fellowship, and Aaron was one who spoke for me. We exchanged letters, and in 1942 I obtained the Fellowship, but I could not come until the war was finished. Toward the end of 1945 I arrived in New York, and I met Copland often at concerts. He introduced me to many people, and especially Mrs. Claire Reis, head of the League of Composers. One time at a party, I was in conversation with other people speaking English, and I was looking very diligent. Copland said, "I never saw anyone like Ginastera, who can put his face like somebody who understands everything, and I know that he doesn't understand anything at all!"*

Copland obtained the scholarship for me to go to Tanglewood. My main reason was to study the problems of education and music institutions, and this was very useful for me, because in Argentina I created the first music school of professional level and the first chair of musicology. Copland instructed me where to go to investigate. He told me that one very great experience would be Tanglewood. Just that year of 1946 was a very remarkable year, because there were Latin American composers who became well known, and there was also Bernstein and Lukas Foss. It was one of the years you never forget. And then I attended Copland's classes, because I was very

Hotel Duane

237 MADISON AVENUE
NEW YORK 16, N.Y.
ASHLAND 4-9390

June 19, 1946.

Dear Mr. Copland:

I just received the communi-
cation from Tanglewood, telling me that
they have already reserved a room for my
wife and for me. I write this paragraph
in English because I want you to know
exactly how much I appreciate all you
have done to make possible my visit to
Tanglewood and to give you my thanks
for all your kindness with us.

Ahora continúo en Spanish. Por primera vez en
la historia de la música argentina, los compositores
han respondido a un pedido. Días pasados recibí
unos dibujos y material musical de algunos
de ellos que servirán para el artículo. ¡Ojalá
la calma provinciana sea reemplazada por
el dinamismo estilo U.S.A.! Los dibujos, muy
graciosos por otra parte, pertenecen a los muy
ilustres maestros José María, Juan José y
Washington Castro, Jacobo Ficher, Luis Gianneo
y Roberto García Morillo.

Esperando los agradables momentos que
pasaremos en los Festivales, lo saluda
muy afectuosamente

A. Ginastera

Letter from Alberto
Ginastera, 19 June
1946.

much interested in the teaching of composition. It can be said I was a pupil
of Copland. His spirit is very open and generous. Every time he could help
us in trying to open a certain door, he always did it. These powerful
communications were due also to the fact that he spoke Spanish.

At Tanglewood, Koussevitzky was like the Czar. We were very much
impressed each time we saw him, especially when he wore a cape with red
silk inside. Koussevitzky was like a star in the firmament to us.

Copland and I were on the jury of a competition in Caracas in 1957. By
chance, it was the same people that had been at Tanglewood in 1946, only
Tosar was missing. One day, they took a picture of all of us. It was like the
famous group of Les Six, when one was missing, Auric. We took a picture
of Tosar and put it on our photograph.

In my country, I have been the equivalent of what Copland is in this
country. There is a parallel: our love for humanity and for our countries.
What Copland did could be bigger because it is a much bigger country. I

The 1957 reunion of Copland with the Latin Americans who had been at Tanglewood in 1946: Chilean Juan Orrego-Salas, Spaniard Julián Orbón, Panamanian Roque Cordero, Mexican Blas Galindo, Cuban Harold Gramatges, Uruguayan Hector Tosar (represented by his drawing), Puerto Rican Hector Campos Parsi, Venezuelan Antonio Esteves, and Argentinian Alberto Ginastera.

always say that I am a composer thanks to the United States. When I was thrown out of Argentina in 1952, I was in a very bad situation. But when I returned, I had a group of private pupils, and I also made music for pictures and had a radio program of contemporary music. It was for the last hour of the night. I played many records of the music of Copland.

I have a great admiration for Copland's Piano Variations. *Twenty or twenty-five years ago, it was a work that the public did not understand; now, it is a classic work of the twentieth century. I believe it is very interesting to compare a work in piano form and then arranged for orchestra. I always would have students make their versions and then compare them with Copland's own* Orchestral Variations.

Copland has created American music in the same way Stravinsky did Russian music, or Falla Spanish, or Bartók Hungarian, because he's an artist with a great personality. The following generations have had a great influence from Copland—some have made international music—but, at the same time, lost the American character that is in Copland's music.

Copland is a man full of realism and optimism. I never saw him without a smile. The other day, we saw each other when Queens College named the music school for him. The newspaper had a picture the next day of the two of us, and my look is full of much emotion, but Copland has a big smile—as always—just as the first time I saw him in the forties.

Following the successful 1946 season, applications flooded in for 1947. The word was out that the Berkshires was *the* place to be if you were a young performer or conductor on the way to a professional career. The faculty and administration was essentially unchanged from the previous summer.[12] Arthur Honegger was the European composer invited to share the composition department with Copland. He no sooner arrived from war-torn Paris than he suffered a serious heart attack. Copland again had to find a replacement. This time he asked Samuel Barber, who came to Tanglewood to take Honegger's students for the remainder of the season.[13] Copland taught eight of the sixteen composition students: Sidney Cox, William Flanagan, Jan Novak, Knut Nystedt, Carlos Riesco, Ned Rorem, Russell Smith, and Douglas Townsend. Copland, together with Bernstein and Fine, taught a course in American music, one of the first of its kind,[14] and he coached student composers in presenting their works once a week.

Koussevitzky directed the Festival and the Music Center with great energy and dedication. His pride in Tanglewood led to such statements as "Our student orchestra is one of the best orchestras in the country, as good as Cleveland or Cincinnati," and students were stimulated to play better than they thought they could. When prominent visitors praised Tanglewood as "an American Salzburg," Koussevitzky asked, "Why a Salzburg? Why not Tanglewood, U.S.A.?" The Director's passionate belief that *everyone* should be involved with music had lasting influence on Copland. To achieve his goal, Koussevitzky organized the Center into five departments, the fifth being for amateurs.[15] He incorporated public forums at the Lenox Library into the curriculum, usually planned and moderated by Copland. The forums gave amateurs and audiences the opportunity to discuss topics such as "What relevance does popular music have in today's world of serious music?" and "What is the place of women in music?" Leonard Burkat attended a forum in which BSO manager George Judd,

Photograph by Victor Kraft.

Copland, Koussevitzky, and Arthur Honneger at Tanglewood, 1947.

Stanley Chapple, and Richard Burgin discussed "What opportunities exist for the professional artist in his career under present conditions?" Judd's remarks about "selling" music prompted Koussevitzky to pronounce furiously, "An artist is not a sack of potatoes!"[16]

Koussevitzky also believed that composers should be able to conduct. Copland had a turn, but Koussevitzky was not complimentary and very soon he urged Copland to forget conducting and concentrate on composing. Irving Fine, Harold Shapero (and later, Peter Mennin) were expected to take turns directing the student orchestra. For years, Fine told his favorite Koussevitzky story and it has been repeated by others ever since: Fine was conducting Brahms' *Variations on a Theme by Haydn,* and the

116

performance was unsteady and uneven. Koussevitzky was listening in the wings. When Irving Fine walked off after taking his bows, Koussevitzky called to him: "Fine! Fine! It was *awful!*"

One of Koussevitzky's ideas, carried out each summer until his death, was to conduct the BSO at a Festival concert in a major work by a young American composer. In 1947, it was Copland's *Third Symphony,* played in a season featuring all the Beethoven symphonies. Koussevitzky managed what no conductor has done since: to attract large audiences with outstanding performances of standard repertoire, while including enough contemporary music to make programs interesting and varied. However, Koussevitzky's affection for contemporary music did little to endear him to the BSO's board of trustees (as Koussevitzky called them, *"Trust*ies"). Finances always being a problem, Koussevitzky constantly had to justify himself and to compromise on expenditures.[17]

The amount of music performed during the short six-week session (later expanded to eight, then ten, currently nine) was unbelievable: In the forty-two days of the 1947 session, sixty-one concerts were given, of which forty-one were by the students. With so many performances taking place in such a short time, it was necessary to have a library of scores and parts on the grounds. Space was cleared at the Main House, and Irving Fine recommended to Copland a young assistant librarian from the Boston Public Library.

Leonard Burkat [18]

Irving suggested me to Aaron, then Aaron to Tod [Thomas D.] Perry, who was executive secretary, and Tod got approval from Koussevitzky. I began in 1946, with a six-week leave to work for the Berkshire Music Center for fifty dollars a week plus a fifty-dollar housing allowance. That sounded awfully good to me. I lived with my wife and young child in a cottage down a dirt road around the lake. (Koussevitzky was always complaining that my car was dusty!) When I was invited back for the 1947 season, the library in Boston did not give me leave, so I quit my job to return to Tanglewood for the summer.

The library there took up much of the first floor of the old house, and Aaron's studio was right above it. I was tested by Aaron. He would ask what I thought about Mahler's symphonies, when they were hardly known at all, and about a Schumann symphony, I remember, and he was surprised when he found that I really knew the scores. Later, when Stravinsky's Agon *first came out and we were looking it over, Copland said, "Everybody who wants to compose from now on will have to know this score."*

Koussevitzky was our lord and our master. This was his place. He had thought it up—invented it—and brought it into existence. He made it exactly what he wanted it to be—a kind of meeting place for people he considered to have the best musical minds and the greatest musical skills and the highest artistic aspirations. He threw them all together with very broad instructions, saying to us, "Do something! Here are all these young people. Make them think and work the way you do, and maybe even live the way you do." For Koussevitzky, it was important to live on an elevated plane and to conduct everyday affairs with the same seriousness of purpose that went into conducting a concert. He was an elevated personage of the kind that there were very few of then—and there are many fewer now. This was the Koussevitzky ethic with which Aaron fit so well. As for the rest of us, if we were not capable of at least aspiring to do the things Koussevitzky wanted done, we just didn't belong there. The effect that he had on the students, on us, and on the musical life of this country is inestimable.

I quickly got involved in doing more than running the library, and acquired a variety of responsibilities at Tanglewood and in Boston. After Koussevitzky died, Judd fired me a couple of times, but [Charles] Munch and Harry Cabot, the president of the trustees, rehired me. Judd soon retired, Tod moved up into his job of general manager, and I became artistic administrator of the orchestra and principal administrative officer of the Music Center. Without Koussevitzky's advocacy, the trustees were unsure that they wanted to spend the money needed to keep the school alive, and I helped get it over that crisis.

That kind of thing could not be Aaron's burden, but he was responsible for a great deal, more than anyone ever knew, especially in the early years. Many of Koussevitzky's composer discoveries were people whom Aaron brought to his attention. Aaron never claimed any great credit for it. It was just what he did when he thought the music deserved it; that's all. It became obvious that Koussevitzky relied on Aaron and Lenny a great deal, and more on Aaron because of his age and experience. Aaron didn't want to be involved in too much operating detail himself, but he wanted people around who could be trusted to take care of it. He would not have stood for careless work, and he knew who deserved his confidence.

As administrator of the Music Center until 1963, when I left to take a job with CBS, I consulted with Aaron on many aspects of its operation.

When Paul Fromm offered to support the study and performance of new music at Tanglewood, Aaron, Irving, and I discussed the possibilities and came up with the idea of attaching a group of chamber-music players to the composition department, and these Fromm Fellows of 1957 were the very first "new-music group."

Aaron looked and acted then much as he does now, except that he was firmer of step. His voice was the same. He could always say very serious things in a light way, and he always had that little, amused chuckle. He was kind and gentle—a person as lacking in cruelty, or even harshness, as one might ever encounter in the current musical world.

As programs and activities expanded, new facilities were added to the campus: a student-orchestra rehearsal stage; a cafeteria where the old lunch bus stood; and the Nathaniel Hawthorne "little Red House" used for classroom space, and as an historical site for visitors. Tanglewood's grounds have always been open to the public, and it was Koussevitzky's idea that college students conduct guided tours. It has become a time-honored tradition for children of Tanglewood regulars to lead the tours. Tod Perry (manager of the orchestra from 1954 to 1979 and connected with Tanglewood since 1940) explained: "It is a kind of nepotism, I suppose, although certainly not exclusive. There's quite an alumni of Tanglewood guides— the Bernstein and Silverstein kids, our own, and people such as Dan Gustin and Harry Kraut also."[19] As audiences grew, so did traffic and the constant need for expanded parking facilities and tourist accommodations. As Copland said, "It was a tough job to find rooms for visitors, even for those of us who were Tanglewood 'regulars.' In all the years I spent in the Berkshires, I never felt that the permanent residents of Stockbridge and Lenox ever got used to the influx of so many strangers every summer."

Everyone was much too busy at the beginning of the season to celebrate the Fourth of July, so the Music Center's official holiday was Koussevitzky's birthday (26 July). Everything would come to a halt and a gigantic cake would appear. Each year, faculty and students outdid themselves to surprise Koussevitzky with an original musical program: A conducting student presented "Also Sprach Koussevitzky"; Lenny produced his famous "Koussevitzky Blues" (with the refrain, "Come the Revolution and we'll all wear capes!"); and in 1947, Bernstein conducted a new work, "Fanfare for Bima" (using the tune Koussevitzky whistled to call his cocker spaniel).[20] In addition to Koussevitzky's birthday, the opening ceremonies

Photographs by Victor Kraft.

Above: Copland with students of the Berkshire Music Center on the lawn at Tanglewood.

Right: Copland at the piano surrounded by fellows of the Music Center at Tanglewood, 1948. Darius Milhaud is seated at far right.

and the closing parties at the Curtis Hotel for the faculty were the special occasions. Afterward, Copland would stay on in his Richmond barn to compose and to enjoy a more peaceful time in the Berkshires.

At the end of the 1947 season, Koussevitzky married Olga Naumova, his late wife Natalie's niece, who had lived with the Koussevitzkys and acted as their secretary for eighteen years. Olga, with her quiet and soft-spoken manner, drew composers to her, and several counted her a close friend, among them Berstein and Copland. In an interview a year before her death, Olga Koussevitzky said, "One of Serge's first pupils was Bernstein—young, enthusiastic. And Aaron. Very much at Serge's side. Aaron was always his closest advisor and friend. It was a very wonderful and warm relationship."[21]

Among Copland's composition students when the Music Center re-opened in 1946 was the young Ned Rorem; Rorem returned to study with Copland in the summer of 1947.

Ned Rorem[22]

The first of his music I ever heard was Quiet City *in 1940, and it bowled me over. Except for Chicago composers, Sowerby and Carpenter mainly, the notion of American music hadn't quite taken with me. Now here suddenly was Aaron Copland's gem, at once so French—like all I adored—with its succinct expressivity, yet so unFrench with its open-faced goodwill. So I tried to find as many of Copland's records as possible, although except for* El Salón México, *there wasn't much available.*

We first met when I was nineteen and a student at Curtis. I used to go up to New York each month to seek various modes of art and fun unavailable in Philadelphia. I knocked on Lenny Bernstein's door (I didn't know you were supposed to phone people first), and we hit it off. He had Copland's Sonata *on his piano, and played it for me, and again I was bowled over, despite—with its almost mean angular aggressivity—its difference from* Quiet City. *So Lenny picked up the phone and made a date for me to visit Aaron. That would have been February of 1943.*

I went next day to the West Sixty-third Street studio, which I recall as a single narrow room as long as the block and compartmentalized by shelves heavy with air-checks and acetates of his various scores. Aaron was affable, immediate, attentive, with that wonderful American laugh; in the four-plus decades since that day, I've seen him behave with the same unaffected frankness not only with other young unknowns but with countesses and Koussevitzkys. He played me a tape (only it wasn't called a tape then) of Of Mice and Men, *of which I was especially touched by the super-simple D-minor moment for solo string, illustrating the death of Candy's dog. I played him a juvenile trio, my* Opus Minus One, *which I still have in a drawer somewhere. We talked about whether tunes came easily, and gossiped about Mexico and Chicago. That was that.*

When I moved to New York the following year, Aaron was a regular fixture at new music concerts, and always surrounded. A few times he came

Photograph by Victor Kraft.

Ned Rorem and Copland, 1946.

*to dine on West Eleventh Street, where I lived with Morris Golde; once with
our mutual friend, the painter Alvin Ross, who did both our portraits. But
it wasn't until 1946 that I really grew to know him.*

*In the summer of 1946, I got a scholarship to Tanglewood and became
one of Aaron's six students. We bunked in one huge stable in a Great
Barrington girls' school along with Martinů's six students and Martinů
himself, who took a fall and had to be replaced by Lopatnikoff. The twelve
student composers had two lessons a week with their respective maestros,
plus two group sessions, plus access to rehearsals. It was the happiest
summer of my life. Aaron lived near Pittsfield and invited me to dine once
or twice, and to see* Fiesta, *an Esther Williams movie that used* El Salón
México *as background music. He also offered me scotch and sodas (he was
never a drinker, but I was) that quite went to my head: Aaron was my
teacher, after all. "Don't tell anyone," said he, "because one can't make a
habit of inviting students out." But what did he really think of me?*

122

*I was always a lone wolf and never became one of Aaron's regular flock,
any more than I became one of Virgil's, except that I worked as a copyist
for Virgil, so I knew him better. Aaron had an entourage, so did Virgil; you
belonged to one or the other, like Avignon and Rome, take it or leave it.
I left it. Or rather, I dipped my toe in both streams.*

*Virgil's "Americanness" predates Aaron's. Virgil's use of Protestant
hymns and, as he calls them, "darn fool ditties" dates from the twenties.
Aaron's use came later. One may prefer Aaron's art to Virgil's, but give
Virgil full credit: Aaron knew a good thing when he saw it. Although he's
had wider influence, he'd not be what he is without Virgil's ground-breaking
excursions. Virgil invented his own folk music (a little as Poulenc and Ravel
did) and left it rough hewn, while Aaron took actual folk music and
revamped it into sheer Copland.*

*I gleaned less out of the one-to-one meetings we had at Tanglewood than
from the classes. The class in orchestration was most canny. Aaron had us
score the same passage—five or six measures—from a piece of his. We did
this, each in our own corner for an hour, then regathered to compare results
against the original. Very instructive.* Appalachian Spring *had just been
published, and we all carried our own little score around like holy writ, the
way the Latin-Americans carried around the Falla* Harpsichord Concert
and the French students Pelléas. *But Aaron, sly fox, had us orchestrating
sections of* Statements, *which we couldn't possibly have known beforehand.
Sometimes he would invite outsiders. For example, Britten came to talk
about* Peter Grimes, *and Harold Shapero analyzed his* Classical Symphony. *We had classes in movie music, and one in modern vocal music.
Aaron had yet to write the Dickinson songs, and didn't feel of himself as
a song composer.*

*He was more interested in other composers than any composer I've
known. That was the season he imported youngish geniuses from all over
South America and listened patiently to every note of every one, then
commented in a very general way. He was less a pedagogue than an advisor—a sort of musical protocol expert. I remember Marc Blitzstein saying
about Aaron that he would sit and listen to these kids play this damn music
and let it go clear to the end of the piece without stopping—he was so
patient!*

*The next summer, I went back to recapture Paradise. You never quite can,
can you? And yet I did. By then, I had already published a few songs and
had a firmer ego than the year before. I remember saying to Aaron during
the class, "You did this last year." And he said, laughing, "Oh, I know, yes,*

but don't tell anybody." I returned to Tanglewood for a few days in 1948 when Hugh Ross introduced my Sappho Madrigals. Then I stayed away until 1959 when I stopped by for lunch with Aaron and Harold Clurman. In the shade of the shed, I shed a tear, and haven't been back since.

I have never been able to squeeze a compliment out of Aaron. He was always willing to write recommendations, always willing to socialize, but my music was nothing he would include on programs. Perhaps I lacked a musical identity (except in the few dozen songs from the mid-forties, which are inimitable) until I started thinking bigger and writing symphonies. What I learned from Aaron wasn't what he taught me per se. Rather, it was through observing how he did what. Aaron stressed simplicity: Remove, remove, remove what isn't needed. That stuck. The leanness!—particularly in his instrumentation, which he, himself, termed "transparent," and taught me the French word dépouillé. Stripped bare. It's the opposite of German, every note's there and you hear it. The dépouillement was certainly something he got from Paris, from Boulanger—but he was not seduced, as I was, by so-called Impressionism. Our respective Frenchnesses were at opposite ends of the scale, and that, I think, put him off.

Aaron brought leanness to America, which set the tone for our musical language throughout the war. Thanks largely to Aaron, American music came into its own. But by 1949 there started to be a give and take between the United States and Europe. Europe woke up where she had left off in 1932, like Sleeping Beauty—or Sleeping Ugly—and revived all that Schoenbergian madness, now perpetrated ironically not through the Germans but through Pierre Boulez, who was a most persuasive number. The sense of diatonic economy instilled in us by Copland was swept away in a trice and everyone started writing fat Teutonic music again. It was as though our country, while smug in its sense of military superiority, was still too green to imagine itself as culturally autonomous; the danger over, we reverted to Mother Europe.

In 1949, when I was living in Paris, Shirley Gabis (now Perle) and I invited a half-dozen people over for Boulez to play his Second Sonata, and Aaron came. At least one of us left the room in the middle, so discombobulating was the performance, but Aaron stuck it out with a grin. On the one hand, he was aroused by the nostalgia of his own Parisian past when everyone tried to épater le bourgeois; on the other hand, Boulez was appealing and sharp as a razor and Aaron would have liked to be taken seriously by the younger man and his bunch. Artists, even the greatest, once they achieve maximum fame, are no longer interested in their peers' reaction *so much as in that of the new generation. Who knows what Boulez thought of Aaron's music? The French have always condescended to other cultures. Except for Gershwin, names like Copland or Harris or Sessions were merely names when I first dwelt in France, and are still (pace Carter and Cage) merely names there. Anyway, that same day, Aaron sat down and played his* Variations, *no doubt to prove he was just as hairy as Boulez, but the effect was one of terrific force and form, and yes, inspiration, thrown at the hostile chaos of the enfant terrible.*

I came back briefly to New York in 1952 and visited Aaron in one of his sublets (this one was deep in the south Village). Patricia Neway was there, rehearsing the Dickinson Songs. *I was terribly interested (and, as a songster myself, maybe a bit jealous) that Aaron kept the verses intact without repeating words not repeated in context, and at how sumptuously, even bluesily, melodic the songs were despite the jaggedly disjunct vocal line. He had already written the* Piano Quartet, *his first leap into the tone-row bandwagon. But here now again was the crystalline (his word) master, clear as mountain dew.*

During the fifties, we saw each other less often, since I lived in Europe for that decade. But whenever he was in Paris, I invited him chez Marie-Laure de Noailles, where I lived, or chez Marie-Blanche de Polignac, who "received" on Sunday evenings. I can still see him in these two extraordinarily beautiful houses, amidst the fragile Proustian society, Renoirs all over the walls, breast of guinea hen all over the table, the dizzy scent of Lanvin perfume pervading the salons, and Aaron so down to earth with his famous contagious giggle, so plain, so—dare I say it?—Jewish, and at the same time cowboyish. For it's notable, maybe even something to be proud of, that the first truly important American composer is a Jew, yet a Jew who never, as Lenny did, wrote Jewish music. Except for Vitebsk. *Always at these functions, he was duly impressed but anxious to get to the sonic core of the situation, meet whatever musicians might be there, or listen to Poulenc, or Jacques Février, or maybe Georges Auric playing four-hands with the hostess. Mostly, though, he was probably unexcited by the tone, anxious for something more current, more vital.*

One of Aaron's letters takes me to task because in my first book, The Paris Diary, *I wrote disobligingly about Boulanger. He wrote me that he simply would not endorse a book that was so vindictive about someone he had always loved and needed. (That slap did me good, and reversed many an exhibitionist stance.) I saw Aaron angry another time—in Rome in 1954. I was sitting with him at a concert, and somebody played a piano sonata* of Georges Auric that went on and on and on. And when it was over, Aaron was just beside himself with impatience and annoyance and said, "What a hell of a piece!" Meaning in a very negative way. He got up and whirled out into the lobby and was very offended.

As Aaron's fame swelled during the sixties and seventies, his influence waned. In January of 1966 when he went to Salt Lake City, where I was teaching, to conduct the Utah Symphony, I told the university that, sure, I'd invite him to give a talk if they would cancel all classes and guarantee a full house. There was a full house, all right, but strictly of faculty and townspeople.

The honors that accrue to Aaron evermore vastly appear so often to be simply praiseworthy, a touch standoffish, treating the man like a saint. Now, to be a saint, you must once have been a sinner, and I feel that it diminishes Aaron to avoid discussion of his various temptations. We all recall his friendly reticence, his hunger for gossip, although he himself was not given, as Virgil was, to gossip. Aaron never said nasty things to others, but I've seen him cool to people who wanted something from him or who were too clinging. People like to talk about how friendly Aaron is. He is easy enough to talk to, but in fact, he knows exactly how friendly to be, and he knows who he is. People who know who they are, are intimidating, because most people don't. I think it's to belittle Aaron to infer that he is a man without temperament. People are inclined to sanctify him, as though he had no temperament or sexual urges at all! I have seen Aaron elated, especially when a new piece was being played (you never get blasé about that first performance). I've seen him struck dumb by the beauty of a passing human being. I've seen him depressed, dark, near tears about the plight of an arrogant friend we both loved; but he never actually talked about his personal life, except elusively. His rapport with Victor Kraft was ambiguous, and, in any case, pretty much deromanticized by the time I knew them both. It's not my place here to speculate on later loves—his generation, even including Auden, was circumspect. Indeed, Aaron is the most circumspect famous person I have ever known, considering how much he encouraged others to let down their hair.

I am thrilled to discover how cyclic our world becomes if you live long enough. In just the past two or three years, I've heard any number of scores by young men and women in their twenties, scores that do more than emulate the wide-open spaces of Aaron's most beloved works—they actually sound—in timbre, tune, and hue—like steals from the master. Always admired by the masses, he's becoming readmired by fickle youth.

Nevertheless, I asked three members of this youth recently, "Is there any composer whose next work you just can't wait to hear?" They had to stop and think. They were not agog as we once were about how the Clarinet Concerto *was going to sound, how the new* Nonet *was going to sound, or how* Inscape *would be received. These were* events. *Aaron Copland wasn't the only one, but he was the chief one whose new works we were all avid to hear. I don't think it was because we were specifically younger. It's that the whole world was younger; there were fewer composers around; the repertory of American works was slimmer, so any new addition was a thrill. Aaron was the king and in a sense still is. There hasn't been another man since then from whom all young composers await each new endeavor with bated breath, and whose endeavor usually doesn't disappoint.*

In 1948 (the spring after Ned Rorem's second Tanglewood summer), it was announced that the French conductor Charles Munch, who had made his American debut in Boston in 1946, would become music director of the Boston Symphony after Koussevitzky's retirement in 1949. Several tributes were made to Koussevitzky marking the occasion.[23] Although Munch would not take over until the fall of 1949—and even then, Koussevitzky had no intention of retiring from Tanglewood—from the time of the announcement of Munch's appointment, Koussevitzky felt that his position was threatened. Those involved with the administration of the Festival and Music Center were aware of the internal politics in 1948 and 1949, but for the public and the student body of the Center, activities proceeded as energetically as usual,[24] and the faculty remained essentially unchanged.[25]

Irving Fine and Copland planned the 1948 lecture course, which dealt with very old and very new music (Julius Herford presented the "old"; Copland the "new"). A new series, "Aspects of Music," was initiated and taught twice a week by various faculty members. Copland again moderated the public forums. Darius Milhaud was visiting composer. He wrote to Copland (27 May 1948), "You are a real darling, and it is nice that you can send a car to fetch the old wheelchaired composer and bring me to Tanglewood." Before Milhaud's arrival, Copland read his autobiography[26] and wrote to Victor, "What a happy childhood he's had, maybe that's why he's so nice now." Milhaud and Copland taught the regular composition students,[27] and a third group from other areas of concentration was taught by either Fine or Foss. Copland taught seven students in 1948. During the

Above: Copland and Darius
Milhaud at Tanglewood,
1948.

Right: Letter from Darius
Milhaud to Copland, fall
1948 (undated).

TELEPHONE CIRCLE 7-1900   CABLE ADDRESS "NORTHHOTEL"

GREAT NORTHERN HOTEL

118 WEST 57TH STREET – NEW YORK 19, N.Y.

Dear Aaron,

How wonderful it was! (Already in the
past.) In Paris we said: how wonderful it
will be.
In Tanglewood: How wonderful it is!

Thanks again —

Hope to see you in California —

How wonderful it will be --

Tell Victor our best affection. I am looking
forward to his pictures.

Madeleine joins me in sending you
notre fidèle amitié —

D.

summer, he heard a piece by a young violin student. Later on, Copland said, "It became clear to me during those years [1948 and 1949] that one of the students at Tanglewood, Jacob (he was then called "Jack") Druckman, was a very talented fellow."

Jacob Druckman[28]

I had always thought of myself as a composer, but in my late teens I thought I would make my living as a violinist playing in symphony orchestras to support the composing habit. I spent the summer of 1948 at Tanglewood as an orchestral violinist and ended up hating it. I also felt that nobody was paying any attention to the music I was writing. After that first summer at Tanglewood, I turned my back on music and spent most of the year working as a commercial artist. Then, just on a fluke, as a kind of last chance, I sent some scores to Aaron, and he accepted me as a student and gave me a scholarship to study composition at Tanglewood. (Aaron had heard my first string quartet during the summer of 1948.) The whole path of events changed after that.

Aaron was a huge presence at Tanglewood. It was, in those years, one of the most glamorous places ever. In the middle of it was Aaron, not only as the important *American composer at the time but also as the person reaching out to other composers. When I first went to study with him, I thought of Copland as representing a kind of neoclassic Americana. My own natural inclinations had very little to do with Americana, and I worried that he would be unsympathetic to other kinds of music. I remember in an early lesson my bristling when he said, "How come you always use intervals like minor thirds and major sevenths? Why don't you ever use a perfect fifth?" And I thought, This is the Americana bit rising up. But that was not the case at all. He was very erudite and his tastes were catholic. He could criticize twelve-tone composers and had a genuine interest in composers of all kinds of music, as well as those working closer to his own style. Aaron had a wonderful eye and ear for the shape of a piece. He could very quickly recognize the original premise of a work and just as quickly put his finger on spots that didn't live up to the promise of the opening. Copland was really the most amazing teacher.*

By the time I met Aaron, he was already a totally establishment person, and to the young and revolutionary, it could have rubbed the wrong way. I think I was suspect of him a little bit, but I'm not sure whether that was

Copland teaching a class at Tanglewood, c. 1949.

a result of deep conviction or just simply a product of my youth. Aaron's influence on my music was not direct: I don't think my music ever sounds like Aaron Copland's music. The influence was more as an example, particularly in the kind of citizen that he is in the world of music—shouldering of responsibility and not being out for his own personal glory and gain. He feels as though the advancement of the art is his responsibility, and this is a wonderful influence on many of us. Aaron is the kind of person who goes out and creates something that was not there, who invents festivals, invents occasions, invents ways to help young composers. This is the kind of citizenship I am talking about, the encouragement and vision that he has.

Through the intervening years since Tanglewood, I have seen Copland only occasionally. I would visit him and show him what I was up to. He was supportive in the sense of being interested in what I was doing and treating me as though I was a real composer, which was even more necessary for me than the opening of doors. But later, I would hear from people that he mentioned my name and recommended me in various places. I feel very close to Copland, but our relationship has always been one of a certain distance, a certain respect. It took me a long time to bring myself to call him Aaron; in fact, it was not until I joined the Koussevitzky Music Foundation board and found myself sitting elbow to elbow with him.

Aaron's is an enormous personality. It may be a new idea in the history of the arts that we need a personality, that we need an identity, that we need to be able to recognize a composer upon hearing the first few measures of the music, but it is a mysterious thing when it happens. It's that magic that we talk about as charisma. We don't know how it happens but it is wonderful when it does. There are so many composers around that are good, but Aaron's voice is distinctly his. His works have already entered into the mainstream of the repertoire and certainly will continue to be performed. They are beyond the question of this year's fashion.

In 1949, the famous French composer Olivier Messiaen joined the faculty.[29] Copland heard from Milhaud: "I miss the Tanglewood atmosphere very much and specially you and Vic and Lenny and Fine and Lukas and of course Dr. K., the magician of this music land. Now you must take a little time for me and write about Olivier the Messiah." Messiaen made a strong impression on the young composers at Tanglewood.[30] They seemed to find his mysticism a refreshing change from the current twelve-tone vogue. Copland's composition students were Martin Boykan, Joseph Harnell, Edward Lewis, Lee Pockriss, Gerald Kechley, Mark Bucci, and Samuel Adler.

When Irving Fine suggested that the 1949 lecture series be "a retrospective survey of the wild and wooly twenties," Copland agreed, making the comment, "It seems funny that it's all history now." Two events are remembered most vividly by those at Tanglewood in 1949: one, the State Department movie being made for distribution abroad that disrupted the regular curriculum[31] and put Koussevitzky on the warpath; the other, the accident that took place on the Richmond Road when Copland ran into a cow. Almost forty years later (24 July 1987), during lunch at Copland's home, talk was about Copland hitting the cow, and he declared excitedly, *"Just* a moment! You have it all wrong! It was the *cow* who walked in front of my car!" The story has been retold through the years by several people, among them Arthur Berger[32] and Verna Fine, who were both on the scene when it happened.

Verna Fine[33]

At the end of each Tanglewood season, Koussevitzky would give a dinner party on Sunday night at the Curtis Hotel in Lenox for the faculty and their wives. It was always very nice but sad—similar to the last days of summer camp. The most memorable of those occasions was in 1949. Aaron, Irving, and I were driving home to nearby Richmond, where we were sharing a house for the summer. Aaron was driving, I was sitting in the middle, and Irving was to my right. In a car behind us were Arthur and Esther Berger, who were staying with us those last two weeks. It was a very foggy night, so we were going very slowly. Suddenly, there was this huge cow standing smack in the middle of the road. Aaron slammed on the brakes, but it was too late. I let out a great scream, and then we all got out of the car. The poor cow was beyond help. Arthur almost fainted; I lost my voice for three days; but Aaron and Irving were cucumber-cool. Aaron's Studebaker was badly damaged—undrivable, in fact—so we drove on to the house in the Bergers' car, called the police, and returned to the scene of the "crime."

The police, who were extremely hostile, actually wanted to put Aaron in jail! They took him to Pittsfield, and Irving, as a Massachusetts resident, put up bail. We tried to explain the accident to the police, but they wouldn't listen: "We will talk only to the perpetrator of the crime," they declared. Aaron finally got out and returned home with Irving, who "sprung" him at about 2 A.M. The next morning, the news was broadcast on the radio, and the local paper ran the headline COPLAND KILLS COW!

Irving and I had known Aaron since the winter of 1943–1944, when he came to the Harvard University music department to teach composition, replacing Walter Piston, who was on sabbatical. Irving was a faculty instructor. One night, he invited Aaron to our apartment for dinner. It was love at first sight, just as if we had known him all our lives. Aaron was an informal sort of person, and he felt entirely comfortable with Irving, who was, as Aaron often said, very simpatico. Let's face it—at that time, Harvard was a pretty stuffy place! Aaron became like an older brother to Irving. They were both soft-spoken, and they loved to talk about music—I never remember them talking much about anything else. They both gave the impression of being calm and unruffled. They also had in common the fact that they were good listeners, and they listened closely to each other. For years, Irving and Aaron had long-distance conversations once or twice a week. Aaron used to say, "Irving, I can count on one hand the people who call me just out of friendship, who aren't after a letter of recommendation for something or other. In fact, maybe I can count them on one finger—you."

Harold Shapero, Lukas Foss, and Irving—the three musketeers, as we used to call them—were all in the Boston area in 1944. Harold wasn't married yet; Lukas was living in a tiny studio; and although Aaron had a beautiful sublet on Memorial Drive facing the Charles River, it was our apartment in Cambridge where we all got together, and where I did the cooking.

I first saw Aaron conduct that same year. He was invited to do Outdoor Overture with the Boston Pops, and on the podium he looked like a modern dancer. We sat there laughing hysterically. Afterward, the good-natured Aaron made fun of himself: "If I can see the first deskmen, then I can't see the percussion! And if I see the percussion, I can't see the score!" Aaron's conducting improved later when he did more of it (and when he got better eyeglasses).

Aaron was writing Appalachian Spring, and he showed us the sketches and played some of it for us. He invited us to Washington for the world premiere. We stayed at the same hotel as Aaron and went to all the fancy parties with him in a chauffeured limousine. The premiere was a sensational success. When Koussevitzky was to conduct the Appalachian Spring Suite, he had some problems with the rhythms and asked Irving to re-bar some sections. But Irving refused at Aaron's request and eventually "Koussie" struggled through those difficult rhythms.

Irving, unlike many of Aaron's composer colleagues, was never critical of his lighter music, because he felt that Aaron maintained the same integrity as in his serious pieces. Irving thought Aaron had discovered something special and often said he wished he could do something similar.

Aaron suggested to Koussevitzky in 1946 that Irving be brought to Tanglewood to teach harmonic analysis. Because Irving was in the academic world, Aaron often turned to him for teaching and organizational ideas. They did a lot of co-lecturing. Both were good administrators. If truth be known, the courtship in the fifties of Paul Fromm and his support of contemporary music at Tanglewood all germinated over the dinner table when we lived together in the early Tanglewood years. The original Brandeis University Creative Arts Festival was planned the same way. Irving had

Copland with Irving Fine (right), a student, and Professor Erwin Bodky (left) at Brandeis University, c. 1951.

joined the Brandeis faculty in 1950; after Koussevitzky died in 1951, Irving and Aaron got the idea of putting on a festival at Brandeis in June 1952 as a Koussevitzky memorial, one that would also honor the initial graduating class of the newly founded Brandeis University. 34

In the summer of 1946, we didn't live near Aaron, but the next summer, we found a little cabin behind a guest home in Richmond owned by a Reverend Cutler. I made lunches for everyone and took them over to the Tanglewood grounds. Aaron rented a suite with a separate entrance near Reverend Cutler's, and every night we had elegant dinners together prepared by Mrs. Cutler. At the end of the summer, Aaron arranged to rent the Gettys' barn the next summer, and in 1948, we all had our meals together at the spacious Kelley mansion, which we rented for the summer. I got two helpers, one to take care of our new baby, the other to help in the kitchen. I ran a "restaurant" every night with typed menus.

In the summer of 1949, Aaron couldn't get the Gettys' barn, but the Kelley mansion had been remodeled and was even larger and more beautiful. Aaron rented a suite in one wing, Lukas took another, and Irving and I and our young daughter had the main part of the house. Three pianos were moved in, one for each composer. Lenny often came for dinner, and we had

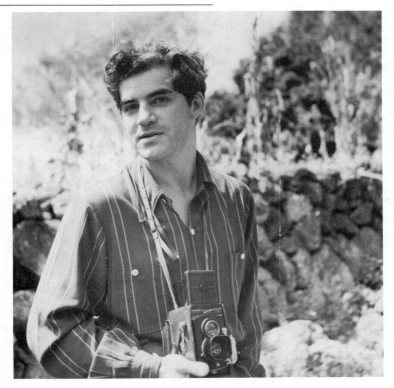

Victor Kraft, c. 1949.

other musicians as guests—Walter Piston, Harold Shapero, and Arthur Berger among them. Once the actor Farley Granger, an old friend of Aaron's, appeared for dinner. Victor Kraft was around a lot. He was moody but charming and handsome and helpful, always working on Aaron's car and taking delightful pictures. I often did Irving's secretarial work, and I also typed for Aaron. He was a pleasure to work for. In 1950 and 1951, we all rented separate places, but we still ate dinner together several times a week.

At Tanglewood, I got to know Aaron's family. I went up to Laurine at a concert in 1947 and said, "Oh, you don't know how lucky you are. How I would love Aaron for my brother!" She looked at me in amazement. I don't think they ever came to terms with how great a man had come from their family. Still, Laurine was charming and beautiful. She and her husband, Charlie Marcus, and Aaron's brother Ralph and his wife, Dorothy, came up regularly every summer to hear Aaron's music. Ralph was very quiet. I noted with surprise that neither Laurine nor Ralph looked at all like Aaron.

After Koussevitzky died, Tanglewood could never be the same. It was my impression that Aaron and Irving lost some of the enthusiasm they had had for the place in the "Koussie" days.

Later on, when Aaron traveled all over the world as a conductor, he always brought back gifts—a Yemenite necklace from Israel for me, books for Irving, and toys for our three daughters. We never saw the thrifty side of Aaron that everyone talks about. As recently as 1980, when Aaron and I traveled back from Washington together after his eightieth birthday concert, he insisted on paying my air fare.

Irving died suddenly from a heart attack on August 23, 1962, in Boston. Aaron flew up for the funeral. A few weeks later, he telephoned to tell me that Lenny planned to conduct the New York Philharmonic in the Adagio *movement from Irving's* Notturno for Strings and Harp *(4, 5, 6, and 9 October 1962). Aaron said he would like to escort me to the opening concert. These were the first subscription concerts of the Philharmonic in its new hall at Lincoln Center. Little did I know what Lenny had planned! Before the performance, a microphone dropped from the ceiling and Lenny gave a moving tribute to Irving. I was overwhelmed, and Aaron squeezed my hand and comforted me.*

The official gala opening of Lincoln Center's new hall had taken place a week or so earlier, when Aaron's Connotations *was given its premiere. Instead of attending with Irving as planned, I had sadly watched it on television at home. When I saw Aaron, he told me the famous Jackie Kennedy story to cheer me up. I asked Aaron what the First Lady said when they went offcamera backstage before the TV camera caught her backing away from that infamous, sweaty Bernstein kiss. Aaron is no mimic, but he managed a passable imitation of Jackie's high-pitched, breathy voice:*

I opened the door for her leading into the TV viewing room and she said, "Oh, Mr. Copland." We took a few more steps and she said again, "Oh, Mr. Copland." At about the fourth "Oh, Mr. Copland," we arrived backstage. What do you think she meant, Verna?

I replied, "Aaron, it's obvious; she hated your piece!"

Aaron called me often after Irving died, and when I was in New York, we would meet for dinner at the Harvard Club or go to a concert together. When I moved out of the Boston area and came to New York, we saw each other often at Peekskill as well as in the city. I was always included in important celebrations or when Aaron would receive an honor.

One night several years ago at dinner, Aaron confided, "I don't feel comfortable with the twelve-tone system, but I don't want to keep repeating myself. And remember, Verna, I don't have a Robert Craft. Stravinsky was lucky that he had a young guy around showing him Webern, bringing him music with which he wasn't familiar. I don't have anybody coming to me all the time to show me the new things." I was impressed with Aaron's honesty.

There were a lot of important people in our lives. Many were Irving's friends, who "dropped" me after he died. Yet I couldn't have predicted that Aaron would have stayed so close. He was, and still is, wonderful to me, and I have felt devoted to him all these years. It was good to know that Aaron liked me for myself, not just because I was Irving's wife. Aaron is not only a great composer; he is a great human being. What a combination!

In 1950, French composer Jacques Ibert shared the composition program with Copland,[35] who wrote to Victor (6 July):

> Ibert has arrived. The barn is okay. I lead a life of lonely grandeur in Richmond. I eat at Fines three times a week and scrounge the others. De Sabata is coming in spite of Kouss, not because of him.[36] The fireworks can be expected that week. . . . Kouss doesn't look very well. He is amazingly insecure about the future of himself as director. . . . Lenny due 19th. *Salón Méx* for student orch.

Copland's brother Ralph wrote (20 July): "Another summer has rolled around and we are again 'Tanglewood conscious.' The ladies have put the burden of finding accommodations on you." Copland invited his family for their annual visit to Tanglewood when *El Salón México* was being performed. Also scheduled were student performances of the *Violin Sonata* and *Sextet* (the latter was studied under Foss but considered too difficult to perform with the allotted rehearsal time).

Copland reported at the August faculty meeting that he was well satisfied with the composition program. He lectured on the music of Roger Sessions in a series called "Music: Pro and Con," in which modern works were presented by students, and speakers were asked to attack or defend each work.[37] The Tanglewood Festival celebrated the two hundredth anniversary of Bach, and the popular "Tanglewood on Parade" featured Eleanor Roosevelt narrating Prokofiev's *Peter and the Wolf.* Ralph Berkowitz went to coach Mrs. Roosevelt at Hyde Park. Leonard Burkat recalls her first rehearsal with the orchestra: "Mrs. Roosevelt's voice and accent

Copland at a rehearsal in the Shed
at Tanglewood, and practicing in
the Theater-Concert Hall.

were so strange that halfway through, Koussevitzky turned to the concert-master, Richard Burgin, and asked incredulously in Russian, 'Doesn't she speak English?' " Nevertheless, the performance was a great success, and Mrs. Roosevelt donated her fee to the Music Center and to the Wiltwyck School for Boys ($1,250 to each).

Bernstein was away for part of the 1950 season, leaving Richard Burgin, Carvalho, Foss, and Howard Shanet as Koussevitzky's assistants.

Howard Shanet [38]

My presence at Tanglewood came about through Copland. I telephoned him at a mutual friend's suggestion, and I went on at length about how much I wanted to go to Tanglewood. It suddenly occurred to me that I hadn't made it clear to Aaron that I meant in conducting! Here I was talking to America's best-known composer, and I couldn't make myself say that I didn't mean to study with him at all! When Aaron said, "My class is filled, but you may get into Martinů's group," I thought I had better go along. I dug out whatever scores I had and sent them along with an application. To my surprise, I was accepted as a composer to study with Martinů, and returned the next year in Honegger's class.

One of my jobs was to organize the student composers' concerts. On one occasion, I had to conduct a quintet because no one else would take it on. Afterward, Aaron came up and said, "Why didn't you tell me you were a conductor?" I said, "That's what I have been trying to do all this time!" Aaron offered to tell Koussevitzky about me.

Koussevitzky was an idealistic man who was accustomed to having his own way. That means there was a pragmatic side to Koussevitzky, and Aaron had to live with both sides. For someone to remain in Aaron's capacity of running Tanglewood without infuriating Koussevitzky, he had to be a special kind of personality. A consummate administrator. Aaron always had to maintain a diplomatic stance. I don't think any of us ever witnessed Aaron in a disagreement with Koussevitzky; they always seemed on superb terms. Nevertheless, Aaron's own personality was strong. He could be firm without being abrasive. These same qualities made him a good teacher of composition. He could make his own opinions known, yet accept each student's different style. He would not impose his own ideas.

There were two things about Tanglewood that concerned Koussevitzky most: one, that he should be separated from the place at all, ever; the other, that a kind of vulgarization was creeping in. There was already talk of bus lines, advertising, pop music. When we were in Hollywood on tour, representatives of the cultural community there offered Koussevitzky the chance to have a West Coast Tanglewood. He was tempted, but it was unthinkable for him to leave his Tanglewood. He thought of it as his own child, which could not be replaced with another. He even addressed those of us who worked with him as "Kinder"—perhaps because he did not have children of his own, he was always warmly interested in young people. Koussevitzky called me "Hovardt"; Seymour Lipkin was "Lipushka"; and Lenny was "Lenushka."

In the summer of 1952, I was a junior faculty member at the Music Center. At a staff meeting, I spoke my mind about what I viewed as an abandonment of certain of Koussevitzky's ideals. Maybe I said too much. It was not Aaron's style to speak out. He doesn't work by making a hassle, and maybe he didn't see it my way. I was young and brash. I asked for a leave and after that, I didn't return to the Tanglewood faculty, although I remained on good terms with my colleagues there and went to visit once in a while.

Following the 1950 season, Koussevitzky wrote a letter to the Boston Symphony trustees (18 November 1950): "I ask that you protect Tanglewood from influences foreign to its initial ideal. I ask the Trustees as long as I am living and able to carry on the responsibility of Tanglewood, to entrust me with the full, undivided artistic authority as Director of the BMC and the Festival." The board agreed, without knowing that Koussevitzky would not live long enough to direct his beloved Tanglewood through another season. He became seriously ill in Phoenix, Arizona, where he and Olga were staying after his conducting tour. After he returned to Boston and it was clear he would not recover, the Fines wrote to Copland in Italy (30 May 1951), but the letter did not arrive in time. Therefore, Copland had a terrible shock when he heard the news from his cook the morning after Koussevitzky's death (4 June 1951). A service for Koussevitzky was held in Boston at the Protestant Episcopal Church of the Advent on 7 June; the funeral was the following day in Lenox at the Church on the Hill. Copland sent a telegram to Olga Koussevitzky, who wired back, "Thank you, dear Aaron, awaiting your return." Copland decided he could best honor Koussevitzky by carrying out a commitment to produce a Koussevitzky Music Foundation concert in Rome (11 June).

Knowing Irving Fine was at home completing arrangements for the up-coming season, Copland wrote (15 June), "If I were after a job of course I would drop everything here and dash home. But I'm not." Copland advanced his return date by a few days, arriving in time to face opening the Music Center without Koussevitzky (24 June 1951). The trustees had decided not to appoint a new director. They released the following announcement:

> We propose to create a Faculty Board which would assume powers of leadership for the 1951 season. This board, composed of Aaron Copland (who was nominated chairman), Leonard Bernstein, Hugh Ross, Gregor Piatigorsky, Boris Goldovsky, Richard Burgin, and William Kroll, met on six occasions for consideration of the school's work-in-progress as well as with an eye toward the Center's future.

The opening exercises of 1951 were of a commemorative nature (1 July). Copland and Bernstein spoke. The following is part of Copland's talk:

> We sense our loss more than anyone else can. I was a friend of Dr. Koussevitzky for about twenty-eight years. It seems to me that his spirit is so clearly among us that it would be impossible for us not to carry on our work in the meaning of that spirit. I think that above all things Dr. Koussevitzky would have wanted us to talk about the future of our school rather than about the past and about the possible accomplishments of our school rather than his past accomplishments. It was his vital personality which inspired all of us to carry out the plan born in his mind. In this spirit, at this moment I want you all to rise for a moment of silence in memory of Dr. Koussevitzky.[39]

A memorial concert was presented with representatives of all the departments of the Center; every year since then, a Koussevitzky Memorial Concert has been included in the Festival, usually conducted by Bernstein.

Copland settled into his barn in Richmond and got to work. Bernstein, who was to have been on leave, changed his plans and took charge of the conducting classes. Foss, Burgin, Carvalho, Lipkin, and Shanet were all on hand, and along with the other regular faculty members, they did their best to make things seem normal. Luigi Dallapiccola arrived as visiting guest composer,[40] and William Kroll came to assist Piatigorsky with the chamber music program. The students studied and played Copland's *Vitebsk* and *Statements for Orchestra,* conducted by Copland.

Charles Munch, as music director, was not greatly involved with the Center and seemed willing to have those who had administered it continue to do so. As Tod Perry pointed out:

Aaron's role took on major importance and was even more essential. I was always interested in the Music Center and continued active in it, and Leonard Burkat, of course, who became administrator in 1954 when I succeeded Judd as manager of the orchestra. Leonard was helpful to Munch since he spoke French.[41]

In the years immediately following Koussevitzky's death, those who had been chosen by Koussevitzky as his Tanglewood "family" kept the Music Center running smoothly, despite periods of serious financial difficulties. Nevertheless, Koussevitzky's death marked the end of an era.[42] One of his greatest achievements had been the founding of Tanglewood and the Berkshire Music Center. With the burgeoning of summer festivals throughout the country, there is still nothing like Tanglewood. Although many changes have taken place through the years, the basic aims and spirit as conceived by its founder have remained constant. Tanglewood is still Koussevitzky's dream come true. His sense of mission, old-fashioned as the word may seem, has never completely faded. Moreover, Tanglewood's unchanging beauty seems to imbue the place with a presence of its own, a grandeur that presides over the many and varied activities on its sweeping lawns and beneath the towering trees. When David Del Tredici returned in 1986 to hear one of his works performed during the Contemporary Music Festival, he gazed out over the distant views and commented in amazement, "I haven't been here for over twenty years, and it looks exactly the same—not even a leaf is out of place."

Serge Koussevitzky
(1874–1951).

Photograph by Victor Kraft.

For Aaron Copland
from a fan
Clare Boothe Luce

Around the World

1949-1953

Europe was coming alive again in the world of the arts. I could hardly believe it had been twelve years since I had been abroad! I planned a trip for May and June of 1949. Erik Johns traveled with me to England, France, Italy, and Belgium.[1] Our first stop was London, where I visited old friends Ben Britten and Peter Pears. I wrote in my diary, "Benjie's charm is still potent and derives from a combination of severity and boyishness." After Michael Tippett came to call at our hotel, I wrote, "He is charming with a very un-English warmth at first sight. He has a sort of British Roy Harris personality." Juan Orrego-Salas was in London, and we met for lunch. He had just come from the Palermo Festival, and I was interested in hearing about the struggle between "progressive" Italian musicians and the twelve-toners. Of the people I met for the first time, I was most interested in composer-critic Wilfrid Mellers: "I am impressed with this pixie-like individual who seemed to know more about American music than anyone I have met in a long time."

Erik and I drove into the countryside one day to have tea with Leslie Boosey of Boosey & Hawkes. I lectured in Birmingham and visited Cambridge, returning to London to attend a rehearsal of *In the Beginning* for a broadcast by the BBC, and for receptions in my honor by the English Speaking Union and the British Council. Many composers attended, even William Walton and Constant Lambert. Erik saw to it that we visited the museums and theaters. Of most interest to me was *The Heiress*, with Peggy Ashcroft in the leading role.

Paris seemed more hectic than I had remembered, yet wonderfully the same. I took my first walk on the boulevard St. Germain to the Café Flore and felt nostalgic in a nice way. On the first night, I went for dinner (the restaurant David Diamond and I used to enjoy in the thirties) with younger composers Charles Strouse, Bill Flanagan, and Gary [Gerhard] Samuel. We talked about Nadia, and the following day, I met all the new

145

Boulangerie when I went to see her on the rue Ballu.[2] Nadia had returned from the States, where she spent the war years—first in California, then Boston. I always had my scores sent to her as they appeared, and I continued to send promising students to study with her. Each year, Nadia counted on my advice in choosing the annual composer awards of the Lili Boulanger Fund. It struck me that Nadia had become rather set in her ways. She remained rigidly aloof from the current excitement about serialism, claiming that such music failed to move her. She would not open herself to students using the method. (Nadia never addressed the issue with me, but it must have been shocking for her when both Stravinsky and I began to use serialism.) During my 1949 visit, Nadia had scheduled a concert by Leo Preger, and I was hard put to see what she was so enthused about, but we had a joyful reunion. We went together to the Champs Elysées Theater and to visit Poulenc in his charming apartment. Before I left Paris, Nadia invited twelve guests for a formal dinner in my honor, among them François Valéry and my old friend Marcelle de Manziarly.

Pierre Boulez was the topic of conversation wherever music people got together in Paris. I met him for the first time when John Cage took him along to a party given by Gary Samuel. Noel Lee played some of Boulez' new music, and the evening had a French intellectual atmosphere quite different from New York gatherings. Boulez was cordial and invited me to a soirée at his apartment later in the week. I described the evening in my diary:

> Cage and Merce Cunningham were there. Typical artists garret apt. Boulez impressive. Young man of twenty-four. He played parts of a piano sonata—seemingly unplayable. Pupil of Leibowitz and Messiaen. He has learnt much from both. Piece rhythmically schemed on a nonmelodic twelve-tone row basis. I said in mock despair, "But must we start a revolution all over again?" *"Mais oui,"* says Boulez, *"sans pitié."* It adds up to a new way of organizing music, such as the fugue must once have been. If one listens for melodies, one is lost. There are patterns of sound, some monotony, but also much conviction, particularly when Boulez himself plays it. How another pianist might do it is hard to say, and public reaction impossible to predict. Anyhow it's new, and therefore exciting. Boulez turns his back on the Satie line, adores Webern. The French are obviously unpredictable.

I saw Boulez on another occasion in Paris—when he played parts of his *Sonata* for some of the Boulangerie. They were quite obviously disapproving. I found myself in the odd position of defending Boulez after he left the gathering! It occurred to me that the Boulangerie had its limitations.

They seemed to have a conservative-modern attitude, much influenced by the Messiaen–Leibowitz axis. Of the young Boulangerie, Noel Lee impressed me most—he was charming and obviously gifted.

My friend Peggy Bernier was in Paris! She put on a swanky reception in my honor to which *tout* Paris came—Poulenc, Auric, Messiaen, Nadia, the Vicomtesse de Noailles (27 October 1949). I wrote, "Messiaen seemed very self-concentrated and looked somewhat seedy, but poetic. Auric was friendly and Poulenc amusing." Peggy told some scandalous tales about composer Florent Schmitt, intending (with some success) to shock Nadia. Messiaen invited me to visit him in the organ loft at the Trinité during a regular noon church service. I went and was shocked to hear him improvise everything from the "Devil" in the bass to what sounded like Radio City Hall harmonies in the treble. I couldn't understand how the church allowed it!

A visit to the Boosey & Hawkes office in Paris proved disappointing—they had very few of my pieces available. I was to find the same story when we got to Rome. As for performances of my music, there was only one in Paris when I was there—Franz Waxman conducting *Lincoln Portrait* (1 June). The audience was so meager that he canceled a second scheduled performance.

Since Sir Adrian Boult was conducting my *Third Symphony* in London (3 June), I returned for the occasion. Boult was at first disturbed by various difficulties in the piece, but the broadcast performance went well. I wrote my impressions: "Boult was not 'fired' by hearing the music and his conducting took on a 'pompier' quality. But he tried hard, which is something." We had a minor tragedy when Erik lost his passport in London. I had to leave him there to work it out. He made it back to Paris in time for a formal reception at the ambassador's home, where neither of us knew a single soul. Later, we had dinner with Paul Bowles, Bob Fizdale, and Arthur Gold. Bowles was bored with Paris, having become interested only in Africa. He thought I was going to be upset with him because he had abandoned music for writing novels. When he saw that I was not, he invited me to lunch with Alice Toklas and for a visit to the Stein–Toklas apartment to see the paintings.

Upon our arrival in Rome, we were met by composer Alexei Haieff, who showed us around and took us to the American Academy.[3] During the next few days, there were the usual receptions and sightseeing. I was interviewed on the radio and somehow managed to reply in Italian after some heavy coaching. We left Rome for Florence, which seemed nice and small townish compared to everywhere else we had been. I spent some time with Luigi Dallapiccola, and wrote, "He is a lively character, a milder version of the young Villa-Lobos. Same vivacity and sharp tongue. I should think Florence would be too small for him. Am anxious to know his music better." I also saw Newell Jenkins, who was conducting some of my works, and he told me, "The Italians don't really care a fig about knowing American music, and are completely unaware of it, except for Gershwin."

After a few days in Venice, we traveled to Nice and then on to Brussels, where I played the *Piano Variations* and *Four Piano Blues* for a radio broadcast. When we returned to London for the trip home at the end of June, Erik was so enamored of Europe that he stayed on, while I got back just in time for the 1949 Tanglewood season.

I stayed on in the Richmond barn when Tanglewood was over, to work on a piece commissioned by The National Broadcasting Company for the first anniversary of the "Universal Declaration of Human Rights" of the United Nations. (The Declaration had been adopted and proclaimed by the General Assembly, 10 December 1948.) The short piece for orchestra and speaking voice was to be performed at Carnegie Hall (10 December 1949). It was not difficult to compose, for the words, which were drawn from the United Nations charter, were in themselves inspiring:

> We, the peoples of the United Nations, determined to save succeeding genera-
> tions from the scourge of war, which twice in our lifetime has brought untold
> sorrow to mankind, and to reaffirm faith in fundamental human rights, in the
> dignity and worth of the human person, in the equal rights of men and women
> of all nations large and small, and to promote social progress and better stan-
> dards of life in larger freedom, have resolved to combine our efforts to accom-
> plish these aims.

Preamble is a patriotic work of under six minutes duration. It was originally conceived as a hymn, which explains why the tempo is slow and stately. An introductory fanfare for brass is taken up by other instruments of the orchestra. The principal melody is announced quietly by violas and a muted horn. *Preamble* has occasionally been likened to *Lincoln Portrait* because of the narration, but the musical style is quite different. It is a more formal work and without the inclusion of any folk song material. (The only similarity is the C major climax at the finale of both works.)

Formal invitations went out from the Secretariat of the United Nations for the special event, which also included the premiere of *United Nations March* by Shostakovich and the finale of Beethoven's *Ninth Symphony.*

Performers were The Collegiate Chorale and the Boston Symphony Orchestra, conducted by Bernstein. Sir Laurence Olivier read the narration in *Preamble.* The audience included U.N. delegates, who were addressed by General Carlos P. Romulo, president of the U.N.; Mrs. Roosevelt, who had played a vital role in drafting the Declaration of Human Rights; and Trygve Lie, Secretary General of the United Nations. Prior to the concert, a forum was held on the topic "Freedom of Information." The entire program was televised by NBC and broadcast coast to coast the following day.

Preamble was heard again on the ninth birthday of the United Nations, conducted by Charles Munch with the Symphony of the Air. The program was the first public concert ever held in the General Assembly Hall, which held 2,500. Another memorable performance was when Duke Ellington spoke the narration in a concert of all-American works during the French–American Festival at Philharmonic Hall, Lincoln Center (30 July 1965).

After the specific occasion for which *Preamble* was composed, I revised the accompaniment so that it can be played by orchestra alone (with a similar version for band and another for pipe or Hammond organ.)[4] The title was changed to *Preamble for a Special Occasion.* The orchestra and band arrangements are used occasionally, sometimes with a different narration, such as during the Bicentennial, when James Stewart read the Preamble to the Constitution to the accompaniment (15 January 1976). The organists have been most inventive in their use of *Preamble,* for various degree programs and as a recessional.

I had been sketching ideas for my *Quartet for Piano and Strings* for several months but only began to work on it in earnest during my sixth visit to the MacDowell Colony in June 1950. After a slow start, I made real headway on the first movement. There were few distractions at the Colony—Lukas Foss and Vittorio Rieti were in residence but both were deeply engrossed in their own projects. I spent most evenings reading at the Colony library or in my own room. I wrote to Claire Reis, "I am intrigued with a biography of P. T. Barnum and surprised nobody's done a musical comedy on his life!" The social highlight of my month was a visit with Mrs. MacDowell. She was still sharp as a whistle at age ninety-two. The realization that she hadn't started the Colony until she was fifty made me feel quite young and energetic about starting something new as I approached my fiftieth birthday.

Manuscript, a page showing twelve-tone series, inversions, and chords for the *Piano Quartet.*

From the MacDowell Colony, I went to Tanglewood and worked furiously on the second and third movements of the quartet when the season was over. The work had been commissioned by Mrs. Elizabeth Sprague Coolidge to commemorate the twenty-fifth anniversary of the Coolidge Foundation and was to be premiered by the New York Quartet during the

Eleventh Festival of Chamber Music at the Library of Congress.[5] I wrote to Irving Fine (22 September), "I played the first movement for Schneider and he didn't turn a hair." And again I wrote (19 October), "I should be done with the *Piano Quartet* tomorrow. Oy—what a relief!" I inscribed "To Elizabeth Sprague Coolidge" on the title page and at the end of the forty-three-page score: "October 20, 1950, Sneden's Landing, N.Y." The premiere was 29 October, a mere nine days later!

I was, of course, well aware that serial composition was the dominant method of composition during the years following the war.[6] Among young composers, it was considered the "new" music. I cannot say that I admired much of what I heard—so often it seemed that individuality was sacrificed to the method. Boulez effectively demonstrated that the method could be retained without the German esthetic. It was twenty years since I had composed the *Piano Variations,* in which I had explored certain possibilities of serial composition and adapted the method to my own use. I was interested in trying it again with the hope that it would freshen and enrich my technique. The *Quartet for Piano and Strings* seemed like an ideal opportunity: I felt able to explore a more abstract and esoteric idiom with chamber music than I could with other types of music.

Composing with all twelve notes of the chromatic scale can give one a feeling of freedom in the formulation of melodic and harmonic ideas. In addition to the fact that there are more notes to work with, taking a different perspective produces material you might not come up with if you were not thinking twelve-tone-wise. It's like looking at a picture from a different point of view. It was not the contrapuntal possibilities that interested me in serialism, but the opportunity it gave to hear chords in a different way. My use of the twelve-tone method in the *Piano Quartet* did not adhere strictly to the rules, particularly as regards repetition of the row. I sketched various rows and chose to use an eleven-note one that would lend itself to development and flexibility.[7] Portions of the row are employed in several places (and in various alterations) motivically, in contrast to the usual practice of the composers of the Second Viennese School. Also, the feeling of tonality or of tonal center is rarely missing.

In the first movement, *Adagio serio,* which has been described as "fugal," the row is announced in an outright manner at the start of the piece by the violin. The second theme, announced by the cello, is a retrograde form of the row. The second movement, *Allegro giusto,* longest of the three movements, is a fast-moving scherzo with jazz-derived rhythms. In some passages, all of the instruments play high in the treble of their registers (the violin has harmonics and pizzicati); in other sections, there are big leaps between the voices. The third movement, *Non troppo lento,* is in a simpler mood. It is in five flats, and is the only movement with a key signature. The form is episodic, with sections loosely based on the original theme. Its beginning resembles the first movement in that it opens with strings alone. In place of the traditional contrasting second theme, I used two motives derived from the series. Toward the end of the *Quartet,* ten notes of the series are presented in a figure of descending whole-tone scales in parallel major sixths. The piano writing is at times far above the treble staff and characterized by wide leaps. In two places, I ask the pianist to use "a glassy tone" and the strings to play "impassively and somewhat draggingly." The *Piano Quartet* ends quietly, *pp. morendo.* [8]

The *Quartet* was intended for the cultivated listener. Most audiences find the work puzzling, some find it moving, others find it puzzling *and* moving. The audience for the premiere was of the puzzled variety.[9] However, they at least seemed to enjoy the ending of the *Allegro.* Critic Lawrence Morton caught the idea of what I was after: "It [the final movement] dwells in regions of immobility, impassivity, and quietude, except for a few impassioned outbursts." Other critics debated whether the *Quartet* was a breakthrough to a new style or a return to the old one of the *Piano Variations.* In any case, they were less than delighted. Olin Downes wrote in *The New York Times* (1 November 1950), "It is Copland on one of his most intellectual jags, and we submit that it is neither beauty nor convincing art." Arthur Berger speculated about whether I was trying to reconcile the two camps of Schoenberg and Stravinsky, formerly considered irreconcilable. I was certainly not consciously attempting any such thing. But Arthur was right on the mark when he said I was developing certain principles of serial treatment with which I had already come to grips.[10]

I had had very little direct contact with Arnold Schoenberg, but I had respect for him and interest in his ideas. It was ironic that in 1949, just as I was using the twelve-tone method invented by him, a statement appeared in the *Herald Tribune* by Schoenberg, accusing me of making "malicious remarks" about him![11] Schoenberg attacked me ". . . for giving students advice to use 'simple' intervals and to study the masters. . . . It will certainly take a generation of sincere teaching until this damage can be repaired. . . ." Schoenberg proceeded to compare me with Stalin! I wrote a response to the newspaper (25 September 1949), after which Schoenberg made a rather grudging apology: "If my words could

February 21, 1950

Mr Aaron Copland
River Road Palisades
New York, N.Y.

Dear Mr Copland:

Your letter from February 13 pleases me
very much. True, I am a fighter; but not an at-
tacker. I "backfire" only when I have been attacked. Otherwise it is very easy to live in
peace with me. I am always inclined to do justice
to every merit and to sincerity. I am sure that
the Hungarian pianist   who played your
music, (and Bartók's) for me, about a year ago
in my home, will have told you that I appreciated your music without restriction.

On the other hand, there is at least one man here
in Los Angeles who goes around forbidding people
to "make propaganda" for Schoenberg, when they
only speak about facts which should interest a
musicologist. CBS has evidently intended to hit
at me when they ordered "no controversial music"
to be broadcast - while they broadcast quite a
number of controversial music from other composers.
You might know also about the attitude of publishers, who, if possible, try to counteract performances of my music. There are many other similar
cases.

You will perhaps understand then, that I considered it as malice, when you uttered surprise about
my large audience in Los Angeles, in contrast to
New York. How am I to know that this might be only
gossip to sow discord? I believe that there are
people who aim for production of enmity between
public figures. Considering the abovementioned
facts, I have no way of discrimination.

When I said at the beginning of this, that your
letter pleases me very much, I can repeat this
now, adding that I am always ready to live in
peace. I strongly believe that at least my sincerity
deserves recognition and respect. So, I am in the
position to consider the merits of other composers
with kindness.   I am most sincerely, yours

Arnold Schoenberg

53/ 68/

be understood as an attempt to involve Mr. Copland in a political affair, I am ready to apologize—this was not my intention." Finally, the affair was settled amicably: I wrote to Schoenberg directly (13 February), and he responded (21 February 1950), "I am always ready to live in peace."

The first New York performance of my *Piano Quartet* was at a League of Composers all-Copland retrospective at the Museum of Modern Art, marking the end of my chairmanship of the League (5 November 1951).[12] Lawrence Morton, director of the Ojai Festival in California and an active promoter of contemporary music in the Los Angeles area, programmed the first West Coast performance (6 May 1951) and several others.[13] I used to joke with Lawrence (somewhat wistfully) that were it not for him, my *Piano Quartet* might not have been heard at all!

Lenny Bernstein did not hear the *Quartet* until some time after the premiere, when someone sent him the recording on which it was paired with the *Clarinet Concerto*. He wrote from Cuernavaca, Mexico:

> I rejoice particularly in the scherzo, because I think it is the longest sustained piece of continuity you have written in a long time, and it is really continuous, yes really, and it goes and goes in a remarkably convincing way. I feel rather close to the tonal way in which you are handling tone-rows (I've done it too, here and there); and I find that this movement is a real triumph. The last movement is beautiful, too, in a way which has already become awfully familiar to Coplandites, so that it is not such a thrill as the second. And the first is lovely, but I never did go for you and fugues, especially here where the opening is so reminiscent of the third Hindemith Quartet. Imagine, Hindemith? Who'da thunk it? But it makes a fine piece, especially for records, because you want to hear it again and again (of course, with two or three mambos in between): And I still think you are a marvelous composer.

Twenty-five years after the premiere, I was back in Washington at the Library of Congress (23 and 24 October 1975) as pianist in the *Piano Quartet* with the Juilliard Quartet. In 1978, when I was composer-in-residence at the Cabrillo Festival, the *Quartet* was performed with Dennis Russell Davies at the piano, and the next day a critic wrote, "What has happened to the smiling, dignified gentleman we've been seeing around town the last few days? These are the strange harmonies of youth on the prod, defying convention."

The premiere performances of the *Piano Quartet* had kicked off the celebrations in honor of my fiftieth birthday. If I *had* to have a fiftieth birthday, the benefits in terms of performances and articles in the magazines and newspapers outweighed my reluctance to face the fact that I had

Left: Copland and Minna Lederman at his fiftieth birthday party, 5 November 1950.

Right: Copland cutting the cake with friend Esther Berger.

reached the century's halfway mark.[14] A gala black-tie party was given by Alma Morgenthau on the evening of 14 November after a League concert in my honor, just when the entire East Coast was being buffeted by violent hurricane rainstorms. Traveling was hazardous, and I almost missed my own party! We were without electricity and heat at Sneden's for four days. I missed only one birthday celebration—in Philadelphia, where Ormandy was conducting the *Clarinet Concerto,* but when it was repeated in New York, I managed to get through the flooded streets and highways into the city (28 November 1950). The performance was good enough, but I had to conclude that Ormandy had little feeling for jazz style. Weather

Left to right: Composers Leon Kirchner, Copland, John Lessard, and Harold Shapero at Copland's home in Palisades, New York, 1950.

Composers meeting at Copland's home, Sneden's Landing, New York, 1949 (left to right, standing): Gerhard Samuel, Donald Fuller, Arthur Berger, Jerome Moross; (seated): Leon Kirchner, Copland, Israel Citkowitz, David Diamond, and Elliott Carter.

notwithstanding, I delivered several out-of-town lectures,[15] returning home to find forty-five birthday telegrams and cards to acknowledge.

I attempted to sum up the previous decade in an article for *The New York Times,* titled "The New 'School' of American Composers."[16] I pointed to the fact that young composers of the forties had grown up with an American, rather than a European, influence, instead of what my generation had—the other way around. Composers were only now beginning to look to Europe again. I put myself on the line (as I had at the end of the twenties and thirties) by naming those representatives of the new generation I considered most promising. They were: Robert Palmer, Alexei Haieff, Harold Shapero, Lukas Foss, Leonard Bernstein, William Bergsma, and John Cage.

The *Twelve Poems of Emily Dickinson* was composed mostly at Sneden's Landing at various times, from March 1949 to March 1950. I wrote a few songs before turning to the *Piano Quartet,* for which I had a deadline. When the *Quartet* was finished, I returned to the songs. My friends kidded me about carrying books by and about Emily Dickinson around Sneden's Landing for months.[17] The house and grounds were old-fashioned and romantic and somehow just right for the nineteenth-century New England poet with her love of nature. I played some of the songs for Lukas and Irving during the summer of 1949 at Tanglewood. By the end of the year, I was finally up to number eleven, and I felt myself bogged down. As a break, I arranged five American folk songs. I wrote to Irving, "No one else may like them, but Hawkes [publisher] is delighted! The Dickinson cycle is done except for a fast song in the middle (why didn't you tell me fast songs are hard to write!)."

I had never thought of myself as a vocal composer. As a student, I had composed several songs for voice and piano, but my music really developed from essentially instrumental techniques. I had not composed for voice and piano since 1928. I am not sure why—perhaps because I did not come into contact with suitable texts. I read quite a lot of poetry but rarely found a poem with sympathetic subject matter and language not too complex that I felt was appropriate for setting to music. I had always liked the poetic prose of Gerard Manley Hopkins and at one time had the idea for a song cycle to Hopkins' poetry—a male singer intoning the poem without accompaniment and with interludes that would be purely instrumental. I even had a title ready: *Readings from Hopkins.* After abandoning that idea, I thought about setting some American poetry, perhaps influenced subconsciously by the songs of Charles Ives. I thought of Walt Whitman, especially the poem "Come, Heavenly Death," but gave that up because the poem's own rhythm seemed to defy musical setting. Then, while looking through an anthology, I came upon a poem by Emily Dickinson that appealed to me. There was something about her personality and use of language that was fresh, precise, utterly unique—and very American.

Emily Dickinson, born 1830 in New England, was a recluse after the age of twenty-three. After she died in 1886, it was discovered that she had written hundreds of poems, of which only seven were published during her lifetime, and those anonymously. I once went to visit the Dickinson house in Amherst, Massachusetts, and actually walked upstairs to see what she saw out of that window—she wouldn't come down, and even had her meals up there. I was surprised to see that from her window one could see the main crossroads of the town, and I remember thinking that the view must have given her some idea of what was going on in the outside world.[18]

Originally, I had no intention of composing a song cycle using Emily Dickinson's poems. I fell in love with one poem, "The Chariot." Its first lines absolutely threw me: "Because I could not stop for Death, he kindly stopped for me; the carriage held but just ourselves and immortality." The idea of this completely unknown girl in Massachusetts seeing herself riding off into immortality with death himself seemed like such an incredible idea! I was very struck with that, especially since it turned out to be true. After I set that poem, I continued reading Emily Dickinson. The more I read, the more her vulnerability and loneliness touched me. The poems seemed the work of a sensitive yet independent soul. I found another poem to set, then one more, and yet another. They accumulated gradually, and when I had perhaps more than six, I began to think about how I would order them. But when I had twelve, they all seemed to run to their right places.[19]

The poems themselves gave me my direction, one that I hoped would be appropriate to Miss Dickinson's lyrical expressive language. Her poetry, written in isolation, was folklike, with irregular meters and stanzas and many unconventional devices.[20] The songs center about no single theme, but they treat subject matter particularly close to Miss Dickinson: nature, death, life, eternity. It was my hope, nearly a century after these remarkable poems were conceived, to create a musical counterpart to Emily Dickinson's unique personality.

Titles for the songs derive from the first line of each poem, except for "The Chariot." This poem, the first I started with, became the last in the cycle. The song I finished first was "The World Feels Dusty." Each song is meant to be complete in itself and can be sung separately or in smaller groupings, but I prefer them to be sung as a cycle. They seem to have a cumulative effect. Although the songs are commonly referred to as a "cycle," only two are related musically—the seventh and twelfth. When thinking about a title for the group of songs, I kept in mind that it was Emily Dickinson and her poems that should be in the forefront. Looking at my sketches, I am reminded of the various titles I considered: *Emily's World, Amherst Days, Dickinson Cycle, Toward Eternity.* I finally settled on *Twelve Poems of Emily Dickinson.* However, the work is most often referred to as the *Dickinson Songs.* [21]

The *Twelve Poems of Emily Dickinson* constitutes my longest work for solo voice, having a performance time of approximately twenty-eight minutes. The songs were composed for a medium-high voice and require a singer with a rather wide range. I gave a great deal of thought as to how my essentially instrumental style of writing could be adapted for vocal purposes. Since I was accustomed to composing for piano, it was the vocal lines that were my real challenge. I followed the natural inflection of the words of the poems, particularly when they were conversational. There is a certain amount of what is called "word painting"—an occasional bird-call, flutterings, and grace notes in the introduction to the first song, "Nature, the Gentlest Mother," the bugle-like melody for the voice in "There Came a Wind Like a Bugle," and so forth. In a few instances, the meaning of a line led me to use a melisma. The harmony is basically diatonic, with some chromaticism and polytonality, and much of the piano writing is contrapuntal. [22]

Ives, Mahler, and Fauré have been mentioned as influences on the *Dickinson Songs,* particularly the romantic fifth song, "Heart, We Will Forget Him," which has been likened to Mahler. Miss Dickinson's poems are preoccupied with death, as is so much of Mahler's work. But as important to my work as these three composers have been, I see no direct influence. Perhaps I am too close to the picture; it is certainly possible that they were part of my working apparatus. The *Dickinson Songs* (and the *Piano Quartet* in the same year) stem more from other impulses and influences. I have always had an aversion to repeating myself. In retrospect, I must have felt subconsciously that I had gone as far as I could with the full-fledged style presented in *Appalachian Spring* and with full-scale conventional symphonic work as in the *Third Symphony.*

In May 1950, when the *Twelve Poems of Emily Dickinson* was

finished, I "premiered" it for a group of composer friends who had been meeting informally on Sunday evenings to listen to and discuss new music at the home of Alma Morgenthau. I wrote to Leo Smit, "They seemed to 'go over' as a cycle. Think of it—twenty-eight minutes' worth of songs!"

The next task was to find the right voice for the first performance—a singer with the appropriate range (a traditional soprano would have to change keys or at least transpose certain passages),[23] an above-average security of rhythm, and an enthusiasm for contemporary music. Douglas Moore, who arranged the Sixth Annual Festival of Contemporary American Music at Columbia University, at which the *Dickinson Songs* would be sung for the first time, asked Virgil Thomson for suggestions. Virgil mentioned Alice Howland, and since both Moore and Thomson thought she was wonderful, I agreed to the choice. They were right—she *was* wonderful. The premiere took place at Columbia's McMillin Theater (18 May 1950). The program opened with songs by John Edmunds and Howard Swanson. My songs followed the intermission.

Alice Howland[24]

I was singing contemporary music and Virgil Thomson knew my work, so it must have been how Copland heard about me. I sang Ives songs and that might have influenced Copland, too. But I don't think he ever heard me sing before he gave me the music for the Dickinson Songs. *I took the score home to study and got together with Aaron a few times to rehearse. It all seemed very compatible. We just hit it off right away and had no difficulty at all. The songs have some unusual leaps and intervals, but compared to some of the composers I sang—Ives, Křenek, and Schoenberg—the* Dickinson Songs *were not so difficult.*

I did not know the poetry of Emily Dickinson before the Copland songs. It was my introduction to her, and I liked them very much. When Aaron set them, he avoided anything too sweet or melancholy, which could have been easy to do. They have a kind of naïve quality that he captured. I think if Aaron had written more songs, he would have had more experience about singers—they are taught to choose only songs that show their voices off best. Of his twelve Dickinson songs, a singer would have a few that fit best, a different few for each singer. I think that is why they have not been per-

formed as a cycle more often. For my voice, the best songs were "Heart We Will Forget Him," "The Chariot," and "Going to Heaven!".

The premiere was a special event. After all, Copland was already an established composer. The piano parts are strong, but he was thoughtful about not covering my voice. It was a wonderful experience singing the songs with him playing! We had no trouble at all, and we were well satisfied with the performance. But the Dickinson Songs *were not a popular success from the first, and no one seemed very eager to hear them again right away. I soon retired from concerts and went on to teaching. I never had the opportunity to sing Copland's* Dickinson Songs *again.*

The critical reception in the newspapers for the *Dickinson Songs* the next day was not overly enthusiastic.[25] Even my admirers admitted to being disappointed. I wrote to Verna and Irving Fine, saying, "I s'pose you heard my songs were done and got a panning in the press. Never occurred to me that they were *that* hard to hear—but taken all of a piece, apparently they are. I dedicated the nicest song to you. So there!" (Each song is dedicated to a composer friend in the following order: David Diamond, Elliott Carter, Ingolf Dahl, Alexei Haieff, Marcelle de Manziarly, Juan Orrego-Salas, Irving Fine, Harold Shapero, Camargo Guernieri, Alberto Ginastera, Lukas Foss, and Arthur Berger.)[26]

Perhaps it was because of the fact that these songs were composed as "art" songs that they were not readily accepted. They are not folk in style and contain no extramusical associations or quotations. Virgil Thomson, expert vocal writer that he is, criticized my "cruelty" to the singer, while admiring "the wide melodic skips, which are in themselves highly effective in a declamatory sense and strikingly expressive." Virgil had caught the fact that I meant for the range to be rather extreme. A few of my composer friends admired the songs right away, even in print. William Flanagan wrote:

> Probably the most important single contribution toward an American song literature that we have to date. Above all, Copland's songs really sing, and in their singing they set standards of accomplishment and stylistic integration that American composers of songs will find difficult to ignore in the future.[27]

Henry Cowell praised the songs,[28] as did Irving Fine.[29] It was not until the *Dickinson Songs* were around for a while, however, that they were more fully admired by others. I sent them to Irving before they were published, and with my permission, he played them for Koussevitzky, who (according to Irving) liked only certain ones—"Dear March" and some of the slow ones. Irving wrote me that Koussevitzky did not think that the music fit the words for "Going to Heaven!". But he wouldn't let Irving take the music home and insisted on keeping the score to study them better.

Personally, I always felt very well satisfied with the *Dickinson Songs*. I am often asked which are my favorites: I am particularly fond of "The Chariot"; "Going to Heaven!" is so different that it's fun to play and to sing for an audience; I like "Sleep Is Supposed to Be" a lot, and "Dear March" as it breezes along. Encouraged, I could fall in love with all of them!

Two years after the premiere, when I accompanied Patricia Neway at Town Hall, the audience and critics responded more warmly than they had when the songs were first heard. In 1954, Pat Neway and I made a short concert tour on which the *Dickinson Songs* were included, and we drew crowded houses in Detroit. In the middle of the night on the sleeper to Pittsburgh, Pat woke me to whisper that she had lost her voice. She continued on to New York in a dejected state, while I frantically telephoned Washington, D.C., for Katherine Hansel to fill the breach. She did, dear girl, by meeting me in Pittsburgh and singing the *Dickinson Songs* without time to even rehearse them. All went off well.

I always thought of the *Dickinson Songs* as being sung by a female, but when a recording by a male singer was sent to me from England, the singing was so musical and with such excellent diction, I liked it, even though it did seem strange to hear a man singing those words. After all, they were written by a woman from a woman's point of view.[30]

I began orchestrating the *Dickinson Songs* in 1958, hoping they might have a wider hearing. I found that only eight of the twelve were suitable.[31] The orchestration calls for thirty-nine players (or a thirty-two member ensemble with a reduced string section). I didn't finish the orchestration until 1970, just in time for the songs to be premiered for a seventieth birthday concert at the Metropolitan Museum of Art in New York by the Juilliard Orchestra, Michael Tilson Thomas conducting, Gwendolyn Killebrew as soloist.

Several fine singers have been drawn to the *Dickinson Songs*[32]: one was Adele Addison, with whom I made a recording and a television film[33]; another was Phyllis Curtin. Phyllis and I enjoyed performing the *Dickinson Songs* together in the sixties and seventies.

Phyllis Curtin [34]

I was Phyllis Jane Smith in 1946 when I first met Aaron Copland at the Berkshire Music Center. It was my first summer at Tanglewood, and my big moment came when I took the part of one of the two nieces in Britten's Peter Grimes, *which was given its American premiere that summer. Tanglewood is the closest thing I have to a musical alma mater, and Aaron was, of course, always on the scene. He gave me the* Dickinson Songs *in Boston when he was Charles Eliot Norton Lecturer at Harvard in 1951–1952. From time to time I looked at them, but I really couldn't sing them. I didn't have enough character and presence in the middle of my voice to make those songs do what I felt they had to do. About every five years or so, I'd take them out to see if I had grown to the point where I could sing them.*

One time I saw Aaron during that ten-year period, and he said, "Do you ever sing my songs?" I replied, "No, I never do, but it's not because I don't like them, it's that I can't sing them." He asked, "Why don't you transpose them?" I almost fainted, because most composers I knew were offended if you even suggested such a thing. That was such a nice easy free thing for Aaron to say. But I answered, "Well, I think because I like the keys they're in. It's just the right speech for those songs." It was about fifteen years after I first saw the Dickinson Songs *that I sang them. By that time, my voice had grown and developed and they really fit beautifully.*

The first thing those songs did for me was very interesting. I had never liked Emily Dickinson. I used to read her and get very exasperated. I didn't like her personality—I thought she was unnecessarily quirky and coy. But as soon as I could sing Aaron's songs, I began to understand Emily Dickinson! It is my conviction, after having sung these songs hundreds of times, that nobody has ever understood her as Aaron does. If anybody ever sent Emily Dickinson's "Letter to the World," it's Aaron Copland. It was Aaron who found the musical voice for Emily Dickinson, and the times when I sang them best, I had the feeling that she was speaking.

I sang Aaron's Dickinson Songs *often with him at the piano. I never felt anything but delight when we did them together. Aaron never varied much from the score. Sometimes he played klinkers or sometimes with less grace and smoothness than other times, but I never once felt uncomfortable. It was always real. Together, we might move a little faster in one performance than another, depending on several things—our disposition, our nerve, or*

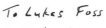

Above: Manuscript, first page of the voice and orchestra version of "Going to Heaven!" from the *Twelve Poems of Emily Dickinson.*

© *Copyright 1950 by Aaron Copland; copyright renewed. Boosey & Hawkes, Inc., Sole Publishers and Licensees.*

Left: Phyllis Curtin and Copland taking a bow after a performance of the *Dickinson Songs* at Tanglewood, 1972.

Photograph by Eugene Cook.

how much Aaron had practiced. If he wasn't in finger, things would change a little in the performance. I would accommodate to that. But you don't think about those things, you feel them. I liked singing with Aaron at the piano. I have always preferred strong pianists. I don't care much for the ones who shy back and don't live with the music.

There were funny little interpretative things once in a while. I remember the first time we ever rehearsed the Dickinson Songs *together; when we got to "Going to Heaven!," he stopped me and said, "Phyllis, but that's so strong!" I said, "That's just how looking at the music makes me feel. And you dedicated this piece to Lukas Foss, and that's how Lukas' rhythms always make me feel." Aaron said, "Oh, that's interesting." We did it again and it was fine with him. Just his asking me about it probably made me think slightly differently. I sang a wrong note in the first song and he pointed that out to me, saying, "Do it again." I did, and he said, "I kinda like it that way. Sometimes I find my best music on other people's pianos." Of course, from then on, I sang his note. But it was a sweet little exchange.*

I never had a single bad review of any kind for me or for the music in all the times I sang the Dickinson Songs. *I usually did them as the second half of a recital. I don't know that I think of them as cyclical, but I think of them as all part of Emily's life, as part of her personality, as part of her living in New England, so that they progress one to the other, but not in a story form. Only occasionally did I split the* Songs *up, singing perhaps three. I did that once on a program when Helmut Schmidt went to the White House, and one of the songs was "There Came a Wind Like a Bugle." A fierce July thunderstorm came up soon after I started! When I sang the entire cycle once at Marlboro, Blanche Moyse said, "This is the American* Winterreise!*" I agree—it is a major song cycle of this century— no question about it. And it is so marvelously American. To my thinking,* Twelve Poems of Emily Dickinson *is Aaron's major work.*

I don't find difficult leaps in the vocal writing. Maybe that was part of waiting until I felt really right for it, but once it happened, there again it seems to me one of the geniuses of this piece that I don't even think of it as having intervals. I think of it as having words, *words such as "the world feels dusty"—nobody ever set the word* dusty *in that way. There are similar things all the way through that to me are the shape of words, so I can't even tell you what intervals are in it anymore. "Sleep Is Supposed to Be" really worries a lot of students. Well, here is Emily's whole idea about all those people when she was in her teens, those who were standing up and declaring for Jesus. That's what those intervals are to me. They are part of a wonderful*

165

New England sermon. It is the pattern of Emily's remarkable speech that Aaron understood absolutely.

I feel about Aaron's orchestrated version of eight of the songs as I do about Alban Berg's Seven Early Songs. *I couldn't wait to sing those with orchestra, and some of it is very lovely. But there is more color with the piano than there is with the orchestra, and that's exactly how I feel about Aaron's* Dickinson Songs. *I think they were hatched in his mind with piano, and that's what does it best, which is not to say that he didn't do a brilliant job of orchestrating. Perhaps if a singer learns them first with the orchestra, she might not feel the same way at all. Once, I did the* Songs *with orchestra at Tanglewood, Aaron conducting (1972), and we had to wait while the orchestra rehearsed Charles Wuorinen's* Violin Concerto. *It was so loud I thought I would lose my mind. I finally said to Aaron, "I can't sit here and wait. I don't think I'll be able to hear when it gets to be my turn." Aaron kind of giggled and said, "This is the first time I have ever felt like a nineteenth-century composer."*

During the winter of 1950, I took a break from the *Dickinson Songs* with the hope of recharging my inspiration. I set a group of American folk songs, calling them *Old American Songs.* The five songs in the set are drawn from completely different sources. "The Boatmen's Dance," a minstrel show tune by Daniel Decatur Emmett, composer of "Dixie," is from the Harris Collection at Brown University. I composed the accompaniment in imitation of minstrel banjo playing. "The Dodger," a satirical political song, was found in the John and Alan Lomax book, *Our Singing Country.* It dates from the presidential campaign of 1884, when Grover Cleveland defeated James G. Blaine. "Long Time Ago" is a sentimental ballad, also from the Harris Collection.[35] "Simple Gifts" is the Shaker song used in *Appalachian Spring,* arranged in a style closer to the original, with a direct and straightforward melodic line and simple hymnlike harmonies. The last of the five songs, "I Bought Me a Cat," is a children's nonsense song resembling "Old MacDonald's Farm." I learned it from the playwright Lynn Riggs, who had sung it as a boy in Oklahoma (we had hoped to use the song in the ill-fated *Tragic Ground* theater project). The accompaniment imitates barnyard sounds in the choices of harmony and figurations. Paul Moor has reminded me that I used to sing "I Bought Me a Cat" for friends, and that I always clapped my hands twice before the last line of each stanza—"and my cat says fiddle-eye-fee."[36]

I sang the songs for Peter Pears and Ben Britten when they came to visit, promising to send them on to England when I finished them. Peter told me, "I like them *very much* indeed—we shall do them first at Aldeburgh June 17, then Amsterdam June 30th; then again here in July; probably Edinburgh Festival September 3rd, & in London in October—So you see! They will, as singers say, prove a most useful addition to my repertoire! I am still a little inclined to make the cat say 'fiddle *my* fee!' " Peter and Ben did the premiere performance of *Old American Songs I* (17 June 1950) at the Aldeburgh Festival and made the first recording.[37] The following winter, the baritone William Warfield and I gave the American premiere at Town Hall (28 January 1951). Warfield's ability to sing in a variety of styles, and his warmth and sense of humor was an ideal combination for these folk songs. Warfield could be gentle and lyric one moment, playful and humorous the next. We made a recording of *Old American Songs I* together with the Columbia Symphony Orchestra for Columbia Records; it was paired with the *Clarinet Concerto,* and reissued in 1980. I always enjoyed playing or conducting the songs with Warfield. I have heard other singers treat these songs in a more formal lieder style. Recently, a baritone performed "Simple Gifts" on a television show and there was nothing at all "simple" about it! But Warfield always brought genuine warmth to the songs.

Everyone seemed to enjoy singing and hearing *Old American Songs I* so much that I decided to arrange a second set in 1952. *Old American Songs II* also includes five songs from diverse sources: "The Little Horses," a children's lullaby from the South based on a version from Lomax's *Folk Song U.S.A.;* "Zion's Walls," a revivalist song (originally meant for *Tragic Ground* and later used in my opera), with original words and music credited to John G. McCurry; "The Golden Willow Tree," a variant of a well-known Anglo-American ballad often called "The Golden Vanity," which I heard on a Library of Congress recording for banjo and voice; "At the River," the 1865 hymn tune everybody knows and loves by Reverend Robert Lowry, and "Ching-a-Ring Chaw," a minstrel song from the Harris Collection at Brown University. I had to change the existing text of "Ching-a-Ring Chaw," not wanting to take any chance of it being construed as racist.[38] William Warfield and I premiered *Old American Songs II* at Castle Hill Concerts in Ipswich, Massachusetts (24 July 1953).

I arranged both sets of songs for medium voice and small orchestra. Warfield sang the first performance of the orchestral arrangement of *Old American Songs I* with the Los Angeles Philharmonic under Alfred

Wallenstein (7 January 1955) and Grace Bumbry premiered *II* with the Ojai Festival Orchestra, myself conducting (25 May 1955). Various choral arrangements have been published.[39] It pleases me to know from my publishers that *Old American Songs I* and *II* are in demand by college choral groups around the country.

William Warfield[40]

Shortly after my debut at Town Hall in 1950, I met Aaron and he showed me the Old American Songs I. *I sang them on my second Town Hall recital (28 January 1951). It was the American premiere of the first set, and they were a tremendous success. Aaron was an excellent pianist and, of course, knowing the flavor of them so well, it was a tremendous experience working with him. When we were rehearsing for the recording of the first set, we had a discussion about singing "Simple Gifts." He wanted it simple, almost recitative-like in quality, so you wouldn't feel it as a rhythmic, bouncy thing. The way it is written in the original, it seems obviously very rhythmic, but Aaron even put the chords on the off-accented beat to be sure it wouldn't be sung with that regular rhythmic feeling.*

When we rehearsed "I Bought Me a Cat," I stopped at "I bought me a cow," because the sound written in the score is "bah, bah." I said to Aaron, "It doesn't sound right to me"—I think it should be "moo, moo." He grinned and said, "Okay," and that's the way we recorded it. You ask me about "Ching-a-Ring Chaw": I never thought of it as a minstrel song and never saw the original words. I didn't know until right now that Aaron had changed some of the words.

I did the premiere of the orchestrated sets (eight songs) with the Los Angeles Philharmonic, Wallenstein conducting (7 January 1955), and I have performed them many times since then: once with Ormandy on tour in Europe (that's when Aaron was in Paris and came to hear them); more recently, I sang a few of the songs with orchestra at the Kennedy Center Honors in Washington when Copland received his award (1979). I don't have a strong preference, but if I had to make a choice, it would probably be toward the orchestrated version, especially for "I Bought Me a Cat," where you have all these wonderful barnyard sounds in the orchestration.

We have had a tremendously wonderful relationship that has lasted all these years. It has included Lincoln Portrait, *which I have narrated with*

168

Photograph by Victor Kraft.

William Warfield and Copland during the recording of *Old American Songs I,* 1955.

Aaron conducting and with Bernstein also. I was doing Lincoln *at the Kennedy Center at the time of the Bicentennial, and Lenny said, "Why don't you come on tour with us [the New York Philharmonic] in Europe?" He had someone do the translations so they retained the feeling of Lincoln's words in other languages. We did it in French in Paris, German in Vienna, and English, of course, in England. A videotape was made of the one in Albert Hall, and a record was issued having to do with Bernstein, and it included my narration of* Lincoln *from that tour.*

I was feeling the urge to spend some time in Europe, so I applied for a Fulbright Fellowship for 1951. I was offered two million lira, and for two exciting minutes I thought I was a millionaire! Then I rushed for a pencil, and it turned into $3,250! But the crossing was paid for, and I would be staying at the American Academy in Rome beginning 1 January. Before leaving on the *Queen Elizabeth* (23 December 1950), I had many arrangements to make. First the house: I wanted it lived in while I was away. Victor was in Brazil taking photographs, and Erik Johns hoped his visa would arrive so that he could go along to Italy with me. I wanted to sublet the house to defray some expenses (without Hollywood, my income had returned to a more normal low in 1949 and 1950).[41] I was delighted when Bob Fizdale called to ask whether I knew a place he and Arthur Gold might rent. They needed a place right away, so I suggested they come and stay with me. There was more than enough room. They split some of the bills, helped me during a few violent storms, made sensational meals, rented the house while I was away, and later on, rented it for three years after I moved out.[42]

Erik's exit visa arrived just forty-eight hours before sailing. Fizdale and Gold gave us a going-away party complete with Christmas tree and trimmings and drove us to the boat. I was feeling rather pleased to leave a known life behind for an unknown one ahead. The crossing was surprisingly smooth for that time of year, but the ship was very empty. Erik's dance partner, Luisa Krebs, was with us, and the two of them ate themselves silly. I got some rest, and we all saw a lot of movies.

After landing at Cherbourg, we went on to Paris, and on New Year's Eve, I took the train alone to Rome (Erik and Luisa joined a dance company for a European tour). A representative from the American Academy met me at the station. An hour later, I was dining at a villa with a count and twelve countesses! I was given an apartment that was beautifully situated—overlooking all of Rome. It came with a cook and a good Bechstein grand piano. The main trouble was the barely adequate heating system. Everyone in Rome seemed to take that kind of problem for granted, but I was condemned to cold feet for several months! Sonny Shapero and Lukas Foss were at the Academy when I arrived, and Leo Smit was also in town.[43] They all helped to get me acquainted with things Roman.

I hoped to get started on a piano concerto, commissioned by the Louisville Symphony for William Kapell. The commission fell through, but I continued to compose piano music without a definite plan for its final form. "Life," as I wrote to Esther and Arthur Berger, "was almost too soft." I was to find that there was not much music going on in Italy by American standards, but as I wrote to Claire Reis, "It's a heavenly town."

When Erik and Luisa arrived after their tour, it was a great problem finding a place for them with a wooden floor for dancing—practically every floor in Rome is made of stone or cement. We finally found them a place on Via Margutta, full of artists and sculptors. Then I took a big plunge

and bought a car—a green Morris-Minor—on Shapero's advice. I wrote
to my sister (3 February 1951); "Dear La: Today I get the tiny car I bought
for a thousand dollars—it's said to get thirty miles on a gallon—and since
gas is eighty cents a gallon here, everyone buys small cars for economy sake.
Also, many streets are so narrow that a Buick wouldn't fit!" From the time
the car arrived, I composed mornings and went exploring most afternoons
with Erik, Luisa, and Leo. We went to see and hear the Pope in St. Peter's
Square (everybody in Rome kept telling me that the Pope and I looked
alike!). We drove to Naples (I had accepted duties for the State Department that included lectures on American music in various cities in Italy),
and afterward, down the coast to Pompei and Paestum. We enjoyed the
beautiful Amalfi coast, although my car almost balked on one of those
mountains!

It was a small musical world in Italy. When Leo gave a recital at the
Academy, there were too many Americans present and not enough Italians. The same situation held when I gave my first lecture on American
music, with Leo playing the musical examples. Among the few Italians I
saw was Dallapiccola in Florence, who had earlier accepted an invitation
to teach at Tanglewood in 1951. I found him personally charming but
became less interested in his music the more I heard of it. Edwin Denby,
who was living in Ischia, came to visit me in Rome, and once or twice,
I went to see Ashley Pettis, who had left the music world to become a
priest. I wrote to Arthur Berger, "You ought to see Ashley Pettis in a
priest's garb. Complete transformation! When he came to lunch at my
place in his priestly robe, he scared my cook!"

As usual, after a short time away, I felt starved for news of New York.
When I didn't see the music page of *The New York Times,* I felt deprived.
I did hear the news when Gide died. Somehow, I did not feel sad about
it—I guess because he had so fully expressed himself in a long lifetime.
What more can one ask?

From Rome, I made my first visit to Israel.[44] It had been arranged by
Eleazar de Carvalho, then conductor of the Israel Philharmonic Orchestra.
Carvalho had played *Appalachian Spring* ten times at the end of 1950 in
Tel Aviv, Haifa, and Jerusalem, and was planning fifteen more perfor-
mances during a three-month tour in the States. I found the two and
one-half weeks in Israel immensely stimulating. My first lectures were in
Tel Aviv. What impressed me most were the young people on the beach
on the Sabbath, all jabbering in Hebrew and looking healthy and happy

Above: Copland planting a tree on
his first trip to Israel, April 1951.

Right: Program from
the Ein Gev Music
Festival.

SATURDAY, APRIL 21, 1951 — OPENING CONCERT
CHORAL CONCERT
by the
TEL-AVIV VOCAL ENSEMBLE
(Eytan Lustig, conductor)

conducted by
AARON COPLAND and EYTAN LUSTIG
Soloist : NAOMI ZURI (mezzo-soprano)

PROGRAMME :
Three Peasants' Songs for mixed chorus and piano (1948) ...
Erich Walter Sternberg (born 1898)
(After ancient folksongs, Hebrew : Joseph Achai)
First Performance.
Cantata No. 4 (composed for Easter Sunday, 1724) ...
Johann Sebastian Bach (1685-1750)
(Original Text by Martin Luther. Hebrew version: Ephraim
Dror).
Sinfonia — Chorus — Duet (Soprano, Contralto) — Tenor solo —
Chorus — Bass solo — Duet (Soprano, Tenor) — Choral.
—Interval—
In the Beginning (Genesis, ChapterI : 1 — II : 7), for mixed
chorus a cappella with mezzo-soprano solo (1947) ...
Aaron Copland (born 1900)
First Performance in Israel.
Conducted by the Composer.
Soloist : Naomi Zuri.

THE OPENING CONCERT
Ein Gev's musical programmes for the 1951 Passover Festival
open with a choral concert by a vocal ensemble that has made
history in the musical life of Israel. This is the Tel-Aviv Vocal
Ensemble (founded and conducted by Eytan Lustig), the nucleus
of the larger Tel-Aviv Chamber Choir, to which the country owes
the first local performances of a great many Bach Cantatas; of
religious works by Pergolesi, Delalande, and Mozart, of ancient
operas in concerted form; and of a number of important Israeli
compositions, among them works by Sternberg, Ben-Haim, Orgad,
and Seter-Starominski. To-night's concert receives special significance by the only guest-appearance as a conductor made in the
country by Aaron Copland, who leads the ensemble in the first
Israel performance of his recent choral work based on the first
chapters of the Bible.

and very un-Jewish. The children were unforgettable. I was moved by
merely walking along the beach in Tel Aviv.

I conducted *In the Beginning* at a concert on the shores of the Sea of
Galilee—a very appropriate setting. I had never conducted a chorus
before, but nobody there seemed to notice. We were only two kilometers
away from the Syrian border. At 2:30 A.M., I was awakened by sporadic
firing, generally referred to as "border incidents." The radio announced

each day that the Festival at Ein Gev would continue, "and Aaron Copland is there." I spent *Pesach* (Passover) at the kibbutz with six hundred people. For five days, I lived with thirty Israeli composers in an art colony, Zichron Yakov, outside of Tel Aviv, and listened to their music, which was enthusiastic but not exportable. It turned out that I was the first composer to have visited there from abroad, and the reception was very warm. I went to Jerusalem for two days. It is absolutely silent by 9 P.M. each night. From my hotel room at the King David, I could look inside the walls of the Old City, but as the Arabs of Transjordan owned it, it was impossible and frustrating not to be able to get inside! Everyone seemed to be having a terrific adventure, however. I wrote to Victor, "It could make a Zionist out of a Hitler." And when I visited Haifa and Lake Tiberias, everyone seemed so fully alive! In fact, the whole of Israel seemed to be developing at presto speed.

Often questioned about what seems a lack of "Jewish" material in my compositions, I decided not to dodge the issue: In Jerusalem, I delivered a lecture called "Jewish Composers in the Western World" (15 April 1951)[45] I admitted that the subject was controversial, because it brought into consideration the racial consciousness of the artist, the assimilation theory, and the role of the nonassimilated artist. I made it clear that I was speaking as a composer from my own experience, not as historian, ethnologist, or expert on Jewish affairs. I knew in advance that this audience would have liked to hear that Jewish artists who affirm their Jewishness come off best. I pointed out, however, that "The facts are more complex: Of the specifically 'Jewish' composers in Western countries, no leading figure emerged with the possible exception of Bloch."

After opening remarks stating my position, I sketched for the audience the contributions of Jewish composers who wrote music of interest to all the world: in the nineteenth century, Mendelssohn, Meyerbeer, and Offenbach; in the twentieth, Mahler, Schoenberg, Bloch, Milhaud, Gershwin, and Weill. I closed my talk by emphasizing that "a man doesn't create art because he is a Jew but because he is a man. The truly Jewish composer need not worry about his Jewishness—it will be evident in the work."

When I returned to Rome, I conducted a work by another composer for the first time—David Diamond's *Rounds* in a concert also featuring my *Clarinet Concerto* (1 May). When the Rome radio invited me to conduct an all-Copland concert, I accepted, and found the orchestra surprisingly

good, so much so that Leo and I decided to program the *Piano Concerto.*
The outcome was that we recorded it for the Concert Hall label.

In mid-May, I lectured in Bologna and Genoa, before traveling on to
Paris. From Paris, I wrote to Victor, "Every street and shop is full of
memories for me." I wanted to stay longer but only had time to see Noel
Lee and hear some of his new music. I had to be in London to discuss the
renewal of my contract with Boosey & Hawkes. Ralph Hawkes had always
looked out for my interests in the past. His sudden death in September
1950 was a serious loss. Leslie Boosey was friendly, but I sensed some
opposition among the other Londoners. I spent a week settling the contract satisfactorily and visiting Ben Britten and Peter Pears. I returned to
Paris for lunch with Clurman and then took the Simplon Express to
Trieste to conduct an all-Copland program (4 June).

Being so far away and traveling from one European city to another as
I did in May, I had no idea that Koussevitzky was so seriously ill. I had
written him from Rome, saying, "It is slow work to get the Italians
interested in American music, but one must begin somewhere. I have been
giving lectures." I wrote again from Israel: "Everywhere we spoke of
you—in Zichron Yakov, in Ein Gev, in Jerusalem." After hearing the news
of Koussevitzky's death, I wrote to Irving (8 June 1951), stating, "I felt
sorry that neither Lenny, nor Lukas, nor I myself were around at the end."
What an irreplaceable void Koussevitzky's absence would leave in the
world of music! All of the implications would take time to realize.

Taking stock of the six months abroad, I had to admit I hadn't finished
composing anything—perhaps because I was traveling so much—somehow, the incentive wasn't there. I arrived home to find many changes. In
addition to Koussevitzky's absence (I kept expecting him to appear at
Tanglewood), I no longer had the house at Sneden's Landing; Victor was
planning to get married to Pearl Kazan; and Lenny Bernstein announced
his engagement to Felicia Montealegre Cohn. After seeing Pearl in New
York, I wrote to Victor, who was still in Brazil (19 August): "Everybody
admired the ring you had sent up. What with Lenny's announcement,
everyone agrees there's a trend."

Everyone thought Victor's news was a great surprise, but I had realized
long before his marriage that it was important for him to go it alone, or
better still, with a woman to help him. I wrote him so, and we continued
to stay in touch regularly. Erik suggested that we give Pearl and Victor a
special wedding gift—the green Morris-Minor from Italy. I agreed and
wrote (14 September 1951), "Dear P & V: No family was ever more

excited about a far-off happening than us at the marriage finals. Hope you both like the idea of a Morris-Minor as a wedding gift. It's really a ducky little car—lightish green in color and hasn't given us a day's trouble. I plan to put it in dead storage about October 15 (for you). Please don't ask to have it mailed to Brazil!"

I wrote to Lenny (5 November 1951): "Victor writes very enthusiastic letters from Rio. Seem pleased with himself and Pearl and Rio and job. It's a miracle and I'm awfully pleased." But in less than a year, Pearl and Victor were already parting—before they had even received their wedding gift! I wrote to Victor (15 August 1952), "I will sell the Morris-Minor and split the amount between you."

I was more than surprised to receive a letter while in Rome that I had been chosen to deliver the Charles Eliot Norton Lectures at Harvard during the academic year 1951–1952. Stravinsky had delivered his *Poetics of Music,* and Hindemith *A Composer's World,* but this was the first time a native-born composer had been chosen for the Poetry Chair established a quarter of a century earlier. Although it would mean living in Cambridge for six months, I accepted. After all, the Norton Poetry Chair is one of Harvard's most prestigious honors and a very high responsibility. I immediately began to worry about what I could possibly say! I tried to get started on the lectures while abroad. Fortunately, there was a good library at the American Academy in Rome, and I went often and read on aesthetics, hoping to stimulate my thoughts.

I am not a professional writer. My literary output is a byproduct of my trade. As a kind of salesman for contemporary music, I frequently spoke and wrote (sometimes wrote and then spoke) about issues relating to my product. Although I tended to think that music was either too hard to write about or not worth writing about at all, I periodically published articles and books, sometimes developed from lectures. For example, in 1949 an article appeared in *The New York Times Magazine*—"A Modernist Defends Modern Music"—that was stimulated by a lecture of a few months earlier at Town Hall. Looking ahead, I hoped the book to be published from the Norton Lectures could be edited directly from my talks. I took warning from my friend Thornton Wilder, Norton Lecturer the previous year, when he told me he was having a heck of a time writing a book from the sketchy notes he had used for his lectures.

Fortunately, a free interpretation of the title "Norton Professor of Poetics" made it possible for me to discuss the one thing I know something about—music. Nevertheless, it was a bit frustrating and scary because I feared that my words might not be eloquent enough. I gave up composing music entirely and worked on the lectures in much the same way I composed—that is, thinking about ideas in advance and jotting them down for future use. By the time I left for Tanglewood in 1951, I had sketched a rough draft. I wrote and polished the final manuscript after Tanglewood and while moving my things out of the attic at Sneden's Landing in the weeks before leaving for Cambridge. Up in the attic at Sneden's, I came across a very stimulating book by I. A. Richards, *Coleridge on Imagination.* It gave me the title of my lectures: "Music and the Imaginative Mind."

An advance trip to Cambridge to see the rooms at Adams House, where I was supposed to stay, convinced me to find something less dreary. I decided to take the top floor of the Edward Forbes house at Gerry's Landing. Mr. Forbes was a grandson of Emerson; furthermore, Stravinsky and Boulanger had both lived in that house while in Cambridge. The place had a nice hidden-away feeling but was only five minutes from Harvard Square. I moved to Cambridge (3 October) and was given an "office" in Widener Library that was reserved for the Norton Professor. To my amazement, I found a chair in it clearly marked "Charles Eliot Norton"! I never sat in it.

The Norton Professorship Committee gave me a cordial reception. I had known professors Archibald MacLeish and A. Tillman Merritt for many years. It was MacLeish's idea to include a program of music after each lecture—an innovation for the Norton lectures. The programs, which I would arrange, were made possible by the Elizabeth Sprague Coolidge Foundation. I was delighted, for as I pointed out in my second lecture, "The Sonorous Image," music must "sound." The post-lecture concerts would help to dispel that vague and unsatisfactory sensation that always follows on any mere discussion of music.

It was not so difficult to write the lectures as I had anticipated. I discovered I really did have some fresh things to say and some others that bore repeating. The value of these lectures depended partly on the overall shaping of the material. I thought of them as similar to a musical composition with two large movements (the two sets of lectures), each including three separate but related sections. In the first three lectures, which were delivered in the fall of 1951, I attempted to develop in a logical way the subject of the imagination in connection with musical experience; in the second set, delivered in the spring of 1952, I was concerned with the public rather than the musical imagination.

The audience for my first Norton Lecture (13 November) had applied for tickets far in advance and seemed interested in what I had to say about the art of listening: "Listening is a talent, and like any other talent or gift, we possess it in varying degrees. . . . All musicians, creators, and performers alike think of the gifted listener as a key figure in the musical universe. The ideal listener, above all else, possesses the ability to lend himself to the power of music." The concert following the first lecture featured vocal music by Stravinsky, Berlioz, and Bizet.[46] A week later, the second lecture, "The Sonorous Image," dealt with the overriding preoccupation of the composer with sound, no matter in what age or what the state of technology and engineering. Music by Mozart, Couperin, and de Falla followed. The third lecture (27 November) explored the linkage of creation and interpretation. I described the composer in the throes of composing and the kind of detachment that follows later, after a work is performed. Music following the talk was by Schubert, Ravel, and myself.

The second set of lectures, "Musical Imagination in the Contemporary Scene," might be considered a guide through Europe and the Americas. I began with "Tradition and Innovation in Recent European Music" (5 March 1952). The music afterward was by Webern and Tippett. The second lecture, "Musical Imagination in the Americas" (12 March), was concerned with Latin America, and appropriately included music by Chávez, Villa-Lobos, and Caturla. The audience also heard recorded music by jazz artists Lennie Tristano, Dave Brubeck, Bud Powell, and Oscar Pettiford (a hoped-for "live" presentation proved impractical). My final presentation, "The Composer in Industrial America" (19 March), dealt with what a composer feels and experiences in twentieth-century America. The musical portion included Ives, Thomson, and myself.

I need not go very fully into the content of the six Norton Lectures because I can refer the reader to their publication by Harvard University Press. In *Music and Imagination,*[47] my fourth book, the lectures appear substantially in the same form in which they were read to the students and general public at Cambridge. *Music and Imagination* received favorable critical reviews when it was published in 1952.[48]

In addition to the Norton Lectures, I was responsible for a course, "Music in the Twenties," which was open to the public. I was delighted that it drew five hundred people. I could not help but notice that everyone in Cambridge seemed to be over fifty or under twenty-one. I wondered where the middle-agers were! Life was peaceful in Cambridge and I enjoyed the quiet academic atmosphere around Harvard. Widener Library was a big drawing card. There I examined scores of George Chadwick and was rather surprised to find how varied in style his orchestral works were. I made a note at the time: "I am convinced that there are many amusing discoveries awaiting the more adventurous musicologist."

It was blissful not to travel for a change. I went down to New York only once to attend the League of Composers' "retrospective" in my honor. Otherwise, I stayed in Cambridge and got together with friends in the Boston area—the Fines, Bergers, and Shaperos. Characteristically, Irving was mulling over his notes; Sonny was teaching at Brandeis; and Arthur was putting the finishing touches on his book about my music. My old friend from Fontainebleau days, Melville Smith, played in my *Organ Symphony* (7 February 1952), and Lukas Foss came to town, bringing along his new *Piano Concerto* and a wife, Cornelia. An all-Copland concert was given at Sanders Theater (20 February). I was treated so well at Harvard that when it came time to leave, I regretted departing from Cambridge and the comfort and privacy of Gerry's Landing.

Just as *Music and Imagination* was about to be published, my brother Ralph died. The book is dedicated "to the memory of my brother Ralph Copland, 1888–1952." I knew that Ralph had not been well: He had been depressed for some long time and seemed to be on the verge of a nervous breakdown. In fact, Laurine and I were having lunch to discuss the situation the very day Ralph plunged from his sixteen-story office building (24 March 1952). Ralph was sixty-three, twelve years my senior. He had been practicing law for many years. He and his wife, Dorothy (my old childhood friend), lived in Brooklyn. They had no children. Ralph was such a mild-mannered individual that I could never have dreamed that he—of all people—would do such a thing! My siblings were all older than I, and Ralph was the first to go. I wrote to Victor, "I am shocked and shaken by it."

When I returned from Cambridge to New York, I was again without a home of my own. I had stayed in Greenwich Village with Erik during the midwinter break from Harvard and again in the spring, but the place was really too small for both of us to be working in at the same time. I was looking for a house in earnest and wrote to Victor (28 May): "How does one *ever* decide where to settle *forever!*"

Erik had hoped to be joining the Martha Graham studio, but an old knee injury was keeping his dance career in the balance. He was painting and working on a project he and I had been talking about—an opera for which Erik would write the libretto. When I left for the MacDowell

178

Colony in June 1952, I took with me a draft of the libretto. Erik wrote (14 June), "Have you let anyone read the lib?" But I was determined to keep it very sub rosa until I knew definitely that we were going ahead. I wrote only to Victor, since he was in Brazil and would keep it to himself (20 July 1952):

> It's an opera for the college trade, about one and a half hours long, I guess. Some of the *Tragic Ground* material can be utilized, which is part of the attraction, since it makes it seem easier to do. Also, I feel the need of more "trials and errors" before launching into a real "grand opry" . . . I keep telling everyone I'm writing a long piano piece, which I am.

The summer of 1952 was the tenth session of the Berkshire Music Center, as well as my tenth year at Tanglewood. An uneasy feeling that the Center might not survive Koussevitzky's death was dispelled when the trustees voted to continue the school, but it was made clear we were to keep expenses down. After Charles Munch became director, he endorsed the reappointment of the faculty board as constituted the previous summer. I received my usual official letter of appointment from George Judd (1 February 1952): "Your duties will be to serve as teacher of composition and assistant director of the Music Center."[49] I had written an article for *The New York Times,* "Tanglewood's Future," describing a new scholarship program that would remove the burden of tuition fees from any student accepted for work in the advanced departments.[50] Tod Perry, Lenny, and I met in New York at the Harvard Club to discuss the Tanglewood Revolving Scholarship Fund and to work on plans for the upcoming season.

For the first time, a visiting composer was invited to return to the Music Center: Dallapiccola again shared the composition program with me. Among his nine students were Luciano Berio, Salvatore Martirano, and Leonard Rosenman. I had seven.[51] Several foreign countries were represented in 1952: Egypt, New Zealand, Israel, and Turkey. The five Composer Forums of student works, which I led, were performed by other students from the Music Center. The "Aspects of Music" series by the faculty continued, and I delivered three lectures in a new series, "Classical Forms in Modern Music," which was taught once a week.[52]

The senior faculty remained essentially the same, except that Irving Fine was on leave.[53] Lukas took over Irving's work as well as his own. I wrote to the Fines, "One week gone. We miss you. All goes well. A lively crowd of composers. Dallapiccola more relaxed than ever; Lukas inspiring all and sundry. Me—starving at dinnertime—but alive." Ingolf Dahl arrived from California for his first Tanglewood year and accomplished the impossible by revamping Department V, henceforth "The Tanglewood Study Group." Lenny did a terrific job conducting the student orchestra in my *Third Symphony* (9 August).

I stayed on in the Berkshires until mid-September, when I returned to Erik's Greenwich Village apartment to work with him on the opera. On weekends, we went house hunting, and in November, I found a house in Ossining, New York, called Shady Lane Farm. It was a remodeled barn just one hour up the Hudson from New York City, near Croton, with a nice view of the river. Tod Perry wrote from Lenox (10 November): "Congratulations on the house. I didn't know composers ever bought houses. Seems very unusual, but an excellent idea." Erik and I got busy buying furniture and drapes and trying to convince the telephone company to install a phone. I moved in on the first of December 1952. The next day there was a big snowstorm, and there I was snowbound without a telephone! After getting settled, I had a big housewarming party (10 October 1953). I was thrilled to have a place of my own, and I lived at Shady Lane Farm for the next eight years.

I finally owned a house, my opera was beginning to take shape, a piano piece was in the works, and two books about me were in preparation for publication. Nineteen fifty-three held promise of being a fine year. But these were the years of the Cold War, and of Senator Joseph McCarthy. Of all things, I became a victim of a political situation! I tried to carry on as usual. I conducted my *Third Symphony* in Minneapolis (February 1953) and finished *Old American Songs II*. I even attended the opening of Lenny's show, *Wonderful Town.* Afterward, I wrote to Verna; "Looked to me like a smash hit. He was wearing Koussie's cape at the opening!" But I lost a great deal of time and energy (not to mention lawyers' fees) preparing to defend myself against fictitious charges. It was not a happy time. What can one do but go through it and carry on?

Interlude III

Everywhere people met, talk turned to the McCarthy hearings: who was being "called," what they said, who they "named." One of Senator Joseph McCarthy's pet peeves was Harvard, and Copland, having just recently delivered the Norton Lectures, was close to the Harvard scene. He and his Boston friends were shocked at the threats to intellectual and academic freedom. The Cold War was escalating rapidly. Revisionist history and post-McCarthy detractors have claimed that the dread of Communist infiltration was exaggerated during the fifties, but historian Irving Howe reminds us that the fear of communism was warranted after the Second World War. In his book *A Margin of Hope,* Howe devotes a chapter, "Ideas in Conflict," to the difficult decisions that intellectuals faced during the Cold War.

> Wherever Stalinism conquered, freedom vanished. . . . The socialist intellectuals either went underground or abandoned socialism. The more thoughtful tried to work out a system of opposing both communism and McCarthyism. The sudden upsurge of McCarthyism was to prove a crucial test for the intellectuals.[1]

Many people Copland knew were called to testify before the House Committee on Un-American Activities (HUAC), including two close friends, Marc Blitzstein and Clifford Odets. Copland became vaguely anxious, knowing he had been connected with Popular Front groups such as the Composers Collective in the thirties. Copland's political thinking derived from a time when it had been a matter of pride for artists and intellectuals to be connected with the socialist movement. Copland was not a registered member of any party; he continued to think of himself as liberal and to depend on Harold Clurman for discussions of a more worldly nature than the music community offered. They talked about literature, ideology, and politics. In an interview, Clurman described his political situation preceding and during the McCarthy years:

I read more political material than Aaron. I was moving very far to the Left. I never joined any party or anything like that. No intent, no thought of ever doing so. But I was interested and sympathetic to the Soviet Union, what I thought they were going to do, what I thought they believed. And I did read. I read Lenin, some Marx, the literature—and I did feel, yes, the working class must do something. I said to Aaron that there was a political ignorance, an enormous ignorance both of the Left and the Right in this country. I think it's one of the most politically obtuse countries in the world. We talked of these things; I talked to Aaron about everything.[2]

Copland was always impressed with intellectuals, feeling that because he had not gone to college, he did not qualify as one himself. He was some-what in awe of people such as Arthur Miller and Lillian Hellman; in fact, he had become involved with the pro-Russian film *The North Star* largely because Hellman had written the script. Another left-winger Copland admired and worked with briefly was photographer Ralph Steiner: Cop-land had helped Steiner edit two films, H_2O and *Surf and Seaweed*.[3] Although Copland thought of himself as a loyal American, even a patriotic one, there was a "new" crime—"guilt by association"—and Copland had associates to whom McCarthy could point: composer Hanns Eisler, who had been deported because of his Communist Party activities; Marc Blitz-stein and other former members of the Composers Collective; the Group Theatre crowd; and Copland's liberal-minded colleagues, Bernstein and Diamond. Clurman said, "I used to kid Aaron. 'Oy!' I would say, 'Wait til they hear about "Into the Streets May First," published in *The New Masses* yet!' Aaron didn't think I was so funny."[4]

Copland's involvement with Russian organizations can be traced to Koussevitzky, who tried to help his countrymen whenever possible. When Koussevitzky asked Copland to lend his name or his efforts to a cause, such as the Friends for Russian Freedom, the National Council of American-Soviet Friendship, and its outgrowth the American-Soviet Music Society, Copland never wanted to refuse him. These organizations would be pointed to by McCarthy in 1953 as Communist fronts.[5]

The popularity of Russian composers in America began when Russia was an ally, and sympathy for them continued under the Stalin regime. Cop-land and other American musicians were impressed with Shostakovich. In 1935, they heard his opera that was banned in Russia, *Lady Macbeth of Mtsensk*, in a production at the Metropolitan Opera House.[6] In 1946, Copland delivered a lecture at Tanglewood on "Shostakovich and the New Simplicity," in which he said, "Shostakovich is enormously musical—not

Board members of the American-Soviet Music Society (left to right): Mordecai Bauman, Morton Gould, Betty Bean, Serge Koussevitzky, Elie Siegmeister, Margaret Grant, Copland, and Marc Blitzstein.

a deep thinker, not strikingly original by comparison with Stravinsky, and sometimes unnecessarily trite. But he has a personal note all his own and enormous facility and brilliance."

When Shostakovich came to the States in 1949, his activities were restricted. Copland was the only composer allowed by Russian authorities to meet Shostakovich at the airport, and the two composers were shown together in newspaper photographs (26 March 1949) at the banquet at the Waldorf-Astoria ballroom, where the Russian composer (through an interpreter) addressed delegates of the World Peace Conference (25–27 March). Lillian Hellman, Copland, and Harlow Shapley, chairman of the conference, spoke to the audience of two thousand. Also at the head table were Olin Downes and Henry Wallace. The atmosphere was tense, with heavy police guards at the dinner and anti-Russian war veterans picketing outside the hotel and Carnegie Hall, where the conference continued. Claire Reis described the scene at the Waldorf:

Shostakovich was guarded by two men from Russia, one who interpreted for him. When he said "Stravinsky is not a good composer—he does not compose

Shostakovich and Copland at the Conference for World Peace, New York, 26 March 1949.

for the masses," it was rather a shocking statement. At the end of the program, Arthur Miller made an announcement: "Will all the audience keep their seats, so as to let the honored guests go down the elevator?" Well, the Waldorf elevators were pretty big, but besides Shostakovich and his guards, nobody was allowed to go. Shostakovich was not allowed to call Koussevitzky or go to Boston to see him, though he was very anxious to do so.[7]

Following the Peace Conference, *Life* magazine published an article, "Red Rumpus," with photographs of fifty people who attended. Under the heading "Dupes and fellow travelers dress up communist fronts," Copland's photograph was included. The Peace Conference of 1949 was one of the Communist front gatherings attacked by Joe McCarthy.

McCarthyism was a central issue in the 1952 presidential campaign. After Dwight D. Eisenhower was elected, *The Washington Post* announced the program for the inaugural concert, which would take place at Constitution Hall on 18 January 1953:

The concert will include Jeannette MacDonald and James Melton. A third
artist will be either pianist Vladimir Horowitz or violinist Yehudi Menuhin.
The master of ceremonies for the concert will be Walter Pidgeon, who will read
Lincoln Portrait, by Aaron Copland, with accompaniment by the National
Symphony.

On the evening of 16 January 1953 in New York City, Claire Reis picked
up her evening newspaper and was shocked to see an announcement that
Copland's *Lincoln Portrait* had been removed from the concert because
Congressman Fred E. Busbey of Illinois had questioned Copland's political associations. Mrs. Reis immediately called Copland and read him the
news. He, too, was shocked. He had not heard that Congressman Busbey
had addressed Congress (3 January):

> There are many patriotic composers available without the long record of ques-
> tionable affiliations of Copland. The Republican Party would have been ridi-
> culed from one end of the United States to the other if Copland's music had
> been played at the inaugural of a President elected to fight communism, along
> with other things.

Congressman Busbey's statement had been read into the *Congressional
Record.* 8 Claire Reis said to Copland, "We've got to do something
quickly. It's only a day and a half before the inaugural concert." She
advised Copland to call his lawyer, and with Copland's approval, she sent
a wire in the name of the League of Composers protesting the ban. A copy
of the telegram to *The New York Times* resulted in an article the following
day. It was headed: "Ban on Copland work at Inaugural scored. The
League of Composers of 115 West Fifty-seventh Street protested yesterday to the Inaugural Concert Committee in Washington against the
dropping of Copland's *Lincoln Portrait.*"

Copland noted in his appointment book on 16 January: "Busbey Attack!" A few weeks later, concerned that the League had not had the
opportunity to approve what was done in its name, Copland sent a letter
to the board (9 February 1953):

> I think I owe our organization a word of explanation. I want it to be known
> by you that I read of this incident in the papers, after it was called to my
> attention by Claire Reis. . . . I have no past or present political activities to hide.
> I have never at any time been a member of any political party: Republican,
> Democratic, or Communist. . . . We are becoming the targets of a powerful
> pressure movement led by small minds. It is surely a sign of the times that a
> musical organization like our own should have become involved in an affair such
> as this.

Paul Hume, music critic of *The Washington Post,* intending to make the absurdity of the issue plain, informed Congressman Busbey that Air Force bands and other tax-supported orchestras constantly played Copland's works. Busbey professed surprise and shock: "We must look into that!" he cried. Hume followed up with an article headed "Music Censorship Reveals New Peril." Hume's attacks spurred Busbey on to expand his remarks about Copland and to read into the *Congressional Record* a long list of allegedly suspicious Copland affiliations.[9] Finally, in his review of the inaugural concert (25 January 1953), Hume suggested that some substantial American music was in order for such occasions, ". . . provided, of course, that by 1957 we will have surmounted the idea that music by various American-born composers is to be banned if Congressmen protest."

Several people wrote to music critic Virgil Thomson asking why the New York *Herald Tribune* ignored the Busbey incident. Thomson explained: "I very much fear that public protests and similar manifestations might result in merely publicizing the incident to Mr. Copland's disadvantage. . . ." To Ernst Bacon, Thomson stated: "Roy Harris has been having similar troubles . . . and I have not publicized them either. . . . I know that agitational or editorial protest can be a two-edged weapon."[10] Copland himself decided to release a statement to newspapers and radio stations.[11] For the usually moderate Copland, the tone was decidedly angry.

> This is the first time, as far as I know, that a composition has been publicly removed from a concert program in the United States because of the alleged affiliations of the composer. I would have to be a man of stone not to have deeply resented both the public announcement of the removal and the reasons given for it. No one has ever before questioned my patriotism. My music, by its nature, and my activities as a musical citizen must speak for me: Both have been dedicated to the cultural fulfillment of America. Isn't it strange that if the record of my affiliations in the past were so "questionable" it should have escaped the notice of all the government officials except the representative from Illinois? . . . I cannot for the life of me see how the cause of the free countries of the world will be advanced by the banning of my works. . . . Bad as our situation may be, no American politician has yet called for the banning of an American composer's work because of its aesthetic content, as is the case in Russia today. I'd a thousand times prefer to have my music turned down by Republican congressmen on political grounds (or because I voted for Stevenson) than have it turned down for aesthetic reasons. It is easy to see why this is so: My "politics"—tainted or untainted—are certain to die with me, but my music, I am foolish enough to imagine, might just possibly outlive the Republican Party.

Copland then composed a letter to President Eisenhower:[12]

> I am an American composer of symphonic music and the composer of a musical portrait of Abe Lincoln. I write to you because an incident occurred during the ceremonies attendant upon the inauguration of your administration too small to have come to your attention, certainly, but too large in its implications to be passed over lightly. If I did not think it transcended in importance my own personal stake in the matter, I would not be writing to you now. . . .

Reactions followed: Howard Taubman, chief music critic of *The New York Times*, wrote an article supporting Copland. It was entitled "Portrait of President Deeply Patriotic—Composer's Stature Not in Doubt" (1 February 1953). The ACLU [American Civil Liberties Union] Anti-Censorship Council protested to the inaugural committee about the Copland ban (along with the suppression of Charlie Chaplin's *Limelight*). Historian Bruce Catton wrote a long piece in *The Nation* (31 January 1953), quoted here in part:

> A leading item on the program was to have been Aaron Copland's *A Lincoln Portrait*, for speaker and orchestra. At the last minute, however, this number was quietly expunged because Representative Fred E. Busbey of Illinois lodged a protest, on the ground that Copland had been accused of associating with Communist front groups. The chairman of the arrangements committee said that the number was dropped as soon as the protest was made, "because we didn't want to do anything to bring criticism." So the Copland number was not heard, and if this was in the end something less than a fatal blow to the evil designs of the men in the Kremlin, it at least saved the assembled Republicans from being compelled to listen to Lincoln's brooding words: "Fellow Citizens, we cannot escape history. We of this Congress and this Administration will be remembered in spite of ourselves."

Copland received many personal letters of support. Composer Elie Siegmeister, who had his own difficulties with HUAC, wrote (21 January 1953):

> Just a few lines to tell you Hannah and I feel with you and are very indignant over the incident of last week. What the hell goes on anyway? Will they soon be forbidding Walt Whitman and the Declaration of Independence?

Edwin Denby wrote to Copland, "Marc B. just came into Minna Daniel's office in a great state about *Lincoln* being taken off the inaugural program." Denby pointed to the fact that "the idea of playing the piece in the first place was *theirs*, not yours."

187

~~the fifth:~~

Dear President Eisenhower:

I am an American composer of symphonic music and the composer of a musical portrait of Abraham Lincoln. I write to you because an incident occurred during the ceremonies attendant upon the inauguration of your administration, too small to have come to your attention, but too ~~~~ in its implications to be passed over lightly. ~~~~ If I did not ~~think~~ it transcended in importance my own personal stake in the matter I would not be writing to you now.

The Inaugural Concert Comm. did me the honor of choosing my Lincoln Portrait for their program on Sunday Jan. 18, 1953. I read of this in the newspapers. On Jan 15, two days before the concert was to take place, I read ~~~~ that my composition would not be played, the reason being that a Congressman from Illinois said I had a record of questionable affiliations:

This is the first time, ~~as far~~ as I know, that a composition has been publicly removed from a concert program ~~because~~ in the U.S. because of the alleged political ~~record~~ "affiliations" of a composer.

I am a musician, not a politician. I have never at any time been a member of any political

Draft of unfinished letter from Copland to President Dwight D. Eisenhower (undated).

After the list of alleged affiliations was read into the *Congressional Record* by Congressman Busbey, Copland released another statement:

> I understand that the Un-American Activities Committee has a record of my alleged affiliation with Communist-front organizations. I wish to state emphatically that any interest that I have ever had in any organization has been through my concern with cultural and musical affairs. I had no knowledge or reason to believe, from my own experience, that any such organization was subversive or communistic. I say unequivocally that I am not now and never have been a Communist or member of the Communist Party or of any organization that advocates or teaches in any way the overthrow of the United States Government. As one who has benefited so greatly from the unique opportunities that America offers its citizens, not only on a financial but also on a spiritual and artistic level, I am far too grateful for the privilege of being an American to become a member of any organization that I believed was merely a forum for Communist propaganda.

The National Symphony Orchestra would play Copland's music frequently in years to come; in fact, when his conducting career escalated in the sixties, it was the National Symphony, of all American orchestras, to which Copland felt closest. A decade after the composer was banned from Eisenhower's inaugural concert, Copland conducted the National Symphony from the West Lawn of the White House, facing the nation's Capitol in a Fourth of July concert that began with the national anthem and continued with his own music. Ironically, the National Symphony has never played a Copland piece at an inaugural concert. It seems there is a rule that once a composer is banned by an inaugural committee, always banned. At the second Nixon inauguration, *Lincoln Portrait* and "The Promise of Living" from Copland's opera *The Tender Land* were included, but they were played by the Philadelphia Orchestra, brought in at Nixon's request to share the inaugural concert program. Nixon's preference had nothing to do with Copland's situation.

On 1 November 1986, Aaron Copland was awarded the Congressional Gold Medal, an Act of Congress and the highest civilian honor in the land. The citation was read into the *Congressional Record,* and the award was presented at a concert by the National Symphony Orchestra conducted by Rostropovich.[13] No one seemed to remember the Busbey incident of 1953. At the time, however, it was unpleasant in the extreme and had repercussions into the sixties.

Considering the Busbey incident, Copland could not have been totally surprised when the dreaded telegram arrived from McCarthy. Copland

WESTERN UNION

1201

:(15)

W. P. MARSHALL, PRESIDENT

The filing time shown in the date line on telegrams and day letters is STANDARD TIME at point of origin. Time of receipt is STANDARD TIME at point of destination

1953 MAY 22 PM 5 34

.:NA248 GOVT PD=SN WASHINGTON DC 22 412P=

:AARON COPLAND, CARE BOOSEY AND HAWKES:

=30 WEST 57 ST=

:YOU ARE HEREBY DIRECTED TO APPEAR BEFORE THIS COMMITTEE
ON MONDAY MAY TWENTYFIFTH AT TWO THIRTY P M ROOM 357 SENATE
OFFICE BUILDING WASHINGTON DC=

    :JOE MCCARTHY CHAIRMAN SENATE PERMANENT SUBCOMMITTEE
    ON INVESTIGATIONS=

THE COMPANY WILL APPRECIATE SUGGESTIONS FROM ITS PATRONS CONCERNING ITS SERVICE

Telegram from Senator Joseph McCarthy to Copland, 22 May 1953.

knew that he had been listed in *Red Channels: The Reports of Communist Influence in Radio and Television* and that Henry Moe of the Guggenheim Foundation had been questioned about him by the Select Committee to Investigate Tax-exempt Foundations (11 December 1952). When asked about Copland's affiliations, Mr. Moe spoke in Copland's favor, concluding, ". . . we are not God and we can't foresee the future. But with respect to Mr. Copland, sir, I would not think that there could possibly be anything wrong with him from the point of view of this committee."[14]

Copland's 1953 appointment book shows a memo for 22 May: "McCarthy wire received!" The telegram was telephoned to Copland at 7 P.M. on Friday evening. It instructed him to appear in Washington the following Monday. When Copland responded that he needed time to secure counsel, the hearing was delayed one day. Whoever recommended Oscar Cox (of Cox, Langford, Stoddard & Cutler) did Copland a great favor. Cox's firm was knowledgeable about the hearings, and Cox himself was a gentleman and a music lover who knew about Copland and admired his music. Cox agreed to see Copland Monday evening before the hearing (Tuesday, 26 May). His interest and respect made Copland feel more comfortable with the situation he was facing. Cox explained that he was involved with another case at the time and had to appoint an associate, Charles Glover, to attend the hearing. Copland said later, "My lawyer was a rock-ribbed Republican who understandably did not want to appear himself." Cox kept closely in touch with the proceedings, and when the difficult year of 1953 was ending, Copland wrote to Cox, "It was my lucky day when I walked into your office. . . ." Cox responded, "It was *our* great luck when you walked into our office."[15]

Several fascinating documents exist concerning the dean of American composers and the senator from Wisconsin, foremost among them being the actual transcript of the privately held hearing.[16] Even today, the transcript of the two-hour interrogation makes chilling reading. It shows Copland responding to hostile interrogation in a controlled, proud, and occasionally even humorous way. Furthermore, the document answers the question of why Copland was called to testify at all. Some have claimed it was McCarthy's intention to use Copland to get at others, such as Hellman, Eisler, and Bernstein. Harold Clurman said:

> What they hunted was not Communists but publicity, and Aaron was the music star. . . . I couldn't take seriously any of the "cases" involving my friends and acquaintances. I knew the truth: Communist Party members or not, they were sentimentalists with little practical understanding of any political issue. . . . They were all on the side of the good.[17]

Copland did not keep a personal diary except when traveling, but he felt motivated to write about the McCarthy hearing the following day. From Copland's description and the transcript of the hearing itself, it is clear that McCarthy was really interested in the U.S.I.A. and who in that organization was responsible for choosing Copland to represent America in an educational capacity abroad. The Information Agency controlled the Voice of America and some two hundred information-center libraries in about ninety countries and was responsible for film services, exhibits, lectures, and exchange programs. At the close of 1952 and the beginning of 1953, McCarthy was convinced Communists had infiltrated the propaganda agency. He saw to it that the average number of books shipped abroad monthly dropped dramatically for lack of clearance of the authors and that thirty thousand volumes by what he considered Communist authors were cleared out. Not only was there a blacklist of authors, composers, and artists but a private "graylist" as well—those who were pending screening and clearance. Copland was on that list of 141, along with

Dorothy Parker, Malcolm Cowley, Roger Sessions, and Edgar Snow. According to an article in *The Nation* by "Scrutiner" (pen name for the newspaperman who covered the Washington scene for the magazine), the list read like a "Who's Who in the Realm of American culture."[18]

The Copland hearing was comparatively mild. Here is a typical exchange:

THE CHAIRMAN: I am not criticizing you for joining these organizations. You may have been so naïve that you didn't know they were Communist controlled or you may have done it purposely, but I can't believe that this very long list used your name time after time as a sponsor of all these outstanding fronts. I can't believe they forged your name to these petitions—borrowed your name unlawfully time after time. However, I am only interested in knowing why they selected you as a lecturer when we have many other people available as lecturers. . . . We must find out why a man of this tremendous activity in Communist fronts would be selected.

MR. COPLAND: May I reply on two points? I think I was selected because of the fact that my employment as a lecturer had nothing to do with anything but music.

THE CHAIRMAN: If you were a member of the Communist Party, let's assume you were, and you were selected to lecture, you would be bound to try wherever you could to sell the Communist idea, wouldn't you?

MR. COPLAND: No doubt.

THE CHAIRMAN: So that I believe you and I would agree that in selecting a lecturer, even though they are an outstanding musician, before we put our stamp of approval on them, we should find out whether they are a Communist or sympathetic to the Communist cause. Is that right?

MR. COPLAND: Well, I would certainly hesitate to send abroad a man who is a Communist sympathizer or a Communist in order to lecture. My impression was that my political opinions, no matter how vague they may have been, were not in question as far as the Department of State was concerned. I assume if they had been in question, I would have had some kind of going over.

THE CHAIRMAN: You were never asked about any of these alleged Communist-front activities?

MR. COPLAND: Not to my memory.

THE CHAIRMAN: I may say, for your information, you did get security clearance.

MR. COPLAND: Did I really? How does one get security clearance?

McCarthy did not answer that question, perhaps failing to see the ironic humor in the exchange. After the hearing, Copland released a public statement:

> On late Friday afternoon, I received a telegram from the Senate Permanent Subcommittee on Investigations to appear as a witness. I did. I answered to the best of my ability all of the questions which were asked me. I testified under oath that I never have supported, and am now opposed to, the limitations put on freedom by the Soviet Union. . . . My relationships with the United States Government were originally with the Music Advisory Committee to the Coordinator of Inter American Affairs and later as a lecturer in music in South America and as a Fulbright Professor. In these capacities my work was limited to the technical aspects of music.

More interesting is Copland's entry in his private diary, which concludes with typical Copland humor, comparing McCarthy's entrance into the hearing room with Toscanini's arrival onstage. The entry is published here for the first time:[19]

> Impressions of the hearing before the Senate Permanent Subcommittee on Investigations, Senator Joseph McCarthy, Chairman, May 26, 1953. (Exchange of Persons Program of the State Department under Investigation)
>
> Arrived Washington, D.C., 6 P.M. accompanied by V. K. [Kraft]. Dinner and evening spent with Oscar Cox and two assistant lawyers (C. Glover and H. Packer). I was coached and warned and instructed by the trio after I had outlined my "situation." Subsequent events proved that we were on the right track.
>
> Appeared before the subcommittee in private executive session. When we entered the room, only Senator McClelland was present, lounging about. Next arrives the general counsel, Roy Cohn (age twenty-six!), accompanied by a young man in his teens who was introduced to the senator. Finally the "great" man himself, Senator McCarthy, entered. I was inwardly and outwardly calm enough. (C. Glover accompanied me as counsel.) The nervousness of the days previous (I had received the committee's wire only three-and-a-half days before) was gone. One hates to be thought a fool or worse still, a gullible fool. The list of so-called affiliations was long—nervous making. But my conscience was clear—in a free America I had a right to affiliate openly with whom I pleased; to sign protests, statements, appeals, open letters, petitions, sponsor events, etc., and no one had the right to question those affiliations.
>
> The hearing was conducted comparatively politely. McCarthy prefaced by explaining the committee's self-made rules of procedure, which are so much criticized. His manner was direct and patient enough. (It was Cohn who seemed to be chafing under insufficient stimulus for a show of personal animus.) His tough-guy radio manner only showed briefly when he hit upon favorite themes.
>
> It is fascinating to try humanly to estimate such a man as McCarthy on so brief an encounter (two hours to be precise). If I didn't know him by his works, I'd be somewhat disarmed. I suspect he derives strength from a basic simplicity

Impressions (May 27/53) of the Hearing before the Senate Permanent Sub committee on Investigations, Senator Joseph McCarthy, Chairman May 26, 1953. (Exchange of Persons Program of the State Dep't under Investigation)

Arrived Wash. D.C. 6 P.M. accompanied by V.K. Dinner & evening spent with my attorney Oscar Cox and 2 assistant lawyers (C. Glover + H. Packer) I was coached and warned and instructed by the trio after I had outlined my 'situation'. Subsequent events proved that we were on the right track.

Appeared before the Sub committee in private Exec. Session. When we entered the room only Senator McClelland was present, lounging about. Next arrived the general counsel Roy Cohen (aged 26'), acc. by a young man in his teens who was introduced to the Senator. Finally, the 'great' man himself – Senator McCarthy, entered. I was inwardly and outwardly calm enough. (C. Glover accompanied me as counsel.) The nervousness of the day previous (I had received the Committee's wire only 3½ days before) was gone. One later stated thought a fool or worse

The first page of Copland's "Impressions of the Hearing . . . ," 27 May 1953.

of purpose; power; and a simplicity of rallying cry: the Commies. The power grabbing is subtle—he seems to enjoy his position as if he was himself a spectator of his amazing rise to importance in the world political scene. Something about him suggests that he is a man who doesn't really expect his luck to hold out. It's been too phenomenal, and I suppose, too recklessly achieved. When he touches on his magic theme, the "Commies" or "communism," his voice darkens like that of a minister. He is like a plebian Faustus who has been given a magic wand by an invisible Mephisto—as long as the menace is there, the wand will work. The question is at what point his power grab will collide with the power drive of others in his own party. *A voir.*

My impression is that McCarthy had no idea who I was or what I did, other than the fact I was a part of the State Department's exchange program at one time. He seemed to show little personal animus. The attitude of the others seemed to be one of studied indifference. (It occurred to me to say to Glover as McCarthy entered that it was similar to the entrance of Toscanini—half the battle won before it begins through the power of personality.) During the hearing, McClelland left, and Senator Mundt wandered in. Only McCarthy was present throughout.

In addition to the transcript itself and Copland's diary entry, another interesting document is the list of affiliations put together by the Senate subcommittee. Obviously, a team of thorough researchers went to great lengths compiling such information, with which those called to testify were faced with no time to prepare responses. Copland was astonished when he saw the list, and said, "It was impossible within those few hours to check whether my name appeared with my consent. It was well known that Communists made unauthorized use of well-known names." Copland admitted only to being involved in the World Peace Conference of 1949. He stated, "I had the hope that by demonstrating that relations are possible on a cultural plane, we might encourage talks on a diplomatic plane. I sponsored no further so-called Peace Conferences, being convinced that they were being engineered by Communists."

Following the hearing, Copland's work with his lawyers began in earnest. When Cox's office went through the transcript, they found ninety-seven technical errors.[20] Cox wrote to Copland (20 May), "You will note that there is grave doubt about the accuracy of the transcript, since the stenographer has already admitted that she omitted one entire paragraph." The paragraph in question put the chairman in an embarrassing light: He had been drilling Copland about the notorious Communist Party leader, Eisler. Copland responded, "Surely you must be referring to Gerhart Eisler. . . ." McCarthy continued, demanding to know what Copland knew about this Eisler fellow, "who had jumped bail, gone to East Berlin, and

Item No.	Date	Page	Source	Allegation
27	3/7/45 II	✓	Report to the National Council of American-Soviet Friendship by the Director	Named him vice chairman of the musicians committee of that organization.
28	11/18/45 III	✓	National Council of American-Soviet Friendship *meeting addressed by State Dept official*	Spoke at an American-Soviet cultural conference.
29	3/13/46 IV	✓	Letterhead of NCASF	Sponsor.
30	3/18/46 V	✓	Memorandum of NCASF	Sponsor.
31	12/17/47	7 /	Daily Worker *Possible fellow musicians, civil rights matter*	Signed a petition to the Attorney General on behalf of Hanns Eisler, a Communist.
32	2/28/48	✓	Release, All-Eisler Program at Town Hall, New York	Sponsor of the Hanns Eisler concert 2/28/48.
33	May/48 VI	9 ?	Pamphlet, How to End the Cold War and Build the Peace.— *NC·A·S·F·*	Signer of statement praising Henry Wallace's open letter to Stalin – May 1948.
Exh. 34	6/21/48 VII	3 ✓	Daily Worker	Signed a statement calling for a conference with the Soviet Union sponsored by the National Council of American-Soviet Friendship.
35	10/19/48	7 ?	Daily Worker *, no recollection, possible*	Signed a statement in support of Henry Wallace, issued by the National Council of Arts, Sciences and Professions.
36	2/28/49	✗ ✗	Daily Worker *NoFALSE, incorrectly reported DID NOT in Cngr. Record SPEAK*	Spoke at a meeting of the National Council of Arts, Sciences and Professions.
Exh. 37	2/21/49 3/13/49	9 9	✓ Conference Program ✓ Daily Worker *Attended, and criticized S.u. artistic policy*	Sponsor and speaker at the Cultural and Scientific Conference for World Peace held under the auspices of the National Council in N.Y.C. – 3/25-27/49.
38	4/27/49	✗	Schappes Defense Committee (This committee was cited as Communist by the Attorney General in his letter to the Loyalty Review Board, released April 27, 1949.) *Definitely No*	Sponsor, on an undated letterhead and pamphlet, In the case of Morris U. Schappes (p. 10). *a statement taking exception Signed a Declaration of War to on Finland Amer. Council on Soviet Relations*
39	no date	✗	no source —— *No recollection*	

(See references to Copland in Eisler testimony before House Un-American Activities Committee, on page A180 in the Congressional Record for Jan. 16, 1953).

A sample page from the HUAC list of alleged Copland affiliations, showing checkmarks and notations by Copland.

become a minister of information." Copland repeated that he knew only Eisler the composer and author of a book Copland admired, *Composing for the Films*. The interrogation went on for some minutes before McCarthy discovered his error. Harold Clurman describes the incident in his book *All People Are Famous,* calling it, "a good example of the employment of the Big Lie."[21]

Also omitted from the transcript of the hearing was McCarthy's questioning based on the erroneous assumption that Copland wrote an article actually written by Hanns Eisler. It seems extremely unlikely that a stenographer would have made the independent decision to remove these sections. One wonders how far McCarthy's editing went with other transcripts.

Copland had to drop everything to prepare the detailed explanations McCarthy required within one week's time, before a public hearing was to be held. With Victor Kraft's help, Copland went furiously through correspondence and financial files and returned to Washington to work with his lawyers. A letter went from Cox to Roy Cohn (5 June) pointing to the ninety-seven errors in the transcript, and a long and detailed letter was sent from Copland to McCarthy responding to each item that had come up in the hearing. Having been asked by McCarthy to "name names" of Americans at the 1949 World Peace Conference, Copland prepared a separate statement: "I have read over *The New York Times* account of the fine arts panel of the conference. . . . I do not personally remember having seen anyone at the conference who is not listed in those published reports."

Walter Winchell broadcast that the McCarthy committee planned a public hearing on the State Department Interchange of Persons Program (9 June). Copland assumed he would be called to testify, but the hearing came and went, and Copland heard nothing further from the committee. Cox's office kept in touch: "We still have no word about a public hearing. We have not thought it a good idea to check in with them constantly to remind them that you are still under subpoena. . . ." As days stretched to weeks, and weeks to months, it seemed less likely that Copland would be called to testify again. However, when Copland left for Tanglewood, he still feared a telegram from McCarthy might arrive at any moment.

At the end of July, Copland's name was mentioned in *The Washington Post* when the subcommittee questioned Senator Fulbright (25 July 1953):

FULBRIGHT: "You say you've found one. You've got a whole corps of people looking around for some time and you've found one Communist. . . . Nobody is perfect." McCarthy said he has "a sizable number of other cases." Among them . . . composer Aaron Copland, who, McCarthy said, "have a great record of Communist activity." Later, McCarthy corrected that to "Communist front activity," and he called the Fulbright program the "half-bright program."

Copland's philosophical nature kept him from becoming bitter at his treatment during the McCarthy period. His friend Edwin Denby wrote (28 June 1953):

> It is extraordinary [that] even now I can't detect a sign in you that you have been through any trouble. I mean in the sense of wanting comforting. It is only by imagining how grueling it would be to me to be questioned by the police on suspicion, even if I were sure of my innocence, that I can imagine anything. To me, it seems more a hideous humiliation, as far as I can think it, than any sort of objective harm.

Copland admitted to Denby and other friends that the affair was very tiring. Arthur Berger said, "Aaron told me the McCarthy thing took a lot of energy and emotion—that sense of being pursued. . . ."[22]

Copland thought the matter was essentially over with the hearing. Little did he realize how much more time and energy would go into the matter of his passport. When he asked his lawyers about a trip to Mexico planned for the end of August 1953 to help direct a series with the Orquesta Sinfonica Nacional, they saw no reason he should not go, as long as he could be reached easily. Cox wrote (16 August), "There is a slight question as to whether you are still under subpoena. It is true that the State Department has a policy of not issuing passports to individuals who are under subpoena. But, as you point out, the trip which you are taking does not require a passport." Nevertheless, before leaving for Mexico, Copland was required to make sworn statement to a notary: "Aaron Copland of Shady Lane Farm is not a Communist." Copland's passport situation became a long-standing issue, one in which Cox's office played an important role. Reading through the voluminous correspondence, statements from Copland and his lawyers, reports of meetings, and other documentation that continued for several years, until Copland's passport was reinstated, one cannot help but wonder at the extraordinary patience and control displayed by both Copland and Oscar Cox.

The Passport Office requested that Copland furnish evidence of affiliation with avowedly anti-Communist organizations and that he supply affidavits from citizens on his behalf. Copland got to work again, even citing the America character of his music, and he asked Henry Moe and Olga Koussevitzky for supporting letters. Oscar Cox wrote to Copland (7

November 1953), "Mrs. Koussevitzky's affidavit is a jewel." The Passport Office again "tentatively disapproved" Copland's application, "unless Copland could submit evidence that he had not consistently adhered to the Communist Party line." Copland cited an invitation from the Congress for Cultural Freedom to appear at an International Conference in Rome (5–15 April 1954): "If my passport is not promptly renewed, I will have to withdraw my acceptance." He also mentioned invitations to conduct in Barcelona and London. Finally, Copland compiled a list of twenty-one "American" organizations "of which I was an active member during the period 1935–1952." Along with Copland's request went a lengthy dossier from the firm of Cox, Langford, Stoddard, & Cutler.

Cox personally reviewed all the papers with the Passport Office. Even then, however, questions were posed. At long last, a limited passport renewal of six months was obtained. The irony of Copland's passport difficulties is that they coincided with his appearances as the major representative of American music in Europe and South America during 1954! In January 1955, Copland's passport was renewed for one year, rather than the normal two-year period.

Letters from Oscar Cox and his office were always typed. But a handwritten note from Cox arrived at Shady Lane Farm before Christmas 1953: "To you, Louise and I wish a good Xmas and New Year of even more fruitful production unhampered by the madness of the small hearts and minds." The following year, when Cox had to inform Copland that his passport had not yet been cleared, Cox sent along the following lines paraphrased from Ecclesiastes 12: "The daughters of musick shall not be brought low / Nor the sun, nor the light of the moon, nor the stars be darkened."

Copland was not billed by Cox's office for legal fees until early 1954. The amount was substantial, and when Copland asked whether it could be paid over a period of two years, Cox responded, "From our standpoint, you can take longer if you wish. . . ." Cox so admired Copland that he talked to people he knew on the boards of the National Symphony and the New York Philharmonic to have them invite the composer to conduct his music. Cox had connections in Cuba and Mexico and wrote to highly placed individuals for Copland to be decorated by both countries. Oscar Cox kept in touch with Copland regularly, especially when the Busbey incident and McCarthy hearing came back to haunt the composer. Whenever Copland went to Washington to conduct, he got together with the Cox family.

The first public reactions to the Red-baiting of Copland came from the South. The University of Alabama had invited the composer to speak and conduct at a three-day Composers' Forum planned for April 1953. The withdrawal of the invitation typified the atmosphere of fear and repression in academic institutions at that time. Copland and Gurney Kennedy, chairman of the Composers' Forum Committee, had been in correspondence since October 1952. Kennedy wrote (7 March 1953):

> I regret to inform you that the recent allegations of Communist sympathies on your part as set out on the Extension of the Remarks of the Honorable Fred E. Busbey . . . and the inaugural concert affair in Washington make it inadvisable for us to have you as our guest.

Copland responded with a lengthy letter (12 March) in which he attacked Busbey's tactics and expressed his regret "for the loss of academic independence that such an action implies. It makes clear that freedom of thought is endangered in America if a large university such as yours can be intimidated by the allegations of a single individual." Copland expressed the hope that the university would reconsider its action. He wrote:

> At this juncture it seems enormously important to me that you and I reaffirm our right to talk music to American students without fear of interference on alleged political grounds. The only way to do so is to put it to the test. It goes without saying that I cannot accept an honorarium for work I have not done, and I am therefore returning the check for three hundred dollars.

Gurney Kennedy, a great admirer of Copland and his music, took the liberty of ending his next letter, which informed Copland that the university would not reconsider its withdrawal, with a personal opinion: "Also I want you to know that I, too, deplore the intrusion of a political counterpoint, which to my mind is sadly out of key in any artistic enterprise." Kennedy's supportive sentence caused remarkable difficulty and embarrassment within the university and impelled the dean of music to write a lengthy explanation and apology to his superior, ending with, "May I repeat that all of us in this matter have been motivated by the desire to protect the university from criticism."

In 1967, after Gurney Kennedy moved to Jacksonville University in Florida, the College of Music and Fine Arts there honored Copland with a Contemporary Music Festival and a Doctor of Fine Arts Degree. Dr. and Mrs. Gurney Kennedy were moved by the citation and by their meeting with Copland, and they commented on how far removed the occasion was from the events in Alabama of 1953.[23]

The next reactions came from the West Coast: The Hollywood Bowl Committee canceled a Copland performance scheduled for March 1953 without explanation. Lukas Foss, who was teaching at UCLA and conducting the Los Angeles Chamber Orchestra, had invited Copland to conduct his music. Several members of the board disapproved of Copland's politics. Foss was furious and wrote Copland, "Cornelia and I have stayed up all night talking about whether I should resign. Who wants to be associated with such an organization!" When asked in a recent interview whether he, himself, had had trouble with McCarthy, Foss responded laughingly, "I wasn't famous enough for anybody to bother me! McCarthy liked Mr. America Incorporated. You can't be a better American than Aaron."[24]

The University of Colorado had invited Copland as Reynolds Lecturer for January 1954. The offer was rescinded on the grounds that the university decided not to hold the lecture that year. No reason was given, but Copland learned months later that the decision was due to his alleged Communist front associations. The *Colorado Labor Advocate* printed a story headed "Another Smear Victim," and *The Colorado Daily* sent Copland a telegram: STUDENTS AND FACULTY INTERESTED IN ORGANIZING MOVEMENT FOR YOU TO SPEAK ON CAMPUS. WOULD YOU ACCEPT? UNDER WHAT CONDITIONS? CITY EDITOR. Copland did not go to Colorado in 1954, but he accepted when reinvited in 1961.

In February 1956, citations voted to Copland from the Borough of Brooklyn and ASCAP were canceled. When television personality Ed Sullivan broadcast a performance of *Lincoln Portrait* in honor of Lincoln's birthday, he did not credit the composer. William Schuman wrote to Sullivan afterward:

> The only disturbing feature was that you neglected to mention the fundamental thing about this composition, namely, that it was composed by Aaron Copland. It is not only that the music for this fine work was written by Copland but that he chose the excerpts from Lincoln's writings and wrote the connecting prose passages which are so effective.

Not surprisingly, the American Legion caused some difficulty. Copland had an appointment as Slee Professor of Music at the University of Buffalo in 1957, and the UB authorities were questioned by the Legion chairman, "Is this the Aaron Copland who. . . ." Cameron Baird, head of the music department, resisted the attack, but the controversy was reported in the *Buffalo Evening News* (2 February 1957). (When the university dedicated their new music building, the letters between Baird and the American Legion were sealed into the foundation stone.)

In 1960, anonymous cards were mailed to the Dallas Symphony trustees and management protesting a Copland concert, causing a board member to cancel a postconcert party. In 1962, the American Legion of San Antonio, Texas, questioned Copland's lectureship appointment at the University of Texas and an award from the San Antonio Symphony, but the activities took place as planned. As late as 1967, a letter was sent to the Rutland, Vermont newspaper protesting Copland's appearance there as guest conductor of the Buffalo Philharmonic in April 1968. An editorial appeared against the protest, and the concert was given without further incident.

These few disturbances did not change Copland's life. If anything, he was more in demand on the lecture circuit than ever, and invitations to conduct were increasing. Copland's first book, *What to Listen for in Music,* was published in Hebrew and in Italian. *Music and Imagination* appeared in Spanish and Italian versions. He wrote articles for *Musical America, Musical Courier,* and *Saturday Review of Literature.* Within a few years of the McCarthy hearing, Copland received prestigious degrees and honors, among them membership to the fifty-member American Academy and Institute of Arts and Letters in 1955 and the Gold Medal in 1956,[25] a year in which he also received an honorary degree from Princeton University, followed by Brandeis in 1957, and Illinois Wesleyan and Oberlin in 1958.

When Copland was asked about the McCarthy hearing by friends at social gatherings, he would treat it lightly, imitating McCarthy's deadly seriousness and Roy Cohn's way of repeating the word *Cooooommunist.* [26] In private, Copland told friends that it was no joke, and he would bemoan the amount of time the affair had cost him. Most of the people Copland knew and with whom he worked were sympathetic to him and critical of what McCarthy represented. Directly after the hearing, Copland attended a family party and prepared to leave for Tanglewood (he had hoped to take leave in 1953 but thought it might be construed as being connected to the McCarthy hearing). He returned to work. The pace at Tanglewood left little time for anything but music, and afterward, the opera project, which Copland and Erik Johns were already deeply involved with, became enormously demanding.

This opera, *The Tender Land,* is counted among Copland's "Americana" works. Except for one moment in the plot, there is no trace of the bitter taste left from the McCarthy hearing and its aftermath. The music for the opera is in Copland's "accessible" style. However, ten years after *Appalachian Spring,* the music and plot seemed nostalgic for a more innocent time in America, a time before the Cold War and Senator Joseph McCarthy.

The Tender Land

1953-1954

Verso: The original production of *The Tender Land,* New York City, 1954.
Photograph by Gus Manos.

Opposite: Copland, c. 1954.

I had hoped to take leave from Tanglewood in 1953 to get to work on my opera, but friends pointed out that my absence might be construed as being connected somehow to the McCarthy business. And Charles Munch was not happy about the idea of my being away for the entire summer, so I decided against it. Lenny Bernstein was also ambivalent about Tanglewood in 1953, but there we were at the opening exercises as usual.[1] I introduced Carlos Chávez as visiting composer to the students and faculty. Chávez' presence cheered me—being used to the erratic political situation in Mexico, he took a philosophical attitude toward the McCarthy hearing. We shared composition students more than when a visiting composer was someone I did not know so well. Chávez and I agreed that the outstanding composition student in 1953 was a young Japanese, Toshi Ichiyanagi.[2] Chávez made a good impression, and there was interest in his music, especially after my lecture in the Aspects of Music course, titled "Chávez and Mexican Music."

Munch conducted *Appalachian Spring* with the BSO (31 July) and Lenny did *Billy the Kid* with the Music Center orchestra (25 July). I played piano in my *Piano Quartet* (9 August), and Sam Barber came up that weekend. He wrote afterward (12 August), ". . . you are a marvelous host. Thanks for pepping up a dull midsummer with such glamour—Dear Aaron: Have we become friends, perhaps? It would be nice."

Immediately following Tanglewood, I left for Mexico to help direct a festival with the Orquesta Sinfonica Nacional. I wrote to Claire Reis from Mexico, "I have been through the wringer but I am beginning to get my equilibrium back." One of my Tanglewood students, Jack Kennedy, met me for a week of sight-seeing in Oaxaca and Taxco. With no word from the McCarthy committee, I decided to stay in Mexico for another ten days to help open the symphony season (I conducted Roy Harris' *Third Symphony* and Chausson's *Poème*). I wrote to Victor, "The men played

Copland at Tanglewood, 1953.

like—Mexicans. That is, out of tune half the time with mistakes and flashes of very good sections. . . . I am learning a lot about conducting."

I returned from Mexico refreshed and ready to work on my opera with Erik Johns. I stayed close to home, except for a trip up to Boston for an unusual performance—Lenny Burkat had convinced Munch to revive my *Piano Concerto* after many years of neglect. Leo Smit was the pianist. It was an exciting event. My Boston friends all attended, among them Arthur Berger, who told me that his book *Aaron Copland* was about to be published.[3] An entire book about me! Arthur, an accomplished composer and experienced writer, had discussed various aspects of the book with me over the past few years. *Aaron Copland* is divided into two parts: biographical and musical. Arthur's main focus was on the musical section. He chose a few pivotal works (the *Piano Variations* and the *Third Symphony*) and concentrated on the form and structure of each. Arthur is expert at analyzing music in technical terms, something I have never done very well myself. *Aaron Copland* was reviewed by Harold Clurman in *The Saturday*

208

Review of Literature (28 November 1953), and by William Schuman in *The New York Times Book Review* (8 November). I particularly liked the part where Bill wrote that "Mr. Copland is but a promising youngster of fifty-three. We can, therefore, look forward to many more years of his fruitful activity and to exciting additions to his list of major works." I wrote to thank Arthur (9 December): "Think of me the next time you pass those Harvard Sq. bookshops. I went in to buy something and a stranger came up and asked me to autograph your book for an Xmas present! Good sign, no?"

Arthur Berger [4]

Do you ever get Aaron to talk about his music? When I was working on the book, I tried to get him to talk in specific musical terms, but he obviously did not at all relish doing so. Perhaps he did not want to give his secrets away! Stravinsky was the same way about discussing his music. Aaron was critical of what I wrote about the Piano Sonata *in* Partisan Review, *and later about the* Piano Fantasy *in the* Juilliard Review. *I didn't use the most specialized language you find in, say,* Perspectives of New Music, *but nonetheless Aaron made the observation that he was not comfortable with the analytic part of the* Fantasy *article. I always had the feeling he felt that way about the technical side of my book—not that the analysis was on a particularly profound level. Clurman's review of my book reflected the same sentiment. Aaron took exception, furthermore, to the sharp distinction I made between his music for an elite audience and his music for a larger public. He thought I was perhaps responsible for starting the whole idea of a bifurcation in his output.*

I met Aaron through Jerome Moross and Benny Herrmann, my fellow students at NYU, way back in the early thirties when we all got together for those meetings of the Young Composers Group at his place—meetings that were very stormy indeed, both musically and politically. [5] I refrained from putting the names of the Group's members in my Copland book because it was published during the McCarthy period. Aaron's politics were mild compared with the orientation of some of the Group's members! We young composers worried that Aaron might get away from the strong austere qualities we so much admired. They were difficult to reconcile with Aaron's more popular music. I tried to convince myself that Aaron's writing for a wider audience was just as significant as his other music, but for me, as far

Copland with
Arthur Berger,
c. 1953.

as the more popular pieces are concerned, you go through them too fast—
they don't last as long.

I have never considered Aaron to be my teacher—very few can claim him
as a teacher, although many composers have studied with him briefly or
attended his lectures at Tanglewood. At first, when I showed Aaron my
music, he would want to know what organizing principles I thought of when
I wrote. I learned certain things from Aaron, but mainly from observing his
music; for example, the spacing of intervals and coming back to a given
chord for punctuation. My Woodwind Quartet *of 1941, which is dedicated*
to Aaron, shows a little of his influence, although it is neoclassic in a way
that Aaron never was.

When I was with the Herald Tribune, *I used to go up to Tanglewood*
as a reviewer quite regularly, and I sometimes stayed with the Fines, with
whom Aaron, their neighbor in Richmond, had his meals. My first wife,
Esther, and I were in the car behind him in 1949 when he hit the cow, and
we were with him when he was severely interrogated by the state police.
Aaron was fond of Esther, and he never got used to the idea that she had
died. (He kept sending regards to her.) There were so many times I spent

with Aaron, I can't remember them all. It's funny how one occasion comes to mind: In 1958, Aaron and I went by train to Illinois to participate in some festival. There was a coal strike, and we couldn't take the train back, so Aaron said, "Let's fly." It was my first time and I was reluctant and scared, but Aaron, in his thoughtful way, kidded me and gave me a silver dollar for luck. You know, I felt very protected because Aaron was there with me.

I was really up against a deadline: The premiere of my opera was scheduled for 2 April 1954 by the New York City Opera, and I had promised the finished product by the beginning of February. I was still composing in mid-March, and the orchestration was not completed until a few days before the premiere. Jerry Robbins, who directed the opera, thought it was very "cool" of me not to go to rehearsals, but the fact was, I didn't have time!

When I was a student in Paris in the twenties, nobody was interested in opera—nobody, that is, who cared about "new music." We were all interested in ballet. Later, in just the same way, everybody wanted to write an opera. But full-length opera is an enormous challenge for a composer! You spend years on the work, and then it's all over and decided in a few hours. It is such a tremendous effort that I waited until I was over fifty to do it. Even then, my opera, *The Tender Land*, was not meant to be a big dramatic opera. It was for young people to perform, and for that reason, it is rather simple in musical style and story line. I admit that if I have one regret, it is that I never *did* write a "grand opera."

Composers fall into two categories: those who are "hopelessly" opera composers—such as Rossini, Wagner, and Puccini—and those who debate whether and when to write an opera. To have the courage to cope with it regularly, you have to feel as if you were born to do that particular thing. The urge has to be so strong that because of some inner drive, little else in music attracts you—and then you are an honest-to-God opera composer. I am not such. For me, opera was really a very problematical form—*la forme fatale*—as I called it after my experience with *The Tender Land*. [6] Most composers will agree that opera is a risky medium even before putting a note on paper. However, the reward for writing a good opera, or even one that just brings attention to the composer, is so great that the temptation is to forget the problems and barge ahead.

The basic difficulty of the lyric stage, I think, comes from the fact that there are so many imponderables. Primary among these is the nature of

Page from Copland's 1952 appointment book listing commissions offered, with "Opera-L of C" (League of Composers) checked.

the forces at your command. When I wrote a symphonic work, I had in the back of my mind the Boston, the Philadelphia, or the New York Philharmonic—I knew these orchestras and their capabilities in advance. But writing an opera, even for the Metropolitan or City Center, one never knows what singers might be engaged. Each time you get a group of people together, the resultant production is full of uncertainties. A composer may have some say about who sings for the premiere of his opera, but there is no control over casts in the future. A composer may very well have to put up with tastes that differ from his own. For example, I prefer a voice with a certain objectivity, a certain purity in the presentation of the vocal line. I don't like to feel that I'm being personally involved in a performer's private emotions. A voice that is deeply emotional makes me cringe! Others may feel differently. (Lenny Bernstein was shocked when I wrote that "I hate an emotion-drenched voice!"—he had never heard me express so strong an aversion to anything in music.)

I once asked Ben Britten what he thought was the most important requisite in composing opera. I was sure he would say a sense of drama, ability to indicate the meaning of a scene musically in a matter of seconds. What he said was that the most important thing a composer must have is the ability to write many kinds of music—chorus alone, chorus with orchestra, soloists separately, soloists in ensemble, and so on. The needs are so varied that one must have terrific facility to handle them all.

My own feeling is that one of the prime requisites in writing an opera is to keep a sense of the flow of the action. Just as in any long sustained piece of music, it is very hard to keep going in such a way that one feels inevitably carried along. I have noticed with some composers (especially Puccini) that the sense of movement is often supplied not so much by the vocal line as by the orchestral accompaniment. The opera composer has to calculate his accompaniment very carefully. It is one way of solving tricky dramatic problems. The sustained melodic line in operatic vocal writing is comparatively rare in contemporary composition. Britten used it on occasion, as did some of the other British composers, such as Walton and Tippett. But it's not easy for a contemporary composer to write the kind of luscious, long, singing tunes that opera composers used to depend upon.

I believe that opera *can* be composed in a contemporary musical idiom. Kurt Weill wrote opera in a different style and got away with it, even though not everybody thought it was opera. And I don't think anybody has trouble with Douglas Moore's *Wings of the Dove* and Hugo Weisgall's *Six Characters in Search of an Author,* which has a certain daring about it that I find stimulating. All operas do not have to be done in the same way. I have noticed that it is usually composers with the experience of writing several operas who can bring one off. But the big bottleneck is that so few operas get produced. The cost and complexity of production have escalated to the point where, although younger composers are writing operas, they're wasting their time unless a way is found to get them performed. It is very hard to move on to the next point in one's development without hearing and seeing what has already been done.

Then there is the matter of the libretto. Where and how does one find a really professional librettist? We don't have people in this country who

St Jean de Luz   Easter morning 1950

Dear Aaron:

You've got a short memory. We've been over all that before.

I'm convinced I write a-musical plays: that my texts "swear at" music. That they're after totally different effects; that they delight in the homeliest aspects of our daily life; that in them even the life of the emotions is expressed contra musicam.

Music and particularly opera is for the unlocked throat! the outgoing expressive "idea and essence" behind our daily life! I hope my plays don't lack that idea and essence but they singularly shrink from any explicit use of it. They are homely and not one bit lyrical.

But I'm delighted that you are applying yourself to opera and the musical play and very proud that that born impresario, Rudi Bing has expressed this good opinion of me. Give him my regard. And you — find a suitable text — and all good courage and best wishes to you.

Cordially ever

Thornton

P.S. Just got here from attending the Holy Week procesiones at Valladolid — great theatre in the best sense — and all surrounded by the great motets of Victoria whose wonderfully plangent type of musical phrase just suits that week's events

Letter from Thornton Wilder, "Easter morning," 1950.

do nothing but write librettos for operas! Librettists usually don't know much about music, unfortunately. I think they would write better librettos if they could imagine what the music is going to do to their words. Composers frequently look at plays in order to find a libretto, but the requisites are different. I was constantly on the lookout for suitable libretto material. I knew and admired the works of several poets and playwrights, and I discussed with them opera librettos and other theatrical projects with music. Among them were Archie MacLeish, Robert Lowell, Bill Inge, and Edward Albee.[7] Clifford Odets was one of the first writers to whom I talked (Clurman always thought that we should collaborate). Cliff and I did some work on his 1938 play *Rocket to the Moon* before abandoning the idea of turning it into an opera. I remember that the main character in the drama was a dentist, and all the action took place in this dentist's office. We also worked on a kind of dramatic concert presentation, *Noah*. Clurman took me to see Arthur Miller to discuss *The Crucible*. I thought about turning Dreiser's *An American Tragedy* into an opera, and I seriously considered a script by Stephen Crane, a writer out in San Francisco. For some reason, I gave that one up, too. In 1948, after seeing a production of my high school opera, *The Second Hurricane*, Thornton Wilder criticized the libretto (6 September 1948): "What I did get from it, though, is—as I would expect—that you have a faultless ear for spoken rhythms and could set the telephone book." I responded by asking Thornton whether *he* would consider writing a libretto for me. I suggested *The Legends of the Chasidim*, but that did not appeal to him. I wrote to Thornton again in 1950, because Rudolf Bing, then general manager of the Metropolitan Opera, had offered me a commission for making *Our Town* into an opera. Thornton responded (April 1950):

> I'm convinced I write a-musical plays: that my texts "swear at" music; that they're after totally different effects; that they delight in the homeliest aspects of our daily life. . . . Music and particularly opera is for the unlocked throat, the outgoing expressive "idea and essence" behind our daily life. I hope my plays don't lack that idea and essence but they singularly shrink from any explicit use of it. They are homely and not one bit lyrical. . . . But I am delighted that you are applying yourself to opera and the musical play.

Mr. Bing said that for once he did not agree with Thornton Wilder and suggested I search for another librettist; but I could not imagine an *Our Town* without Thornton Wilder.

While I was at Harvard delivering the Norton Lectures in the spring of 1952, Claire Reis wrote that I was the League of Composers' first choice for a commission (one thousand dollars) from Richard Rodgers and Oscar Hammerstein II to compose an opera for television.[8] I was intrigued with the idea of composing opera for an exciting new medium. Claire added a personal comment: "It would be wonderful to have you help the League celebrate its thirtieth anniversary and it would be wonderful if I could whisper to Rosenstock [Joseph, general director] perhaps the City Center might have a work of yours in the near future."[9] This seemed like good preparation for the "grand" opera I hoped to write someday. Since Erik Johns and I had been talking about working on a project together, we decided to give it a try. I wanted a simple libretto, and it appealed to me to work with someone I knew without having to worry about changing a famous writer's work or doing damage to a preconceived play or story.

Erik Johns[10]

I took the name "Horace Everett" as a pseudonym because I had a dancing and a painting career at the time of The Tender Land, *and I did not want to confuse the two activities. (Horace Everett was a name that had more to do with my real life than the name Erik Johns, which I had taken as a pen name much earlier, since Horace was my real given name and Everett my father's middle name.) I had never written a libretto or a play, only poems and various stories and sketches. Aaron had had the idea of composing an opera for a long time, and we had often discussed my writing a libretto for him, but as to a specific theme, time, or locale—nothing seemed to material-ize. I knew that Aaron felt that opera was uncharted territory for him. "All those notes," he would say, "and that awful bugaboo, dialogue." Then one day he played me several songs from the abandoned folk musical* Tragic Ground, *and he showed me a book he greatly admired,* Let Us Now Praise Famous Men, *by James Agee, with photographs by Walker Evans. They were of a sharecropper's family in the South. Aaron suggested a libretto duplicating the pilgrimage of Agee and Evans, who lived and worked with a poor sharecropper's family. I derived the basic idea of the libretto from the book—two men from an outside world "invading" the inside world of a provincial family. The two men became migrant farm workers. I carefully examined the photographs in the book and kept coming back to the faces of the mother and young daughter: one, still a mother but passive and stony; the other, not yet hardened by the grim life. What effect would the entrance*

Copland with
Erik Johns,
1953.

of two strangers have upon these lives? The answer to this question came
to be my plot.

The locale changed from the south to the midwest in the mid-1930s in
June, spring harvest time. The story is about a farm family, the Mosses—a
mother, a daughter Laurie about to graduate from high school, her ten-year-
old sister Beth, and the grandfather. When the two drifters come along
asking for odd jobs, Grandfather Moss is reluctant and the mother is
alarmed because she's heard reports of two men molesting young girls in
the neighborhood. Nevertheless, and with Laurie's urging, Martin and Top
are hired. The first act closes at sunset with the main characters looking
forward to Laurie's graduation party. Act II opens with the party. Laurie and
Martin fall in love, but there is something of a complication: Laurie associ-
ates Martin with freedom, while he associates her with settling down.
During the evening, Martin and Top are accused of being the molesters.
Although it soon is proven that the accusations are false, Grampa Moss tells

A sharecropper mother and daughter from *Let Us Now Praise Famous Men,* the book that influenced the characters and plot of *The Tender Land.*

Photographs by Walker Evans. Courtesy the Library of Congress and Beinecke Rare Book Library, Yale.

them they must leave at daybreak. In the course of the night, Martin and Laurie make plans to run away together, but Top convinces Martin that the roving life is not for Laurie. The two drifters steal off. When Laurie discovers she's been jilted, she decides to leave home anyway. At the conclusion, the mother looks to her younger daughter as the continuation of the family cycle that is the reason for their existence.

The action was developed in a series of plot outlines that were quite complex at first, and were then simplified as I went along. I was not used to thinking in terms of time and space plausibilities or of literal justification for actions. I soon discovered another aspect of libretto writing—reading time and singing time are quite different. Also, I learned that the presentation of a "finished" libretto to the composer is not the end of the librettist's job. Aaron might need an extra line to fill out a melodic phrase, and I would find that such a request could take more effort than a dozen verses.

When Aaron returned to Cambridge to deliver the second series of lectures on his Norton Professorship, I stayed in New York to work on the libretto and sent sections off to Aaron. He would cut and make suggestions for changes and additions. By Easter, I had a second draft of the final scene

218

of Act I, which incorporated the quintet "The Promise of Living" for the first-act curtain. I wrote to Aaron, "Lord help you if there are other serious changes." The second act progressed with less difficulty. Aaron came down to New York from Cambridge to play the love duet and a dance number for me, and I made suggestions about the dances, having been a professional dancer myself.

The music for Tragic Ground was gradually dropped out of the opera. It was too popular in style, perhaps too folksy. Other changes were made as we went along—a name change, words cut or added as Aaron needed for the music, the title changed twice: from Graduation Harvest to Picket Fence Horizon to The Tender Land. [11] At one time we considered including a murder or rape scene to add dramatic impact, but the idea seemed at odds with the modest pastoral quality of the work. The most dramatic scene was when the drifters are falsely accused, and then a few moments later discovered to be not guilty. Aaron had just been through the McCarthy business and we were definitely influenced by that. When Grandpa Moss says to the boys, "You're guilty all the same," we were thinking about all the false McCarthy accusations and the effect they had on innocent people.

After working separately, Aaron and I got together in the spring of 1954 before he left for the MacDowell Colony, followed by Tanglewood. We went up to Canada for a few weeks, still working on the opera, and returned with a script finally ready to submit to Peter Herman Adler at the NBC television workshop. Well, Adler turned it down cold! We almost gave up the whole thing, but Aaron asked Clurman to read the libretto, and he liked it and made some suggestions, which we incorporated. We decided to go ahead.

In order to give a clear idea of what we had in mind for the opera, we included a memo, "Suggestions Toward Production," in the score:

> The Tender Land was conceived with an eye to modest production and intimate scale. These increase the effectiveness of the work and make presentation possible for smaller operatic groups. The sets should be poetic rather than naturalistic, simple rather than complex. Overdramatic lighting should be avoided. . . . The nature of the opera allows for varied treatment. Dialogue sections move naturally. . . . The dance should be rustic and "untrained." Spontaneity is important.

It was a very exciting time when the opera went into production with the New York City Opera Company. I had never had an experience like it before. Seeing The Tender Land on the stage, Aaron and I felt that it needed more dramatic tension in various areas. Because the premiere was in the opera house instead of the intimacy of the television screen, our

*original concept of a very small gentle work, to which Clurman had re-
sponded with his suggestions, did not really work. It needed things made
more explicit—things that we had in our heads but that weren't shown on
the stage. That was just our inexperience. Aaron's commission from the
League and the commitment of the City Center had made us go a little
faster with the production than we should have. We might have been able
to troubleshoot it a little more with more time.*

Many people who know the recording of scenes from The Tender Land
find it very meaningful, as I do. [12] *Aaron has such a strong lyric gift and
his lines sing. He really intended to do another opera; people wanted him
to do another; and I thought he should. It just didn't happen.*

In writing *The Tender Land,* I was trying to give young American singers
material that they do not often get in the opera house; that is, material
that would be natural for them to sing and perform. I deliberately tried
to combine the use of traditional operatic set pieces—arias, duets, choruses, etc.—with a natural language that would not be too complex for
young singers at opera workshops throughout the country. I wanted simple
rhetoric and a musical style to match. The result was closer to musical
comedy than grand opera. The music is very plain, with a colloquial flavor.
It is primarily diatonic, with dissonance used only in a few instances for
dramatic tension. The orchestration is not complex, nor does it call for
special effects.

The Tender Land and the *Dickinson Songs,* composed close together
in time, were different in intention. Both are recognizably mine, but they
are two different solutions to setting texts: The songs are discreet, intellectual; the opera, simple and folklike. *The Tender Land* is not the kind of
work to be pulled apart for study of its counterpoint and harmonies.
Besides, who cares about tearing an opera apart? It either functions, jells,
and works—or it doesn't!

I think of *The Tender Land* as being related to the mood of *Appalachian
Spring.* Both the ballet and the opera take place in rural America: one in
the southern Appalachians; the other in midwest farm country. Both make
use of folk materials to evoke a particular landscape in a real way. I adapted
several folk songs for inclusion in the opera, among them "Ching-a-Ring
Chaw" for the square dance number and "Zion's Walls" for the quintet
that closes Act I. A funny thing happened while I was working with
"Zion's Walls": I began to develop a countermelody of my own and

became more interested in my own tune than in the Revivalist one, and the piece ends up being more about my tune than the borrowed one.[13] A more direct arrangement of a folk tune in the opera is "I Was Goin' Acourtin'," sung by Top, one of the migrant workers.[14]

We did not write *The Tender Land* with the City Center in mind, but nevertheless, I was pleased to have it accepted for production there. The talented Thomas Schippers conducted the premiere (1 April 1954), and the cast included Norman Treigle (Grandpa Moss), Rosemary Carlos (Laurie), Jean Handzlik (Ma Moss), John Crain (Martin), Andrew Gainey (Top), and Adele Newton (Beth). Jerry Robbins accepted the job of staging the opera, his first work outside of dance. Oliver Smith, who had designed *Rodeo* and was to have done *Tragic Ground,* designed the set. John Butler was choreographer and Jean Rosenthal was lighting designer.

The Tender Land was in two acts with two scenes in Act II. The total duration was about an hour and a half. After two years of work, I had an opera that absorbed only two-thirds of an evening. It was necessary to fill out the program. For the premiere, my opera was followed by Menotti's already very successful short opera *Amahl and the Night Visitors.* It was a rather odd combination! As though foreseeing the future, Clurman's good-luck telegram read, "Hope this is a smash and runs at least five performances." The first-night audience must have been a houseful of friends, for despite what seemed like an enthusiastic reception, the reviews were not good. Olin Downes of *The New York Times* criticized the libretto and the second act, describing the ending as "inconclusive and unconvincing." He found the roles of the women undefined and wrote that my music told the audience very little about their feelings and inner lives. As did other critics, Downes praised the production and some of the music, particularly the quintet and the love duet. *Time* magazine concluded: "*The Tender Land* is a step along the road to a full-evening opera." Obviously, this was not the opera the critics were waiting for me to write—if they *had* been waiting. On the other hand, B. H. Haggin wrote in *The Nation* (24 April 1954):

> I was struck first by the loveliness that was being achieved with the assured mastery one is always aware of in Copland's operation; then as the work continued, by the variety and unfailing adequacy for the dramatic purposes, the power when this was called for; and in the end by the rich profusion of the invention and elaboration.

I considered we had a flop on our hands and told Erik so. I am convinced that the conditions for the initial entry of a particular work into the world

A page from the revised version of *The Tender Land*, Act III, pre-orchestral score with pencil markings toward the orchestration.

© Copyright 1954 by Aaron Copland; copyright renewed. Boosey & Hawkes, Inc., Sole Publishers and Licensees.

of music have a great deal to do with its future. In this country, we put so much emphasis on premieres and reviews of first performances that it can take a long time and a terrific struggle to turn a negative first impression around, if that is possible at all. It is particularly unfortunate when it comes to complicated opera productions where first performances are seldom the most polished. I have often thought that opera companies should copy Broadway, with out-of-town openings and previews in New York before critics are allowed to get their hands on a piece.

I was not sorry to have a legitimate reason to leave town soon after the premiere of *The Tender Land*. (I had agreed to perform in my *Piano Quartet* for the International Society for Contemporary Music in Rome.) I traveled to Milan, Geneva, Zurich (where I conducted an all-Copland radio orchestra program), and London. Erik kept me posted. He wrote (24 April 1954), "After seeing the second performance I am sorry to tell you it was even rougher than the first, which is not surprising considering the lapse of a month and one brush-up rehearsal. I went backstage after, for which the singers were grateful. They had thought they'd been deserted."[15]

Erik, being younger and more energetic than I, was convinced that the opera was worth revising. He began suggesting changes. "What my mistake was," he wrote very honestly, "was not to more clearly develop relationships which were indicated, such as Laurie's 'feeling strange inside,' and her mother's resignation at the end. I'm certain that the motivations must come in the first act. That's what I'm working on." Erik got my enthusiasm going again: "Be prepared for lots of work after May 10th," he warned. After I returned from Europe, we worked on a revised version to be tried out at Tanglewood in August 1954. *The Tender Land* became a three-act opera, with more passion in the romance of Laurie and Martin and a more clearly focused ending. We moved some things around and added a new scene in Act I. The Tanglewood production was directed by Frederick Cohen, acting head of the opera department, with Frederic Waldman conducting.

At Tanglewood, *The Tender Land* fared little better with the critics. Jay C. Rosenfeld of *The Berkshire Eagle* wrote, "Copland can do better and must try again." However, the audience and the cast were enthusiastic and to this day, I have heard people who were at Tanglewood that summer say they were moved by the production. Erik and I were certainly more satisfied with the new version, which seemed closer to our original intentions.

223

The final revised version was presented by the Oberlin College opera workshop (20, 21 May 1955) under my supervision. I wrote about it to Jack Kennedy, who said, "Make changes now and try them out. . . . *This is your last chance!* You really should have the help of someone far more competent than Erik or I." With the exception of a few minor changes and more polishing, I felt *The Tender Land* was in its final form and ready for publication. I sent the published score to Richard Rodgers and received a cordial letter of thanks, but I never knew how he felt about the opera, or whether he and Oscar Hammerstein ever saw it.

Certain colleagues admired the opera. Arthur Berger, who had always been an outspoken supporter of my more austere works, surprised me with praise for *The Tender Land*. [16] And Israel Citkowitz wrote:

> The curiously tentative reception accorded *The Tender Land* tempts one to speculate still further on the cognoscenti vs. Aaron Copland. For, is not the opera house still another precinct for the sacred cow? I think Laurie is lovely. It's clear that we weren't dealing with Lulu or Lady Macbeth.

Bill Flanagan found much to his liking (5 May 1956):

> Someone will do this opera again in N.Y. and if the present regime of poisonous criticism dies off—or, better still, is shot to a man—it will be the success that it should be. I couldn't be convinced that there is a composer living who could move me as you do with the music of the mother's closing song.

Soon after the original premiere in 1954, I arranged an orchestral suite from *The Tender Land*. It does not represent a digest of the dramatic action of the opera, but it proceeds from the second act to the first in a three-movement sequence. The first movement, longer than the other two combined, is comprised of the introduction to Act II and the music of the love duet. The second movement is the lively square dance from Act II, and the last movement is the music of "The Promise of Living," the vocal quintet from the end of Act I. Fritz Reiner conducted the premiere of the suite, Chicago Symphony (10 April 1958). When I conducted it with the BSO in Boston (10–11 April 1959) and then New York (21 November), the reviews were far better than they had been for the opera. Even my conducting was praised, which led me to conduct the BSO for a recording in 1959 [Victor]. I prepared arrangements of "Stomp Your Foot" and "The Promise of Living" for chorus (sometimes used with the orchestral suite) [17] and for piano four-hands. "Laurie's Song" is arranged for high voice and piano.

The opera has been produced by various college opera programs through the years. [18] Bill Schuman, as president of Lincoln Center, had the unusual idea of presenting a full concert version of *The Tender Land* during the French-American Festival of 1965 (31 July). I conducted the New York Philharmonic and Norman Treigle sang the grandfather's part as he had in the premiere. From that performance, the recording of excerpts was made that brought *The Tender Land* more public recognition.

It was not until 1975 that *The Tender Land* was heard again in New York, mounted by the Bronx Opera Company at Lehman College. The Michigan Opera Theater of Midland, Michigan, produced the opera at the time of my eightieth birthday and invited me to conduct. The performance was televised and shown nationally on PBS. Unfortunately, what works for an audience in an opera house or theater may not work when a camera comes in close and shows a middle-aged male lead in the role of a very young fellow! The story seemed to lose all sense of reality in the television version.[19]

Surprisingly, it was a summer production in 1976 at Banff, Canada, that was most satisfying. It was a very modest affair with no orchestra and with amateur singers. Nevertheless, the opera seemed to work in a way that I had never seen before. It was very touching. The girl who sang Laurie was sweet and modest and fit the part beautifully. It brought tears to the eyes. I never would have expected I could have been moved that way by it. It all seemed so very real, and everybody seemed to have had the same reaction. It wasn't just myself being satisfied by renewed contact with my own opera.

Murry Sidlin, conductor of the New Haven Symphony, had admired *The Tender Land* for some time and wondered why it was not heard more. In 1985, Sidlin asked whether he could reorchestrate the score in a thirteen-instrument arrangement for a revival of the opera by the Long Wharf Theatre in New Haven, Connecticut.[20] I responded to Sidlin's request (17 May 1986): "I think it is a very good idea, from a creative as well as a practical point of view." Long Wharf Theatre director Arvin Brown was enthusiastic. With Brown as director and Sidlin as musical director,[21] *The Tender Land* was given over fifty performances in the spring of 1987.[22] Brown returned to my original two-act form, and he and Sidlin included two songs from my *Old American Songs* in the party scene of Act II: "Zion's Walls" and "Long Time Ago." When I saw a matinee performance, I thought it worked like a charm! Erik Johns accompanied me, and he remembered every word he had written. At first, we missed the full orchestra sound, but then we agreed that Sidlin's version worked exceedingly well.[23] After the performance, when Arvin Brown announced

Photograph by Charles Erickson.

Discussing the 1987 Long Wharf Theatre production of *The Tender Land* (left to right): Copland, Vivian Perlis, Arvin Brown, and Murry Sidlin.

that we were in the audience, everyone stood and cheered while we took our bows. Later, we greeted the cast onstage. These talented young musicians had been living with our work constantly for months. One by one, they came up to see us, and it was clear by the look in their eyes what *The Tender Land* meant to them.

When Erik and I were writing the opera, we had great trouble naming it. When we finally settled on *The Tender Land,* I wrote to Esther and Arthur Berger (9 December 53): "How you like? I've had good reactions to it—so I hope you both approve. It's worse than naming a baby." I was well satisfied with the name and never thought it would be so adaptable to changes. The BSO players sometimes refer to my opera as "The Tender Gland"; and I have received several amusing fan letters: One praises "The Tender City"; another is addressed "To the composer of 'The Tender Hand.'" But the best is the letter that arrived in 1987 referring to the "Tenderloin Suite."

226

New Horizons,
New Sounds

1954-1957

Nadia Boulanger's 1953 birthday greetings included a request for two songs: "Next year is my fiftieth of teaching. This would be a 'commission' had I the funds. . . . But we are very poor, every year a deficit. . . . Therefore, it is *a present* I am expecting. . . ." I responded, "Of course, of course, I shall write the two songs you ask for as a *petit cadeau—microscopic cadeau* is a better word—for such a fifty years. (Fifty? Impossible!)" I heard from Nadia again (May 1954): "This is not to hurry you, but my eagerness to receive your songs cannot be misunderstood. Your music means so much to me, since the old far-gone days when one could see come to light a *real* composer, even at the very first steps. . . . I am impatient as when one expects a child in a house!" I wrote one song and sent it off in June with an explanation: "Because of revisions in my opera, which must be ready for a Tanglewood production this summer, I was not able to compose more than one song. I hope you will like it, and that it sings well."

The text for Nadia's song, "Dirge in Woods," is by George Meredith. It is for soprano and piano and of about three and one-half minutes duration. "Dirge in Woods," performed first in Paris during the summer of 1954, had its New York premiere in a recital of American music by Adele Addison at Carnegie Recital Hall (28 March 1955). The concert was sponsored by the recently merged League/ISCM. "Dirge in Woods" is not so grim as one might think from the title. As critic Ross Parmenter wrote, "Its mood is hardly sad. Rather, the feeling is one of serene acceptance. . . . The vocal line is long and floating and the piano accompaniment ripples gently under it." Of Adele Addison, Parmenter said, "She sang this and the four other American songs in a quiet and rapt rendition such as few contemporary songs have the luck to receive." Adele included "Dirge in Woods" in several programs after the premiere, but I cannot say that the song has been taken up by other singers.[1]

When the League of Composers' board decided to merge with the U.S. Chapter of the International Society for Contemporary Music in 1954, I was not at all convinced that it was worth continuing under such an arrangement. I felt that the organization had served its purpose well for many years and that perhaps it was time for other groups to take over. However, mine was not the majority opinion. The League/ISCM was established, with headquarters in New York and chapters and juries in various cities around the world. Former board members were invited to stay on the board, such as Roger Sessions, who had been active in the ISCM, and Claire Reis, who continued to work on various committees.

David Walker, who had become my assistant in 1952, went up to Tanglewood with me in 1954. He stayed in Lenox and was given the job of organizing the Sunday night Composers Forum Concerts, acting as general liaison between the composition department and the administration. David also helped with *The Tender Land* production in August. Lenny B., who had been promising to stay away from Tanglewood for a summer, finally did. The place did not seem the same without him.[2] Lenny wrote from Martha's Vineyard, where he and Felicia had a house (29 July):

> I miss you. That's the long and the short of it. I don't miss Berlioz or the crowds or the pewpils or the scenery or the meetings on the green, green furniture of Seranak, or even the hot crowded Sunday forums. I miss you, ecco. And Lukas.

Ingolf Dahl had written to me the previous November: "I have to make a choice of either getting my orchestra piece for Louisville written or coming back to Tanglewood." As a composer, I was sympathetic to the problem, but it seemed a shame to interrupt the successful launching of the Tanglewood Study Group so soon. Lukas Foss took over as acting head, and, along with his composing duties, did a terrific job with the TSG.

Ernst Toch shared the composition department with me. Toshi Ichiyanagi and Jack Kennedy returned in my group; Barney Childs and Jack Gottlieb were among my new students.[3] Teaching, lecturing (I spoke on Berlioz), preparations and rehearsals for *The Tender Land,* and Leo's [Smit] performance of the *Piano Concerto* with the BSO (18 July) kept me hopping all summer. I have been asked whether I ever took a vacation that did not have to do with music-making. The idea had always seemed boring to me; but after the schedule of Tanglewood 1954, I did enjoy a brief trip to see Martha's Vineyard, Nantucket, and Newport.

Returning to Ossining refreshed, I tackled some of the things that had been left unattended during preparations for *The Tender Land,* such as lectures for Smith and Amherst colleges and a Town Hall Forum with the musicologist and *Herald Tribune* critic Paul Henry Lang. By November, I was off again to Caracas, Venezuela, for the First Latin American Festival of Contemporary Music. I arrived there to find a very lively scene: Chávez, Varèse, Villa-Lobos, Juan José Castro, Virgil Thomson, plus five of my ex-Tanglewood students.

Within two and a half weeks, forty symphonic compositions from seven Latin American countries were performed in a series of eight concerts. It was a major effort for all concerned, especially the courageous musicians of the Orquesta Sinfonica Venezuela. A prosperous oil economy was being enjoyed, and the festival reflected the Venezuelan largesse. Three prizes totaling twenty thousand dollars were offered for symphonic pieces. They went to Castro, Chávez and Orbón. Villa-Lobos and Chávez confirmed their reputations as leaders of Latin American composition. It was my opinion that the program planners had overemphasized the folklore side of Latin American music. As I pointed out in an article in *The New York Times* (26 December 1954,) a few gripes were in order: Chile was inadequately represented; Guarnieri from Brazil was absent, as was the young Chilean Juan Orrego-Salas. Most of all, one missed an experimental note. Of dodecaphonic music, there was not a trace. But all in all, the Festival was a great success and Caracas was already planning another for 1957.

I returned to the States just in time to see Martha Graham and her Company dance *Appalachian Spring* in the full orchestra version conducted by Ormandy in Philadelphia. Back in Ossining, from December 1954 to April 1955, between various lecture, writing, and conducting assignments, I composed a work commissioned for the opening of the new Kresge Auditorium at MIT. I had started to collect some ideas while in Caracas, but now I was pressed for time. I began looking through my notebook and files for something I might use. I came across sketches for a choral work made in 1949 utilizing the lines "Let us now praise famous men, and our fathers that begat us. . . ."[4] These famous biblical words intrigued me, as they had James Agee and Walker Evans, who titled their book *Let Us Now Praise Famous Men*. I used the text and my musical sketches of 1949 as the basis for my new piece for chorus and orchestra.

Canticle of Freedom is fourteen minutes long, and, as I wrote to Victor, "It makes a big noise." I joked about the title to Irving Fine: "Maybe I'll call it 'Inauguration Overture,' and dedicate it to Rep. Busbey!" I wrote to Lenny about it, too (3 April 1955): "It's called *Canticle of Freedom*. Sounds subversive, no?" Lenny responded from Italy, where he was conducting at La Scala:

It's good to hear that you have a new piece. That's always an occasion for me. *Canticle of Freedom*, though: I thought we had had that era. But this sounds well for the times: A new interpretation can be laid on it. I'm eager to hear it.

The premiere was conducted by the director of music at MIT, Klaus Liepmann, with the Institute's chorus and orchestra at the Kresge Auditorium (8 May 1954). Before leaving for a six-month stay in Europe, I went up to Cambridge for a rehearsal. I inwardly despaired of Liepmann getting results from the forces with which he had to work, even though, knowing the limitations of a nonprofessional chorus, I had confined myself to two-part choral writing and to introducing the chorus only in the final third of the work.

Canticle of Freedom is scored for normal-sized orchestra, with percussion instruments requiring five performers. It is in two main sections: an orchestral prelude followed by a choral portion with orchestral accompaniment. The first part, mainly for brass and percussion, presents the principal melodic material, heard first in imitative fashion in the woodwinds; it concludes with a full orchestral statement of the main material as it appears again later with the chorus added in the final coda. A transition, using chords from the introduction, leads to the choral finale, which brings the materials of the first part to an intense climax.

The first New York performance of *Canticle* was conducted by Lenny Bernstein with the Symphony of the Air (formerly the NBC Symphony) and the Schola Cantorum at Carnegie Hall (9 November 1955). At the rehearsal I attended, the piece seemed to have no conviction; the playing and singing were very tentative because the performers had no chance to familiarize themselves with the music. It was obvious that Lenny had cut the rehearsal time for my work in favor of Mahler's *Resurrection Symphony*. I told him so and threatened not to go to the performance—and didn't. David Diamond was shocked when I wrote to him about it: "AAAAAARON! Not you!"

Critics reviewed *Canticle of Freedom* as a *pièce d'occasion*, which it was. I meant to revise the piece, and when Robert Shaw asked me for a piece to open the 1967–1968 Atlanta Symphony season, I offered him a revision of *Canticle of Freedom*. The revisions were made only in the orchestral introduction; the choral finale was kept intact. Shaw conducted the premiere (19 October 1967). In addition to the revised version, an arrangement of the choral finale with piano accompaniment is available.[5]

I was feeling the need for a change. For whatever reasons, perhaps the McCarthy business and the disappointing reception of *The Tender Land*,

I seemed to be having what writers call a "block." I could not seem to move ahead with the fast sections of the piano piece. Instead, I worked on lectures and articles: One was a response to musicologist Henry Pleasants, who had come to the conclusion that modern music, with the exception of jazz, was finished. *The New York Times* magazine published an article giving both sides of the story: Pleasants on "Modern Music: 'A Dead Art' '"; Copland on "Modern Music: 'Fresh and Different.' '"[6] I still could not make headway on the piano piece, so I decided to take the break from Tanglewood that I had been promising myself. I planned a six-month trip to Europe, from April through September 1955.[7]

My friends Bob Cornell, Jack Kennedy, and Victor saw me off at the airport. The first stop was Monaco, where I was on the Olympic Hymn Jury at Monte Carlo (18–25 April). Nadia presided over eight representatives from European countries and myself.[8] She seemed her old self—energetic and running the show at age sixty-eight. Nadia did most of the jury work, reading through 389 scores, of which very few were from American entrants. We were all invited to lunch at the palace—quite a show! There were twenty-six guests, pictures of ancestors on the walls, and Prince Pierre himself was host—a nice youngish fellow, seemingly working hard at his job.

I spent all of May in Paris and wrote in my travel diary, "Everything seems the same as in the twenties except for the traffic and the prices—both of which horrifies an old Parisian resident like me." I stayed in my old *quartier* and kept running into people I knew—Gerald Sykes and his wife Buffie—and Clurman came over from London for a reunion. He couldn't understand why I was spending my time correcting proofs for *The Tender Land:* It aggravated him that I would do such a thing while in Paris! I visited the Musique Concrète studios, which did not seem to have made much progress since I was there last—the same few composers using the same methods. I went to the Paris Opéra with Marcelle de Manziarly to hear a concert in which *Old American Songs* were sung by Warfield, conducted by Ormandy. I noted, "Marcelle was very taken with my orchestration. I rather liked the way it sounded myself." Before leaving Paris, I conducted the Radiodiffusion orchestra in an all-Copland concert, which included the *Third Symphony.* At the end of May, I made a brief but hectic trip to Milan to see Lenny, who was conducting there, and searched in vain for a place to rent at Lake Garda for the summer.

Jack Kennedy met me in London as planned. I gave two BBC talks and conducted the complete ballet version of *Appalachian Spring* twice with the BBC Orchestra. Jack and I attended the opening of a play Clurman was directing, and then we left London for the the ISCM Festival at Baden-Baden. I noted:

> Of all the music, the Schoenberg Var. Op 31 left the strongest impression. Boulez' *Le Marteau Sans Maître* has striking sounds and peculiar rhythms (nonrhythms would describe it better). I worked hard to get him one of the prizes—but lost out in the end.

I bought a German Ford, and Jack and I drove south in it through Switzerland and into mid-France. We had no luck in finding a villa in Aix-en-Provence, so we continued on to the Riviera and there found a beauty of a place in the hills above Cannes in the small town of Le Cannet. The villa, "L'Orangerie," had two pianos, a cook, a car, and a distant view of the Mediterranean. I wrote to Victor, "Now! Let's see if it brings forth some music." I was finally able to move ahead nicely on the piano piece and wrote again to Victor, saying, "If it turns out well, it should be one of my best things."

I thought about Tanglewood and wrote to Olga Koussevitzky to find out how things were going without me (16 July 1955): "I will be here 'til Aug. 31. How's the Tanglewood season shaping up? Has anyone noticed yet that I am not there??" Olga responded (August 21), ". . . we all missed you at Tanglewood—the season was most successful. . . . Roger Sessions was delighted with and excited by the spirit of Tanglewood, and, I think, put his heart into the task you left him to carry out." (Roger was taking my place as the American composer; Boris Blacher was the visiting European.)

We left France for Venice and a delightful visit with Gian Carlo Menotti and Tommy Schippers. Then on to Munich. Jack left to return to New York. Paul Moor was in Munich and he showed me around and took photographs while I was conducting the orchestra. I listened to tapes of music by Hartmann [Karl Amadeus] and Henze [Hans Werner] and was impressed with Hartmann, but Henze put me off. I wrote, "Henze is generally thought of as the white hope of young German music. This tells more about the state of German music than about Henze."

I conducted eleven different works with five orchestras in five weeks—Munich, Baden-Baden, Helsinki, Stockholm, and Oslo. The most enjoyable was the *Short Symphony* in Baden-Baden. I was beginning to feel out of the amateur class as far as conducting was concerned. Helsinki was an odd experience because for the first time ever I couldn't talk to the orchestra at all, except in translation. I gave radio talks, newspaper interviews (which I found frustrating because I couldn't read them), and played chamber music—my *Violin Sonata* three times with three different violinists in three different languages.

In Baden-Baden, I heard radio tapes of the enfant terrible of young music—Karlheinz Stockhausen. I wrote my impressions in my diary:

> It seems to me pointless to have an opinion about this sort of music—it is just too soon. Stockhausen is starting music again from the beginning—with notes strewn about like member disjecta. There seemed an end to continuity in the old sense and an end of thematic relationships. In this kind of music, one waits to hear what will happen next without the slightest idea of what will happen, or why what happened did happen once it has happened. Stockhausen's only chance is to mesmerize the listener. No one knows where it will go, and neither do I.

In Helsinki, I gave a talk for a mixed group of Finns and Americans, recorded my *Violin Sonata* with an excellent local violinist, and played the *Piano Variations* for a radio broadcast. Tapes of recent Finnish music were very disappointing. I wrote, "The Finns are rather backward in music, and I suspect that the figure of Sibelius, who is still alive, is overimposing." The boat to Stockholm went through a series of lakes, and then the city appeared at the end of all that inland water. It was more inviting than Helsinki. A nice surprise was to find the Juilliard Quartet there! The American Embassy invited me to a party for them. I rehearsed and recorded the *Clarinet Concerto* with Ib Erikkson, and feeling more confident about my conducting, I did Ives' *Unanswered Question* and felt that it went very well.

In Copenhagen, my lecture at the Royal Conservatory had a very thin audience—no students whatever! The interest in new music was very faint, although they had the best orchestra in Scandinavia. I played the *Dickinson Songs* with a singer at an ISCM concert to a small but enthusiastic audience, as well as the *Piano Quartet* and *Violin Sonata*. When I heard Carl Nielsen's music from recordings, I recognized an original mind who thought his own thoughts and I wrote, "What a tragedy that Koussevitzky had not gotten to know his work!"

In Oslo, I found the Norwegian Symphony better than expected: We did *Lincoln Portrait* in Norwegian, *Outdoor Overture*, and *Quiet City* without difficulty. I received compliments on my conducting from the local conductor. I wrote to Victor (6 October 1955):

> This reminds me very much of my two South American tours. I hope the traces I leave are as lasting. Everyone has been very nice and sort of took the attitude

that I was honoring them with my visit. In the four main towns, the composers' societies gave me a dinner or lunch—and I said "skol" until I was blue in the face explaining shamefacedly that I'm not much of a drinker. The Norwegians are even worse than the Finns, I think—aquavit, red wine, cognac, and beer all at the same meal, and "skol" by golly, every time.

Victor had returned from Guatemala and was living in Brooklyn, but he made trips out to Shady Lane Farm to keep track of the house and to run the Buick once in a while. David Walker sent important mail on to me. There were three offers for movies: I turned one down because of the script—*Alexander the Great* did not appeal to me, nor did William Wyler's film about the Quakers, *Friendly Persuasion* (it seemed to falsify Quaker ideas as I understood them). I decided to terminate my arrangement with MCA and sign with the William Morris Agency for theatrical contracts and with Arthur Judson for conducting. As a starter, Judson got me a contract ($1,250) for a concert at the Ravinia Festival the following summer. It was about this time I began to realize that I might make good money conducting.

Shady Lane Farm looked grand after six months of traveling! I returned just as a new biography of me was published. It was by Julia Smith and called, not surprisingly, *Aaron Copland.* Julia had been in touch with me since about 1945, when as a young composer and graduate student at New York University, she chose me as her topic for a thesis for the degree of Doctor of Music. We met several times: Julia asked the questions and I responded. I was amazed when she told me that she had also been a pupil of my teacher Rubin Goldmark! Julia worked hard on her thesis, and when it was finished and accepted, she prepared it for publication in book form by E. P. Dutton. Julia Smith's *Aaron Copland* is more a biography than a technical presentation of my music. In that respect particularly, it differs considerably from Berger's book of 1953. Both books have been helpful, each in its own way, in supplying information to the public about my music. I was certainly pleased when, on 30 November 1955, Julia Smith met me at the Harvard Club and presented me with the first published copy of her *Aaron Copland.*

My plan was to stay home from October 1955 to January 1956. I had to get right to work on the revision of the *Symphonic Ode,* commissioned by the Koussevitzky Foundation for the seventy-fifth anniversary of the BSO, to be celebrated with a concert conducted by Munch in Boston (3 February 1956). Koussevitzky had introduced the *Symphonic Ode* twenty-five years earlier. It was a work he had admired. For the new version, the shape and character of the piece remained the same, but the size of the orchestra was reduced and notational changes of the difficult rhythms were made.[9] At the time of the premiere of the revised *Ode*, I was on a conducting and lecturing tour that took me to Washington, San Francisco, Vancouver, and Chicago. Irving Fine sent me the reviews, even though they were awful. The critics' reception for the New York performance that followed was not much better. I wrote to the Fines, "I'm sorry to say the N.Y. performance of the piece was sort of stiff and unconvincing. I guess Munch got self-conscious. Oh well—publication is assured, so it's in the hands of the gods. But I sure do wish I could hear it conducted by an American." (I conducted the *Ode* myself with the New York Philharmonic in June 1980.)

In the spring of 1956, I received two special honors. At the annual May ceremonial of the American Academy and Institute of Arts and Letters, I received the Gold Medal in Music, presented by Virgil Thomson.[10] In June, I became a Doctor of Music for the first time with the honorary degree conferred on me by Princeton University. I felt highly honored. Between conducting and lecture assignments, I was working to finish the piano piece. I had to put it aside again to write a few overdue articles on American music: one for *The Washington Post*, another for *Musical Courier*, and a third for the Associated Press.[11] I was told that the AP piece would be "put on the wires" with a photograph on Sunday, 15 July, and that I would have 47 million potential readers! How could I resist?

David Walker came out to Shady Lane Farm regularly to help with all the paper work and correspondence. Being a composer himself, David knew his way around scores and parts—sometimes I even asked him to write parts out for me.[12] As time went on, David became my loyal and indispensable assistant. He helped organize all my manuscripts and files and is the the most knowledgeable person about my scores and my musical activities. David has composed his own music through the years, never talking much about it. I was amazed when in 1979 I attended a concert in Greenwich Village entirely of music by David Walker!

David went up to Tanglewood with me in 1956. I was surprised (and relieved) to see how little the Music Center had changed—everything seemed the same as when I had left in 1954. I still stayed in the barn in Richmond and had my meals with Verna and Irving Fine and their three girls. Most of the regular faculty returned to the Center.[13] The composition department was the largest ever, with four in faculty: Goffredo

Petrassi from Italy, Lukas, Irving, and myself. Among us, we taught twenty-three students.[14]

One major difference sparked a fresh and lively atmosphere: the involvement of philanthropist Paul Fromm, a successful wine and liquor importer and merchant from Chicago, originally from Germany. Fromm had a passion for contemporary music. Just the man we needed! He had set up a foundation in 1952 to assist the performance of contemporary music and to commission new works. Paul Fromm had written to me (17 February 1956), saying, "You can plan boldly since we do not intend to sponsor contemporary music in economy size over the thrift counter." The Fromm Foundation's two concerts of "modern chamber music" took place on Monday evenings in July in the Theater-Concert Hall with members of the BSO. Four Fromm-commissioned works were played.[15] Enthusiasm ran high; Fromm was so pleased that he promised to continue his support. It was a big step forward for contemporary music. We began to talk about adding a seminar to the contemporary concerts the next season.

The BSO presented my revised *Symphonic Ode* and *First Symphony* as a continuing celebration of the seventy-fifth anniversary of the orchestra. But the event everyone was talking about in the summer of 1956 was Lukas' opera, *Griffelkin*. Friends invited themselves up the first weekend in August to hear it, among them were Erik Johns and Jack Kennedy, and I played host. Unfortunately, *Griffelkin* was not an immediate success.

After Tanglewood, Jack Kennedy and I drove up the Maine coast, after visiting Sam Barber in Nantucket. I played some of my new piano piece for him, but I desperately needed some uninterrupted time to bring it all together. That meant the MacDowell Colony. From Peterborough, I wrote to Victor (19 September 1956), "If you're in the midst of new scenes and new faces, I'm in the midst of old ones. The Colony looks just like it always did, but the faces have changed. It's still as conducive to work as ever, and I am plugging away at my piano 'number,' as usual." After a few solitary weeks, I wrote to Verna, "This monster *must* be tamed!" I made headway at the Colony, but it was not until four months later that I inscribed the date of completion at the end of the last measure of my *Piano Fantasy:* "January 19, 1957."

The *Piano Fantasy* has a long history. Way back in 1951, Bill Schuman had offered a commission from the Juilliard for a work to be premiered during an American Music Festival in celebration of the school's fiftieth anniversary. I had responded to Bill's request (22 July 1951): You sure are a planner—to be thinking about 1954–1955 in 1951. But the idea sounds *grand.* I know what I'd like to do—and the next time I see you I'll discuss it with you. But it needs a text." At that time, I had in mind a choral piece, a kind of cantata, and I was thinking about Walt Whitman (as I had before when composing the *Dickinson Songs*).[16] I made some sketches using sections from *Leaves of Grass,* but occupied as I was with *The Tender Land* in 1952 and 1953, I proceeded no further. In 1953, I received a letter from Bill (17 June): "This note is by way of a gentle, friendly, but firm nudge." I took out the sketches and made a few attempts to move the cantata along, but it soon became clear that the idea was not working. When I had Bill's go-ahead to submit a different type of work for the Juilliard commission, I began to think about the piano piece I had been composing since the early fifties.

I had developed some material for a concerto for William Kapell to play with the Louisville Symphony Orchestra. The commission fell through, but as I wrote to Victor from Italy (28 February 1951), "Perhaps I will do a big piece for piano alone. I have material for it that tempts me—a kind of Fantasy or something." Then Willy Kapell died in an airplane crash, 29 October 1953. I wrote to his wife, Anna Lou:[17]

> When William died he was expecting a new piano work from my pen. It was a promise I had gladly given him. It is a promise I intend to keep, and when the work is written I can only hope that it will be worthy of the best in William Kapell.

The Juilliard anniversary seemed an ideal occasion for the premiere of the *Piano Fantasy* to be dedicated to William Kapell. Bill Schuman suggested a performance date during the American Festival in the spring of 1956. I made some progress on the piece while on my six-month trip to Europe in 1955. I had written to Chávez about it from the Park Lane Hotel in London:

> I have been battling with the piece. It is, as we say, a very hard nut to crack! The no repetitions and no formulas makes the piece hard to get hold of. By the time I have figured out the notes, I cannot hear the music. I have to be inside and outside of the work at the same time—lost in it yet watching the composition being led.

I heard again from Bill Schuman (22 November 1955):

> My great pleasure in seeing you again perhaps covered up my genuine disappointment in learning that there is some question about your piece for the Festival. Surely, as one of your great admirers I would not want you to rush the composition and run the hazard of premature birth. But—couldn't you stop all

your other activities, such as baton wielding, lecturing, and committee trotting. Stick to the farm, work long hours and eat Wheaties. Just to make you feel worse, I told the entire faculty that we confidently expected your piece. We will hold up the final copy of our program until December 15 when you should be in a position to know more. As things now stand, your work is scheduled for Monday, February 20. With so much time, I refuse to be discouraged. Just make believe that JSM is MGM and you'll finish.

I was having trouble with the *Fantasy,* particularly the fast sections. To put it plainly, I was stuck! There was nothing to do but take a forced hiatus with the hope that my ideas would be fresh when I returned to it. It was important to me to have a sense of not repeating myself, sorry as I would be to disappoint Bill and the Juilliard. I asked to postpone until late spring and received another of Bill's "gentle but firm" notes (20 January 1956): "Spring begins on March 21 and your work will not be performed until April. I hope you will consider that this is reasonably late spring." But the piece was still not finished—spring and summer came and went and so did Juilliard's American Festival and the date of its fiftieth anniversary. It was the month of September 1956 at the MacDowell Colony when I began to feel the *Piano Fantasy* really begin to come together. When I finally sent the score off to Bill Schuman in February 1957; it had been almost six years after the commission was first offered! Bill wrote (12 March 1957):

> I immediately took it home and placed it next to my writing desk. This was a fatal error. . . . I was in the position of having ten minutes of music to compose in less than a week. And, blast you, in every moment of weakness I would put down my pen and take up your *Piano Fantasy.* Clearly, it is a major Copland work, which is another way of saying, an important addition to music's literature.

Since I had missed the date for which the *Piano Fantasy* was commissioned, Bill arranged a special concert for its presentation (still in honor of Juilliard's fiftieth anniversary) to take place 25 October 1957. Lucky for me that the president of Juilliard was a composer!

I was invited to write an article for *The New York Times* at about the time of the premiere of the *Fantasy,* [18] and I was grateful for the opportunity to explain certain aspects of this particular work as it related to my career. I was well aware that I had become typecast as a purveyor of Americana in music. I knew this was not the whole story, or even the best of the story. I wrote:

Juilliard School of Music

cordially invites you to attend the world premiere of

Aaron Copland's

"PIANO FANTASY"

on Friday evening, October 25, 1957, at 8:30 o'clock
in the Juilliard Concert Hall.

This work, commissioned by Juilliard on the occasion
of its fiftieth anniversary, will be performed by William
Masselos. The "Piano Fantasy" is the sole work on this
program and will be repeated following an intermission.

R.S.V.P.
on the enclosed card.

William Masselos and Copland in the CBS recording studio, New York, 1957.

A composer in our time is comparatively helpless as to the picture of himself that will be presented to the listening public. Commercial exploitation of serious music is by definition plugging the "well known." By and large, performances are restricted to a narrow list of one's most accessible works, and this restriction often obtains in concert and broadcast performances.

As my *Piano Variations* of 1930 and *Piano Sonata* of 1939, the *Piano Fantasy* belongs in the category of absolute music.[19] It makes no use whatever of folk or popular musical materials. My purpose was to suggest the quality of fantasy; that is, a spontaneous and unpremeditated sequence of 'events' that would carry the listener along, while at the same time exemplify clear, if somewhat unconventional, structural principles. To give free rein to the imagination without loss of coherence—to be "fantastic" without losing one's bearings—is venturesome, to say the least. Yet a work of art like the *Piano Fantasy* seems to me the ideal proving ground for just such a venture.

I wrote in the program notes for the first performance that the musical framework of the entire piece is based upon a sequence of ten different tones of the chromatic scale. To these are joined, subsequently, the two unused tones of the scale, related throughout as a kind of cadential interval. Thus inherent in the materials are elements able to be associated with the twelve-tone method and also with music tonally conceived. To describe a composer as a twelve-toner, I felt, was much too vague. The *Piano Fantasy* is by no means rigorously controlled twelve-tone music, but it makes liberal use of devices associated with that technique. It seemed to me at the time that the twelve-tone method was pointing in two opposite directions: toward the extreme of total organization with electronic applications, and toward a gradual absorption into what had become a very freely interpreted tonalism. My use of the method in the *Piano Fantasy* was of the latter kind.

I decided not to play the first performance of the *Fantasy* myself, as I had with the *Variations* and the *Sonata*—my friend Lawrence Morton was right on the mark when he said it was too hard for me! I had to practice whenever I played the *Variations,* but as I admitted to Ben Britten when writing to him about the new piece, "The *Fantasy* is quite beyond me." William Masselos, a Juilliard alumnus and one of the most talented young pianists around, was unusually committed to the performance of contemporary American music. He had been responsible for the premieres of several outstanding American works, Ives' *First Piano Sonata* and pieces by Ben Weber, for example. Masselos was without doubt the choice pianist for the premiere of my *Piano Fantasy,* and I was delighted when he agreed to do it. After hearing Bill play through the piece one day while he was testing pianos in Steinway's basement, I really got excited: Masselos was a composer's dream.

William Masselos[20]

I started doing American music in 1939 at my debut. There were the Copland Variations *and the Griffes* Sonata. *When I started working on the* Piano Fantasy *in 1957, I fell in love with the piece. It's a wonderful addition to the big contemporary piano literature, in a Lisztian–Copland style. We performers need big works, ones that can be performed in Carnegie Hall, and this is certainly one of them. It seems to me an "American" piece—very open-faced and through-and-through Copland.*

It is the work, of all I have played, that needs the most carefully chosen piano. I put all my body weight into the beginning, into the announcement of the first ten notes of that row. Some of the newer pianos become shocked, jarred by that. There's something that happens—they get paralyzed and there's no sound. I would go to the Steinway basement to see the technician, Bill Hupfer, and say "I need a Copland piano again." He understood what that meant—a piano I could really lean into that would take the thrust. It meant a riper, older piano, one that could take a slugging, particularly in the bass, a piano that's almost ready to go to the piano hospital, one that's in the autumn of its existence, before it gets rehammered. Number fifty-five was like that for a while. That was one of my favorites for Copland's Piano Fantasy.

When I was learning the piece, I asked Aaron to tell me more about it. He said that the row is announced in the first ten notes, and that he'd saved the other two notes for special occasions. Then he said, "It's vaguely in three sections. You don't need to know any more." That's all I got. It wasn't that Aaron couldn't describe the Fantasy, *but he wanted me as the performer to have plenty of room for personal expression.*

I don't remember too much about the premiere.[21] I have always been a nervous kind of performer. But I remember that the program said "Aaron Copland, Piano Fantasy (World Premiere). Intermission. Aaron Copland's Fantasy." It was scary, because when I walked out onto the Juilliard stage, I saw that the audience was made up of practically all the great musicians in New York. You're relieved if you get through it the first time and then immediately have to wonder whether you can do it again! Somebody booed from the balcony. I am told it was Morton Feldman.[22] *Aaron took a bow with me at the end. In the year following the premiere of the* Fantasy, *I traveled fifty thousand miles just doing that piece. And I was the only guy who knew it. For a little while, the* Fantasy *was virtually my exclusive property. As I wrote to Aaron after the premiere, "Now I'm going to be jealous of everyone that plays it. It's my piece."*

I played the Fantasy *for the thirtieth anniversary concert of the Copland-Sessions Concerts (10 May 1958) and at the ISCM Festival in Strasbourg (June) to represent the United States. I even played it in a program of the National Catholic Music Educators Association. Most of the Fathers and Sisters loved the piece—at least, they seemed to—the ending sounds almost biblical. I recall playing it in Mexico City on a beautiful Hamburg Steinway; and for Nadia's seventieth birthday celebration in Washington.*

I recorded the Fantasy *in 1958 and wrote to Aaron, "I think I chose a dreamy piano (the one we used at Juilliard died of a broken plate). 'Course I'm shaking in my boots. Think of all the decisions I'll have to make alone. Recording piano in a studio is so different from a concert hall performance." It was not until 1960 that the record came out together with the* Variations *and then I learned the* Sonata *in time to play all three major works for Aaron's sixtieth birthday celebrations at Tanglewood and at Juilliard. These pieces are always part of me, so Aaron always feels close by, even when we do not see each other or write so often as we did for a while.*

The *Piano Fantasy* is a large-scale work in one movement. If you write a work such as this that lasts half an hour without pause, you would be foolish to imagine that everybody is going to love it—or play it every day. Just for a listener to be able to sit for one half hour, without letup, and connect in his mind what the composer began with from the first note through to where he comes out at the end, takes a considerable amount of concentration and musical sophistication. Such a composition is therefore by its nature not going to win over the kind of audience that a *Salón México* is able to attract. For the composer, a long and continuous one-movement form is one of the most taxing undertakings.

The *Piano Fantasy* was received as I hoped it would be: a serious major work. One always hopes that *The New York Times* review will be favorable. In this case, Howard Taubman seemed to have a good idea of what I was after. He wrote (26 October 1957):

AARON COPLAND
SHADY LANE FARM
OSSINING, NEW YORK

Next Day

Dear Bill:
         It was an 'occasion' —
it really was!
    I'm grateful as can be
for the way the whole evening
went off, and to your generous
part in it. (And I'll always
remember your excited letters
before the performance.) And
also thanks to the staff for
so ably aiding and abetting — the
program and the party and

even the bron was perfect.
So, here for once, is greetings
to you from one satisfied
composer!

         Best

         Aaron

JUILLIARD SCHOOL OF MUSIC

130 CLAREMONT AVENUE

NEW YORK 27, N. Y.

OFFICE OF THE PRESIDENT   October 28, 1957

Dear Aaron:

            What a charming note and what a
wonderful evening. It was just about the
happiest occasion ever. Accepting your
gracious comments about our efforts to
present the work in its proper setting before, after and during does not in any way
obscure the fact that it was your music
and only your music which made everything
else seem right. Please know that I
spent hours yesterday studying the score
while the sounds were still so fresh. This
work is for keeps.

            Affectionately,

            Bill

Mr. Aaron Copland
Shady Lane Farm
Ossining, New York

> The *Fantasy* . . . is one of Mr. Copland's most significant compositions. . . . This is an intensely serious work, but it is not forbidding. . . . He has given his imagination wide range, but a cultivated mind and ear have been in control of the selection and development of material. The listener who has any experience with the contemporary world of music and who gives his attention to Mr. Copland is carried along. This *Fantasy* has a largeness of scope that reminds one of the fantasies of Mozart and Schubert, though its idiom is a far cry from theirs.

Taubman went on to praise Masselos. He described the audience as one of the most knowledgeable that could be assembled in New York. "At the end of each performance it hailed composer and performer. There were a couple of boos from avant-gardists who regard Mr. Copland as an old conservative. They couldn't be more wrong." Irving Fine wrote after the premiere (30 October 1957): "I should imagine you must have mixed feelings about being referred to as the grand old master who can show those young whippersnaps a thing or two. We must have the *Fantasy* done up at Brandeis."

Among the many congratulatory notes received after the premiere was one from Anna Lou Kapell, which touched me deeply (19 October): "Willy would have been deeply moved and excited to carry your new *Piano Fantasy* about the world. It is a great privilege of which he was deprived. I was profoundly touched that you should have remembered him in this way. Thank You. Anna Lou."

Leo Smit soon learned the *Piano Fantasy* and gave the West Coast premiere in the Monday Evening Concerts series. Leo wrote (14 January 1958):

> It worked! Cheers, bravos, four calls etc. . . . Your telegram made me so happy. When I finished there was a stunned silence, then a long gasp . . . and finally the outburst. I was thrilled myself.

My friend Lawrence Morton (director of the concert series) wrote (13 January 1958):

> I would call the whole thing a triumph for both you and Leo. And a triumph for Monday Evening Concerts, too—as for myself, I have no words. But I congratulate you with all my heart for this, your "late Beethoven," and I rejoice that you have been able to deliver yourself of a work so tragic as this.

Later, he sent a few reviews:

> I send them with little pleasure. But this is the usual treatment we get for our concerts; we're eggheads. These critics would not be excited by the Crucifix-

ion—they'd say it was not original, too staged, and too stark—even if there were
background music by Tiomkin. But everybody who matters knows that the
Fantasy matters.

Among the pianists who have performed my *Piano Fantasy* are Noel Lee,
who played all three of my larger piano works at Hunter College (16
February 1966) and recorded the *Fantasy* and the *Sonata* in France
[Valois]; Andor Foldes; Joel Shapiro; Charles Fierro, who played and
recorded the *Fantasy* with other of my piano pieces [Delos]; and Shura
Cherkassky. Cherkassky wrote from France (22 May 1958) to ask for
advice about interpreting the work:

> I will play your *Piano Fantasy* everywhere next season. I am studying the work,
> and simply crazy about it. However, some markings, changes of tempi, etc. I
> do not quite understand . . . please be so kind as to drop me a line—your advice
> how to study it, a general outline. The more I practice it, the more I am
> becoming thrilled with this piece—it is the most unusual composition I have
> come across.

In 1965, Leo Smit presented a program in Buffalo, *Keyboard Masterworks
of Three Centuries,* on which he included my *Piano Fantasy.* When I was
there as visiting lecturer in Morton Feldman's class, Leo played my complete works for piano for the first time (1 June 1977), followed by the same
program at Harvard (2 November) and in New York at Carnegie Recital
Hall (5 November). In connection with the Harvard program, Leo interviewed me in front of an audience. An edited version of our talk appeared
in *Contemporary Keyboard* magazine and was reprinted on the record
jacket of Leo's *Aaron Copland: The Complete Music for Solo Piano,*
which was released by Columbia Records in 1979.

Leo Smit [23]

*I met Aaron for the first time in 1943 after he sent me a copy of the newly
published* Piano Sonata *in 1941. I played it for him at his sunny loft and
was surprised how he seemed to prepare himself for my performance, an-
ticipating a pleasurable experience. He stretched out on his couch, whereas
I thought surely he'd pull a chair up to my elbow and watch intently and
mutter all kinds of corrections and suggestions. But he didn't say a word.
I played through the entire* Piano Sonata. *Then he said that he liked
the way I "tasted" the harmonies and the chords, especially in the last*

movement. When I asked for suggestions, he again expressed his pleasure, his satisfaction. Didn't tell me anything. I was quite frustrated because I was seeking greater authenticity. I wanted some hot tips! He simply expressed his own philosophy—that he was more interested in the variety of performances rather than having everyone play his music the way he *thought it should go. That made a very deep impression on me.*

Earlier on, I had worked with Stravinsky, whose ideas were quite different, insisting on strict adherance to his score. But Aaron's way is a more lasting way, because that's the way it ultimately works. With Aaron's dynamics, there's wide margin for personal expression. That's what he's after; especially when it's done with power and conviction and technical backup. Aaron's very different from other composers in that respect. I've heard him express criticism all right, but only when an interpretation went beyond a certain margin—when it really changed the character of a piece.

The next wonderful event was the unveiling of Aaron's new Violin Sonata *at his loft. David Diamond played, and Harold Shapero, Elliott Carter, and Oliver Smith were there—quite a gathering of New York's finest. I played the curtain raiser—a piano transcription of a recently composed orchestral work of my own. Aaron took pleasure in introducing new talent—he was always on the lookout. After Aaron's* Violin Sonata *was performed, Shapero, known for his keen critical ear, sat down at the piano and went through the piece note by note, commenting all the way. Aaron pretended to be scared. He cried out, "Stop that. I didn't write it to be analyzed."*

Aaron introduced me to Lenny Bernstein in 1943, at Carnegie Hall, as I was hurrying backstage to turn pages for Béla Bartók. "You guys ought to know each other," Aaron sang out. Shortly after, I watched Lenny entertain a wildly adoring crowd at a Greenwich Village party, playing everything from El Salón México *to the latest Broadway show tunes—and singing all the words. At that moment, I knew he was going to "make" it big.*

Aaron was interested in my music. I played everything I wrote for him. He was concerned with receiving an overall impression before considering the details. He said to me once, "I like the turn of this cadence." My first ballet was composed in Aaron's loft, which I rented when he went off to Europe. I also made a piano arrangement of The Second Hurricane, *but he thought the music was too simple for concert performance, and he didn't sanction it. And I made a solo piano arrangement of* Danzón Cubano, *which no one has ever played, including me. It's too difficult, but it would*

Leo Smit and Copland, c. 1945.

be a wonderful program finisher. Aaron has very few pieces that end in a bravura style. You know I helped Aaron make the rehearsal records of Appalachian Spring *to send to Martha Graham. I stood behind Aaron as he sat and played the main parts, poking away at an inner part or a difficult run, filling out the score, thus approximating the full sound. At the end of the recording, Aaron said, "Martha, here is your ballet." Then he gave the date and said, "This recording was made with the assistance of Leo Smit."*

Don't be fooled when Aaron says, "Oh, did I do that?" He knew what he meant to say. An examination of his sketches, his work in progress, includes strong writing; the impression of the man was powerful in every way. Everything Aaron has written sounds as if it came out in a burst of joy, but actually he's a very slow, painstaking worker. I think it's because he's extremely critical about letting things through that he does not feel convinced of completely. His inner censor works on a very high level. Whereas, when the work is over, he relaxes his extremely fine critical faculties, except when he's writing an article. And how well those evaluations of other composers' music stand up with time.

Aaron's score markings are often unusual: "Crystalline," for example, is one of my favorites. [24] *"Crystalline" had a few chords to go with the word.*

Aaron built a whole vocabulary to correspond to certain emotions—such as "searing" had a certain harmony, with minor seconds. The kind of harmony you find in Night Thoughts *and in the* Piano Fantasy. *I remember Aaron playing the* Fantasy *for me and entire pages were simply incomprehensible in terms of the printed page, but when you realize the words that he used, such as "freely expressive," "hands go two different speeds," he really meant it—like a Beethoven crescendo—it goes and goes till it roars. "Uncertain" is one of the words Aaron uses. How do you monumentalize that or put that into concrete tones? Aaron explained: "Well, as* if *uncertain. I want* you *to be certain of uncertainness." Aaron's instructions to the performer in the* Fantasy *are so personalized that it's as though he was standing behind you looking over your shoulder. I know of no other work that is so filled with the physical presence of a composer. "Clangorous" is in there and "brooding." At one point, Aaron indicates—"right hand as background"—which sort of upsets the normal balance between the hands. "Heavy staccato" is one of my favorites, and "muttering" and "musingly." I asked Aaron about that one, and he said, "It suggests the sort of touch that will produce a kind of doodling effect. A toying with the note."*

I always admired Aaron's own piano playing because of the clarity with which he was able to convey the intent of his musical thought, without gorgeous tonal quality or brilliant technique. Yet the rhythmic drive, for one thing, had such an infectious quality of joy. It came out of his whole physical being. And his lonely melodies, the sense of isolation and the stopping of time. I thought his playing unique, extraordinary. I didn't mind the harshness of his tone. I'd rather have that than a crooning, "poetic" touch.

I played with Aaron once when we were in Rome in 1951. I brought over the Bach Chorale Preludes, *and we played them four-hands on his spinet. It was wonderful playing Bach with Aaron. He didn't often play classical music. After we played a particular prelude, "Herr Christ, der ein'ge Gottes-sohn," I heard him muttering to himself, "He's the best." A rare and precious bow to the great J.S. It sort of stopped me in my tracks. That particular chorale prelude wasn't one everybody would fall for right away. It had a plainness to it that appealed to him. It was in A major—*Appalachian Spring *key, and the intervals were mostly thirds. Aaron didn't talk much about composers. Mahler was definitely one of his favorites. He spoke about his orchestration and his liberating ideas. Once he said a beautiful thing about Wagner. Instead of putting him down, as so many French-trained musicians did, he said that he found a wholeness in every note and measure, and that Wagner sculpted his ideas. Fauré was one of Aaron's very* *favorites. He mentioned a Fauré song to me, "Diane Selene," the first time we met, and I dashed out and got it right away. Those strange intriguing harmonies. They don't go where they're supposed to. They had a kind of Aaronish quality, and I could understand their appeal to him.*

We had literary discussions, too. Aaron told me once that he read himself to sleep every night. He'd read mostly twentieth-century writers.[25] *He especially liked Gide. One day, he remarked how strange that I loved new music and old books. He referred to me as "a kind of Henry James of music." Isn't that nice? He was also pushing D. H. Lawrence then. To Aaron, Lawrence was a liberated writer exploring themes no one else had. I stuck to Tolstoy, Gogol, and Hawthorne.*

The first present I ever gave Aaron was a necktie. He said, "Beautiful. You can pick my ties anytime." I sensed the kind of quality, elegant but subdued. Not sporty, like Stravinsky, who was very daring, wearing polka dot bow ties and navy pea jackets. And Aaron's first present to me back in 1945 was the Harvard Historical Anthology of Music. *Very special.*

I have two Stravinsky stories about Aaron. I was riding in a taxi with Stravinsky and Joseph Fuchs in New York, and Joe said, "Copland is a very good American composer." Stravinsky immediately reacted and said, "Why American? He is a very good composer." I told that story to Aaron and he was tickled pink. At a party given by Lawrence Morton one wonderful afternoon in Los Angeles, Stravinsky, Aaron, Lukas Foss, Ingolf Dahl, myself, and a few others were all having lunch, including strawberries handpicked by Vera [Stravinsky]. Suddenly, out of the blue, Stravinsky raised his glass and offered a toast to Aaron. Aaron almost blushed, he was so pleased; and he was simply delighted that the old master paid him such a sincere compliment.

Aaron's personality, it seems to me, was expressed at the very outset with such power and conviction that even his twelve-tone music is completely his, completely original and not influenced by the atmospheric world of the modern Viennese masters. The emotional integrity has always been constant, and that's the symbol of his great musical power. That voice, the Mosaic voice. What a drive that man was consumed by from the very start—the confidence, the vision, the ambition! The first time I heard the opening of the Piano Concerto, *I thought of Moses blasting away on the mountaintop. How young he was and already filled with the confidence and the power of his own voice.*

I only heard Aaron say "Dear Leo" once at the end of our interview for Contemporary Keyboard. *So when you tell me that you have heard Aaron call me "Dear Leo" when I'm not around, I am very touched.*

I visit Aaron in Peekskill periodically. I went up to see him with Verna Fine in 1988. At lunch, Aaron began to sing to himself and then said with a laugh, "I wonder where that came from!" After lunch, somebody asked me to play, so I did, putting together a medley of Aaron's music, ending with the last pages of Appalachian Spring. *I played the ending very softly and Aaron cut in, "You left out the last three notes!" So I played them again, banging them out for him,* fortissimo, *and we all laughed like old times.*

Interlude IV

When William Masselos played Copland's *Piano Variations* and *Piano Fantasy* in a retrospective series at the Juilliard in 1960, the spotlight was turned on Copland as a composer of keyboard music. When Noel Lee played all three major piano works at Hunter College Playhouse in 1966, audiences knew that what Virgil Thomson had said in 1946 was true: "Copland has written his most expressive music for the keyboard."[1] Then, along came Leo Smit in 1977, playing all of Copland's solo piano works. Few composers have had the experience of hearing their entire output of piano music played by a talented and knowledgeable performer at a single concert. Pleased as he was, Copland expressed surprise that anyone *could* play all his piano music at one sitting. He exclaimed afterward, "I thought I'd written *more* than that!" Smit took his Copland show on the road, and more important, recorded it. *Aaron Copland: Complete Solo Piano Works,* released by CBS Masterworks before Copland's eightieth birthday, is a landmark in the composer's career, demonstrating a fifty-year span in which Copland made use of a wide range of compositional styles. The album makes Copland's entire piano output accessible and points to its dominant role in Copland's work as a whole.

Copland grew up with the piano; he never wanted to play another instrument. Just as other middle-class Jewish immigrant families at the turn of the century, the Harris Coplands viewed their piano as a symbol of culture. Copland was encouraged to play, and when he showed talent, the family was impressed that their youngest might aspire to the heights of professional concert pianist; not that anyone believed he might appear at Carnegie Hall, but a modest performing career or a teaching profession was within the realm of possibility. Even after he knew he wanted to be a composer, Copland continued to study piano. He was practical enough to realize he might need to make some money by playing piano. Also, he would need the piano for score reading, to demonstrate his works to

On the occasion of the release of *Aaron Copland, Complete Solo Piano Works* by Leo Smit, Columbia Records, 1979. (Left to right): producer Thomas Frost, Copland, and Smit.

potential performers and conductors, and to play the premieres of his own difficult solos. Copland had no illusions about his pianistic abilities and admits that one reason he gave up composing jazz-oriented works was because he was never able to improvise himself. However, from reports of those who heard him, and from recordings, Copland was more than a passably good pianist. Listening to a recording of the *Piano Variations* many years after it was made, Copland surprised even himself: "I can't believe I ever played it so fast!"

Copland's earliest attempts at composition were simple piano pieces, followed by songs and a few cello pieces with piano accompaniment. In some of the juvenile writings, glimmerings of the mature Copland can be detected, particularly as regards syncopated rhythms and percussive sonorities. He drew from ragtime and "salon" pieces that he heard when the family gathered around the piano in the evening for entertainment, and he never lost track of that tradition, composing short piano pieces throughout his career, which were meant to be played without great difficulty by nonprofessionals for entertainment or for study.

At nineteen and twenty, Copland took lessons from the renowned Rubin Goldmark. His studies culminated with a *Piano Sonata* (Goldmark would not allow the young Copland to leave for France until he had mastered sonata form).[2] When Copland began to compose instrumental works under Nadia Boulanger's tutelage, he included piano parts and continued to include them later on, sometimes giving the piano an unusual or unexpected solo passage.[3] Most of Copland's chamber music includes piano; furthermore, the keyboard is an equal partner rather than mere accompaniment. In fact, the *Violin Sonata*'s full title is *Sonata for Violin and Piano;* and the *Flute Duo* is *Duo for Flute and Piano.*

Copland's use of the piano was so integral to his composing that it permeated his compositional style, not only in the frequent use of the instrument itself but in more subtle and complex ways. Copland's habit of composing at the piano always slightly embarrassed him, until he learned that Stravinsky worked the same way. Copland said, "I can't imagine just sitting at a table and composing." He feels that the layman does not understand what it means when a composer talks about composing at the piano. He explained:

> They tend to think that you touch a chord, then ask yourself, "Do I like this? No." Then you touch another, and perhaps you do like it, and so on. It doesn't work that way. The composer knows in advance what he wants before he tries it out on the piano. It's difficult to explain, but it's certainly not pure chance.

Copland's method of composing was to write down fragments of musical ideas as they came to him. When he needed a piece, he would turn to these ideas (his "gold nuggets"), and if he found something appropriate that he thought might develop further, he would write a piano sketch in pencil. For an orchestral piece, he might use three staves, or write it down first for two pianos (for example, *Music for the Theatre*, the ballet *Hear Ye! Hear Ye!*, and *Inscape*). Copland would not think about specific instrumentation until a piece was fully formed and put down on paper. As John Kirkpatrick has pointed out, "It is not difficult to make piano reductions or two-piano arrangements of Aaron's orchestral works, because they can be derived almost directly from his own piano sketches."[4] (Examples of such solo piano arrangements are *Our Town* and "Saturday Night Waltz" from *Rodeo.*) Kirkpatrick made several two-piano arrangements of Copland works—the *Piano Concerto, Billy the Kid* (prior to Bernstein's), and the *Ode.* Kirkpatrick and Copland performed these transcriptions together in the thirties.

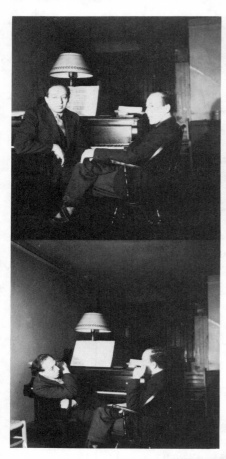

Photographs by Victor Kraft.

Left and above: Copland and David Diamond in the loft, c. 1947.

Below: In Copland's studio, Ossining, c. 1958.

In Copland's studio, Peekskill, c. 1975.

At Tanglewood, c. 1965.

Unlike many composers who wrote less well for other instruments than their own, Copland mastered each genre so that it seemed a natural and brilliant vehicle for him. He intuitively adapted his basic pianistic gestures to the particular purpose of each piece. William Schuman has said, "Copland may have composed but *one* song cycle, *one* choral work, *one* piano variations, and so on, but his *one* is the highest accomplishment of its kind."

Copland's three major piano pieces are not among his most popular works, yet they are perhaps his most characteristic: the lean, craggy, and demanding *Piano Variations* (1930), among the composer's most influential works; the lyrical *Piano Sonata* (1942), in a more faithful classical sonata form, yet individualistic and with one of Copland's most beautiful endings; the more atonal *Piano Fantasy*, Copland's last large-scale keyboard piece, disciplined yet wide-ranging, subsuming most of the moods, techniques, and characteristic sounds and rhythms of all his other piano music.[5] Harold Clurman said in an interview:

> These are mysterious works—the way, in a sense, Aaron is mysterious. They reveal some things about him that he never would talk about. Deeply buried things. He said nothing in words that in any way reflects what is in the *Sonata* or the *Fantasy*. But maybe if Aaron could talk these things, he couldn't compose them![6]

When questioned about why he did not write another large piano work after the *Piano Fantasy*, Copland pointed out that the *Fantasy* had taken years of hard work. He frequently remarked, "I have an aversion to repeating myself." Perhaps Copland meant that he had said what was important for him to say (pianistically) in the three big piano works. What was left he would use for short piano pieces during the remainder of his composing career.

A lifelong aim had been to provide challenging contemporary music for young performers. Copland had done so, starting with *The Young Pioneers* and *Sunday Afternoon Music* of 1936. Eleven of Copland's short keyboard pieces have been edited by Leo Smit and published together in a *Piano Album* for "young adventurous pianists" (1981). (One piece, *Petit Portrait,* composed when Copland was twenty-one, appears for the first time in the album.)[7] Copland had planned a three-volume series to be called *Piano Miscellany* (Book I for children; Book II for teenagers; Book III for adults), but the idea never came to fruition. One piece, composed in 1947

258

and discovered later in Copland's files, was probably meant for that series. It was edited for publication by composer Phillip Ramey in 1977. The title, *Midsummer Nocturne,* was agreed on by Copland and Ramey, to whom the piece is dedicated.[8]

Down a Country Lane (1962) is in the category of "music for young performers," although it is more of a challenge than it may at first seem. Commissioned by *Life* magazine, it was featured in the 19 June 1962 issue with photographs and a homespun type of article headed "Our Bumper Crop of Beginning Piano Players." The article explains, *"Down a Country Lane* fills a musical gap: It is among the few modern pieces specially written for young piano students by a major composer." Copland is quoted: "Even third-year students will have to practice before trying it in public." *Down a Country Lane* begins with instructions to the young performer to play "gently flowing in a pastoral mood"; a brief midsection is slightly dissonant and to be played "a trifle faster"; and the ending returns to the earlier lyric mood. *Down a Country Lane* was orchestrated for inclusion in a Youth Orchestra Series and premiered by the London Junior Orchestra at Royal Festival Hall (20 November 1964).

After the story and music appeared in *Life* magazine, Copland's privacy in Peekskill was temporarily shattered. People searched him out—even for piano lessons! A Texas oil millionaire learned of Copland's whereabouts and sent a telegram: COME DOWN HERE NEXT FRIDAY MORNING AT 9 O'CLOCK TO GIVE MY EIGHT-YEAR-OLD SON A PIANO LESSON. PRICE NO OBJECT.

When the Scribner Music Library commissioned a piece from Copland in 1966, he searched through his files and found a good tune left over from the 1945 documentary film *The Cummington Story.* Copland arranged it for piano and gave it the title *In Evening Air,* after a poem by Theodore Roethke. The theme is pastoral and singable, but the style is undeniably contemporary, with unannounced shifts to new keys, syncopation, and parallel motion of open fifths. Copland so admired the Roethke poem that he chose a few lines to be printed in the score: "I see, in evening air, how slowly dark comes down on what we do."[9]

Another short piano piece, *Night Thoughts,* was composed for the Van Cliburn Competition (1972). It was to be played by each contestant in the 1973 Quadrenniel Competition of Fort Worth, Texas. While not a virtuosic work, *Night Thoughts* presented certain difficulties for the three hundred entrants in the competition who were required to sight-read it:

DOWN A COUNTRY

The Premiere of a

The charming piano piece that makes its debut above is a rarity. It was written especially for LIFE by the dean of American composers, Aaron Copland, a Pulitzer prize winner for music. *Down a Country Lane* helps fill a musical gap: it is among the few modern pieces specially written for young piano students by a major composer. "Yet," warns Copland, "this composition is a bigger challenge than it first looks, and even third-year students will have to practice

LANE by Aaron Copland

Noted Composer's Piece for Youngsters

efore trying it in public." It opens in an easygoing pastoral mood, ut the middle section is slightly dissonant and takes dextrous ngerwork. "The music," Copland explains, "is descriptive only in an imaginative, not a literal sense. I didn't think up the title ntil the piece was finished—*Down a Country Lane* just happened o fit its flowing quality."

This is one of the few pieces of its kind that Copland has written

in all his 61 years and it is likely, considering the number of young pianists, to be his most widely played composition. His other works of course have become standards in the repertoire of orchestras all over the world—the lyrical *Appalachian Spring*, elegiac *Lincoln Portrait*, dissonant *Piano Fantasy*. Though Copland's style is highly varied, it is always stamped with directness and rhythmic ingenuity—even in so innocent a work as *Down a Country Lane*.

CONTINUED

From an article in *Life* magazine, 29 June 1962, featuring Copland and music for young piano students.

Copland working between his desk and piano, Peekskill, c. 1977.

unusual chords, wide spacings, and some complicated pedaling.[10] Copland
said, "My intention was to test the musicality and the ability of a performer to give coherence to a free musical form." The subtitle, *Homage
to Ives,* was added after the music was composed. According to Copland,
"This has not prevented performers and critics from finding Ivesian allu-
sions in the music." (A horncall question at the beginning of the piece has
been pointed to as reminiscent of *The Unanswered Question.*)

For a few years in the early eighties, a manuscript page in pencil sat on
Copland's piano stand. It was dated 1973 and bore the title "Improvisation." When Copland played it, as he did occasionally on request, it
seemed to be music that was meant as the opening of an important piano
piece. Questioned about taking it further, Copland would laughingly reply,
"If only I could!" Composer Phillip Ramey asked Copland whether he could
try to make a short piece from "Improvisation," and Copland agreed. It

became *Proclamation for Piano*. Bennett Lerner edited a second short piece, based on a sketch from 1944 that was in Copland's files. It was given the title *Midday Thoughts* and was dedicated to Lerner when it was published (1982). Both short pieces were premiered by Lerner in New York (2 February 1983) and recorded in his album *American Piano Music*.

Copland cared little for luxurious living conditions, but he could never tolerate the lack of a piano. In describing various living arrangements, it has always been the room with the piano that was most important—from the family home above the department store in Brooklyn, to a hacienda in the Mexican hills, to the studio in his Peekskill residence. The piano is a prized possession, as it was to Copland's parents. He takes great care with the instrument, watching when it has to be moved and pulling the draperies when the sun shines on the case. Copland's first pianos were Steinways. After moving into his Ossining house, however, Copland took advantage of a good offer from Baldwin: They loaned him pianos, which were replaced periodically, with the agreement that the replaced piano could be sold as "a Copland piano."

For many years, Copland as pianist was a familiar sight to audiences of contemporary music. By the end of the fifties, he was not playing very much in public. However, he accepted with pleasure when Stravinsky asked him to play in a performance of *Les Noces*, 20 December 1959 in New York City. Stravinsky wrote (1 September 1959), "I have never conducted *Les Noces* before, and it has always been my wish that it be performed by four of my esteemed colleagues." (The other three were Samuel Barber, Lukas Foss, and Roger Sessions.) Copland described the event to Victor Kraft: "Strav looked frail, came out on stage slowly with a suggestion of difficulty. The audience stood and greeted him with thunderous applause, and at the end, he was hailed as conquering hero."

When television made Copland a recognized figure, it was not as pianist but as conductor. His looks and gestures became part of the American consciousness: the lean figure with the wide grin, the long arms akimbo, the informal stance on the podium, a kind of running jump on and offstage at the end of a piece. Only Copland's close friends, who see him frequently at home, still connect him with the piano. The instrument, piled high with music, dominates the studio. Copland's desk is placed so that he can turn directly from it to play the piano, which he did regularly until his eighty-fifth year. Since then, Copland has played only on occasion (when David

Diamond visited on Copland's eighty-eighth birthday, the two played piano four-hands ad lib). But even away from the keyboard, when Copland speaks of music, his long fingers move in pianistic flourishes, left hand over right, or staccato on a tabletop—an imaginary piano at his fingertips.

Copland, c. 1960.

Photograph by David Gahr

Russia and the Far East

1957–1960

Verso: Copland conducting the Leningrad Philharmonic, 7 April 1960; concert announcement for 10 April 1960.

Opposite: Copland, 1958.

As a young man, one of the writers who had impressed me was Gide. I remember him writing that each person should follow his own natural instincts. For me, it seemed natural and comfortable to do several different things: Composing is a solitary pursuit for which I needed uninterrupted periods of time at home or at the MacDowell Colony; conducting took me out to all kinds of places and usually carried with it lecturing and teaching duties; working with organizations, festivals, and competitions that promoted the performance of contemporary music was also very satisfying. Looking through my notebooks and travel diaries, I am amazed to see the number and variety of places I went during these years—European tours, Mexico, and American cities and college towns, where I conducted, lectured, and taught composition.

Nineteen fifty-seven began with a return to Caracas, Venezuela, for the Second Latin American Contemporary Festival. I had promised to return after the First Festival in 1954. The Institution José Angel Lamas again planned to hand out twenty thousand dollars in prizes for the best works in a competition for Latin American orchestral pieces. Forty-four works were presented during the nine-day festival (18–27 March). The jurors included Chávez (Mexico), Ginastera (Argentina), Juan Batista Plaza (Venezuela), Domingo Santa Cruz (Chile), and myself. We were required to arrive three weeks in advance to choose the prizewinners, whose pieces would be performed on the concluding program. We decided on four prizes: Blas Galindo (Mexico) and Camargo Guarnieri (Brazil) divided the Lamas Prize of ten thousand dollars; and the two other prizes went to Roque Cordero (Panama) and Enrique Iturriagi (Peru).

No expense was spared in arranging and promoting the festival and life was still luxurious in Caracas. We were put up at the posh Hotel Tamanaco. I wrote to Irving Fine:

> If your ego ever gets low, come to Venezuela. They print your picture in the
> papers every other day, plug your music on the radio, interview you till you're

Carlos Chávez and Copland in Caracas, 1957.

blue in the face. Finally, even the American Embassy took note, and is arranging a party for the festival personalities. We are all having a fine time reminiscing about Tanglewood days.

Eight programs were devoted to Latin-American music and one to U.S. composers Gail Kubik, Samuel Barber, Roy Harris, Charles Ives, Virgil Thomson, and myself. I conducted *Lincoln Portrait* with the fiery Argentine actress Juana Sujo as narrator.[1] The quality of the orchestra had deteriorated somewhat since 1954, but the enthusiasm and conviction of the musicians for my piece stirred the audience, so that when the concert was over, they stood and cheered for some time and were reluctant to leave the stone seats in the outdoor amphitheater.

268

One day during the festival, Ginastera got all fifteen visiting composers together in a large room at the hotel to help Chávez finish a score for an upcoming premiere in New York. We took places at long tables and proceeded to copy 430 pages! *The New York Times* critic Howard Taubman wrote that it was ". . . a practical demonstration of inter-American friendship in action . . . a perfect example of harmony"![2]

Lawrence Morton invited me to participate in the May 1957 Ojai Festival in California, which was to revolve around my music. Lawrence suggested that I conduct works by other composers in addition to my own pieces. So I did: Purcell, Diamond, Britten, Grieg, Haydn, Fauré, and Stravinsky. I wrote to Lawrence afterward, "You really started something!" When invited to return to conduct varied programs again in 1958, I accepted. Ojai was the first place I was treated like a "real" conductor.[3]

From California, I went directly to the Brandeis Festival (3–10 June 1957), where I was on the jury for the annual Brandeis Creative Arts Awards. We had met during the winter to plan the programs and choose the winners. The festival, which included an all-Copland program,[4] coincided with the Brandeis University commencement. I received a letter from the president of Brandeis informing me that in this one hundredth anniversary year of the birth of Justice Louis Brandeis, the university wished to confer on me a Doctor of Humane Letters degree. The fact that Irving Fine had initiated the idea, and that he, Verna, and other of my Boston friends were in the audience when the honorary degree was bestowed, added to my pleasure in the occasion.

During the fall-winter semester of 1957–1958, as Slee Professor of Music at the State University of New York at Buffalo, I made nine visits of two or three days each to Buffalo to teach composition to about ten students. At the end of the semester, I conducted the Buffalo Symphony with Leo Smit as soloist (5 January 1958). In the next few years, I was asked to recommend composers for the visiting Slee Professorship: Chávez followed me, and then Ned Rorem. After my tenure at Buffalo, Slee professors were required to live in Buffalo. Ned wrote, "I've never even dreamed before of having so much money [ten thousand dollars]—but somehow I'd rather skimp along just as a composer being happy and poor in New York than as a professor sad and rich for eight and a half months in Buffalo. . . ." Ned asked my advice, I gave it, and off he went to Buffalo. As for myself, I found that I could work while traveling by train. By the end of 1957, I had completed my *Orchestral Variations* (an arrangement of the *Piano Variations* of 1930) and composed music for a television program.

John Houseman and Robert Herridge, producers of the CBS series *Seven Lively Arts,* asked me to compose incidental music for a drama based on five Ernest Hemingway stories that were adapted for television by A. E. Hotchner. The young actor Eli Wallach was to appear in the leading role. I had admired Hemingway since the twenties, when I would see him from a distance in a bookshop or café, and I found the idea of composing for the new and exciting medium of television intriguing. I agreed to a contract of fifteen hundred dollars to compose the music for "The World of Nick Adams."

Composing for a television drama was similar in procedure to preparing a film score. I was sent a script with cues to indicate where and for how long music was required: The first music was to follow directly after a voice announcing, "We call it 'The World of Nick Adams'!" I composed a kind of fanfare for the opener and music for such cues as "When a man comes face-to-face with death," and "It's fun all right."[5] I attended the live broadcast at which Alfredo Antonini conducted my music (10 November 1957). Hotchner told me that Hemingway was abroad and could not see the broadcast, but that he was taking a kinescope of the show for Hemingway to view later. I never did hear what Hemingway thought of it.

It was a commission from the Louisville Symphony Orchestra that stimulated me to put into action an idea I had been thinking about—transcribing my *Piano Variations* for orchestra.[6] I found it a challenge to re-create the piano material with orchestral color in mind. Robert Whitney led the Louisville Symphony in the premiere (5 March 1958), and I was astonished to hear catcalls at the end of the piece! At least the perpetrators waited until the work was over. There is something about a boo you can't forget—I seem to remember more vividly the few times my music was booed than the many times it was applauded! About a month after the premiere of the *Orchestral Variations,* I returned to Kentucky for a festival at the University of Louisville School of Music, where the piece was performed again, this time *sans* catcalls. In 1958 at Tanglewood, Charles Munch conducted the *Orchestral Variations* with the BSO, but it was in William Steinberg, conductor of the Pittsburgh Symphony, that the piece found a real champion. Steinberg conducted it in Pittsburgh in 1959 and on tour during the 1959–1960 season.

Working on a freelance basis, I never knew in advance what my total yearly income would be. I listed payments in a notebook as they came along and then added them at the end of each year for tax purposes.[7] When I totaled the amounts for 1957, I realized with surprise that my income had jumped rather suddenly, and it continued to climb in 1958. The change was not, as one might suspect, due to conducting fees or the CBS TV show, but from royalties and performance fees. It amazed me when I looked at the figures—after all, I was paid to compose the music in the first place!

Nineteen fifty-eight got off to an exciting start—my conducting debut with the New York Philharmonic (30, 31 January) and my television debut (1 February). I conducted the *Outdoor Overture* and part of the finale of the *Third Symphony* for the televising, sharing the program with Lenny Bernstein. At Claire Reis' party after the first Philharmonic concert, she commented that I was becoming addicted to conducting. I had to admit that it was pretty heady stuff. Part of me would say, "Stay home and compose," and I would do so. But after a short time, particularly when fresh composing ideas were hard to come by, I would get bored and want to take off again. I heard from people all over the country who saw the television broadcast—even my dentist, who said my new tooth looked fine—and David Diamond, who had heard about the broadcast while living in Florence, Italy. David wrote:

I hear that you had great success conducting the *Third*. Bravo! But what is this fantastic nonchalance of yours in relation to your own music and performances?. . . . When you clam up . . . especially about your musical activities, your biographers are *sure* going to have a hard time.

The worst part of the composer's life is the fact that he does not feel himself an integral part of the musical community. I had always enjoyed being with people: Young performers stimulated me; travel was interesting; and conducting puts one in a very powerful position. Best of all, it is a use of power for a good purpose. When Arthur Judson suggested an extensive midwest conducting tour for me during the first few months of 1958, followed by a European tour from August to the end of the year, I agreed. I had no plans to give up composing; in fact, when I left for Europe, I took materials with me for a ballet Jerry Robbins and I had been talking about.

I traveled to Europe by ship.[8] As long as the weather cooperated, I could rest, study scores, and read—a biography of George Sand occupied my attention. After a few days in a London hotel, I took a flat in Mayfair and enjoyed seeing old friends (Ben Britten and Peter Pears) and making new ones. This year of 1958 marked the beginning of a long and satisfying

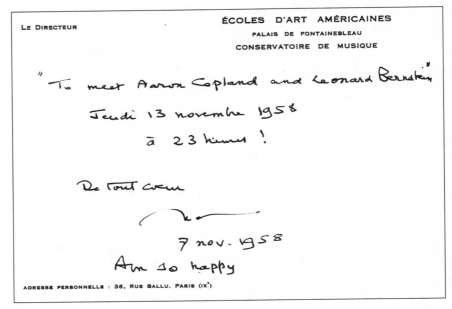

ÉCOLES D'ART AMÉRICAINES

LE DIRECTEUR

PALAIS DE FONTAINEBLEAU

CONSERVATOIRE DE MUSIQUE

" To meet Aaron Copland and Leonard Bernstein

Jeudi 13 novembre 1958

à 23 heures !

De tout cœur

7 nov. 1958

Am so happy

ADRESSE PERSONNELLE : 36, RUE BALLU, PARIS (IX°)

Invitation to a reception for Copland and Bernstein from Nadia Boulanger, Paris, 13 November 1958, with a personal note to Copland.

relationship with the London Symphony Orchestra. I was the only American composer represented at the Promenade Concerts at the Albert Hall in the summer of 1958. I wrote to Leo Smit from London (3 October 1958):

> My visit started off with a bang in August conducting the *Orchestral Variations* and *Rodeo* at the Proms. London musical life is beyond belief conventional. I wrote an attack in the Sunday *Times* and caused a commotion.[9] Then I taught for ten days at Dartington and heard the Berlin Octet murder my *Sextet* there. I've made two forays to the Continent: one to conduct in Copenhagen, and one to conduct in Stuttgart. Stopped off in Brussels on the way back to do a lecture for USIS. Next week to Paris to lecture, hear *Threni* [Stravinsky], see Lenny, Nadia B., Peggy Bernier, etc. As you can imagine, I don't get much composing done in the midst of all this.

David Walker, who had his own place in New York, went up to Ossining periodically to check my mail and take care of routine correspondence and requests. He forwarded important things to me. The house was looked after by Victor Kraft when he was around, or Jack Kennedy, who went up to Ossining once in a while. I was at Shady Lane Farm only the month of December in all of 1958. I really had to scramble to meet some deadlines: radio talks for WQXR in New York; a lecture, "The Pleasures of Music,"[10] for the Distinguished Lecture Series at the University of New Hampshire for April 1959; a foreword to a book, *Portrait of a Symphony;* and the orchestrations for two of my *Dickinson Songs.* The Ossining house and grounds were attractive, but I was not finding the place perfect for my needs, being a converted barn with one big living room and no separate studio. I could not take care of things by myself when I was there, so people were always around, and I did not have the privacy I needed for composing. Chávez, who was in Cambridge as Norton Lecturer at Harvard, offered me his country house in Acapulco. He arranged to have the piano tuned, and wrote, "Acapulco is waiting for you. My sister Chabela is there and she knows how dear a friend you are to me, so everything will be in order." The house was simple but with everything I could possibly need, including cook and housekeeper, and the separate studio had a spectacular view and a very beautiful garden. I arrived in Acapulco (12 February 1959) and got right to work on a piece for orchestra for the Festival of Two Worlds in Spoleto, Italy. I had promised Gian Carlo Menotti a premiere in July.

The music of Latin America had more than a passing interest for me ever since my first visit to Mexico in 1932. Again in 1958, I was stimulated by my surroundings to compose "Paisaje Mexicano" and "Danza de Jalisco," which when put together became my *Two Mexican Pieces.* As it turned out, only the "Danza" was played at Spoleto. Both pieces were performed together for the first time in the United States under my baton at a private invitation concert given by the Pan-American Union in Washington, D.C. (20 April 1965). In 1968, I made a two-piano arrangement of "Danza de Jalisco," which contains a few revisions (for example, the handclapping was made optional). In 1971, after I composed a piece derived from Venezuelan sources, "Estribillo," I added it to the others and the collective title became *Three Latin-American Sketches:* "Estribillo" is the vigorous first piece; the lyrical "Paisaje Mexicano" comes next; and the bouncy "Danza de Jalisco," with its contrasting rhythms of 6/8 and 3/4, is the third. I would describe the character of the *Three Latin-American Sketches* as the title indicates: the tunes, the rhythms, and the temperament of the pieces are folksy, while the orchestration is bright and snappy and the music sizzles along—or at least it seems to me that it does. The entire work is scored for a moderate-size orchestra. The world premiere was conducted by André Kostelanetz in a "Promenades" concert with the New York Philharmonic (7 June 1972).

I wanted to stay longer in Mexico, but certain commitments could not be ignored, one being the premiere of the *Suite from The Tender Land* with the BSO (10 and 11 April 1958). Also, I wanted to be back in New York to talk with Jerome Robbins about the ballet we were planning. When Chávez returned home to Mexico, he wrote (26 May), "This past Sunday I was in Acapulco and thought a lot of you. I wished you back, anytime, as many times as you can. Please remember the polite Spanish phrase is absolutely literal in your case: 'esa es tu casa.'"

Jerome Robbins and I had hoped to work together since 1954 when he directed the premiere of my opera, *The Tender Land.* Under consideration briefly had been a ballet depicting a bullfight, but, as Lincoln Kirstein wrote, "Jerry decided it is too picturesque and pantomimic. Jerry wants to do only dancing with a very simple program to a four-part symphony." Other commitments intervened, and when we got together one evening at the beginning of 1959 to discuss the possibilities, we discovered that we both leaned toward a non-story ballet. Jerry was particularly interested in waltzes, and he followed up by sending a pageful of ideas. The result was that I accepted a commission from him for a full-length ballet score based on a series of theatrical dances.

At first, I called the music *Ballet for J.R.,* as I had called *Appalachian Spring, Ballet for Martha.* Later, the score bore the title *The Dream,* and later still, it became *Dance Panels, Ballet in Seven Verses.* When the piece was finished, I played the music on the piano for Jerry. There was one section that he couldn't see movement to at all. Jerry explained:

> A strange thing happened. I went straight to rehearsal without the music right after Aaron played the score for me. I tried to remember it, but could only recall the counts. When I began working with the company just with counts, I got interested in what they were doing without music. It fascinated me, and I continued working that way. It really moved along. I was sorry I wasn't able to do *Dance Panels,* but in a very real way, Aaron's music was the accidental genesis of my ballet without music, *Moves.* [11]

Dance Panels sat on the shelf until 1962 when I revised it for a ballet by the Bavarian State Opera in Munich for the opening of their new house in November. The spring before the opening, on a trip to London, Berlin, Munich, and Rome, I met with representatives of the Opera in Munich and attended an orchestra rehearsal (19 April 1962). It was curious to hear music I had written so long ago (1959) finally being performed. I was invited to return to conduct the premiere. There was much discussion about who would choreograph the work. Heinz Rosen, music director of

Copland playing *Dance Panels* for Jerome Robbins, New York City, 1959.

the Opera House, thought the best solution would still be Robbins. I thought so, too, and tried again, but Jerry could not be interested. Rosen suggested Eugene Loring or Arthur Mitchell, but Mitchell's price was too high, so Rosen decided to do the choreography himself and to engage guest dancers. I was apprehensive, and my worst fears were confirmed when I saw a run-through. I wrote in my diary, "Has good, balletic things in it, but completely without relation to the quality of my music. More or less what I suspected would happen. A ballet seems to be going on, but you could never guess what the music was like from what you see onstage— Damn!" It was essentially a boy-and-girl idea: The Boy was danced by Arthur Mitchell of the New York City Ballet; the Girl was Liane Daydé of the Paris Opera. I hoped that when Mitchell arrived, he might change the atmosphere somehow, but to top the situation off, he turned his ankle and could not dance for a few days, and at the premiere he had to omit his first solo.

The rebuilt Bavarian State Opera House, a replica of the old one, opened 21 November 1963, and the premiere of the ballet took place there on 3 December. Mitchell and Daydé, a most appealing dancer, were received well. The designer had devised a set of colored screens with changing patterns that was effective when combined with the unusual lighting. When it was all over, I wrote in my diary, "Somebody, someday will make a good ballet out of the piece—it's so very danceable, but I'm afraid it's a lost cause here. Still—it's rather fun to be involved in the putting on of a new stage piece—*any* stage piece." It was rumored that Balanchine was planning to choreograph the music, and I hoped so, since the German affair left much to be desired.

Dance Panels was my sixth ballet score. I seemed to have an affinity for the art of dance, and dancers themselves must have a certain feeling for my music, since each of my ballets, except the first, *Grohg,* was composed at the request of a choreographer. Also, some of my concert music has been considered danceable. *Dance Panels* is a different sort of ballet music from my earlier dance scores. It is more abstract, and it is lyrical and slower in tempo than most of my other ballet music. It does not tell a story as does *Billy the Kid,* or paint a picture of American life as in *Appalachian Spring.* It makes no use of American folk melodies; however, in two of the movements, there is a relationship to familiar genres of our popular music—the quiet sentimental song and a type of stage music used for "tap dancing."[12]

Dance Panels is in seven contrasting sections: the introduction, with long sustained notes, is in slow waltz tempo; a second section continues the waltz rhythm; the third is a light transparent scherzando; the fourth is a melancholy and nostalgic *pas de trois* featuring solo flute; the fifth is characterized by brisk rhythms and jazzy drum patterns; the sixth is a lyrical episode with a finale in jagged irregular rhythms; and the seventh section ends the piece as quietly as it began. Within these confines, the separate sections are varied in character and easily identifiable, although they are to be played without pause. The score begins and ends with related material. The music is composed in a simple and direct style. The lyrical parts are very diatonic, "white-notey," one might say, while the lively and bouncy portions have more complexity of texture.[13]

Dance Panels as a ballet finally had a production in the United States under the title *Shadow'd Ground.*[14] It was performed by the New York City Ballet at the State Theater at Lincoln Center (21 January 1965). John Taras was choreographer, Robert Irving conductor. The story is about two lovers reading epitaphs in a graveyard. The ballet did not fare well with audience or critics. Walter Terry wrote in the *Herald Tribune* (22 January 1965):

Photographs by Serge Lido.

Left: Copland in Munich for the production of the ballet *Dance Panels,* with choreographer Heinz Rosen (center) and dancers (left to right): Liane Daydé, Arthur Mitchell, and Margot Werner. *Right:* Liane Daydé congratulating Copland after the first performance, 3 December 1964.

Whether one wished to or not, he could not help thinking, while stirred by the Copland music, that perhaps this genre of ballet were better left to an Agnes de Mille or to a Eugene Loring or, perhaps, to a Martha Graham. Taras, who has created some attractive ballets in the past, was just not at home with this type of Americana.

The concert version of *Dance Panels,* which is essentially the same as the ballet score, was played first by the Ojai Festival Orchestra, Ingolf Dahl conducting (24 May 1966). With the pauses in the first dance shortened, *Dance Panels* is approximately twenty-three minutes in duration. It calls for a moderate-size orchestra of six woodwinds, five brass, two percussion (but no timpani), and strings. At first, I had some concern about whether the piece would work on the concert stage, and since I was not able to attend the festival, I was anxious for Ingolf's report (26 May 1966):

Thanks for your telegram—it was just the thing to cheer me up at the crucial time! I think the performance went very well indeed. You will be happy to hear that the whole orchestra just loved the music from the first rehearsal. As for me, I am crazy about the work. Every detail, every harmonic subtlety, every finesse of melodic phrasing, not to speak of the fabulous orchestral color, seems to me to be inspired and in every way successful. I am tempted to enumerate all the special places that excited me, but that would make this interminable. Not the least admirable about *Dance Panels* is the act of courage on your part, to be so completely "you." Several of my young composer friends shared my admiration for this courage—a ray of light in the present gloom.

When I conducted *Dance Panels* for Columbia Records, I made slight revisions,[15] and in 1965 I approved an arrangement for solo piano made in-house at Boosey & Hawkes. (The first New York concert performance of the orchestral version did not take place until my seventh-fifth birthday celebration at Alice Tully Hall: I conducted *Dance Panels,* and Dennis Russell Davies conducted *Statements for Orchestra* and the *Third Symphony.*)

Tanglewood became an exciting place again for composers, because of Paul Fromm and his Foundation. Beginning in 1957, the Fromm Players (ten instrumentalists and one singer) were in residence and responsible for playing and demonstrating new music in the weekly Composers Forums, the Aspects of Music lecture series, and the Seminar in Contemporary Music envisioned by Fromm in 1956.[16] Ralph Berkowitz, Tod Perry, Gail Rector, and I met during the winter months to choose the Fromm Fellows. Our job was to find top players with an interest in contemporary music who would become a homogeneous ensemble. They had to be able to read almost anything at sight. We were lucky on all counts. The players included a woodwind quintet plus a string quartet, a pianist, and a soprano: All were outstanding performers. I wrote to Leo Smit (25 July 1957), "Tanglewood is hectic as usual, but we have been having lots of fun with our Fromm Players—at our beck and call—playing oodles of modern music from Varèse and Webern to V.T. [Thomson] and S. Revueltas."

The Fromm Seminar in Contemporary Music was held on Friday afternoons. I was responsible for presenting a general outline and background material in the first lecture, and for delivering one lecture during the series. In 1957, I spoke on "Nationalist Trends—American Phase," and the Fromm Players demonstrated by playing my *Sextet;* in 1958, it was "New Music from Latin America"; and in 1959, "Recent European Piano Music," musical examples by pianist Paul Jacobs (Paul joined the Fromm Players that summer). The atmosphere for composers had never been more stimulating. Having Paul Fromm as our patron was like having our own Prince Esterhazy! The Fromm Players gave composers the rare opportunity to have performers right on hand to test out their works. Student composers could hear their pieces played by instruments separately or in combination. They could hear what happens, for example, if a tune is doubled by five instruments rather than four, or hear a five-note chord for woodwind quintet in twenty different ways before deciding the final way. Students don't often get a chance to hear their works before the ink is dry!

Paul Fromm took pleasure from the fact that the composer was again the central figure, a rare occurrence in the twentieth century. As I told a newspaper critic, "Paul Fromm is the ideal patron. He doesn't mix in or give orders, and when he gets enthusiastic about something, he gives money to support his enthusiasm. The Fellowship Players, for instance. It is a vast luxury. Ask anybody. Ask me."

When I went to visit the Fromm Foundation in Chicago in 1958, I did not know what to expect, but whatever it was, I did not find it. Paul Fromm was an importer of liquor and the Foundation offices were in the wholesale wine district. To get there, one walked through the storerooms of crates filled with wine and whiskey. Paul Fromm had a strong German accent; he was not always easy to understand, but what he said about contemporary music was always so passionate that he got his ideas across in no uncertain terms. What he expressed on that day I visited the Foundation was: "I want to help raise the level of advanced musical studies. I am determined to get a project well under way." Fromm's contributions to the Music Center grew to support forty fellowships a year after the program was established. Many new works were commissioned, and in 1964, the annual Tanglewood Festival of Contemporary Music was initiated.

Milton Babbitt was the visiting composer at Tanglewood in 1957 and again in 1958. Although his appointment meant giving up Koussevitzky's idea of a European composer, the need for a leading serialist was pressing, and Milton Babbitt was certainly one of them. Munch was eager to return to the composer-from-abroad tradition; nevertheless, Leon Kirchner was invited in 1959. Leon promptly fell in love with the place. He wrote to me, "It is the most 'gemütlich' atmosphere anywhere."

I was finding the Tanglewood students anxious about their futures. Most were feeling the influence of Webern and his present-day followers. They wanted to learn electronic techniques, but it was very difficult for them to find enough studio time, and they worried about having an audience for their music if they did write it. One of the most talented of these students was a young Argentinian, Mario Davidovsky.[17]

Whitestone Photo, Heinz H. Weissenstein.

At Tanglewood, 1958 (left to right): David Walker, Mario Davidovsky, and Copland.

Mario Davidovsky [18]

My friend, Efrain Guigui, went to Tanglewood in 1957, and he took with him a clarinet quintet of mine, which Copland heard and liked very much. Suddenly, out of the blue, I had a letter from Aaron Copland. I almost died!

He was a famous man and one of the most important figures as far as promoting Latin American composers. I doubt that any composers came to the States from Latin America without Copland having something to do with it. Copland's letter asked me to come to Tanglewood, but I had tremendous troubles getting financial help in Argentina. Copland practically solved all my troubles. He really helped more than any Argentinian helped me. Meanwhile, I submitted a score to the 1957 competition in Caracas. I didn't get any prize, but I got a letter from Aaron, saying that he liked the piece, although he criticized the melodic material. He said, "I wish that your material could be less derived from European sources."

I made my way to Tanglewood in 1958. Copland was a wonderful teacher. We argued vehemently about procedures and aesthetics. Copland was very critical of my music derived from Europeans, because he very much believed there were tremendous sources in our Latin American traditions to nourish major compositions. My English was double zero, but Aaron spoke fluent Spanish. Tanglewood, being only for the summer, is not the kind of place where very serious work gets done, but Copland's advice was extremely precise, ranging from general formal troubles to the handling of the orchestra. He was quick to know the shape of a piece, even when it was not his cup of tea. He was very open. If he believed in somebody's talent, he would be a staunch supporter, no matter what kind of aesthetic the composer chose to use.

I was young, idealistic, and intense. One day, Marc Blitzstein came and talked to the composers on what it takes to make an opera. I had no idea who he was. Mr. Blitzstein played on the piano and sang excerpts from his own productions. I remember getting absolutely furious. I just could not understand how I, coming from so far away, should have to use my time listening to that kind of light music! I thought it was a travesty, and I stood up and left in the middle. Copland didn't get angry, but he called me up and asked why I was so upset. I explained about my high standards. Copland very patiently talked to me about what Broadway was and the importance of show music. He took the time and trouble to give me examples of local Argentinian tango and Brazilian samba composers to trace a parallel with what Blitzstein was doing. Aaron didn't act as though I was a spoiled brat from Latin America! I remember that with great affection.

I complained to him that many of the composers interested in writing nationalist music, Ginastera and others, were very influenced by Bartók, and that Latin American music was almost one hundred percent Hungarian. He thought that was very funny. I said also that his pieces El Salón México

and Danzón Cubano, *based on Latin American folk tunes, were so successful that they set the standard of how a good Latin American piece should
be written. They became the models, and in the process, to my mind, the
music did not sound so Latin American anymore. Aaron didn't see it quite
that way.*

*Aaron and Milton Babbitt, who was also teaching at Tanglewood, helped
me to come back to the States to work at the Columbia University electronic
laboratory in 1960. After that, I used to send Aaron studies every three or
four months, and he would write me notes with criticism. He would say,
"Even if I really find myself unable to discriminate many things musically
speaking in this kind of music, I like number one better than number two."
And he would tell me reasons. They were always very good reasons why piece
number one was better than number two. Aaron was very perceptive. He was
interested in the electronic field, but he never could understand it. He said,
"How can you people manipulate these machines so elegantly!" He came
several times to Columbia University to visit me, and I explained to him
step by step, because I wanted very much to interest Aaron in writing some
electronic music. I thought it would be a tremendous boost for what we were
doing. But Copland was already a completely solidified composer. It is
difficult at a certain age to open up to such a radical proposition, and Aaron
was already going more and more into conducting. Maybe if the development had come sooner, he might have used it. But he was very much curious
and alert to all the developments and came to our concerts. He even
commissioned me in the 1960s through the Fromm Foundation to use
traditional instruments with electronic sounds. It speaks about his openness
and generosity toward composers in whom he believed.*

I returned to the barn in Richmond each summer, although I rarely stayed
on past the Tanglewood season as I had in earlier years (in 1958, I left
immediately for Europe). The BSO trustees were looking at what could
be trimmed from the Music Center budget. It seemed to be a matter of
who could be kept on. Leonard Burkat had just moved up to become chief
administrator of the Center. Irving helped plan and execute a complicated
curriculum in 1957, reminding me all along that he had not been given
a raise since 1948. Lukas returned in 1958 and 1959. The rest of the faculty
remained about the same.[19] Boris Goldovsky was still with us, but the
opera program was cut back to four weeks, and in 1959, the trustees

decided to suspend the opera program completely, although all agreed that Goldovsky had done fine work for Tanglewood. I called a meeting for the entire faculty (6 July 1959), partly because there had not been one for twelve years, but mostly because of dissatisfaction about the abandonment of the opera program. Also, it seemed the Tanglewood Study Group was in shambles. I had received complaints from several of the faculty about the quality of student talent declining at Tanglewood, and I, myself, felt that the caliber of composition student was not quite as high as in the years when a European guest composer was in residence. A planning committee was elected to deal with the issues before the next Tanglewood season.[20] The time had come for a thorough stock-taking and a rethinking of directions.

In 1960, the State Department wanted two American composers to represent the United States in Russia, with the idea of furthering a cultural exchange program that had begun with five Russian composers and a musicologist touring the United States in 1959. (I took part in a symposium in Boston in November debating with Khrennikov, and in an ASCAP reception for Russian composers in New York.) The State Department chose Lukas Foss and myself as representatives. My plan was to stay in London for a few weeks after touring Russia and then meet up with the BSO as guest conductor for their tour of Japan, the Philippines, and Australia. When the State Department heard about this, they suggested a cosponsored arrangement.

I was required to go to Washington for a "briefing" (2 March 1960). I called Oscar Cox to keep him informed of my activities, since for several years after the McCarthy hearing, I was made to feel anxious about my passport. I would be away for three and one-half months, returning just in time for Tanglewood. Before I left, I had a letter from Sam Barber: "Bon voyage and may the spirit of Olga Koussevitzky see you through such an arduous trip." Sam also thanked me for birthday greetings I had sent for his fiftieth birthday:

> Thank you for your kind wire on that melancholy occasion. It was much appreciated. It was very curious: If you have all the youth of the United States at your feet, at least I have a great following among retired secretaries, janitors, et al.

On 15 March, I left for Amsterdam, where I met Lukas. Together we flew to Moscow via Warsaw.

Lukas Foss[21]

Aaron and I spent four solid weeks together in 1960 when we were chosen to be the two composers to represent the United States in Russia. We had known each other for a long time and were good friends even though there's twenty-two years' difference in our ages. We really got to know each other better on that trip. I first met Aaron when I was only seventeen, but I no longer recall who introduced us. Isn't it amazing the little things one remembers, when so many things are forgotten? Most vivid to me is that I carried with me a bag of dirty laundry to my first meeting with the great American composer at the Empire Hotel! I don't know why—I probably couldn't find a laundry that day—but I recall being embarrassed enough about having that laundry with me that I let Aaron assume the case was full of music. On that first occasion, Aaron played me some excerpts from The Second Hurricane.*

It was really via* Billy the Kid *that I discovered Aaron. He entrusted me with finding all the mistakes in the galleys before it was published, and I found so many that Aaron began to be irritated and bored by my coming in to see him with more and more mistakes the publishers had made. Then Aaron asked me to do a piano arrangement of* Billy. *When I first heard* Appalachian Spring *played on the piano at a party, Aaron asked, "Well, how do you like it?" I said, "I like it, but it's not like* Billy the Kid." *I was a creature of habit. Once I got to love something, that was the bible for me, and the next piece was bound to be disappointing until I conducted it or got into it.*

At Tanglewood, I felt like a refugee at first. But a refugee learns to call anything his home, wherever he is, so America very quickly became my home. (I was born in Germany and studied music in Paris before coming to the States at age fifteen.) Aaron had something to do with that, and so did Carl Sandburg, because I discovered his poetry and then got to know him and set "The Prairie" to music. For about five years, before the neoclassicism of Stravinsky took over, my music was American. Aaron was slightly disapproving of my studying with Hindemith at Tanglewood. I remember he said, "Isn't that like bringing coals to Newcastle?" But I didn't agree with him until later. I would probably have been better advised to have studied with Aaron, but in a way I did study with him, because once I got to know him and his music, I asked him for advice and criticism. Aaron's stamp was even stronger than Hindemith's for me during those years. I had fallen in love with America because of people like Aaron.

At Tanglewood, Koussevitzky was very important to me. All of us profited from his interest in American music. Koussevitzky tried to help me—he even gave me his suits after having worn them four or five times. He would ask me to try one, saying, "You feel rich now, don't you?" I probably did. Koussevitzky got me the job of pianist with the BSO in 1944 when I was twenty-two, so I would have some money. After Koussevitzky died, Tanglewood was different. It's an important legacy, but not quite the same.

By the way, I remember Koussevitzky was very critical of Aaron's conducting. I think he did him an injustice. I always thought Aaron conducted very well. It was Aaron who kept the group of us composers together, not Koussevitzky. During the late forties and fifties in New York, a group of us would go to the Russian Tea Room, where there was one table at which we all gathered after concerts, always with Aaron presiding. On Aaron's right was Elliott Carter, and there were a few other faithfuls, such as Bill Schuman and myself.

We were different generations, Aaron and I, but always very good friends. With Aaron good friends doesn't mean necessarily chummy, because Aaron has that composer's aloofness, which I love. He has it when he narrates Lincoln Portrait: *never emoting, absolutely quiet and sober, and his music is quiet and sober much of the time. So he was as a person. I never had chummy sessions with Aaron. There was definitely that generation gap, and I think that is what a boy needs. Aaron's music actually became like a father figure to me.

Aaron could be very critical. For instance, he felt that the neoclassicism in my Piano Concerto *was really fresh, but a little too schoolish, too classical. He didn't like to see me go that way after The Prairie. Stravinsky was foremost in our minds—Shapero, Fine, and myself—but Aaron didn't completely endorse that school. Aaron was not altogether wrong, because in a sense that classicism was something we had to overcome eventually.

The State Department picked Aaron to go to Russia as an example of the older generation, and me as an example of the younger one. We acted out these parts perfectly. Aaron was the proper ambassador, and I was the enfant terrible. Every evening I would tell him about my exploits, and he would get a vicarious pleasure out of all the naughty things I had done. He enjoyed being what he was, but at the same time, he enjoyed hearing things I was up to. We always had a sort of spy secretary with us—a woman who looked like the kiss of death. She also translated for us at rehearsals. One

Copland and Lukas Foss at
the State University of New
York at Buffalo, 1957.

Letter from Foss to Copland,
Warsaw, 1960 (undated).

Hotel Bristol
WARSZAWA

Dear Aaron

You were very much present in poland
also. I just spent 7 hours rehearsing and
taping for the Radio ---- yes -- El Salon Mexico.
The Radio orchestra of Kattowice is one of the 2
good polish orchestras. In fact it's every bit
as good as the Moscow State Symphony. And I
must say our Radio performance was extremely
decent. Only they found they didn't have.
By the way I did Copland and Bach (Dvunno
concerto) instead of Foss and Foss. Because
there was a mix-up and the parts were not
here. Actually I was overjoyed that I got
to d (for the first time) El Salon, which I
fell in love with all over again. I was lucky
that they had a set of parts. Apparently Antoni
was here 10 years ago,

Lukas

time, I stole out of the hall, grabbed a cab, handed the driver the Pasternak address Lenny Bernstein had given me. [22] He had said, "Lukas, you have got to find out why I don't get any answers, no acknowledgments of the gifts and music I send. . . ." So I handed the address to this driver, but it was in a neighborhood where foreigners are not allowed. The driver didn't like it, but he drove me there anyway and out came Pasternak. I said to him, "Nobody knows I am here." I stayed two hours and the driver came back and dropped me back off in a public place, because I didn't want him to know at which hotel I was staying. I didn't tell anyone except Aaron, but, of course, Pasternak's place was bugged, and when I got back to America, I got a call from the North American Associated News. They said, "We have received a wire with sad news for you. Your friend, Mr. Pasternak, has just suffered a stroke." I said, "What do you mean, my friend?" The wire said: LAST KNOWN WESTERN VISITOR, COMPOSER-CONDUCTOR LUKAS FOSS, KEPT HIS VISIT SO SECRETIVE THAT THE AMERICAN EMBASSY KNOWS NOTH-ING ABOUT IT. All those things I did without permission, I told Aaron about secretly, and the Russians knew about them after all!

On the Russian trip, I carried a collection of songs around with me and played them for Aaron for his criticism and reactions—these eventually became my Time Cycle. I played Aaron's music publicly and for composers' meetings in various places we traveled. Once I got terribly mixed up with El Salón México, thinking I knew it from memory, and Aaron was really very much like a schoolteacher, shaking his head at me and being very stern.

I have conducted almost all of Aaron's works. Lincoln I did with Marian Anderson, Carl Sandburg, and Senator Jacob Javits. For Aaron's eightieth birthday, I did a Copland Festival in Milwaukee, and he came and participated. It was a multimedia festival with film and dance. It was one of the last big trips Aaron took, and he was not feeling very strong, but I noticed how his face suddenly became relaxed when he listened to his music.

After I returned to the United States, I wrote a report and an article titled "Four Weeks in the Soviet Union—1960."[23] In it, I described our musical activities and my impressions of a friendly and genuine people desiring to do everything possible to further friendly relations, musically and humanly. In addition to the official report, I kept a diary, where I jotted down our day-to-day experiences in a more informal way.[24] I described a visit with the Shostakovich family, seeing the great composer at his own home in a

relaxed and charming mood at the dinner table with Kabalevsky, Khrennikov, everyone's wives, and Shostakovich's son, Maxime. I wrote:

> I watched Shostie while Lukas and Kabalevsky played a Haydn symphony
> four-hands. He loves music with a kind of innocent joy I have rarely seen in
> a famous composer. Music must have been a great solace to him through the
> tough days. I was persuaded to play my *Piano Sonata*. At the end, they all said
> *Spasibo* (thank you), with no comment of any kind.

The Leningrad Philharmonic was the best of the orchestras with which
we worked. They showed not the slightest sign of concern about our
"modernisms." I had to repeat the finale of *Red Pony,* and much curiosity
was aroused by that title. While walking in the Nevsky Prospect after the
concert, a man appeared under the light of one of those beautiful street-
lamps they have there and said, "You Copland?" I answered, "Yes." The
young man was a musician and he invited us to his apartment to hear some
music he had written in the jazz style. We went, and the place was like
any little place up in the Bronx and so was the music. The young musician
asked me whether I thought jazz was bad. Lukas was impressed by the
firmness of my "No!"

In Moscow, I gave a radio talk, the first by an American on the air. At
the final concert, I played my *Piano Quartet* with the Borodine Quartet,
and the famous pianist Sviatoslav Richter finished the program. Afterward,
I gave him all the piano music I had carried with me.

I left Russia with a lasting impression of cooperative spirit at all levels.
Our concerts aroused great interest. No surprise was ever shown at dissonance, no matter how severe. But there is active propaganda by those in
authority to discredit twelve-tone atonalism and what is referred to as
"electronic noises." I was not prepared before our visit as to what degree
Russian music is exclusively Russian. There is an extraordinary and all-
pervasive unity of expressive ideal: Over and over again the pathetic note
is struck; the harmonies are fulsome; the melodies clear and singing; the
orchestral coloring familiar.

I flew from Moscow to London for a few weeks, where I conducted the
LSO and the BBC orchestra.[25] A letter was waiting for me there from
Clurman: "I heard from Foss that you were very diplomatic in the
U.S.S.R. But I have never known you to be anything but that everywhere."
An amusing thing happened in London when I got into a taxicab to go
to the Boosey & Hawkes office. As I wrote in my diary at the time:

HE: I see you're an American. What do you do?
ME: Why do you ask?

HE: You look to me like a musician.
ME: That's right.
HE: What sort of musician?
ME: I'm a composer.
HE (in a tone of amazement): *Not Walter Piston?!*

The opportunity to travel with the BSO as guest conductor in Japan, the Philippines, and Australia was one I could not pass up. I was to meet up with the orchestra in Japan via Seattle and Alaska. I had become quite used to all kinds of flying conditions, but this time I really had a scare. While in the air, a propeller conked out, forcing us to return to Alaska and causing a twenty-four-hour delay. Being late in arriving in Tokyo, I had no time to catch up on sleep. My duties with the BSO began that very day (4 May). Charles Munch and Richard Burgin were alternating as regular conductors, and I filled in at various times with a program devised by Munch: Purcell, Haydn, and Copland (partway through the trip, I found myself yearning for an alternate program). One concert I conducted was in Osaka. For fun, I traveled there alone by train to Nara, which was packed with kids touring the shrines. It was a strange feeling being the only Westerner in a train full of Japanese.

We went to various one-night stands—Kyoto and then on an Inland Sea boat trip. At times when it rained, I stayed indoors to write letters and to work on an article I had promised to do about Nadia. Everywhere we went, we were greeted with banners: WELCOME BSO. We stayed in hotels where we slept on the floor, Japanese-style. One day, I was awakened by an earth tremor of worrisome proportions. I was concerned, not having asked anyone just what one *does* in an earthquake! The inland towns in Japan reminded me of Mexico—the people, the mountains, the houses. The small town of Matzuyama had attractions that the big towns lacked. Richard Burgin conducted the evening concert there, including Leon Kirchner's *Toccata* and the *Adagio* from Mahler's *Tenth Symphony*, both big flops. But Tchaikovsky's *Fifth Symphony* always saved the day. Our next stops were Beppu, a dusty resort city; Yawata, a dreary Pittsburgh-like steel center; and Fukuoka, a busy up-and-coming seaport.

In Hiroshima, we stayed in a new hotel surrounded by a park, the former epicenter of the A-bomb. I visited the Museum of the Bomb across from the hotel—it was depressing beyond words, with its photos, statistics, and pieces of clothing—bomb-torn—under glass. I heard half the concert in the new hall, conducted by Munch. It was very strange to sit calmly on the very bomb site listening to a concert! I asked someone what the

Left: Copland conducting a student orchestra in Japan.

Right: A concert program in Japanese and English.

F

1. 弦楽のための幻想曲‥‥‥‥‥‥‥‥‥‥‥‥‥‥‥‥‥‥‥‥‥‥‥‥パーセル
    第2番　変ロ長調
    第4番　ハ短調
      一音符による幻想曲　ヘ長調
2. 交響曲　第1番‥‥‥‥‥‥‥‥‥‥‥‥‥‥‥‥‥‥‥‥‥‥‥‥‥‥コープランド
    前　奏　曲
    スケルツォ
    終　　曲
3. 交響曲　第95番　ハ短調‥‥‥‥‥‥‥‥‥‥‥‥‥‥‥‥‥‥‥‥ハイドン
    アレグロ・モデラート
    アンダンテ・カンタービレ
    メヌエット
      終曲：　ヴィヴァーチェ
4. 歌劇　「テンダー・ランド」からの組曲‥‥‥‥‥‥‥‥‥‥‥‥‥コープランド
    序奏と愛の音楽
    パーティーのシーン
      終曲：　暮しの約束

1. Fantasias for Strings ‥‥‥‥‥‥‥‥‥‥‥‥‥‥‥‥‥‥‥‥‥PURCELL
    No. 2 in B flat major
    No. 4 in C minor
    Fantasia on One Note in F major
2. First Symphony ‥‥‥‥‥‥‥‥‥‥‥‥‥‥‥‥‥‥‥‥‥‥‥COPLAND
    Prelude
    Scherzo
    Finale
3. Symphony No. 95 in C minor ‥‥‥‥‥‥‥‥‥‥‥‥‥‥‥‥HAYDN
    Allegro moderato
    Andante cantabile
    Menuetto
    Finale : Vivace
4. Orchestra Suite from the Opera, "The Tender Land" ‥‥‥‥‥COPLAND
    Introduction and Love Music
    Party Scene
    Finale : The Promise of Living

Left: Copland signing autographs for Japanese fans.

Japanese audience might be thinking, and the response was chillingly obvious: "These people were not here then." I felt that the Dello Joio piece played by the orchestra sounded sentimental and wooshy under such circumstances.

In Nagoya, the fourth largest city in Japan, I finally caught up on my sleep and on my mail. I walked about and visited a large department store filled with people. Back in Tokyo I had calls from three of Lukas' friends who came to play tapes of music by Takemitsu for me. They were members of the recently formed radical Sogetsu Group of Composers. I wrote in my diary that "Toru Takemitsu was the composer who made the best impression. . . . He chooses his notes carefully and meaningfully. . . . I was pleased also by his personality—typically Japanese and yet a character of his own." I rehearsed and conducted (for a later radio broadcast) the Japan Philharmonic Orchestra in *Appalachian Spring* and "Hoe-Down" from *Rodeo.* I also conducted a piece, *Lyric Ode,* by my friend Jack Kennedy. No opinions were expressed by anyone about anything, but there was a very deferential attitude. Finally, before leaving Japan, I did the things one does in Tokyo—I bought a sport coat from a Singapore tailor, shopped at Takashimaya, and bought an etching.

My impressions of Japan were not clear-cut. I was rather disappointed in the general musical reaction of audiences. However, I wondered whether that might be because they show emotion differently from ourselves. In part, it makes for the fascination and in part for the dissatisfaction. From my viewpoint, it was the ubiquity of youth in Japan that was quite unique in my travel experiences. I kept wondering, Where are the old people?

We traveled on to Manila, where I made a big impression on the orchestra and the audience by appearing in a Filipino shirt, beautifully embroidered and with the tails hanging out. It was so hot, I was soaked through! In Manila, the audiences applauded during the music when they liked it enough. They only did this once though, for "Hoe-Down," played as an encore. I met with the League of Filipino Composers sponsored by the USIS. They told me I was the first serious composer to come from the United States. I found the heat so exhausting that I stayed in my room working until we left for Brisbane, Australia (5 June).

At some point in our travels, we touched down in the San Francisco airport at 2:30 in the morning. I got out to stretch my legs. There was a bookstand full of paperbacks and standing at the bookstand was a girl who was carrying two books: *What to Listen for in Music* and a volume of

Copland
in Australia,
1960.

Shakespeare plays. I did something I had never done before, but the night was solitary and I was struck by the coincidence. I offered to autograph the book for her. I said, "Would you like me to write my name in that book for you?" She looked down at both of them and said, "Which one?" I answered, "Well, I didn't write the Shakespeare!" "Oh," she said. She just couldn't imagine that the author of the book she was carrying was standing there in front of her!

I do not like to sign autographs much—it gets to be kind of boring signing your name over and over. I always remember that at one of those post-concert gatherings, some little kid came up to me. I don't know how old he was—eleven or twelve perhaps—with a dirty little piece of paper. He shoved it in front of me and said, "Sign your name." I scribbled my name hastily, handed it back to him, and said, "What are you going to do with that piece of paper?" He looked me straight in the eye and said, *"Treasure* it." Just like that. I've signed hundreds of autographs, but I'll never forget that kid saying, *"Treasure* it," with disdain, as if to say, "You're so dumb, you don't even know what I'm going to do with it!"

In Australia, everything suddenly seemed "normal" again—weather, people, language. But I was afraid it would be quite dull compared to Russia and Japan. I had to study the Tchaikovsky *Fifth Symphony* that I was scheduled to conduct in Adelaide. I shared the program with Richard Burgin. We performed in a boxing stadium, open to the night air, and so cold the men wore topcoats over their dress clothes. I had difficulty concentrating. It was all in such strong contrast to sweltering in Manila! Tod Perry was traveling with us, and I said to him as I went offstage, "Can you imagine what Koussevitzky would say if he knew I was conducting *his* orchestra in Tchaikovsky's *Fifth* in Australia!"

Back in London, I was completely confused as to waking and sleeping hours. My plan was to spend some time in Aldeburgh. I traveled there with composer Harrison Birtwistle and conductor John Carewe. We were put up in rooms without baths or telephones (I always have felt slightly uncomfortable in a room without a phone). My *Piano Quartet* was performed and the Society for the Promotion of New Music sponsored a program at which I spoke. Jack Kennedy met me as planned and caught me up on all the news from home. We were invited to tea chez Benjamin Britten, and it was very posh with the Prince of Hesse and Earl of Harewood present. I was to conduct a new piece at the Aldeburgh Festival, but it was not finished yet; instead, I conducted *Two Pieces for String Orchestra, Quiet City,* and *In The Beginning* at the Blythburgh church. I wrote to Claire [Reis], "The choir sounded like the voice of the Lord!"

Returning to London, I gave a talk for the BBC on Japanese composers. After a visit to Oxford, I flew home and was greeted at the airport by Victor Kraft in my new "buggy"—a Mercedes—bought while I was away (Victor had had an accident with my Buick with "total" damage). I arrived home to find that the country had gotten into a state of excitement and fear over the U-2 incident. Everyone was talking about bomb shelters—I was amazed! The subject came up in Ossining, but having only a few days home before leaving for Tanglewood, I was saved from making a decision. Anyway, I did not plan to stay in Ossining. Victor had been searching around for another house. He had found one in Peekskill and took me to see it. One look at the grounds with the Hudson in the distance, the gardens and woods, and the house with the separate studio, and I was sold! When I first saw the studio, I said that it looked like a room where a composer could write music. The house, "Rock Hill," is not a made-over barn as my previous homes had been. I sold Shady Lane Farm in Ossining in August 1960 and moved to Peekskill after Tanglewood, just before my sixtieth birthday. *Time* and *Newsweek* magazines came to interview me for the occasion. They found me surrounded by unpacked cartons of books, papers, recordings, and music.

I am not much of a "backward looker." My head was full of the recent past—my travels in Russia and the Far East. Nevertheless, for Tanglewood's twentieth anniversary in 1960, I allowed myself a bit of nostalgia in my usual opening address to students and faculty. "Only Randall Thompson's 'Allelulia' is the same," I said. I recalled various images from earlier years: "Ben Britten in the wings at *Peter Grimes;* the excitement of Shostie's *Seventh Symphony* played by the student orchestra conducted by Koussevitzky; young conductors such as Thor Johnson, Walter Hendel, and Lenny Bernstein; and the composers from abroad—Hindemith, Martinů, Milhaud, Honegger, Messiaen, Ibert, Dallapiccola, Petrassi, and Chávez."

I introduced Luciano Berio as guest composer for 1960. He would share the program with Leon Kirchner and myself. The famous Italian composer was a coup for Tanglewood. Leonard Burkat had convinced the Ford Foundation's international relations program to give a grant to make his presence possible. I had written to Berio in Milan (5 Feb 1960): "I have just learned that it is possible to invite you and your wife to be present during these six weeks as house guests of Mrs. Serge Koussevitzky. You probably remember the house itself, which is beautifully situated and should be comfortable. If this plan is agreeable, we would ask you to accept the designation of Composer in Residence." Berio had been a student at Tanglewood in 1951 and 1952 and was familiar with the place. He requested that he have only three or four students (Kirchner had six, I had eight[26]) so that he would be free to produce an open-air electronic concert (8 August). It was the first of its kind in the States.[27] Berio also prepared the premiere of his Fromm-commissioned work, *Circles,* for the Fromm Chamber Music Concert (1 August).

I wrote to Lenny (28 July): "Our summer is considerably enlivened by Luciano Berio who has stirred things up . . . Otherwise, routine reigns. We need you in Tanglewood—but badly!" A few changes in the Music Center in 1960 were the result of the brainstorming meetings in 1959 that had continued during the winter months.[28] Fromm Foundation activities continued with the Sunday Composers Forums. David Walker, who was put in charge of organizing them, described the arrangements.

It was complicated—a composer would leave a note in my box in the library telling the character of his piece, its duration, instrumentation, and so forth. I would put together the players at the right time in an appropriate space. At one Sunday reading, a young student by the name of Seiji Ozawa conducted a piece.[29]

The Friday afternoon Seminar in Contemporary Music began with my lecture, "Music in the Twenties," and continued with sessions by composers Berio, Kirchner, Carter, Blomdahl, and Cage.

Paul Fromm was preparing a radio series, "Composers on Composers— Twentieth-Century Profiles," for WFMT in Chicago, which was to be broadcast by over forty affiliated stations nationwide. The programs featured twelve well-known composers about other composers, as well as composers about their own music.[30] Fromm requested that I prepare a tape to give him at Tanglewood in mid-July. The programs were broadcast during the following fall and winter. Fromm had also written to Lenny Burkat expressing his wish for an all-Copland concert to celebrate my sixtieth birthday. I was apprehensive, thinking that it might seem self-serving, but when Paul Fromm was determined, watch out! Fromm's idea was "to show the three compositional phases of Copland." The result was that one of the two Monday-evening concerts was devoted to my three major piano works played by Billy Masselos. At the end of the season, Fromm wrote to me (11 August), "We are again indebted to you for the planning of our Tanglewood project. It is especially gratifying to me that the Copland recital was the high point of our Tanglewood program."

Ralph Berkowitz circulated a memorandum in 1960 suggesting a change in the name of the Center from Berkshire Music Center to Tanglewood Music Center. Most of the faculty agreed, so Tod Perry sent the request on to the trustees. "After all," said Berkowitz, "No one ever has said, 'I'm going to the Berkshire Music Center.' They always say, 'I'm going to Tanglewood.'" The suggestion was not approved, and the BMC did not become the TMC until 1985. For the public, it is not the Center that is the focal point of Tanglewood, but the Festival. I usually conducted one of my own works with the BSO in the Shed each summer; in 1960, it was the *First Symphony* (13 August).

I left the Berkshires directly after the 1960 season for my first visit to the Aspen Festival. Norman Singer, director and dean, had invited me each summer since 1957, but I had not been able to accept because I was committed to Tanglewood. Singer wrote again (August 1959): ". . . to invite you to be with us next summer when it is our intention to feature your music in celebration of your sixtieth birthday." A compromise was reached about the scheduling so I could fly to Aspen a week before the Aspen Festival, immediately after Tanglewood. Aspen offered a different atmosphere of musicmaking in a very beautiful setting. I conducted the Aspen Festival Orchestra in my *Orchestral Variations* and *Red Pony Suite* and enjoyed it so much that I promised to return if invited.

Every ten years or so, since 1926, I had put myself on the line by naming the most promising young composers in each generation; I attempted a similar assessment of the fifties. However, this decade was more difficult to describe. There were so many more composers active in many parts of the country, and I was that much further away in age from the young composers. Nevertheless, I had a pretty good idea of what was current from summers at Tanglewood and from my travels. I wrote a short article, "1959: Postscript for the Generation of the Fifties," for inclusion in the book I had been working on that was to be published by Doubleday at the time of my sixtieth birthday. In the article I wrote: "The young composer of today seems to be fighting hard to stay abreast of a fast-moving post-World War II European musical scene." By this I meant Pierre Boulez, Karlheinz Stockhausen, and Luigi Nono. I mentioned Elliott Carter as an honorable exception to this trend. The composers I singled out in 1959 as "young talents whose music commands attention" were Billy Jim Layton, Salvatore Martirano, Seymour Schifrin, Edward Miller, Yehudi Wyner, Kenneth Gaburo, and Robert Lombardo. I mentioned Gunther Schuller for his independent use of jazz with serious music and cited others for various reasons: Easley Blackwood, Noel Lee, and Mordechai Sheinkman. After *Copland on Music* was published,[31] I sent copies out to friends and colleagues, including Elliott Carter. He responded, "I rather appreciate never having been singled out in your articles as so many passed-up past masters and dead wood were, since by this it is made more clear than ever that my music has taken an opposite direction—one that can be talked about now and not reminisced about."

Copland on Music includes reprints from earlier publications as well as material written especially for this book (the article on Boulanger, for example).[32] Being away so much of the time prior to publication of *Copland on Music*, I needed an assistant and was fortunate in obtaining the services of Yehudi Wyner, who had given me the original idea for the book. The reception of my book was generally favorable, although there was some criticism that much of the material had appeared elsewhere. My review of René Leibowitz' book on Schoenberg and his school drew interest because in it I expressed my attitude to twelve-tone theory. The essays on Mozart, Berlioz, Liszt, and Fauré were praised for their simplicity and directness. Eric Salzman reviewed *Copland on Music* for *The New York Times Book Review*, which appeared the day before my sixtieth birthday. He wrote: ". . . Aaron Copland writes about music in the same way that he composes. The qualities of clarity, liveliness, elegance, precision, and directness which distinguish his music make him a fine essayist."

My sixtieth birthday was a blockbuster, "a deluge," as Nadia Boulanger called it in her congratulatory letter. I had great trouble making a connection with that number—sixty! It seemed to have no relation to how I felt, thank goodness! In an interview at the time, I said that fifty had been worse. I pointed out that since I had no children with whom to compare myself, I couldn't really tell that I was older. However, no one could accuse me of sitting back and taking it easy on my sixtieth. The weekend before my birthday, I conducted the New York Philharmonic at Carnegie Hall in their weekend subscription concerts. The program included my *Symphonic Ode* and *El Salón México,* as well as pieces by Gluck [Arnold], Franchetti, and the Dvořák *Violin Concerto* (the rather odd program was because the Philharmonic was celebrating violinist John Corigliano's twenty-fifth anniversary with the orchestra, as well as my birthday). Lenny Bernstein had written during the previous summer:

> I have an idea, which will be doing something nobody else can do for your sixtieth, and that is to make a whole TV show for the kids (the Shell series, originating in Carnegie) on the subject of the Venerable Giggling Dean. . . . This will happen on the 12th of November (Sat.) at noon in Carnegie Hall. I want you to participate, do you hear?!

I responded (28 July 1960): "The only thing I don't want to be presented as is grandpa for the kiddies." I appeared with Lenny and William Warfield on the Philharmonic Young People's Concert, "Aaron Copland's Birthday Party." It was taped to be broadcast later on CBS TV (12 February 1961). Lenny was conductor and commentator, and I conducted *El Salón México* at the end of the program. Lenny is a born teacher—he had those young people enjoying every moment.

Television appearances always brought tons of mail from many places. This time, it was the fan letters from kids that delighted me. One twelve-year-old wrote, "My teacher said I should pick someone I don't know anything about for my music assignment. I saw you on TV and don't know anything about you, but I like your fast music. Can you tell me how you write fast music?" Another letter came from a neighbor who had a small store near us when I was growing up in Brooklyn:

> Whenever I heard your name mentioned, I always wanted to see you, but I could never see your face until today on Leonard Bernstein's program. It was a great moment for me and my family to see you on television. We all knew you so well. We were such good neighbors. From our little neighborhood came out a lot of geniuses and good people. I am sure that Boys' High School will be happy to know they had a pupil like you. . . . You've made good for everybody.

The major sixtieth birthday event was a two-concert celebration by the Juilliard, one on my birthday and another the following evening. In the audience was a solid representation of the intellectual life of New York, along with many of my friends and colleagues. I dined with Minna Daniel ("Mink" as I call her for reasons known only to us), and she accompanied me to the concert and the Boosey & Hawkes postconcert party at the Gotham Hotel, at which Bill Schuman delighted the guests with a parody of *Lincoln Portrait*—about me, of course.

The first Juilliard program included *In The Beginning*, the score for my early film *The City, Sextet*, and three staged excerpts from *The Tender Land*;³³ the second program was devoted to my three major piano works played by Bill Masselos. The celebration did not end with the concerts: The entire issue of *The Juilliard Review* (Winter 1960–1961) was a souvenir album containing the concert programs, photographs, and an essay, "The Copland Festival," by Richard Franko Goldman. All in all, it was the most satisfying kind of celebration for a composer.

In addition to the Juilliard concerts, Benny Goodman played the *Clarinet Concerto* with the Orchestra of the Americas (16 November 1960) and concerts were held in my honor in other parts of the country.³⁴ After hearing about the West Coast tribute, I wrote to Leo (24 November), "You've been an *angel* to engage in all this activity—and I'm forever grateful. Lots of fuss here in the east—especially in the newspapers. So I've been spoiled beyond measure."

Boosey & Hawkes prepared an updated catalogue of my works, and Doubleday published my book *Copland on Music* to coincide with my birthday. Columbia Records released two recordings of my works: Masselos playing the *Piano Fantasy* and Lenny's version of *The Second Hurricane* (with *Rodeo* and *Billy the Kid*).

Lenny wrote after hearing the test pressing of *Hurricane:*

> Mainly I'm writing because I'm so impressed all over again with the music. It is lovely and endlessly fresh: Neither the simplicity nor the grandeur stales. . . . I hope you like it; it will be our November release on Columbia, along with *Billy* and *Rodeo,* making a delightful, gay (though costly) birthday package!

It took me over a month to answer all the tributes and greetings, among them ones from Clurman, Stravinsky, Lenny and Felicia, and even a telegram signed "Papa and Mama of Leonard." Messages arrived from England, France, Russia, Argentina, and other Latin American countries, and David Diamond wrote from Italy about the symphony (his eighth) that he was composing in honor of my birthday (9 November):

> I am on the last measures (orchestration) of "your" symphony. I am sure that by the 14th I shall have it done. I am pleased with the work and hope you will be. What these years of our friendship and sustained faith have been is *all* there, in those pages.

I heard from all my family as I did every birthday, even my long-silent cousin Percy Uris, who remembered me as "the young man who lived at 1 University Place and played the piano so vigorously that we had to move him to one of our numerous vacant apartments where the piano playing (I was about to call it noise) would not disturb others."

Bill Schuman's "A Birthday Salute to Aaron Copland" in the *Herald Tribune* (30 October) kicked things off in the press. *Time, Newsweek, Musical America,* and *The New York Times Magazine* followed with articles.[35] I was pleased to tell interviewers that I was in the midst of composing a new piece. It was gratifying to be able to bring forth surprise from the press at its unusual instrumentation: three violins, three violas, and three cellos.

Nonet for Solo Strings was commissioned by Dumbarton Oaks in honor of the fiftieth wedding anniversary of Mr. and Mrs. Robert Woods Bliss (Dumbarton Oaks, with its research library and collection, was presented to Harvard University by Mr. and Mrs. Bliss.) The piece was to have been premiered at a special concert celebrating the anniversary and conducted by Nadia Boulanger, who was a longtime friend of the music-loving Bliss family (14 April 1958). In a letter to Mrs. Bliss, I apologized that the pressure of other commitments prevented me from completing the com-

Copland demonstrating bowing to string players for *Nonet*, Berlin, 1960.

position in time for the event, but I attended the concert with Nadia and participated in a symposium with Walter Piston. When *Nonet* was finished (December 1960), I conducted it at a private subscription concert at Dumbarton Oaks with nine string players from the National Symphony Orchestra (2 March 1961). I also conducted works by Purcell, Handel, and Bach. The program included my *Piano Variations,* Frank Glazer pianist. I wrote to Chávez (March 1961): "My main news is that I completed my

Nonet, and it was premiered at Dumbarton Oaks last week. I wonder how you will like it? I, myself, thought it had a poignant and elegiac sound—almost autumnal in quality."

Nonet is dedicated to Nadia Boulanger, "after forty years of friendship." When composing it, I had looked through my notebook of musical ideas and found two pages that seemed usable: one that gave me my main tune (undated); the other, a half page (dated "5/22/50"). Perhaps *tune* does not accurately describe the thematic material: a series of rather darkly colored three-voiced chords. The nature of these chords gives off a crowded, rather sober, and perhaps somewhat lugubrious feeling that is characteristic of this work and no other I have written. The idea of the particular instrumentation for *Nonet* came from these chords, which I "heard" for three solo cellos. Starting with that, I decided to balance the cellos with a combination of strings, which, in its very makeup, would produce a darkly colored sound. Those first three chords generate most of the harmonic and melodic material for the entire composition.

The one-movement *Nonet* is about eighteen minutes in duration. Its general structure is easily grasped: two slow, rather somber sections flanking a livelier midsection. The opening chords are played first by the three cellos with deadened vibrato. After the material rises and subsides in a slow-moving progression, the violas enter one by one, then similarly, the violins. The longer notes give way to shorter ones until the music reaches a complex rhythmic climax in the midsection. The music then broadens and gradually evolves into another lyric section that bears a linear relation to the vertical chordal beginning, leading back to the music of the opening. *Nonet* is introspective and subjective in mood, less diatonic than most of my earlier music and, therefore, freer in its chord relationships. I like to think it shows a continuing development in the type of harmonies and sonorities employed.[36]

In the year of the premiere, 1961, I conducted performances of *Nonet* at Brandeis University, in Chicago, for a BBC broadcast in London, and the New York premiere at a Composers Showcase concert at the Museum of Modern Art (5 April 1962). The occasion was a memorial concert for Theodore Chanler by some of his friends: Nadia Boulanger, Walter Piston, Virgil Thomson, and myself. When Leo Smit was about to conduct *Nonet* at Ojai, he wrote, asking advice, and I replied, "Try to make the beginning real special in color—a moyen-age gloom (but not dull)."[37] Lawrence Morton heard the performance and deferred an opinion: "You took a long time to write the piece and so you must allow me some to learn it."

the Park Shelton Hotel

WOODWARD AT EAST KIRBY • DETROIT 2, MICHIGAN • PHONE TRINITY 5-9500
• TELETYPE DE-966

Leo, my boy:
                    Awfully pleased to get
your preliminary note about the Nonet.
Your assumptions are quite right about
not hurrying the H.H. Try to make the
beginning (until bottom of p. 1) real
special in color — a moyen âge gloom,
(but not dull.) But you'll know how to do
it all, I'm sure.
        I'm "conducting" it in Wash. D.C.
(Inter-Amer. Festival) to-morrow, and then
again in Brandeis on Friday, and then
again in London May 18.
        At the moment I'm on a little tour:
Peabody Inst., Goucher College, Univ. of Delaware,
Conducting the Phil. Orch at the

IN THE HEART OF DETROIT'S CULTURAL CENTER

Ann Arbor Festival in Orch.
and Tender Land Suite.
        What do you do this summer?
        Let me hear how it went?
                        Love—
                        Aaron—

Letter from Copland to Leo Smit about *Nonet* (undated).

Most praise for *Nonet* came for its unusual combination of instruments and the string sonorities. Ingolf Dahl and Leon Kirchner both admired and conducted *Nonet* [Dahl in 1969, Los Angeles; Kirchner in 1974, Cambridge]. Ingolf wrote (15 March 1969), "What pleased me particularly was the variety of string color throughout. . . . The passage between four and five is particularly lovely, with that bravely sad rise of the seventh in the melody. . . ."

Nonet was subjected to a rigorous analysis in *Perspectives of New Music.* The article, "Aaron Copland's *Nonet:* Two Views," was by Eric Salzman and Paul Des Marais: The former treated the piece as a nonserial work; the latter as a serial composition.[38] I cannot say that I recognized my intentions in either discussion, but I appreciated two views being given, which made the point that music can be analyzed according to whatever system the analyst cares to apply. I had a long letter from Leon Kirchner, full of quotes and musical examples, criticizing both of the analyses (17 January 1963).

It seems that the twelve-tone crowd had hoped I would continue in the direction of my *Piano Quartet* (1950) and *Piano Fantasy* (1957), which made use of serial techniques. Then, here I came along and confused the issue again with *Nonet,* a piece that could not be claimed by either the twelve-toners or the diatonic composers. Since the critics could not categorize *Nonet* as belonging to either my "accessible" or my "austere" style, it has been called "transitional." In an article on *Nonet,* Stephen Plaistow concluded, ". . . it must be observed that the *Nonet* does little to advance the expressive boundaries of Copland's style. . . . More positively it can be said that the *Nonet* is a work of charm and immense technical polish . . . a disappointment from Copland is worth more than run-of-the-mill competence from most others."[39]

In concert halls whose size justifies the use of larger groups of strings, specific larger combinations can be employed when performing *Nonet*— up to forty-eight players in all, but, as I stated in the score, "The work should under no circumstances be performed by a string orchestra as normally constituted." William Steinberg conducted the New York Philharmonic in the expanded instrumentation (19, 20, 21 November 1964). Critic Alan Rich wrote in the *Herald Tribune:* "The augmented version detracts not at all from the work's high quality. It is grave, intense music, beautifully constructed and eloquent."

Interlude V

Dwight D. Eisenhower had been the oldest President to hold office; by the time of the 1961 election, he and the country seemed immobilized. When John F. Kennedy came into the White House, a cultural revolution was about to begin. The forty-three-year-old Kennedy held out the promise that America would come alive again. Economist John Kenneth Galbraith foretold it in his popular book of 1958, *The Affluent Society:* America had limitless resources, and Jack Kennedy was the man to put them to use.[1] The Kennedy years would be ones of activism, commitment, and, above all, idealism.

The American people fell in love with the handsome young President and his beautiful family, and for artists and intellectuals, it seemed as though the messiah had arrived. The Kennedys really cared about education and culture. No wonder Washington in the Kennedy years was called "the new Camelot!" The President and First Lady promptly made their artistic interests known by holding a White House Gala in honor of Pablo Casals (13 November 1961) to which they invited outstanding figures in the arts, Copland among them. He described the occasion in a diary:

> I sat between Mrs. Walter Lippman and Mrs. William Paley. Pierre Salinger and Senator Mike Mansfield were at our table. President Kennedy was in full view the entire time, while ten violins played through dinner. Surprised at his reddish-brown hair. No evil in the face, but plenty of ambition there, no doubt. Mrs K. statuesque. A ceremonial entry with the presentation of colors preceded dinner at which guests were presented to President and Mrs. Kennedy. Seemed to note a glance of recognition from Mr. and Mrs. Kennedy. After dinner we were treated to a concert by Pablo Casals. No American music. The next step.

It did not take long for that "next step." In May 1962, the Kennedys planned a performance of *Billy the Kid* by the Ballet Theatre for a program in honor of the visiting president of the Ivory Coast Republic. With American choreographer Eugene Loring and leading American composer

At the White House on the occasion of the performance of *Billy the Kid* (left to right): John Kriza, Eugene Loring, Copland, President Kennedy, Mrs. Felix Houphet-Boigny (wife of the President of the Ivory Coast Republic), and Mrs. Kennedy, May 1962.

Aaron Copland as honored guests, American dancer John Kriza in the role of the quintessential western cowboy, and the glamorous Kennedys and the handsome entourage from Africa—all in formal attire in the elegant surroundings—the White House proudly displayed American arts and creativity to the world.

The Kennedy administration offered hope for the revitalization of the arts in America: Lincoln Center for the Performing Arts was scheduled to open in 1962, and plans were in progress for other large art centers around the country; individual artists were experiencing the heady sensation of support and approval from the top. The "nothing is impossible" Kennedy spirit infiltrated the arts. What could never before mix, could now be tried. Multimedia events became popular, and in all the arts, lines were developing and crossing in many directions.

Those who had lived under the shadow of McCarthyism could finally believe the nightmare was over. For the first time since 1953, Copland renewed his passport without apprehension. As one of the most gifted and articulate musicians of the time, now entering his sixth decade, Copland

WESTERN UNION
TELEGRAM
W. P. MARSHALL, PRESIDENT

NO. WDS.-CL. OF SVC.	PD. OR COLL.	CASH NO.		CHARGE TO THE ACCOUNT OF		TIME FILED

Send the following message, subject to the terms on back hereof, which are hereby agreed to

To Aaron Copland   August 19, 19619

Street and No.
Care of or
Apt. No. _____ Place _____

I AM DELIGHTED TO LEARN THAT YOU WILL RECEIVE TODAY A MEDAL
FOR DISTINGUISHED SERVICE IN THE FIELD OF MUSIC FROM EDWARD
MACDOWELL ASSOCIATIO . YOUR CREATIVE MIND AND IMAGINATION HAVE
BEEN A SIGNIFICANT FORCE IN THE CULTURAL LIFE OF THIS NATION
AND OF THE WORLD'S COMMUNITY. IT IS MOST HEARTENING THAT THE
CEREMONY IS TAKING PLACE AT THE MACDOWELL COLONY WHICH HAS
PROVIDED FOR YOU AND SO MANY OTHER AMERICAN ARTISTS SUCH A
FINE ENVIRONMENT IN WHICH TO PURSUE YOUR WORK.
WITH ALL GOOD WISHES.
                              s/ John F. Kennedy

Senders's name and address (For reference)   Sender's telephone number

Congratulatory telegram from President Kennedy (19 August 1961) on the occasion of the awarding of the MacDowell Colony Medal to Copland.

was refreshed and stimulated by the optimistic atmosphere during the Kennedy years. On behalf of the President, Secretary of State Dean Rusk invited Copland to join a small working committee "whose purpose is to prepare a recommendation by July first for the State Department advising on philosophy, concept, and criteria for an international cultural project. They need your wisdom and hope you can serve." Copland was pleased to accept.

The brutal assassination of John Kennedy was a tragedy of such proportion that the circumstances of how and where the news was heard is remembered by every American who heard it that November afternoon in 1963. Copland recalls that he was in the opera house in Munich rehearsing the orchestra for the premiere of the ballet *Dance Panels*. He said, "I stayed on that day to watch the other ballets. The orchestra suddenly became silent. I thought some local person had died. Then the director, Heinz Rosen, came over to tell me, "Your President Kennedy has been killed!" Copland recalls his feelings at the time: "I was shocked. At such a moment one wants to have a fellow countryman nearby. It was sad to be alone and hard to believe. Even when I attended a memorial service at Amerika House the next day."

The sixties are described as a decade of radical change and upheaval. The most profound changes followed in the wake of the Kennedy assassination, which caused sustained and debilitating trauma to the country. In the aftermath of the nation's grief, "the Kennedy legend" was kept alive for a while, a fact that Lyndon Johnson had to live with during much of his administration, sometimes uncomfortably. Johnson did not care greatly for the arts, and he rated low with intellectuals. Nevertheless, the National Council on the Arts was established in Johnson's administration (1964) and following the inauguration, under pressure from former Kennedy supporters, Johnson agreed to hold The First White House Festival of the Arts (24 March 1965). When several prominent artists refused to participate as a gesture of protest against the Vietnam War (poet Robert Lowell in the forefront), Johnson was so incensed, he vowed to stay clear of "those people" during the remainder of his time in office.[2] Copland, who had received the Medal of Freedom the previous September and had attended the Johnson inauguration concert in January 1965, was not invited to participate in the Festival of the Arts. Because of the Vietnam protests, the Johnson people were being careful about associating with those who had confrontations with McCarthy. (Ironically, the liberal playwright Arthur Miller had been asked to speak at the festival before the political implications surfaced, and his invitation could not be rescinded without embarrassment to the President.)

During the ensuing Johnson years, there was a good deal of discussion about government support of the arts, but it was known and felt that the President himself was not committed. As the decade progressed, Copland, as an artist and public figure, was affected by the changed spirit and the upheavals in the country, but his personal life and career were neither turbulent nor changeable. The pattern of his life had been set earlier, and it continued: conducting tours, lecture and teaching engagements in the United States and abroad, interspersed with quiet periods at home among familiar faces and unchanging surroundings.

At the start of each new year, a red leather appointment book, with "Aaron Copland" and the year imprinted in gold, arrived mysteriously at Copland's house in Peekskill. (No one can recall who was responsible for sending it.) One year, the diary failed to arrive, and Copland exclaimed in mock horror, *"Mon dieu,* how can I go on without it?" (It was a great relief when delivery resumed the following year.) After Copland transcribed fixed dates, such as quarterly tax payments and birthdays of friends and relatives, into his new diary, the year was ready to begin. Taken individually, these appointment books reveal useful details of time and place; over the decade, they show the continuity and stability that was essential to Copland's sense of well-being. The diaries also demonstrate a gradual change of emphasis away from the solitary life of composer toward a more public one of conductor.

The pattern of Copland's day-to-day existence can be reconstructed from the regularity of certain diary entries: trips to New York—"reserve at Harvard Club," "Philharmonic rehearsal," "B & H meeting," "ASCAP." For out-of-town dates—"Pick up plane tickets and tux," "pack scores." Or for times at home in Peekskill—"DW coming to work," "meet Clurman at train." At the back of each appointment book, Copland listed the commissions offered, marking rejections with an *X,* acceptances with a checkmark. These lists make interesting reading, considering some of the music that might have been. Asked whether he regretted not accepting more of the commissions, Copland responded, "Good Heavens, no! I'm lucky to have composed the one or two a year I *did* accept."

The birthdates marked by Copland into his appointment books were of the same friends and colleagues every year: "Clurman, Mink [Minna Daniel], Claire [Reis], LB [Bernstein], BS [Schuman], DD [Diamond], Alvin [Ross], DW [David Walker], V [Victor Kraft], Chávez, Olga [Koussevitzky]." The list changed only when someone died, which occurred with increasing frequency as Copland grew older. The greatest shock was the sudden death of Irving Fine in 1962. Fine was a younger colleague and dear friend. Irving, Verna, and their three daughters were the closest Copland had to a family of his own.[3] He wrote to Boulanger (September 1962): "Now—after Teddy Chanler and Mel Smith—another sad loss— Irving Fine." When Clifford Odets died in 1963, Copland heard from David Diamond (17 August): "I am just sick about Cliff; and I know how you must feel." Then Colin McPhee and Marc Blitzstein both died in 1964. In a tribute to Blitzstein, Copland wrote, "I feel saddened to realize how little his music was known by the current generation. It was ironic, with all Blitzstein's accomplishments, to think that his fame rested on his talent as translator of *The Threepenny Opera.*"[4]

Copland's own health was excellent, and his yearly checkups with his doctor, Arnold Salop, duly notated in his appointment books, were routine. Only once during the sixties was he hospitalized, for a prostate operation, from which he recovered rapidly. Copland's doctor, lawyer, accountant, dentist, publisher—all stayed the same through the years. David Walker,

Copland with great-nephews Matthew and Daniel Levey, and the dog, Nadja, 1977.

who became Copland's assistant in 1952, is still his close friend and colleague. Victor Kraft, an intimate friend for many years, was remarried in 1960. The couple had a baby boy and Copland was named godfather. They lived close by, and Victor continued to take care of the grounds and the car at Rock Hill when Copland traveled. Even when Victor became difficult and demanding, Copland would never abandon him. As for Copland's family, he sent checks on birthdays and for special occasions and he helped take care of his sister-in-law Dorothy. "Dot" appears regularly in the appointment books, as does "La" (sister Laurine). Not having a family of his own, nieces and nephews (nine in all) received his attention, and as time went on, grandnieces and nephews. The oldest of these, Roger Levey, said:

> Uncle Aaron was never too busy or too far away to remember the family. When I got married, he wrote from the Connaught Hotel in London, and we heard from him when each of the children was born. We went to see Uncle Aaron

Copland at his desk in the seventies.

Photograph by Victor Kraft.

conduct at Tanglewood several times. Once (I must have been about ten years old), I was impressed with seeing him wearing a white tuxedo and conducting in the Shed and the next thing, we were all back at his place and he had on a white apron and was carving a turkey, acting as host. He liked to do that kind of thing at home. There was always a very warm feeling between Uncle Aaron and the family. If he thought any of us was interested in music, he went all out. He left his Steinway at our apartment once when he was between houses, and there it stayed because I was taking lessons.

After settling into his new home in Peekskill, Copland gave one big housewarming party in the fall of 1961. Thereafter, he enjoyed inviting friends and colleagues individually or a few at a time for lunch or dinner. He took pride in showing the place and liked to walk around the grounds or in the woods with his guests. For several years, a Belgian couple (Mireille and Gaston Varaertenryck and their poodle "Poupette") kept the house and grounds in good order. Copland was upset when they decided to leave, and delighted when they returned after a brief stint with another employer.

Few changes were ever made in the Peekskill house: If something wore out, it was likely to be replaced with the same or a similar item. When Copland moved in, he brought with him from Ossining his favorite desk, which someone had put together from a large piece of wood balanced on

Copland and Ralph Hawkes at Tanglewood, c. 1949.

carpenters' "horses." Copland has used it in his studio ever since. He has one of each piece of clothing—a black overcoat, a beret, one dark suit, a tuxedo. His car, once a Mercedes, remained a Mercedes.

Copland never considered staying anywhere in New York City but the Harvard Club, his "home away from home." One day when he entered the dining room and heard recorded music being piped in, he was appalled to think he might have to find a new place to take guests to lunch or dinner. (Perhaps other members complained, too, since a week later, the Harvard Club dining room was silent as usual.)

Boosey & Hawkes has been Copland's publisher from the time Benjamin Britten introduced Copland to Ralph Hawkes in 1938. This long-standing association, so much in character with Copland, has been an important one in his career. Through the years, various people at Boosey & Hawkes have been in charge of Copland's catalogue,[5] but no one person is as knowledgeable about rights, royalties, contracts, and the myriad details surrounding Copland's music as Sylvia Goldstein.

311

Sylvia Goldstein[6]

I began working at Boosey & Hawkes in 1940 and have been concerned with Copland's account since then. In 1945, I attended law school at night and got my law degree, but I never left the firm as I had intended. This is a different kind of firm. We represent only a small number of important composers. My contract work has been with all of them, but Aaron has always been an important part of our activities. Working with him was different from the other composers. Aaron liked to stay out of the limelight. He was a good businessman, precise and careful. He always wanted copies of his contracts, and he knew where everything was. He was easy to deal with, but not easily led. Aaron always knew what he wanted.

I remember he used to work very hard on titles, from Lincoln Portrait *to* Inscape. *Not that they meant a lot in terms of the music, but he was convinced titles have a lot to do with the way the public reacts to a piece. Only the ballets he left to the choreographers to name.* Appalachian Spring *was always* Ballet for Martha *until Martha Graham named it. Aaron gave it to her as a gift, and as long as Martha danced it, she didn't pay for it.*

Aaron brought back thoughtful gifts when he traveled, and he gave them to me along with nice notes: a painting, Jensen jewelry from Europe, a bowl, bangle bracelets. And when he returned from his first trip to Israel, he gave me a shofar.

Aaron came to rely on my judgment. He would ask my opinion about requests to use his music. One time when we were having a change in personnel, he said, "If Sylvia goes, I go!" He wanted to know there were people he could trust taking care of his music. Aaron was worried about the continuity. He liked the sameness of things.

Stuart Pope, president of the American branch of Boosey & Hawkes from 1964 to 1984, became closely involved with Copland's music and career.

Stuart Pope[7]

Aaron was the most civilized person with whom to work. He was certainly the most businesslike of composers. He understood the business aspects of

Copland with Stuart Pope, 1979.

music publishing, which is most unusual in composers. The first question Aaron would ask when a proposal concerning his music came up was "Can we make any money out of it?" If the answer was yes, we would then look further and deal with the matter seriously. When Aaron got his annual financial statements, he went through them and then made an appointment to go through them with us. I mean he went through them from line to line with questions. "Why have we sold this piece more this year than last?" "Can't we do something about the Dance Symphony?" *And so on.*

Aaron's contract had been standard, with his royalties higher than they would be for an unknown or unestablished composer. Not long after I arrived at Boosey & Hawkes' New York office, Aaron's contract was due for renewal. It was in 1965 or 1966, and Aaron's lawyer, Abe Friedman, and I negotiated a rather special deal, under which we took a kind of mercenary attitude, gambling on Aaron's longevity. Not having heirs to be concerned about, he was to receive higher royalties for ten years or life, and on his death, the royalties would drop below normal. (This is, of course, aside from ASCAP, which is the usual 50–50 arrangement.) It has worked out far better for Aaron than for B & H, but they have done very well with Aaron. Everything of Aaron's has been published, so they no longer have major expenses with his music.

We always had a lot to talk about, and most of our meetings were at the Harvard Club. I was a musician, but Aaron really only cared that his publisher be a good businessman, as was Ralph Hawkes, who was not a musician. It is a disappointment to me that so few of the remaining serious music publishers today cannot see the responsibility to do more promotion of their composers—so many publishers take on a piece rather than a composer.

I made an effort to develop the American list at B & H. I inherited two composers and brought ten others in. I recall that Aaron met me on my first visit to Tanglewood. Roger Sessions was with him, and they showed me around. In the course of conversation, I said to both of them, "Who are the young composers I should be hearing?" Sessions said, "Never mind about the younger ones, how about me?!" A year or so later at Tanglewood, Aaron asked, "Do you know the music of Jacob Druckman?" He advised me to hear the concert on which Jacob's Dark Upon the Harp *was being played. I signed Jacob as a B & H composer that very day. Aaron also recommended David Del Tredici and Barbara Kolb. He cared deeply about other peoples' work.*

Copland tried to keep au courant with what was happening in the music world, no easy task at a time when there were many composers and no dominant musical style. Copland's thinking at the time can best be discerned from his own writings. From an unpublished journal entry, it seems Copland was in an introspective mood (1961):

On "depth" in music: How can notes—mere notes—project philosophically profound thoughts? And yet, certain composers by comparison with other composers do appear to be more deeply serious, more able to handle "thoughts" that dig deeper, seeming to reflect ideas that evoke a world of philosophy. I have thought of this more than once, curiously enough, while listening to the works of Shostakovich. Whatever else I might say about Shostakovich's many musical qualities, it strikes me that he is not at all the deep thinker in the sense I indicate here. It is all the more strange in that he often puts on the role of the "philosopher," musically speaking. . . . What is "deep" in music? My mind thinks first of all of the *Orgelbuchlein* of Bach. But why are these short organ pieces "deep?" How does Beethoven break "depth" in the slow movements of the late string quartets? Or Mozart or Palestrina or Purcell? It would seem that they touch within each of us some deep well of sensitivity, an area of musical empathy that even their own music does not always reach.

These thoughts of mine suggest that when musicians insist that music is "just music," and that one shouldn't attempt to read "meanings" into mere note patterns, they are not probing "deep" enough.

In an unpublished article, "Where Are We?" (1963), Copland compared the contemporary situation to earlier years:

> The preoccupations we had in the twenties find almost no echo today. For example, the desire some of us had to establish America's voice in the context of serious concert music. The use of folk tunes and jazz as a basis for a specifically native music has been completely abandoned. It was established and so it isn't needed any longer.

Copland told Walter Piston (1963), "People always want to shove me into the Americana idea more than I really want. Nobody wants to be an 'American' composer now as they did."[8] To another friend, he said, "Young composers today wouldn't be caught dead with a folk tune!"[9] An unpublished typescript, prepared for a lecture in Buenos Aires, "The Aesthetic Climate of Today," shows Copland questioning the validity of music journals that were filled with analyses and theories understandable only to those with scientific knowledge. He wrote (1963), "The composer asks himself whether he ought not go back to school to study physics, acoustics, and higher mathematics, if only to save music from being 'taken over' by the engineers and technicians."

Copland's conducting career was escalating: city orchestras and college groups around the country; European tours almost every year, sometimes twice yearly; Mexico periodically. With London as his European base (where many of Copland's recordings were made), Copland frequently toured elsewhere: Yugoslavia, Portugal, and Spain (spring 1961)[10]; Japan (1962); a State Department tour of Latin America (1963), where Copland was surprised to see many of his old friends[11]; and Israel (1968).[12] When Copland returned from these trips, his mail was awesome. That he continued to answer it all personally is little short of astonishing—the number of requests for Guggenheim Fellowship recommendations alone was staggering!

One of the continuing activities in Copland's life was Tanglewood. For twenty-one years, since 1940, he knew that come spring, it was time to prepare for the upcoming session of the Music Center. Retirement from Tanglewood in 1965 would be a major change, one that was to be accomplished gradually. Tanglewood was Copland's channel to young composers. Teaching was a learning process for him as well as for his students. Copland may have heard more serial music than he might have wished, but by constant exposure, he became genuinely interested in what the system might do for his own music.

Copland at a recording session, London, c. 1960.

Tanglewood was the closest Copland ever had to a steady teaching position. There were many offers, but only one had seriously tempted him: In 1945, William Schuman, recently appointed president of Juilliard, had invited Copland to join the faculty. Copland accepted, but when it came to actually fixing his name to the agreement, he had second thoughts. What Copland wrote to Schuman at that time held true for the rest of Copland's career (2 January 1946):

> I've been having the great inner struggle of all time. At the eleventh hour, faced with the prospect of tying myself down to a thirty-hour-week job, I got the jitters. . . . My deepest inner concern seems to be a need to think of myself as free to move about when and where I please and to let my mind dwell solely on my own music if I happen to feel that way. I hope this won't come as too great a shock. You'll probably think it uncharacteristic of me to not know my own mind for so long but put it down to my real wish to work with you and your own potent charm.

316

Copland knew that the decision was right for him, but he admitted to feeling a sharp pang of regret when the Juilliard bulletin appeared without his name. Similarly, in 1965, Copland knew the time had come to retire from Tanglewood. He would miss the exposure to young composers at the Music Center, the Berkshires, and his barn in Richmond. Nineteen sixty-one was Copland's last full season at the Music Center[13]; in 1962, when Erich Leinsdorf came in to replace Munch as music director, Copland took a leave of absence, and when he returned, it was on part-time basis. Leonard Burkat left to take a position with Columbia Records, and his assistant, Harry Kraut, took over as administrator of the Music Center.

Harry Kraut[14]

An alienation took place between Aaron and Tanglewood, which everyone tended to blame on Erich Leinsdorf, but actually it preceded him somewhat. In 1960, Aaron went on tour with the BSO to Japan. Aaron enjoyed it no end; the orchestra thought it was about okay, but unfortunately, no one, not even the public, was enthusiastic about Aaron in the role of conductor. Everyone loved him as a composer and was appreciative of what he had done at Tanglewood, but, at the price of inviting him to conduct the BSO, there was great hesitation. So by the time Leinsdorf came on, the decision was already pretty much made: with Aaron embarked on a conducting career, it would be too embarrassing for him to be at Tanglewood but not invited to conduct in the Shed. I was a partisan of Aaron's, because he played a really vital role (that wasn't filled at Tanglewood by Munch) by conducting his own music and other American music. And Leinsdorf had too much of an eye on the box office to want to do an awful lot of American music.

Leinsdorf was deeply interested in the school, if not much interested in Aaron's kind of music. The structure had remained the same all during Munch's time, and it was getting harder each year to maintain a high level of student quality. There was not the volume of good string players then, and many were going to other summer places. They were given the impression by their teachers that if they were really good, God forbid they should show interest in playing in an orchestra! There were not so many good composition students applying, either.

Leinsdorf was given a mandate by the BSO trustees to do something about the Center. My juggling the numbers persuaded them it would not cost that much more money to keep it going. The simple change that was made between 1963 and 1964 was that Paul Fromm's money was used as the main support for the entire performance program, and all the contemporary music activities were melded into the performance program rather than being separate. Fromm approved, agreed, and increased his support. This enabled the underwriting of the new Fellowship Program, and attracted the best students.

Tod Perry stayed through all the changes—he is still a trustee of the orchestra—a remarkable man and a great fan of Aaron's. It was Tod who offered me a full-time job with the BSO in 1958. Beginning as Burkat's assistant, I got to meet with Aaron Copland to discuss the student applications and scores, and was impressed with just sitting in the same room with him! As I came to know him, I saw what we all found—a very nice fellow who would listen to whatever one wanted to discuss—music, management, organization, public relations. Aaron was able to strike right to the core of an issue and set us straight. He was never self-promoting or egotistical about his own work. In fact, very much to the contrary: If someone suggested a whole Copland program, he would recommend incorporating other works.

I hired Dan Gustin as my assistant in 1965, and he has carried on the continuity: Dan is also a great Copland admirer. With Ozawa as director, it became a different scene again. Aaron was invited back after he retired, but there were fewer invitations than he might have liked. Perhaps he thought that his friends in the BSO had deserted him, and in fact there were few of them left around Tanglewood, except for Tod, Dan, and myself. The new people were interested in the international music scene rather than anything nationalistic and American. Aaron was having a wonderful time conducting all over the world, and it may have been hard for him to understand why Boston and New York did not pay the same attention to him as a conductor.

Being a good disciple of Aaron Copland and taking seriously his writings on musical meaning, I felt like the wrong guy in the wrong job, trying to like (let alone promote) some of the serial, atonal music better. When William Steinberg came in as director of the Boston Symphony, he wasn't interested at all in the school. I finally left Boston myself to work for Leonard Bernstein in 1971. I remember what Aaron said when I told him I was going to work for Lenny. "Well! That will keep you busy!" I was never quite sure what he meant, but he was right, as usual.

In 1963, when Copland announced to Erich Leinsdorf that he wished to be in residence for the month of August only, Leinsdorf's reaction was "Since you really exploded a bomb by saying you wished to devote only half the summer to Tanglewood, I am most anxious to see you and discuss that problem and what becomes of your position as chairman of the faculty." Copland suggested that Gunther Schuller become acting head of the composition department. In addition to Schuller and Copland, the composition faculty included Foss, Paul Jacobs, and visiting Greek composer Yannis Xenakis from Paris.

After a hiatus in Paul Fromm's involvement during the changeover from Munch to Leinsdorf, fourteen Fromm Players were reinstated in 1963, and Fromm began working toward a major Festival of Contemporary Music to begin the following season.[15] Copland, aware that offerings at the Center in the past were in need of updating, drafted ideas for courses in electronic music, serial techniques, and percussion. In the summer of 1963, David Del Tredici was a composition student at Tanglewood, and Copland recognized in him a special talent.

David Del Tredici [16]

I might be the last composer Aaron supported in a tremendous way. I had just come to New York from California and was floundering around in the usual way. On a lark, I sent a tape of my music to Aaron. A few months later, mysteriously, I received a letter offering me a Fromm commission. So I was off to Tanglewood in 1963 and met for the first time the great man who was to become a friend. To this day, Aaron has never said there was a connection between the tape I sent and the commission, but I have a strong feeling there was.

Aaron was using serialism when I first got to know him. By then, I think he'd tired of his tonal Tender Land *style and serial procedures seemed fresh. The way Aaron made serialism work for him was interesting. He had just written* Connotations, *and in our class, talked about the opening pages. The piece begins with three statements and each gets a little louder than the last. The idea, Aaron said, was to suggest that the music was as loud as it could possibly be each time, while at the same time saving something in reserve for an even stronger second and third repetition. It was a simple concept that made a big impact on me. No one had stated musical principles so simply before.*

Copland greeting David Del Tredici in New York City, 1984.

*Every time I wrote a piece after that summer of 1963, I went with it up to
Rock Hill. Aaron would never say much, and often I would have to draw out a
comment, but what he did say was always frighteningly accurate. If I played
a piece, he'd say something noncommittal at first, such as "It's very nice."
Maybe an hour or so later, at dinner, he would turn to me, apropos of nothing,
and say, "I think the bass line is too regular, and the percussion should not
always underline the main beat and would you pass the butter. . . ." It would
always be something I had been worrying about—Aaron was usually right
on target and went to the musical core; but he preferred what he said to be
by indirection. He didn't ever want to seem to know too much. There was
an enigmatic quality to Aaron: his knowing yet not expressing.*

    *Aaron was the same way about his own music. If I asked specific ques-
tions, he'd be reluctant with answers. Aaron once told me that when he was
composing and with a close friend, he'd like to carry on a conversation while
continuing to improvise at the piano. I asked him what he got from that,
and he said that his musical ideas often took surprising turns, just because
part of his brain was casually involved. All Aaron really cared about was
what got him to get the music out. It had nothing to do with some regular
procedure. It has nothing to do with understanding the process or being able*

even to describe it. One day, while talking about the Piano Concerto, *Aaron said, "No one plays this right." He jumped up and played the opening of the second movement for me. I realized when I heard him that there was no way to write it down exactly as he played. It was so idiosyncratic—like trying to write down a jazz improvisation; there's no notational equivalent.*

Aaron was nurtured by the French school, but he didn't have the terrifically quick ear that is supposed to be part of French compositional technique. Lenny has it. Aaron had of course a wonderful ear, but it didn't show in any facile way. My ear is more like Aaron's—very different when I am composing than when I am not. (One's ear gets good when it must.) When Aaron is through with the struggle of composing a piece, he sort of floats away from it—disengages. Maybe it's been too personal, too upsetting. Or maybe he's just glad to be rid of it! Also, Aaron never seemed to be much of a reviser. Because I revised an awful lot when I was younger, I asked Aaron about himself, hoping to make myself feel better. Aaron's reply, however, was simply that he worked on a piece until he was satisfied and rarely felt the need to revise afterward.

Aaron conducted one of my earliest orchestral pieces, The Lobster Quadrille, *in London on November 25, 1969, while he was on a conducting tour of Europe. I went over the score with him beforehand and he was very open to suggestions. As might be expected, he had none of the typical conductorial vanities.*

When people ask me who influenced me, I always say Aaron. Ironically though, when critics accuse me of sounding like this or that composer, they have yet to mention Aaron! I suppose it was not so much his music that shows up in mine, but his way of dealing with music and composing that had a profound effect on me. Aaron trusted his musical instincts completely. He was untouched by academic ways. He never let the enormous effort of composition show. It all just seemed to happen. "Remember, David, it is the illusion of inevitability that we are all after, as though all those notes just fell from heaven." I have tried to emulate that.

In 1964, Copland again spent only the month of August in the Berkshires. He relinquished his position as head of the composition department at Tanglewood to Gunther Schuller. Thirteen composition students were taught by Copland, Schuller, Foss, Jacobs, and Berger. As usual, a few Copland works were performed by students and by the BSO.[17] The Fromm Fellows now numbered twenty-two, and Fromm supported a group of nine composers to be commissioned for works to be performed in the week-long Festival of Contemporary Music. The "Fromm Week," supervised by Schuller, became an important annual event in contemporary music. After the first festival, critic Eric Salzman wrote, "For once, the composers really are young . . . and all but a couple have something to say. There's talent in these here hills and there's a music of the future and it's here right now."[18] A feature of the festival in 1964 was a panel of five composers, with Copland as moderator, discussing "Problems of Materials."

A festive dinner was held after the gala anniversary concert celebrating Tanglewood's twenty-fifth year, which opened with *Fanfare for the Common Man* and included *Outdoor Overture*. Lukas Foss wrote to Copland afterward (18 September), "I knew then that it was a farewell dinner as well. . . . And sad as it is for Tanglewood, I cannot blame you. Enough is enough. Your time will be spent better without all that summer activity." In 1965, the "Fromm Week" featured music by composers who had attended the Music Center in past summers. One of the highlights was a retrospective Copland concert (17 August).[19] During intermission, Leinsdorf announced Copland's retirement from the Music Center and the appointment of Gunther Schuller, age thirty-nine, as head of contemporary music and composition. The thirty-three-year-old concertmaster of the BSO, Joseph Silverstein, was named chairman of the faculty. Many in the audience viewed Copland's retirement as the end of an era at Tanglewood. He was given a standing ovation, but he made no speech of farewell, choosing to allow his music to speak for him.

Copland wanted to spend more time on the recording of his music. He recognized the importance of recordings to a composer's career, and he always tried to accommodate his schedule when a recording opportunity was involved. Leonard Burkat's new position at Columbia Records was fortunate for Copland; Burkat saw to it that Copland's music was systematically recorded by Columbia. He said, "Aaron's series of Columbia Masterworks Records was something I thought up when I was head of the label. It was approved by the president, Goddard Lieberson, and produced by John McClure. Public announcement was made (28 April 1964) in my apartment with press and lots of friends from the music world in attendance."[20]

Copland received major awards in the sixties, among them the Edward MacDowell Medal for lifetime achievement (1961) and the Medal of

A reception to celebrate Copland's recording contract with Columbia Records, at Leonard Burkat's apartment, New York City, 28 April 1964. (Left to right): Bernstein, Burkat, Copland, and Felicia Bernstein.

Freedom (1964). Among the honorary degrees,[21] one from Harvard in 1961 was especially meaningful, considering Copland's long association with the university. Also in 1961, Copland was voted president of the MacDowell Colony, a position he held until 1967. Toward the end of the decade, two books about Copland for young readers were published.[22]

Following the brief glory years for the arts during the Kennedy administration, contemporary American music retreated to its familiar position: a sharp division between popular music (almost completely rock by the end of the sixties) and concert music (serial, electronic, and chance operations). Diversification and experimentation continued to an extent, but the best of Kennedy's intentions to create an atmosphere of artistic and academic freedom ended with the student riots of 1968. Many composers, who depended on university positions, suddenly found themselves in uncertain and unsympathetic situations. Small groups were formed in the cities to promote the performance of contemporary music. Not unlike the 1920s and 1930s, they drew from the limited segment of the population that had a particular interest in new music.

Young composers were not very much interested in Copland's music. Paul Moor described the difference between going to concerts with Copland in the sixties and what it had been earlier:

> In the forties Aaron was like a magnet and had to stay in his seat for fear of being overwhelmed at intermission, but not so, later on. At one concert of his music in the sixties, Copland commented almost wistfully, "Do you realize that there is not a single young composer in the audience!"[23]

Leonard Bernstein recalls a similar remark from Copland backstage after he conducted the premiere of Copland's *Inscape* in 1967. Bernstein said, "I recognized that as the moment Aaron really stopped composing."[24]

Removed as young composers might have felt from Copland as the generation gap widened, they looked to him with wonder: an American composer whose music got played regularly by the major orchestras, almost all of it recorded; a composer making a substantial living from being a musician without a regular teaching position. If Copland was no longer the enormous influence he had been on younger composers in terms of actual composition, he was a role model, an example of the good citizen in music, a man tolerant and open to what others might want to do.

No one replaced Copland as the leader among younger composers. Perhaps a single figure was no longer appropriate or necessary. But the enduring qualities in Copland's music and the stability of his personality took on special meaning in the fast-changing, violent sixties, when values changed from day to day and heroes disappeared as suddenly and quickly as the shot of a gun.

The Music Within

1961–1969

Early in 1961, a young director by the name of Jack Garfein approached me about composing the music for his film *Something Wild*. I explained how busy I was, and so forth, but Garfein said, "Please! Just see it before you decide." Well, the film was already shot, and I was curious and thought it couldn't hurt just to see it before refusing. I went to United Artists and sat in the projection room watching this unusual production. It was so vivid that it gripped my imagination. Then I saw it a second time. Garfein was so eager for me to compose the score that he agreed to anything I asked—yes, he was willing to wait until I had an opening in my schedule; yes, he would supply a Moviola so I could work at home in Peekskill; and yes, he would hire wonderful musicians, almost twice as many as was usual for a film. Finally, I agreed to spend about six weeks on the score and to supervise the recording.

Something Wild was my eighth film score and the first since *The Heiress* twelve years earlier.[1] I had been offered seven movies during that time, but none seemed to give opportunity for musical treatment that could serve the picture in a meaningful way. In my view, Garfein's film had that potential. Based on a novel, *Mary Ann*, by Alex Karmel, *Something Wild* was adapted for the screen by Karmel and Garfein, produced by Prometheus, an independent company, in collaboration with United Artists. In the starring role of Mary Ann Gates was the young and beautiful actress Carroll Baker (Garfein's wife), who had made a big hit in the movie *Baby Doll*. Ralph Meeker was Mike, the costar in this psychological drama set in New York City. Also in the cast were Mildred Dunnock as the girl's mother and Jean Stapleton in the role of a prostitute.

Something Wild was about feelings—the loneliness and despair of a young girl learning to live with violence—and it was about the moods of the city; in fact, the original title of the film had been *Something Wild in the City*. The story was basic: On the way home from school choir practice one summer evening, young Mary Ann is raped. She runs away from home and exchanges her safe, ordinary life for a job in a chain store and a room in a squalid part of the city. When she attempts a suicide jump from a bridge, she is saved by a man who then offers her the spare bed in his basement room. He keeps her a prisoner, something like Beauty and the Beast. By the end, they have fallen in love and get married.

Something Wild had lengthy stretches of silent action without dialogue, which invited musical comment in a way that imbues the whole picture with a certain musical "tone." It goes without saying that the composer must have a free hand for this kind of score. Jack Garfein assured me of this, as did George Justin, the producer assigned to the film from United Artists.

In most films, the composer's prime opportunity comes at the very beginning, for the so-called "title music." The composer is expected to do his best work accompanying the long list of screen credits. At this point, the audience, of course, knows nothing about the film but its name. In the case of *Something Wild,* I was given something more tangible, since the title and credits were superimposed on action shots of the city and on some drawings. I had the chance to compose the equivalent of a big-city profile. The opening chord taken by itself was meant to give a sense of power and tension. I worked on that chord to make it sum up what the picture is all about.

Having been shot on location in New York City, the film was interspersed with every variety of city noise—trucks, taxis, subways, police sirens, slum kids shouting. In one scene I tried to outshout a bulldozer and bridge traffic. It proved a hopeless task, so I decided to work with the sounds by allowing the percussion to improvise along with it. For the bucolic scenes set in Central Park, I also had to use some ingenuity. Take, for example, the segment where our star is discovered asleep in the park in the early hours, against a background of skyscrapers. What I tried for there were pastoral sounds edged with a steely quality, hoping thereby to suggest the country in the midst of the city.

The most difficult hurdle of all in *Something Wild* was keeping the audience guessing as to the underlying emotions and intentions of the two principal characters. For much of the film, we don't know what their relationship implies. The trouble with music is that when it speaks, it can tell too much. I had to exercise continual discretion in order not to give away the real motives of the characters too soon. It is comparatively easy to reflect physical action in musical terms; more challenging are those moments when one attempts to think unspoken thoughts musically. *Something Wild* took the question even further: What does one do when a character is unable to think consecutive thoughts, such as when Ralph Meeker returns to his apartment one night completely drunk? Natural musical sequences would not convey the foggy, disjointed nature of his mental processes. I decided on an unconventional solution: unexpected silences that abruptly disconnect the musical texture. When we recorded that scene, the musicians were perplexed at why they were expected to stop and start so fitfully. Another scene where I made explicit use of silence was the rape of the heroine. Garfein was surprised when he heard what I intended, but he went along with it. I thought that the girl's shock suggested a kind of "stop dead" treatment. I wrote about that in my diary at the time:[2]

> Study clinical reaction to rape. The music, if possible, should enter and leave curiously; as if in a series of non sequiturs (somewhat "confused" perhaps.) The sudden outbursts of shouted dialogue may well be reflected in sudden bursts of music, like a radio turned on too loud. A moment of discomfort for the audience, followed by relief at return of normal sound levels.

David Walker, as a composer familiar with electronic music techniques, was copying out the orchestration for me. I suggested to him that the score could possibly be enhanced by a few electronic segments subtly layered over the orchestral sound. A perfect spot was the scene on the bridge when Carroll Baker is close to throwing herself into the swirling water. David composed two or three electronic sections and played them for me while we were at Tanglewood in 1961. Unfortunately, Garfein vetoed the idea for financial reasons.[3] He had agreed so readily until then to everything I requested, I could not insist.

Jack Garfein[4]

The famous literary agent Audrey Wood brought Mary Ann *to me. From the first reading, it had an emotional impact. I kept thinking about that girl. The idea of invisible forces in the city and how they affect a person fascinated me. I optioned the book and started on the script myself. I was thirty-one years old and had done only one other film. It was difficult to convince Hollywood to support such a film, but finally United Artists agreed, if we could do it on an acceptably low budget.*

Photograph by Sam Shaw.

Above: Copland at
the Moviola with
director Jack
Garfein, discussing
Something Wild,
Peekskill, 1961.

Right: Garfein,
Carroll Baker, and
Copland in the
recording booth.

Photograph by Eugene Cook.

*Usually you choose the composer before shooting a film, but I knew that
the music would give the viewer a sense of the soul of this girl and that we
needed to find a great composer. Someone recommended Morton Feldman,
and we met a few times and Morty played some music for me, but I couldn't
imagine his kind of music for this story. I got in touch with Aaron Copland,
and although he was all booked up with his own projects, I convinced him
to see the film. It was one of the first screenings I ever had for anyone, and
was I nervous! I was completely in awe of Copland. He said he liked it and
would think about it: "Call me tomorrow." When I called, Copland told*

330

me he couldn't get the film out of his head, but if we wanted him, we would have to wait six months and pay a hefty fee. The music costs came to almost ten percent of the budget—unheard of then. United Artists thought it was insane, but it worked out in an unusual way. Carroll [Baker] was by then a star at Warner Brothers. She wanted Aaron also, and she agreed to guarantee his fee through her contract at Warners.

Aaron and I went over the script together, and he put me at ease by asking questions that I hesitated to answer. I was afraid he would compose something just to please me. When I told Aaron that, he just laughed and said, "Don't worry. I've never done anything just to please someone." Only at one point did we disagree. That was the rape scene, where Aaron said, "No music here. Not until she gets home." That turned out to be absolutely masterful. And in the drunk scene, where Aaron wanted the music to stop and start abruptly, I at first thought it was mirroring the action too much, but again, his instincts were dead right.

We shipped the Moviola up to Peekskill and Aaron got to work. I only talked to him twice during the six months. Once he called to ask about the segment when the girl escapes from the apartment and wakes up in Central Park: He thought there should be contrasting music between the park and the city, and wanted to discuss it with me. The next time he called, it was to tell me the score was ready and would I come up to Peekskill to hear him play through some of it on the piano. I couldn't get the sense of it at all from that, but Aaron just said, "Don't worry. We'll take care of everything at the recording session. Whatever time you give me, we'll do it with corrections and everything."

I was so taken just seeing Aaron Copland conducting for my film and listening to the music that I had to remind myself to pay attention to the screen. Every decision Aaron made was right—his timings, his use of the real city sounds. Extraordinary. Somehow Aaron had locked into the girl's feelings and touched on some things I couldn't express in the film. It is not too much to say that Aaron made me realize things about my life I had not confronted.

Carroll Baker[5]

When Jack and I formed our production company, Prometheus, it was at a time when films were beginning to cost a great deal. Movie studios wanted some low-budget films. One of our ideas was to make a quality film in New

York City and bring it in with a budget of about $100,000. We made the deal through United Artists, and if we wanted anything beyond actual production costs, we had to go to them and ask. It was Jack's idea that Aaron Copland could add something specifically to a story about New York City. When Copland showed an interest, it was partly because New York was like another character in the story. Copland named his price and we went to United Artists, but they did not feel that such a film as ours warranted a pricey big-name composer. We wanted Copland so much that I agreed United Artists could take my services as collateral: I would have to make a film for them for whatever amount Something Wild *went over budget. I actually ended up having to do* Mr. Moses *with Robert Mitchum in Africa in exchange for Copland's fee for* Something Wild! *But at the time, I was very happy to find a way for Copland to do it.*

In all truthfulness, I do not believe that the story was quite as strong as it should have been. It was a mood piece more than an exciting story. If one takes on something like this, it is usually a financial loss. That style of film was something the French had an easier time selling. In America, you either hit success immediately with a film or it's dead. But we believed in it and were not in it for the money. Our producer, George Justin, used to laugh at me about the fact that I did not feel free to use the hairdresser, and he'd say, "Carroll was in there counting the bobby pins."

I had never been to a recording session before, and I was ecstatic at what the music added to the film. Afterward, I went over to Mr. Copland and told him what I felt: "Your music makes me a wonderful actress."

A limousine arrived each day to take David Walker and me to the Fine Studios in Bayside, Long Island, where I conducted and recorded the sound track. Four television monitors were placed around the room so the musicians could follow the action and mood as we played. In three days, we recorded 40 minutes of music, a little more than one-third of the total 110-minute film. United Artists wanted to invite representatives from the record companies to these sessions, but I suggested we play tapes for them afterward. When *Something Wild* was ready for its first screening in New York, the music was played at a high level to emphasize my involvement to the press.

Something Wild met with mixed reviews. Bosley Crowther, film critic of *The New York Times,* found the story unconvincing. He claimed it was hard to believe that a girl like Mary Ann would not find one person to sympathize with her in the whole city of New York. *Something Wild* was a commercial flop, probably because it was ahead of its time, although serious filmgoers recognized its remarkable qualities. Garfein and Miss Baker were awfully disappointed. Harold Clurman wrote a review for *Show* magazine, claiming that it was the only existentialist film in the United States, but the magazine's editor refused to run it, and Harold told me later that he always felt guilty about not insisting.

United Artists refused to record my music after the film was released. It seems that they never thought the film had a chance commercially. I asked Garfein to set up a meeting with the producers and told them, "Every recording of mine has been successful and has made money." But when the head of the music department was called in for an opinion, he said, "It won't sell." Garfein asked what kind of music *was* selling, and the response was, *Birdman of Alcatraz.* When we went down in the elevator from that meeting, I told Jack, "Don't worry. I will do whatever I can about the music."

I retrieved the rights to my score from United Artists and had a studio recording made of the sound track. A copy was sent to Senator Jacob Javits, because after seeing the film, he had written:

> I wanted to let you know how much we loved the score of the Carroll Baker movie, *Something Wild.* It would be wonderful if it could be made into a symphonic suite called "New York"—what could I do to help bring that dream into reality? If you'd let me know, I'd do my best to do it.

As it turned out, the music for *Something Wild* was not used for New York, but to satisfy a commission I had received from the London Symphony Orchestra for a piece in honor of their sixtieth anniversary season in 1964. I wrote to Ernest Fleishmann, manager of the LSO: "My intention is to incorporate parts of the film score in a new composition composed for the L.S., somewhat in the manner of Vaughan Williams in his *Antartica Symphony,* in which work he also makes use of previously composed film material." Fleishmann agreed, but when I sent the title, "Music for New York," he countered with, "How about *Symphony No. 4?*" We compromised, choosing the title *Music for a Great City.* I felt that the music could be thought to portray any large city, even though it had been composed with New York in mind: To me the "great" in the title meant large and noisy. In any case, I did not intend to follow the cinematic action of *Something Wild* when adapting the music for the London commission.[6]

novements of *Music for a Great City* alternate between
big-city life with its external stimuli and personal reactions
periences. The first movement, *Skyline,* opens with a broad
for full orchestra, followed by a percussion solo to introduce
ented theme presented by brass, piano, and pizzicato strings.
For the second movement, *Night Thoughts,* I reduced the full orchestra
scoring to chamber music orchestra for what might be called a series of
free contrapuntal variations. The reality of big city life returns in the third
movement scherzo, *Subway Jam,* which, as one might suspect, includes a
great deal of brass and percussion. (One reviewer wrote, "There is not a
string player to be found in this rush-hour crowd.") The final movement,
Toward the Bridge, presents contrasting ideas, some jazz-inspired, that
build to a big climax, followed by a coda with material from the introduction to the first movement. *Music for a Great City* calls for an extra
complement of percussion, such as slapstick, cowbells, sandpaper, maracas,
ratchet, and conga drum. The work is dedicated to the members of the
London Symphony Orchestra.[7]

Preceding the premiere, Victor Kraft met me in London. His job was
to take photographs during preparations for the premiere, to be used along
with interviews and rehearsals for a television documentary by the BBC.
From the time we arrived in London, the director, Humphrey Burton, had
the cameras follow us everywhere. I found the LSO responsive and well
prepared. They had looked at their parts in advance and the general
atmosphere was of keen interest. In addition to the new piece, I conducted
Stravinsky's *Ode,* Britten's *Sinfonia da Requiem,* my *Lincoln Portrait,*
with Sam Wanamaker narrating, and the *Clarinet Concerto,* with Gervase
de Peyer. I described the concert, which took place at Festival Hall, 26
May 1964, in my journal:

> The LSO played a beautiful Britten (he sent a wire from Aldeburgh). They
> seemed to be playing both for me and with me. De Peyer did an excellent *Clar.
> Concerto.* Wanamaker couldn't be heard in the LP (mike mismanagement),
> and he muffed one whole section. (Oy!) Rapt attention during the *Ode.* The
> new piece was very well played, much public enthusiasm at the end. All-round
> my best public appearance as conductor thus far.

The audience gave a terrific ovation, so I was a little surprised when I saw
in the papers the next morning that the critics were not thoroughly
pleased. They thought I had not done myself justice by playing the more
popular side of my output. If they only knew how programs are really

made! Sure enough, every critic mentioned that the precise locale of the "great city" in the title was Manhattan, not London.

A few weeks after the premiere, I recorded the piece with the LSO for Columbia Records (John McClure in charge), together with *Statements for Orchestra.* Reviewers gave varying opinions of *Music for a Great City,* but all agreed that the fresh recording of *Statements* was welcome. On my last day in London, I saw the BBC documentary and was pleased with the editing. I commented at the time, "One watches oneself for sixty minutes and is never quite the same. A rare form of egomania results!"

I conducted the London Symphony for the American premiere of *Music for a Great City* at Constitution Hall, Washington, D.C. (13 October 1964), and Antal Dorati conducted it with the BBC Symphony Orchestra at Carnegie Hall (15 May 1965). Howard Klein wrote in *The New York Times:* "It is tight as a drum and a potently dramatic work . . . it reflects the anxiety and tension of the present." *Music for a Great City* did not catch on quickly. I was reminded again how much the fate of a work depends on the circumstances surrounding its launching. A work composed for a special occasion is not as likely to be taken up by conductors for regular programs. I programmed *Music for a Great City* whenever I could—it seemed to have a freshness, but that may be precisely because it was not played as often as my other works.

The offer of a commission from the New York Philharmonic to compose a work for performance at the opening concert in its new home sparked my writing *Connotations for Orchestra.* It was the first purely symphonic work since my *Third Symphony* of 1947. I worked on sketches during 1961, and promised myself to stay home in 1962 for uninterrupted composing time. But I could not resist an invitation to return to Japan for a State Department conference at the beginning of the year to be combined with conducting in Seattle and Vancouver. To gain some composing time, I took leave from Tanglewood in 1962. As I wrote to Chávez (25 June): "I am working day and night on my symphony for the Philharmonic commission. It is in three movements and I have just finished the last, the first being more than half done." Chávez invited me to Mexico for some conducting, but mostly to continue composing. From there, I wrote to Leo Smit (4 July), "I'm not finished with my piece and so I have a very hectic five weeks ahead of me after my return from Mexico, Rio, and Montevideo. Damn! Having a hell of a time trying to find a title, and they need it tomorrow."

Manuscript, first page from the sketch score of *Connotations*.
© Copyright 1962 by Aaron Copland. Boosey & Hawkes, Inc., Sole Publishers and Licensees.

Connotations was completed just in time for orchestra rehearsals. Carlos Moseley, then managing director of the New York Philharmonic, wrote (12 September 1962), "My sigh of relieved joy at hearing from you that the work is completed was probably registered on seismographs throughout the Northern Hemisphere."

Knowing that other music on the gala Philharmonic program would represent earlier and more traditional aspects of musical culture, I preferred to compose a work expressing something of the tensions, aspirations, and drama inherent in contemporary living. I have frequently been asked why I decided to make use of twelve-tone principles in this particular work. I can only say that the method seemed appropriate for my purpose. I had used it for my *Piano Quartet* of 1950 and again in 1957 for the *Piano Fantasy* and both seemed to work. In those two works, the row is first presented as a theme; in *Connotations,* the row is first heard vertically in terms of three four-voiced chords with, needless to add, no common tones. When spelled out horizontally, these chords supplied me with various versions of a more lyrical discourse.[8]

After I wrote to David Diamond about *Connotations,* he responded from Italy (14 August 1962): "Is it a variation form? It will confuse some, I am sure, and wish you could come up with a better title. It's not—it seems to me—even provoking as a title—and somewhat forced, no?" An early sketch reminds me that my temporary working title had been *Music for a New Hall,* and that other titles had been considered.[9] The dictionary states that the verb *connote* means "to imply," to signify meanings "in addition to the primary meaning." In the case of *Connotations,* I explained (to David Diamond, and to Chávez, who thought the title too abstract) that the skeletal frame of the row is the "primary meaning"; it denotes the area of exploration. The subsequent treatment seeks out other implications—connotations that come in a flash or connotations that I might have only gradually uncovered. The listener, on the other hand, is free to discover his or her own connotative meanings, including perhaps some not suspected by the author.

The twenty-minute work was dedicated to the members of the New York Philharmonic and to its music director, Leonard Bernstein. It is scored for large orchestra, including a percussion group of five performers to deal with various special percussion effects and a piano solo. David Diamond had not been far off in speculating about the structure of *Connotations,* which comes closest to a free treatment of the baroque form of the chaconne with a succession of variations, based on the opening chords

Above: Copland discussing the score of *Connotations* with Bernstein at rehearsal for the premiere, Philharmonic Hall (later renamed Avery Fisher Hall), New York City, 1962.

Left: Jacqueline Kennedy and Copland backstage at Philharmonic Hall after the premiere of *Connotations.*

and their implied melodic intervals, supplying the basic framework. The variations are sometimes recognizably separate, one from another, sometimes not. As in the *Orchestral Variations,* the problem was to construct an overall line that had continuity, dramatic force, and an inherent unity. It has been pointed out many times that the dodecaphonic method supplies the building blocks but does not create the edifice. The composer must do that.[10]

The gala opening week of Lincoln Center's Philharmonic Hall (later Avery Fisher Hall) featured thirteen concerts (23–30 September 1962). The first program was conducted by Bernstein and included works by Beethoven, Vaughan Williams, Mahler, and my *Connotations*. In the fourth concert of the celebration week, *Lincoln Portrait* was performed with Adlai Stevenson narrating and Eugene Ormandy conducting.

Since Philharmonic Hall was the first of the Lincoln Center complex to be completed, the opening concert was a momentous occasion, happening amid gaping holes and construction rubble. The Metropolitan Opera House was no more than an excavation. There would be other openings, but this being the first, it was special. There was an air of glamour and excitement as an imposing array of national and international celebrities arrived by limousine. They included John D. Rockefeller III (chairman of Lincoln Center), Jacqueline Kennedy (looking particularly stunning), Secretary of State Dean Rusk, Governor and Mrs. Nelson Rockefeller, Mayor Wagner, and many other dignitaries. Harold Schonberg of *The New York Times* wrote the following day, "It was a highly formal audience, the kind that quite naturally said, 'There's Jackie,' or 'There's Adlai'—not because it was namedropping, but because to this audience they *are* Nelson, Jackie and Adlai."

General agreement was that the premiere was not a congenial circumstance for *Connotations for Orchestra.* It was an occasion when the music was not as important as the hall itself; the interest was on acoustical sound. The critics also were less involved with the music than with questions such as: "Did the sound work?" "Was it as good as Carnegie?" and so forth. I had not wanted to present something bland and traditional for this occasion and to such a distinguished audience. My gesture was not appreciated at the time: *Connotations* was not what was expected. The piece does have, after all, a rather severe and somewhat intellectual tone, but my hope was that it is also intense and dramatic. When it was over, a confused near silence ensued.

The evening's gala tone quickly resumed and it all ended with champagne being served to the entire audience of 2,588 guests. Leo Smit told me afterward that he was impressed when Governor Rockefeller shook his hand, until he realized that the governor didn't know who he was and was shaking everyone's hand, campaign style! I had arranged for my closest friends and family to attend, and Laurine wrote afterward, "I still haven't come down to earth. It was most exciting for us to be there in person." The event was televised by NBC and broadcast nationwide.[11] I was asked to speak to the television audience while the cameras alternated between me and a shot of the music manuscript. I said:

It seems to me that there are two things you can do when listening to any new work. The most important thing is to lend yourself—or to put it another way—try to be as sensitive as you can to the overall feeling the new piece gives off. The second way is to listen with some awareness of the general shape of the new piece, realizing that a composer works with his musical materials just as an architect works with his building materials in order to construct an edifice that makes sense. Let me show you the opening manuscript page of my *Connotations for Orchestra*. At the very start, you will hear three rather harsh-sounding brass chords that climax almost immediately into silence. Each of these three chords contain four different tones, so that they add up to the twelve tones of the chromatic scale. These form the basic working materials of the entire composition. Later on, after a passage for the solo piano, the tension subsides. At this point you should watch for the moment when all the strings of the orchestra except for the basses, sing these same twelve tones as a melodic line. Here you have a page of my score as illustration. These are the same tones as those in my three primary chords, spelled out horizontally. In listening to the work as a whole, some of you may wonder why I chose to create a work that reflects drama and tension and even desperation on so gala an occasion as this. The reason is simple: In inaugurating this beautiful new hall, I wanted to remind our listeners that we are dedicating it not only to the rehearing of the great music of the past but also to the more challenging music of our own day. I wanted to speak in a musical idiom of our own day in a hall of our own making.

To my great surprise, my little talk was interpreted by some as an apology for the piece. I certainly did not mean it that way. Moreover, I was surprised at the vehemence of the letters that began to arrive from across the country after the broadcast. For example: "If last night is any criterion of what can be expected in Lincoln Center, it should be called 'Center of Jungle Culture' "; "Dear Mr. Copland, Shame Shame Shame!" *Connotations* did not fare quite so poorly with the critics. Louis Biancolli wrote in the *New York World Telegram*, "It struck me as a turning point in his career, a powerful score in twelve-tone style that has liberated new stores of creative energy." John Molleson wrote in the *Herald Tribune:*

This is a difficult work and like most music difficult to understand at one hearing . . . this listener had the feeling that these connotations are couched in terms of a present crisis over what to do with serialism. But this piece has flesh where others have only skin, and there was a good deal of arresting lyricism.

Virgil Thomson commented that counterpoint was totally lacking in *Connotations.* I wrote to him (27 November 1962), saying, "You must have been in a homophonic mood not to have heard the pages of two-part counterpoint in the fast section (and sometimes maybe even three-part)."[12] Reviewers had only praise for Lenny's conducting of the entire program.

Connotations was certainly not an immediate success, but then, I did not expect it to be. I had gone through this kind of thing earlier in my career and was not concerned about the piece itself in the long run, although I did make some minor modifications after the premiere. I am reminded that once, when crossing the Atlantic several decades earlier, I was approached by a fellow passenger. "Mr. Copland," he announced, "I don't like your music." "Well," I said, "I don't think any more highly of you for that!" No matter how much recognition I have received, there always have been my tough pieces I can't seem to sell to audiences. There were at least some who understood my intentions with the new piece. Claire Reis, who attended a rehearsal in addition to the premiere, and Minna Daniel, who wrote to me afterward:

> I think *Connotations* was exactly the right piece for the place and occasion—indeed the only one properly related to them. It sounds a good deal like certain aspects of the building—big, spacious, clear, long-lined, and it sounds very like you. . . . To those familiar with your music, the characteristic, identifying moods are perfectly apparent. The special Copland eloquence is there.

Marc Blitzstein wrote from Bennington College, where he was teaching, that he was "all for *Connotations* as a work, and as a picture of growth. It makes me happy." Composer Bill Flanagan wrote (1 February):

> You were swallowed up by the blue and gold reaches of Philharmonic Hall yesterday before I had the chance to tell you how glad I was finally to hear *Connotations* . . . the work makes perfect sense to me; I reject the Total Gloom descriptions that I've heard. . . . I think it's an impressively vital and absorbing piece of music.

Lenny programmed *Connotations* again a few months after the premiere for the regular Philharmonic subscription concerts during the first week of 1963, and on the orchestra's February tour in London. The European premiere was more successful than the New York reception. Lenny explained at a press conference, "*Connotations* is Copland looking back at earlier works from the vantage of 1962—and the 1962 point of view is a twelve-tone one." In response to the lengthy ovation after the piece in London, Lenny announced he would conduct another Copland work. To cries of "Oh oh," he said, "But this will be a very different style." He then conducted "Hoe-Down" from *Rodeo.*

I conducted *Connotations* myself in 1966, 1967, and 1968 around the United States, including the Musica Viva series in San Francisco, the Baltimore Symphony, the National Symphony in Washington, and the Buffalo Philharmonic. I spoke to the audiences with humorous accounts of the work's adverse effect on droves of letter writers, who had heard the original performance, in person or on TV. Then I asked the brass section to illustrate the opening chords, and the strings to show how they sounded. Before they knew it, the audience was sympathetic. My purpose was not to sell the work but to demonstrate it.

Connotations was recorded on the commemorative album of the opening of Lincoln Center, along with an impressive booklet containing articles and photographs (Lenny recorded *Connotations* again in 1973 with the Philharmonic for Columbia, paired with my 1967 *Inscape* and Elliott Carter's *Concerto for Orchestra.*)

A decade after the premiere, Pierre Boulez conducted *Connotations* with the New York Philharmonic (1973–1974). The auspices were similar, but ten years had changed audience perception enough so that *Connotations'* revival was a different story. In a review in *The New York Times* headed " '62 Copland Piece Gets Cheers This Time," Harold Schonberg wrote, "*Connotations* is Boulez' kind of music." Nevertheless, the piece is not programmed often. After a 1987 hearing at Juilliard's "Focus!" series at Tully Hall conducted by Joel Sachs, critic John Rockwell stated, "*Connotations* holds up very well indeed—a genuinely powerful piece that once again reveals Mr. Copland's exploration of Serialism to have been an extension, not a denial of his musical personality."

Choreographer John Neumier asked me for permission to use *Connotations* for a ballet, *Der Fall Hamlet (The Hamlet Affair),* in which he would also use some of the *Piano Variations.* Baryshnikov danced Hamlet, and other stars appeared in various parts: Marcia Haydée, Gelsey Kirkland, and Erik Bruhn. The world premiere was by the Ballet Theatre (6 January 1976). Despite the impressive roster of dancers, the ballet was not successful and has not been staged again.

Soon after the Philharmonic premiere of *Connotations,* I accepted an invitation to participate in a Latin American conference at the Huntington Hartford estate in Nassau, and I admit to using it as an excuse to recover from the excitement and to celebrate my sixty-second birthday by basking in the sun for five days.

I have often called myself "a work-a-year man": 1963 was the year of the ballet *Dance Panels* in Munich and 1964 belonged to the band piece *Emblems*. Among the invitations I received to compose new pieces was one from clarinetist Keith Wilson, who was president of the College Band Directors National Association (CBDNA), for a work to be played at the organization's national convention (December 1964). Wilson wrote, "The purpose of this commission is to enrich the band repertory with music that is representative of the composer's best work, and not one written with all sorts of technical or practical limitations." I hesitated for a moment but accepted when I was told that the piece would be bought sight unseen by at least two hundred bands!

I began the piece in the summer of 1964 (after conducting in Holland and Scotland in June) and finished it a few weeks before the premiere (while on a guest-conducting tour of Washington, Rochester, Chicago, and Pittsburgh). The premiere was played by the University of Southern California band, The Trojans, conducted by director William Schaefer.

I tried to keep Keith Wilson's injunction in mind while still making *Emblems* challenging to young performers. Schaefer made a few recommendations: substitution of bass clarinet for my original baritone sax; and cueing of the piano part. After receiving the score, he wrote (7 December), "We find it challenging, but hope to have it well prepared. The item of greatest resistance is the blending and resolution of intonation problems in the doubling of high E flat clarinet and flute. We trust that we shall live up to the honor of giving the first performances of this significant work." I explained the title *Emblems* in the program notes:

> An emblem stands for something—it is a symbol. I called this work *Emblems* because it seemed to me to suggest musical states of being: noble or aspirational feelings, playful or spirited feelings. The exact nature of these emblematic sounds must be determined for himself by each listener.

Emblems is tripartite in form: slow-fast-slow, with the return of the first part varied.[13] Embedded in the slow sections may be heard a brief quotation of the well-known hymn tune "Amazing Grace." Curiously, the harmonies had been conceived without reference to the tune. It was only by chance perusal of an anthology of tunes that I realized a connection existed between my harmonies and "Amazing Grace!"

Schaefer sent me a tape of the premiere, which took place in Tempe, Arizona (18 December 1964), and he expressed gratitude on behalf of The Trojans, but I sensed that the work was received with some disappointment. I did not hear *Emblems* played until the New York performance by the combined bands of Columbia and Harvard universities at Carnegie Hall (10 February 1965). Alas, my new band piece was not taken up by two hundred bands! I had purposely avoided serial composition; nevertheless, *Emblems* was at first considered dissonant and angular. In time, it has come into the college-band repertory. When in Cleveland in November 1965 to conduct the orchestra there, it happened that the Baldwin–Wallace College Band was rehearsing *Emblems* for a performance, so I went to Berea to hear them. The band director had posted a notice—"Aaron Copland will attend rehearsal." One student was heard to mutter, "Yeah, and next week, Shostakovich." I had the opportunity to say a few words to the players:

> You must always play absolutely in tune when you play dissonance. We composers take a chance when we write it, because if it is not played absolutely in tune, it sounds like a mistake. . . . Everybody knows a band can play loud. The question here is, How soft can you play?

When rehearsal was over, I told a reporter from *The Cleveland Plain Dealer*, "Baldwin–Wallace has a swell band."

President Lyndon Johnson sent a telegram informing me of his intention to award me a Presidential Medal of Freedom. I was told that it was the highest civilian honor that could be conferred by the President of the United States in peacetime.[14] The citation reads:

> To those men and women prominent in public affairs, business, science, education, journalism and the arts who collectively have made man's world safe, his physical body more durable, his mind broader, his leisure more delightful, his standard of living higher and his dignity important. They are creators; we are the beneficiaries.

The Medal of Freedom was conferred at a White House ceremony (14 September 1964). Among the thirty prominent recipients were Secretary of State Dean Acheson, John Steinbeck, Helen Keller, Edward R. Murrow, T. S. Eliot, Walter Lippmann, and Carl Sandburg. We were all invited to return to Washington early in 1965 for the inauguration of Lyndon Johnson.

WESTERN UNION
TELEGRAM
W. P. MARSHALL, PRESIDENT

1201 (4-60)

The filing time shown in the date line on domestic telegrams is LOCAL TIME at point of origin. Time of receipt is LOCAL TIME at point of destination

```
CT WWY005 WWZ3      WWZ3 GOVT PD=WUX THE WHITE
  HOUSE 1 NFT=
AARON COPLAND=
  ROCK HILL RFD #1 PEEKSKILL NY=

I AM HAPPY TO INFORM YOU OF MY INTENTION TO
AWARD YOU THE PRESIDENTIAL MEDAL OF FREEDOM. THIS
IS THE HIGHEST CIVIL HONOR CONFERRED BY THE PRESIDENT
OF THE UNITED STATES FOR SERVICE IN PEACETIME.
THE CRITERIA FOR THIS AWARD INCLUDE MERITORIOUS
CONTRIBUTION TO THE SECURITY OR  NATIONAL INTEREST
        OF THE UNITED STATES, WORLD PEACE, CULTURAL
        OR OTHER SIGNIFICANT PUBLIC OR PRIVATE ENDEAVOR.
        THE FORMAL ANNOUNCEMENT FROM THE WHITE HOUSE OF
        THE THIRTY RECIPIENTS FOR THIS YEAR WILL BE MADE
        ON JULY FOURTH. THE PRESENTATION OF THE MEDAL WILL
        TAKE PLACE IN SEPTEMBER AT THE WHITE HOUSE.
          ¶ WITH WARM BEST WISHES AND CONGRATULATIONS=
          LYNDON B JOHNSON.
```

PRECIATE SUGGESTIONS FROM ITS PATRONS CONCERNING ITS SERVICE

Telegram from President Lyndon Johnson offering Copland the Medal of Freedom, 1964.

NEW YORK
Herald Tribune
▽ **Tuesday, September 15, 1964** 23

Medal of Freedom for 30

By The Associated Press

WASHINGTON. Thirty prominent Americans, including a snappily saluting Carl Sandburg, received the Presidential Medal of Freedom from President Johnson in White House ceremonies yesterday.

"Our glory is peace, not war; our greatness is in people, not power," Mr. Johnson said after presenting the nation's richest civilian award to labor leader John L. Lewis, author John Steinbeck, moviemaker Walt Disney and others. The President also said: "On the genius of the individual rests the greatness of America."

When Mr. Sandburg's name was called the 86-year-old poet-historian stood beside his chair and asked the President:

"I salute you here and then walk up?"

The President beckoned him.

Mr. Sandburg then moved in front of the President smartly and said, "Sixth Illinois Volunteers."

Mr. Johnson smiled warmly and pulled Mr. Sandburg—who once served in the 6th Illinois Volunteers during the Spanish-American War—around beside him in the spotlight.

The President had a kiss on the cheek for Mrs. J. Frank Dobie, representing her husband, a Southwestern historian and longtime friend of Mr. Johnson.

There was extra applause from the East Room assembly for journalist Walter Lippmann and for three men whose medals were accompanied by citations of special distinction:

Former Secretary of State Dean Acheson, retiring Rep. Carl Vinson, D., Ga., and Edward R. Murrow, former television commentator and director of the U. S. Information Agency.

DEAN ACHESON	RALPH E. McGILL	SAMUEL E. MORISON	LEWIS MUMFORD	EDWARD R. MURROW	REINHOLD NIEBUHR
CLARENCE L. JOHNSON	THEODORE HESBURGH	JOHN W. GARDNER	J. FRANK DOBIE	WALT DISNEY	WILLIAM DE KOONING
JOHN L. LEWIS	HELEN A. KELLER	WALTER LIPPMAN	FREDERICK R. KAPPEL	DETLEV W. BRONK	AARON COPLAND
A PHILIP RANDOLPH	CARL SANDBERG	LEONTYNE PRICE	JOHN STEINBECK	CARL VINSON	HELEN B. TAUSSIG

THE HONOR ROLL

Announcement of Medal of Freedom awards in the *Herald Tribune*.

I had been impressed with being invited to the White House from my first visit in 1945, after Franklin Roosevelt was re-elected. Twenty years later, I was still impressed, although the only American music played at the Johnson inaugural concert were excerpts from *Porgy and Bess* and "America the Beautiful." I no longer recall much about the inaugural ball, but I see from my diary that I danced until the wee hours of the morning. I wrote, "Lucy danced the frug, and the President danced."

Directly after receiving the Medal of Freedom, I went to Ann Arbor, Michigan, where I found myself onstage with Lenny Bernstein as we both received honorary doctorates from the University of Michigan (19 September 1964). Traveling home, Lenny was inspired to write a sonnet for the occasion, which he sent to me.

Television, as a new medium for promotion of the performance of contemporary music, interested me, just as radio and film had earlier. An offer to host my own television series on the music of the twenties was too tempting to pass by. I wrote the scripts, conducted the music, and appeared as host. Station WGBH in Boston taped the presentations during 1965 and 1966, and they were broadcast on public television across the country[15] under the title "Music in the Twenties." While I enjoyed doing the series, it was more demanding than I had envisioned. Because of various conducting engagements (Europe in the fall, including Warsaw), I did not compose anything in 1965. That always made me slightly uneasy. I was determined to get back to writing music in 1966. The results were the piano piece *In Evening Air;* an arrangement of *Eight Songs* from *Twelve Poems of Emily Dickinson* for voice and orchestra; a school-orchestra version of *Variations on a Shaker Melody* from *Appalachian Spring;* and music for a television series to be presented on CBS' "Television Playhouse."

The scope of CBS' series was impressive. It was produced by Fred Coe, and I was to compose "signature" music to announce each play. What little music there is to talk about, I would describe as being in the style of a fanfare for brass and percussion. I also composed music for the opening play, Ronald Ribman's *The Final War of Olly Winters.* Seven takes of various short segments were recorded (5 December 1966).[16] To my surprise, the CBS "signature" music received a nomination for an Emmy from The National Academy of Television Arts and Sciences.

LEONARD BERNSTEIN   1964

*Sonnet on receiving an honorary doctorate
with Aaron Copland*

This day, my will demurring, I grew old.
I could have written memoirs on that stage
For the first time. A longwave had unrolled,
And beached me, spent with swimming and with age.

Docta honoris causa. First for him,
A craggy cedar planted by the sea
Since Adam. Then they called on me to swim
Ashore, and simulate that salty tree.

A poor impostor, I. Not even brave,
A plotter with no plan, and less than told.
They fished me, red-eyed flounder, from the wave,
Wounded, rigid, open-mouthed, and cold.

With velvet bait they plucked me from the sea
And dropped me, panting, near a cedar tree.

Much love,

L.

19 Sept 1964

"Sonnet" from Leonard Bernstein to Copland (previously unpublished), 1964.

I was puzzled when people asked why I bothered composing for television. Although I never accepted assignments that did not interest me, there was another factor to consider: Somebody had to pay the rent! It was ironic that when I was younger and really needed commissions, they were few and far between; now, I had ten times more than I could accept. Since

347

Photograph by E. Fred Sher.

Rosamond ("Peggy") Bernier and Copland at the "Gala" celebrating the New York Philharmonic's 125th anniversary.

it could take a year or two to honor a commission for a major work, I occasionally accepted something that did not take long to write but that paid well, such as the CBS "signature" music.

In celebration of its one hundred and twenty-fifth anniversary, the New York Philharmonic commissioned eighteen new works, each to be included on a program during the 1967–1968 season. (The actual anniversary was marked by a gala reproduction of the 1842 inaugural concert (7 December 1967). My commission would be the first symphonic piece I had tackled since *Connotations*, five years earlier. Searching through my notebooks, I came upon several quotations from poets I particularly admired, which I had transcribed into a diary. Among these were the words of the nineteenth-century English poet-priest Gerard Manley Hopkins. Hopkins interested me because of his originality and his experiments with prosody and meter, language and structure. He had also tried his hand at musical composition. Hopkins wrote, "No doubt my poetry errs on the side of oddness. . . . Melody is what strikes me most of all in music and design

348

Copland's diagram of a twelve-tone series used for *Inscape*, 1967.

in painting, so design, pattern, or what I am in the habit of calling 'inscape' is what I above all aim at in poetry."[17]

As I reread some of Hopkins' poetry, I found that his term seemed to apply more truly to the creation of music than to any of the other arts. What appealed to me was Hopkins' ability to see beyond the outward appearance of things to their innermost being and his genius in making the outer appearance itself reflect the inner reality. My idea was to write

349

music that would attempt to do just that, music that seemed to be moving inward upon itself, and (as I wrote in the score of my new piece) "a quasimystical illumination, a sudden perception of that deeper pattern, order and unity which give meaning to external forms." I was reminded recently that these were the principles Nadia Boulanger talked to me about so long ago—order, unity, discipline. I set out to find a different way of expressing these principles. I felt that I could accomplish this with serialism, which had opened a wide range of possibilities and combinations.

The material for *Inscape* comes from two different series of twelve tones that give rise to a number of subsidiary serial patterns of less importance. One of these dodecaphonic tone rows, heard as a twelve-tone chord, opens and closes the piece. All twelve notes of the row are equal and free of either tonal or serial considerations, while frequent use of thirds and triadic groupings creates a sense of diatonic center, giving *Inscape* more tonal orientation than is customary in serial composition; indeed, there is quite a lot of two-voice writing that suggests tonality. *Inscape*, scored for large orchestra, is in one continuous movement of about twelve minutes duration. It begins simply in an andantino tempo, becomes more complex as it proceeds to an allegretto, before gradually returning to the opening tempo and material.

Examining the rough sketches of *Inscape* in my files, I see that I drew on some materials from 1963.[18] When I began to put the piece together, I found that I needed more time, so having accepted various conducting dates, I carried the *Inscape* materials along with me and composed whenever I could—on planes, trains, in hotel rooms, and in college practice rooms. *Inscape* was completed in Peekskill (August 1967).

I am not certain when I made the decision to use Gerard Manley Hopkins' privately invented word for my title. In any case, I have never felt audiences should attach too much significance to titles. *Inscape* is a suggestive word, that's all. The idea of a "scape" of any kind—a landscape, or an inscape, or an escape—seemed to lend itself in a general way to a music piece, because it *is* so general. To the uninitiated, the word "inscape" may suggest a kind of shorthand for "inner landscape." Hopkins, however, meant to signify a more universal experience. *Inscape* shares an extramusical relationship with *Connotations* insofar as both compositions derive motivation from literary sources. Because I allowed myself more tonal implications within the twelve-tone procedure with *Inscape*, it is a more relaxed piece than *Connotations* and therefore has been compared to *Quiet City* and even *Our Town* in feeling, although it is considerably more dissonant than either.

Lenny Bernstein wrote to me from Italy (August 1967):

> A letter from the Philharmonic contains programs, rehearsal schedules, etc., wherein I find the word *Inscape*. Nobody told me, least of all you—good title. You might conceivably drop a line about it and what it's like and how it goes and how it feels to be writing an inscape at almost sixty-seven.

Lenny had good reason to be interested, since it was he who would conduct the premiere performances with the New York Philharmonic on their preseason tour, beginning 13 September 1967 in Ann Arbor, Michigan, where the university was celebrating its sesquicentennial. Thirteen performances were given in all, including five upon the orchestra's return to New York. *Inscape* was positioned between Beethoven's *Eighth Symphony* and Tchaikovsky's *Second Symphony*. The audience reception was warm and enthusiastic, and for once, the critics seemed to understand right off that my intention was to make a piece of music in my own way, with my own sound, using the twelve-tone method, instead of creating an example of a perfect serial composition. Irving Kolodin wrote in *The Saturday Review*, "What Copland had undertaken . . . in a search for making Schoenberg's precepts the means not merely for expression, but for self-expression, he has done convincingly." In *The New York Times*, Allen Hughes wrote, "You will admire the workmanship and will respect the composer's ability to make the twelve-tone technique as though it had been invented to create the Copland sound." Although there was some criticism regarding melodic and rhythmic elements, the critics unanimously praised the sonorities and textures.

The serial aspects of *Connotations* and *Inscape* have been commented on more than I consider necessary, but that was due to the time-lag factor between the listener and the composer. For us composers, serialism was hardly a new thing. I was always interested in what Stravinsky was up to, and of course I heard his pieces of the early fifties (*Cantata* and *Septet*) in which he used serial elements. By the sixties, serialism had been around for over fifty years; young composers were not so fascinated with it anymore. It was taking its place with the passage of years. As I told an interviewer for *Music and Musicians* in 1966, "I imagine serial technique is going into history like the fugue form." New things arrived to be ingested and digested before becoming part of the musical vocabulary. We

AARON COPLAND

ROCK HILL R. F. D. 1 PEEKSKILL, N. Y. 10566

Nov 17 '67

Dear Lensk:

What a <u>beautiful</u> letter you wrote me for my birthday! I shall treasure it always. And what a deep satisfaction it is for me to know that we've sustained our feeling for each other all these many years. It's a joy — that's what it is. And just imagine what it means to me to see you prepare and conduct my music with such devotion and love and musical sensitivity — for that alone

I am forever in your debt.

Un abrazo — and love

Aaron

Letter from Copland to Bernstein, 17 November 1967.

composers have access to each new development, and I, for one, never wanted to be limited to one kind of musical language.

When I conducted *Inscape* at Tanglewood (23 August 1968), it made at least one member of the audience happy. Thornton Wilder wrote to me the next day:

> Just a word to say that *Inscape* is a very fine piece. It mounts to a wonderfully eloquent urgency.... The orchestration is of the richest and all so clearly signed by *you*. Of course, I was shocked to hear that you don't obey one of Schoenberg's *first rules* (but no one else does either): in stating a row do not repeat a note until you have given all the other eleven! Cheers. Felicitations. Gratefully, Thornton.

I conducted the first European performance of *Inscape* with the London Symphony on their International Series (24 October 1968). *Inscape* elicited no comment whatever from the players but received a good review from the London *Sunday Times*.[19] While I was composing *Inscape,* I got to know the young composer Phillip Ramey. I invited him to the first rehearsal of the new piece and to the premiere.

Phillip Ramey[20]

When Aaron heard that big crashing first chord of Inscape *at rehearsal, his eyes gleamed with pleasure and excitement. Despite so many years of experience, it was all new to him, every time. I went with him to Ann Arbor, Michigan, for the world premiere. Lenny Bernstein, who conducted, had never been enthusiastic about Aaron's twelve-tone music; but backstage after the concert, he exclaimed, "Aaron, it's amazing how, even when you compose in a completely 'foreign' idiom, the music still comes out sounding like you!" Aaron thought that first performance excellent, the tempi and so on. Then the New York Philharmonic continued its tour and played* Inscape *several times more, on the same program with the Mahler Fifth Symphony, before introducing it to New York. Upon hearing his piece again, Aaron grumbled, "Lenny's been conducting too much Mahler.* Inscape *has gotten too slow." By the time of the recording session, Lenny's version of* Inscape *was somewhat longer than the premiere. Aaron was not pleased but he didn't fuss about it to Lenny.*

I was introduced to Aaron by David Del Tredici at a piano recital in New York early in 1967, and I boldly asked whether I might show him some of

Above: Copland and Phillip Ramey en route from Budapest to Bucharest, 14 November 1969.

Photograph by Phillip Ramey.

Above: Copland at the Teatro Communale, Bologna, Italy, 1969.

Photograph by Phillip Ramey.

Right: Signing copies of the Hungarian translation of *The New Music,* Hungary, 1969.

my music. "Sure," he replied. "Give me a ring." I did, and he invited me to Rock Hill. There, I played for him a recent piece, Piano Sonata No.2. *The dean of American composers told me my sonata, though well made, sounded too like Prokofiev and therefore lacked freshness. The judgment was delivered firmly but not unkindly, for he also pointed out things he liked. (Aaron tends not to be unduly kind to young composers; he's too objective for a grandfatherly role.) The high point of that first visit was his read-through at the keyboard, at my request, of his own* Piano Variations— *which does not sound like Prokofiev, or, for that matter, anyone else.*

As our friendship grew, I often reflected how lucky I was to have one of the century's great composers to consult whenever I wrote a new piece. When I asked for Aaron's opinion, I always found everything he said extremely helpful, even in those few instances when I couldn't agree. He seldom suggested solutions to compositional problems; rather, he took note of material he felt worth keeping and that which might be discarded. He emphatically conveyed to me his ideal of how tightly constructed and economical pieces should be; and his special kind of chord spacing had a certain influence on me. His neojazzy rhythms did not, though I liked them, and he sometimes expressed amazement that such a "warlike character" (his favorite description of me) didn't write more rhythmic music.

When Aaron went to Dartmouth College *as composer-in-residence in the fall of 1967, I went with him, for he wanted a musician as a general assistant. That was the first of our many trips, most of them conducting tours. After Dartmouth, he asked me to go to Europe. In Vienna, during grueling rehearsals of his* Third Symphony, *I had my first demonstration of the famous Copland patience. I remember Aaron complaining about the musicians: "They're so arrogant. Not only can't they play the irregular rhythms accurately, they won't even try." He suspected that their obstructiveness was motivated in part by anti-Semitism. In London, where Aaron's concert with the London Symphony Orchestra was sold out and the musicians played enthusiastically for him, he was more relaxed, always charming (I used to tell him he would have made a fine diplomat, and he would respond, "Or psychiatrist") whether conversing with a young British composer such as Peter Maxwell Davies or with a future prime minister, Edward Heath.*

Two years later, in November 1969, Aaron and I went to Europe again. In Bucharest, he was somewhat annoyed to discover that his agent had neglected to tell him his fee would be in Roumanian lei and couldn't be taken out. [21] I said, "Well, then let's live it up: champagne—morning,

noon, and night! And we can buy lots of souvenirs." But Aaron graciously—
and cannily—decided to use the money to establish a prize in his name for
young composers.

Aaron is one of the few friends with whom I've never had a falling-out.
We took to each other immediately, and we remain close twenty-two years
later. Of course, he's a patient man, which may account for the phenomenon, and he's incredibly loyal to friends. Aaron is most drawn to a different
kind of personality from his own. Lenny Bernstein, for instance—how very
unlike Aaron he is. By different, I don't mean stronger, for under all the
cordiality he is strong as can be, but rather a more assertive, even acerbic,
type. There's no cruel or vindictive side to Aaron; he's genuinely well-
meaning, but he likes people who are more opinionated and outspoken than
he is. I filled that bill.

In *1968*, with the Stravinsky–Robert Craft books in mind, I decided to
conduct interviews with Aaron on the subject of his music, focusing on
specific works, and more than a dozen were eventually published, most of
them as liner notes for the CBS Records series "Copland Conducts Copland." All those interviews were tape-recorded, put together by me from
transcripts and then carefully edited by Aaron. He was enthusiastic about
the project, for he thought it important to leave his own commentary for
future generations. Later, when I became the New York Philharmonic's
program editor, I found our interviews invaluable for my many Copland
annotations.

As an example of how private and emotionally contained Aaron is, there
was the weekend in the early *1970s* when I was at Rock Hill with two
composer friends, David Del Tredici and Robert Helps. After lunch on
Saturday, we played tapes of our latest pieces, and Aaron followed the
scores. Then he disappeared for awhile and reentered the studio dressed in
a suit. "I've got to go out for a couple of hours," he said, and off he went
in his Mercedes-Benz. When he returned, he was a bit subdued and would
not tell us where he'd been, but we had a lively dinner and played four-hand
piano music afterward. The following week, a small article appeared in The
New York Times concerning the funeral, Saturday, of Aaron's beloved sister
Laurine, and it noted that Aaron had been present. I wondered then just
how well I actually knew Aaron, since I hadn't realized that something was
very wrong. Aaron is given to concealing his innermost feelings and, even
so, he wouldn't have wanted to subject friends to a personal trauma.

I never once saw Aaron indulge in sentimentality; but he has a sad core
that is perhaps responsible for the wonderful bittersweet lyricism heard from

time to time in his music (I think especially of the opening of the Clarinet
Concerto *and some of the exposed woodwind writing in* Inscape). *That's
the part of him nobody gets at. At least I never did.*

*In recent years, one of my duties on trips was to make certain Aaron did
not become overtired, along with keeping careful watch over appointments
and rehearsal schedules. At the colleges, he always agreed to listen to works
by student composers. In Kansas in 1982, I wouldn't have wanted to be one
of them. Aaron didn't much like anything he heard and was cool and a bit
clipped. He said to me afterward, "They really should be doing better." I
replied, "You made that quite clear." "Did I?" he asked, concerned. "I
meant to get it across but I hope I didn't sound mean." Yet he had been
intimidating. Aaron won't take the easy way out and be politely noncommittal when asked to evaluate a score, even with friends. Music is too important
to him, and he's always serious about it. He has extraordinary integrity.
That's the real gist of Copland.*

In June 1967, I spent four days on the Oberlin campus for the celebration
of the conservatory's one hundredth anniversary, conducting, attending
recitals, listening to student composers, and speaking informally, in addition to delivering the convocation address. I enjoyed spending time with
the students. By this time, I had talked about twentieth-century music so
often, I could do it blindfolded! For the serious presentations, I did as
other speakers do in similar situations—adapted notes and outlines from
my files. At about this time, I began to curtail lecturing. There is some
danger in that you begin to find yourself believing everything you say!
With conducting, no matter how many times one might conduct a piece,
there would be the excitement of different players, a different atmosphere,
the uncertainty of what might or might not happen. But with lecturing,
as with composing, if indulged in over a very long period of time, one runs
the risk of repeating oneself.

My trip to Europe in the fall of 1967 was scheduled to coincide with Nadia
Boulanger's eightieth birthday party in Monaco, hosted by Prince Ranier
and Princess Grace. Much of the music world was there for the occasion.
I sat with my old friend from the Paris days, Marcelle de Manziarly, for
the concert at the Monte Carlo Theatre. Nadia looked more fragile than
I remembered but otherwise her old self. I had written an article about
her, just published by the Associated Press (3 September) and released

worldwide. It had been seen by many people at the party. I wrote to Nadia afterward, "It was a never-to-be-forgotten occasion."

On my return to London, I conducted a recording of the *Dance Symphony,* the *Symphonic Ode, Our Town,* and *Outdoor Overture.* Phillip Ramey and I had a pleasant country visit with Michael Tippett before returning to Paris. The weather was sunny and warm, and I walked everywhere—St. Germain des Près hangouts from my old days in Paris, Brentanos, the rue de Rivoli, the whole Champs Elysées. I had dinner with Virgil at his place on the quai Voltaire, along with Peggy Bernier and Earle Brown. As pleasant as it was to be in Paris, as far as I could tell, the French had lost all contact with my music. I wrote, "All is *a refaire,* a rather glum prospect."

From Paris I went to Köln [Cologne] to conduct my *Orchestral Variations* with the Köln Radio Orchestra, which had too small a string section and rather weak brass. They also had the same sense of reluctant cooperation, though the discipline was somewhat better than most radio orchestras. Phillip and I traveled on to Venice via Frankfurt and Milan, and from Venice to Bologna, where I had to conduct a third-rate orchestra. Bologna was plastered with posters announcing my arrival. We had a lot of rehearsals for the concert, which went off fairly well. It was repeated the next night to a pitifully small house. I wrote, "Stupid of the management to have thought they could get two audiences for a modern American music program in Bologna. It was an 'experiment' that failed!"

Back in Peekskill by the end of October, I hoped to stay home for a while. A quiet sixty-seventh birthday was enjoyed with friends. I finished the revision of *Canticle of Freedom* and tried to make some headway on a commission for a string quartet I had promised Bill Schuman for the Juilliard back in 1962. It was not moving along, and much as I would like to have had a string quartet in my catalogue, I eventually relinquished the commission.[22]

In 1966, Victor Kraft had suggested I update my 1940 book, *Our New Music.* He wrote, "Isn't it a waste to have it lying around unsold? Wouldn't it be worthwhile to redress the whole thing—maybe even alter the title a bit . . . people are really exposed to our new music in a way you never dreamt of then." I thought Victor had a good idea, so I got to work writing "second thoughts." The revision gave me the opportunity to admit I had not foreseen the enormous influence the twelve-tone system would have on postwar composers. I caught readers up on recent developments, such as chance operations and electronic music, and updated my autobiographical sketch. The title became *The New Music: 1900–1960.*[23]

In connection with the publication, I was invited to appear on NBC's "Today" show with Hugh Downes (13 March 1968) and on WOR radio with the actress Arlene Francis. I don't know how many books were sold as a result, but my family sure was impressed! My sister-in-law Mildred wrote, "You should have seen Leon's face when he watched that wonderful interview." When the family visited me in Peekskill about a month later, they were amazed when I told them that the television show was unrehearsed—except for Leon, who said, "Aaron, you were always that way—when you were three years old you got up on the pulpit at temple—people could just see the top of your head—and you recited 'How would you like to be a dog?'"

After conducting varied programs with the BSO and the Music Center orchestra at Tanglewood (20–25 August 1968), I wrote to Lenny (26 August): "I'm just back from conducting at Tanglewood, where your spirit hovers. But it always hovers wherever I go. American music would have a different 'face' without you!"

The Israel Philharmonic invited me to conduct a series of concerts at the end of 1968 and beginning of 1969. Victor Kraft, recently separated from his wife, went with me. I had not been to Israel since 1951, and not surprisingly, I discovered some changes: a luxurious guest house for visitors of the orchestra and the Mann Auditorium, which seated three thousand. The subscription audience numbered twenty-four thousand for each set of concerts in Tel Aviv, which was calculated to be about ten percent of that city's population! Therefore, the same program had to be repeated eight times, with a ninth in Jerusalem. I wrote in my diary[24]:

> The mere prospect of all those repetitions of the same program is exhausting! The orchestra is cooperating well. Weak elements—horns, some woodwind players. The program [Stravinsky, *Symphony in C;* Ives, *Decoration Day;* Copland, *Orchestral Variations*] is too hard for four rehearsals—my error—damn!

In addition to conducting, I played piano in *Vitebsk* in a chamber music concert arranged by the American consul. Local composers attended and afterward I listened to some of their works and talked with them. My impression was that they had gained considerable self-confidence in an organizational way since 1951.

In Jerusalem, Victor and I stayed at the King David Hotel and visited the Old City, which I found incredibly picturesque. After a visit to Bethlehem, I commented, "The usual sense of unreality about these ancient sites and legends. Most impressed with the *paysage*. Kept puzzling over how it happened that *this* was the Holy Land." During one three-day weekend, we rented a car and toured the countryside, accompanied by a young guide. I wrote:

> Our first stop was again Jerusalem, then Jericho by way of an impressive ride down from the heights to the subsea-level ruins of ancient Jericho and a distant view of the Dead Sea. Unforgettable terrain. Drove for more than three hours back to Jerusalem and on to the kibbutz through rather scary Arab towns and lovely stretches of mountainous roads. Reached the kibbutz in time for dinner. . . . We were shown the children being put to bed in an underground shelter (because of the danger of Jordanian shelling). . . . After a communal breakfast, we were taken to visit a kibbutz right on the border with Jordan. . . . An heroic atmosphere since they are under continual strain of possible attack. We dropped our guide at his kibbutz and headed for Safed on a narrow bumpy road through remote areas of empty hill country—left an impression!

Back in Tel Aviv for the remaining concerts, we spent a quiet New Year's Eve, and then made a one-day excursion to Eilat on the Red Sea. On our return to Tel Aviv, I was greeted by Julius Rudel, who had arrived for the *next* series of nine concerts. After my final concert, I was presented with candlesticks made in Israel, as a momento. Victor was so taken with the country, he decided to stay for a while, but as my plane touched ground in New York (5 January), I wrote in my diary, "glad to be home."

I composed three short musical works in 1969, all of a celebratory nature. One was for the dedication of a very large red stabile by Alexander Calder in a plaza in downtown Grand Rapids, Michigan. The sculpture, *La Grande Vitesse*, was the first work of art in American history to be jointly commissioned and financed by federal and private funds. I knew and admired Sandy Calder and this was a spectacular sculpture, so I accepted the commission.[25] The result was *Inaugural Fanfare*, composed for twenty-four instruments—woodwinds, brass, and percussion—in three sections. The opening is characterized by biting harmonic chords; the middle section is for ad-lib snare drum against a quiet melodic line played by two trumpets; and the closing material resembles the opening.

Calder attended the unveiling of *La Grande Vitesse* in Grand Rapids (14 June 1969), but I could not be at the dedication ceremony. Reviews and a tape were sent to me afterward. One critic quipped, "Copland's *Inaugural Fanfare* was unfortunately gone with the wind." I had aimed for something more than a conventional fanfare, and it seems that the nuances of the piece were lost in the open air. Such events are rarely very satisfactory in a musical sense, and for the Calder dedication, several factors combined to dull the effect of the music, which was played by the Grand Rapids Symphony under their conductor, Gregory Millar. I decided not to release *Inaugural Fanfare* for publication until it could be revised.[26] Other commitments intervened, and I did not get around to doing anything about it.

In 1974, the powers that be in Grand Rapids were installing another Calder, an enormous rooftop painting close to the sculpture in the plaza, which was about to be renamed "Calder Plaza." When they looked for "their" Copland piece in order to perform it again, they found no sign of a score or parts in their files. Gregory Millar had a photocopy of the score; Boosey & Hawkes had nothing; and I had only the sketches from which I had planned to revise the work. The newspapers made a thing about it, joking that at least Grand Rapids could not misplace the Calder sculpture as it had its Copland piece! The situation spurred me on to compose the new version for wind ensemble. I apologized to Grand Rapids for letting so much time pass and soon presented them with the new score, dedication intact: "Composed for the City of Grand Rapids. Inauguration of Calder Statuary, revised 1975."

Another pièce d'occasion of 1969 was *Happy Anniversary,* an arrangement for symphony orchestra of the well-known tune "Happy Birthday," in honor of Eugene Ormandy's seventieth birthday.[27] It was first performed as part of a *Variations on Happy Birthday* by famous composers, conducted by myself in Philadelphia (24 January 1970) at the orchestra's seventieth anniversary concert (Ormandy's birthday was actually in November). The date was planned to coordinate with President Nixon's presentation of the Medal of Freedom to Ormandy at the concert. My score, dedicated to the conductor, was presented in a bound book containing the twenty variations. I never expected to hear anything further about *Happy Anniversary,* but it was published by Boosey & Hawkes in 1972, although it is only about one minute in duration, and the idea was turned around by the National Symphony Orchestra when they played the arrangement for *my* seventy-seventh birthday, on an all-Copland concert, Rostropovich conducting. It was used in the same way at the "Wall-to-Wall Copland" eightieth birthday party at Symphony Space in New York City.

The third tribute I had promised was for the Metropolitan Museum of Art centennial, which was to be celebrated with the performance of an original fanfare to open each exhibit during the 1969–1970 season. (Commissions went also to Virgil Thomson, Walter Piston, William Schuman, and Leonard Bernstein.) I composed it immediately after returning from my 1969 fall trip to Europe (Phillip Ramey accompanied me to Baden-Baden, Budapest, Bucharest, and London, where I reviewed tapes for recordings made the previous year). *Ceremonial Fanfare* is for brass ensemble of eleven instruments and is three minutes and twenty seconds in duration. The piece falls into three connected sections: The first begins with a trumpet line echoed in the trombone, followed by the horns building to a big climax; the middle section is a more flowing passage with canonic and quasicanonic imitation; and the final section is basically a recapitulation of the beginning, except for the final half-dozen bars, which bring the short piece to a quiet close. *Ceremonial Fanfare* is tonal in feeling, using key signatures and a home base of B major/minor.[28] The first performance took place at the museum on my seventieth birthday, for the opening of the exhibit "Masterpieces of Fifty Centuries."

Interlude VI

Following the assassinations of the Kennedys and Martin Luther King, the Vietnam War and Watergate further diminished American pride and self-respect. A loss of confidence in democratic ideals resulted in severe setbacks in education and civil rights. Social historians have compared the disillusionment that characterized the seventies to the Depression, but for the first time in American history, traditional values faltered to such a degree that schools and colleges closed at an alarming rate around the country.[1] As educational standards lowered, the arts were in turn affected. Discouraged by Vietnam and embarrassed by government corruption, American artists preferred to follow international styles rather than ones that would be perceived as national or American.

A key word of the period was *cool*, a term borrowed from bebop and modern jazz. An outward show of emotion or vitality was not admired. Visual artists produced abstract forms and shapes; literature and poetry explored words as sounds, not commentary; and most composers used atonal styles that referred to nothing extramusical: serialism, electronic sounds, chance operations, and minimalism. The fragmentation and pluralism (terms used by historians to describe the diversity of musical activities)[2] would show little change until the eighties, when the prevailing aesthetic would finally swing back toward figurative art, and an old "ism" would reappear in music as "the new romanticism."

Aaron Copland at seventy was cool and contained, tall and spare, craggy-featured and bespectacled, grayer of hair, but still sure of step, speech, and purpose. For his major works of the sixties, he had used serialism, but in ways that are unmistakably Copland. As Ned Rorem, a composer who wrote tonal music during the years when it was not in fashion, explains about *Connotations* and *Inscape:* "We are now far enough away from those pieces to see that, in fact, they still contain the leanness that Copland has always had—like when an airplane leaves the earth, and things

Copland at seventy.

get smaller and smaller in the distance and become more and more one color."³

Inscape was Copland's last major work, although he continued to compose into the seventies. Whether the decline in Copland's composing was connected to the disenchantment of the times is speculation, as are other possibilities—the increasing gap in time between Copland and young composers, the natural effects of aging, or a combination of these. Copland continued to be very actively involved in the music world, and when he turned seventy and was told he hardly looked his age, he responded, "I hardly *feel* it." He said to interviewers (as he would at seventy-five and eighty), "I just don't relate to that number!" Indeed, he was about to go through such a round of birthday tributes that one journalist wrote, "Copland concerts are outnumbered only by Beethoven's."

No manager or public relations firm had ever organized a Copland birthday celebration, but Claire Reis, who was a consummate organizer, discussed Copland's seventieth with William Schuman and Stuart Pope at Boosey & Hawkes in order to coordinate the New York events. Claire's idea was to put together an album of composer tributes from all over the world to be presented to Copland at a birthday dinner after the Juilliard

364

Left: Claire Reis presents a book of composers' letters to Copland at his seventieth birthday dinner, the Essex House, New York City; (right) William Schuman, master-of-ceremonies.

Right: Looking at the tributes with Copland (left to right): Claire Reiss, Michael Tilson Thomas, Mari and Robert Cornell, Olga Koussevitzky, Leonard Bernstein.

Below: Letter from Copland to Claire Reis, 21 November 1970.

AARON COPLAND   1538 L. WASHINGTON STREET PEEKSKILL, N.Y. 10566

Nov 21 1970

Dear Claire,

Many, many thanks for all you did in connection with my 70th birthday. (I don't believe the ↑ even as I write it!)

It was a 'dream' party from my standpoint...

And especially thank you for that magnificent book of letters from my fellow-composers. I've just finished reading them. If any composer of serious music has ever been more generously praised by his peers, I can't imagine who it might have been.

Verily, my cup runneth over! And I have a very good idea as to who it was that first raised the cup.... Or —

Again — many, many thanks — and for the long years of a devoted friendship.

Gratefully and affectionately

Aaron

concert.[4] The gala dinner at the Essex House, hosted by Boosey & Hawkes, was described by Ned Rorem: "The feast . . . followed by *louanges* and presentations from the Great, terminated with *Danzón Cubano* performed at two pianos by Copland and Bernstein with the élan of a pair of drunken sailors, all harmless fun. . . ."[5] Bernstein evidently was feeling no pain, playing exuberantly and smiling away, while Copland looked up and over in alarm at the fusillade of wrong notes. The "presentations from the Great" included the album of composers' letters, the Handel Medalion, "the highest award given by New York City for a contribution to its cultural life," and remarks by Schuman and Bernstein.[6] Copland wrote to Claire Reis afterward:

> Thank you for that magnificent book of letters from my fellow composers. I've just finished reading them. If any composer of serious music has ever been more generously praised by his peers, I can't imagine who it might have been. Verily, my cup runneth over! And I have a very good idea as to who it was that first raised the cup.[7]

According to Claire Reis, every request brought forth a response, except for those sent to Russia. One that particularly pleased Copland read, "Dear Aaron, Seventy is pretty good. Congratulations, Stravinsky."

Copland conducted The New York Philharmonic in a concert of his music, and received honorary membership in the Philharmonic Society of New York, conferred by Carlos Moseley, who said, "Aaron Copland's music has been represented on the Society's programs more than that of any American composer during its history." In addition to the Philharmonic, Copland himself conducted seventeen orchestras during that year.[8] In Minneapolis, he wryly reminded the newspaper critics, who were referring to him as "The Dean of American Music," that many years earlier a Minneapolis critic had called him "Copland the Ogre." Yale University awarded Copland its prestigious Howland Medal (30 January 1970), and honorary degrees were given by the Peabody Conservatory, Columbia, Brandeis, and York universities, as well as by the New York University School for Continuing Education. In July, when the Interlochen Music Camp students presented their annual "Man of Music" plaque to Copland and asked the secret of his success, Copland responded, "These things just *happen* to you!"

Festivities at Tanglewood in July included Copland conducting the Boston Symphony and the Music Center orchestras.[9] In August, he flew to Los Angeles to conduct the Philharmonic in the Hollywood Bowl and the Los Angeles Chamber Ensemble in the premiere of *Appalachian Spring* in its original orchestration. Lawrence Morton wrote in the program book of this concert of Copland's early music (14 August), "This is not inappropriate, for it is only chronologically that he approaches seventy. In heart and spirit he remains the youngest of them all."

In October, the British rolled out the red carpet. André Previn, then director of the London Symphony Orchestra, had been asked to play Copland's *Piano Concerto,* but he demurred, saying it was "because of a lack of time to learn the solo part of your fiendish piano concerto—much as I admire the work." Copland played it himself, afterward vowing not to do so again: "I didn't enjoy it. Hit too many wrong notes. Other people don't notice it, but I do." After the concert at the Festival Hall, Copland received honorary membership in the Royal Philharmonic Society, and a dinner was held in his honor by Ambassador Walter Annenberg, with Prime Minister Edward Heath attending. As critic Peter Heyworth noted in *The Observer* (15 November): "No American composer has made such an impact on English musical life as Aaron Copland. . . ." Copland was so taken with the British, he told Harold Clurman that he was considering buying a flat in London.

Copland's career as composer, conductor, and representative of American music was discussed and evaluated in articles, reviews, radio programs, and on television.[10] Copland enjoyed it all, except for part of an article by Leonard Bernstein, "An Intimate Sketch," in *Hi Fidelity* magazine (November 1970). Lenny praised his close friend, but in the closing paragraphs, he wrote about Copland's current status and situation as composer:

> . . . So Copland stopped composing. How sad for him. How awful for us. . . . All it will take, it seems to me, is another musical turn, this time to a rediscovery of the basic simplicities of art, in which Copland will once more be looked to as a leader, will once again feel wanted as a composer. Happy Birthday, Aaron. We miss your music.

Someone other than Bernstein placed a heading on the article. It read, "Why Has Copland Stopped Composing?" Copland had made no decision or public pronouncements about his composing; evidently, he did not want anyone else doing so, although he had admitted to friends that he was in a composing slump. As he wrote to Carlos Chávez (22 August): "I wish I could tell you of new works of my own—but the truth is that the urge to compose seems to be tapering off. I hope not permanently. Perhaps you have a 'cure' to suggest?" In response to Bernstein's article, Copland was quoted in the the *Daily News:* "Don't know where Lenny got the idea I was stopping composing. *I* never told him that." Donal Henahan of *The New York Times* described an interview with Copland in Peekskill:

> Copland said, "Did you see the piece that Lenny Bernstein wrote about me in the new *Hi Fi?* 'Happy Birthday, Aaron. We miss your music.'" Copland breaks out in a giggle. "I thought it was rather naïve of him to imagine that you can just happily go on doing what you always had been doing and get away with it. . . . Also, the picture he paints of me at the end of the article of having been abandoned by the young composers. Why, that's nothing at all like what I feel." An incredulous laugh. "It's perfectly natural, after all, that when you get to your seventies you're not going to have the same hold on a younger generation as when you were forty or fifty! Why he should seem unhappy for me, I don't know."

Phillip Ramey sent a response to the editor of *Hi Fidelity,* after showing it to Copland. Ramey wrote, "Copland is presently writing, on commission, a sizable three-movement work for flute and piano." (This became Copland's *Duo for Flute and Piano.*)

The relationship between Copland and Bernstein was of such long standing that the contretemps was soon forgotten. Bernstein's own birthday salute to Copland was "A Copland Celebration" (27 December), similar to the sixtieth birthday tribute. It was a broadcast of a Young People's Concert on CBS featuring the *Clarinet Concerto* and excerpts from *Billy the Kid.* Bernstein said, "It's almost impossible to believe that time has rushed by so fast that this year Copland is suddenly seventy. Copland has often been called the 'Dean of American composers,' whatever that means. I guess it's supposed to mean that he's the oldest, but he isn't the oldest—he's just the best." Bernstein also played a major role in a MacDowell Colony dinner and concert in Copland's honor (24 November), along with Isaac Stern and others. (After seven years as president, Copland turned the leadership of the Colony over to Schuman in 1968).

With birthday festivities extending into 1971 (a vocal concert in February by Phyllis Curtin and Jan DeGaetani, films with Copland's music at the Metropolitan Museum), Copland was more than ready to leave for Europe in June, first to Paris, where he had not been for several years.[11] Perhaps because of having reached his seventieth year, Copland was nostalgic in France. He conducted a concert of his works at the Théâtre des Champs Elysées, where he had spent his first night in Paris in 1921, watching the Ballet Suédois in Milhaud's *L'Homme et son désir,* and saw

368

friends from the twenties, including Marcelle de Manziarly and Nadia at Fontainebleau. Copland wrote of Nadia in his diary, "I was struck by the fact that she couldn't see anything anymore. Otherwise, she seemed very much alive. I visited the outside of my 1921 abode. The town of Fontaine-bleau in general and the house in particular looked all spruced up— younger than in 1921!"

Between conducting tours, Copland stayed at home, catching up with correspondence and organizations with which he was involved,[12] and working on various publications and presentations. Ten years at his Peek-skill home, Rock Hill, was enough for him to know that the place really suited his needs: a country house close enough to the city for his purposes and for visitors to come out easily by train or car in little over an hour. Copland managed to keep his housekeepers, Gaston and Mireille, with him until 1973. Once, when he was with Harold Lawrence, manager of the London Symphony Orchestra, Copland pointed out that he could not stay away from home too long. "My rare and wonderful cook and gardener get lonely when I am away," Copland told Lawrence. "Touring is one thing, but a bachelor-composer needs someone to look after him."[13] When Gaston and Mireille finally returned to Europe, Copland found another couple for a short time; then in 1974, a young man who was a talented cook, Sophronus Mundy, came to take over the kitchen and the driving. Professional equipment was installed in the old-fashioned kitchen, and Sophronus proceeded to cook gourmet meals that meant not so much to Copland but were a delight to his guests. Sophronus sometimes accom-panied Copland on trips and to concerts in New York, driving him home afterward.

Invitations and requests continued to fill Copland's mailbox. His name alone on a program or announcement is good publicity for any organization or performing group. His attractive style of public speaking accounted for the many requests to appear as master of ceremonies or toastmaster for special occasions. Copland would always supply the perfect blend of seri-ousness and wit. He could be relied on to be straightforward and insightful, not to ramble or mumble, and always to get a good laugh or two. As with most people who speak with ease and spontaneity, Copland always thought carefully about what he wanted to say, then delivered the message in his inimitably breezy and impromptu fashion. He and Schuman frequently hosted each other's special parties, and Schuman, an exceptional speaker himself, would joke, "I have a second occupation—introducing Aaron Copland at his own birthday parties. It's not lucrative, but it's fun!"

Accepting the Laurel Leaf
Award from the American
Music Center, 1968.

Speaking about "Music in
the Thirties" on stage with
Minna Daniel, Graduate
Center, New York City, 8
May 1979.

Included in Copland's speaking engagements were the inevitable memorial tributes, such as the opening remarks at a concert in William
Flanagan's memory (14 April 1970). Others close to Copland died in the

Copland with Harold Clurman, Lotos Club Dinner, New York City, 1978.

seventies. In 1972, his sister Laurine and her husband Charles Marcus, composer Ingolf Dahl, and Copland's lawyer Abe Friedman. (Copland's *Piano Sonata* was played by Leo Smit at Friedman's memorial service.) Abe Friedman's music clients were turned over to an associate, Ellis J. Freedman, who reported that Copland was wary at first and had asked him, "Do you think you can handle composers' affairs?"[14] (Before long, Copland came to rely on Ellis Freedman as he had Abe Friedman.) Composer Israel Citkowitz and Copland's sister-in-law Dorothy ("Dot") died in 1974; and a year later, the last member of Copland's immediate family, his older brother Leon. In 1979, André Kostelanetz died, and Copland appeared in the New York Philharmonic's concert tribute to the conductor as narrator in the work "Kosty" had commissioned from him, *Lincoln Portrait*. In the late seventies, Copland lost two people who had been closest to him throughout much of his life: Harold Clurman in 1978 and Nadia Boulanger in 1979. Copland never got used to the idea. He would comment, "I just think of them as still being out there."

Copland's own health continued to be excellent. He had rarely been seriously ill, and in all the years of traveling, on only one trip (to Prague in 1973) did Copland need to consult a physician and go to bed for a few days. It caused him to miss an ambassador's dinner and a meeting with Prague's composers, the latter with great disappointment; the former not at all.

Copland continued to travel extensively during the seventies and well into the eighties. He became a familiar and popular figure on the conducting circuit. He had developed his own style on the podium: relaxed, economical, and informal, but with zest and vitality. Audiences liked his obvious physical enjoyment of the music. The English particularly found him a refreshing contrast to their own more restrained conductors. Above all, Copland's performances possessed rhythmic energy. When an interviewer asked how it felt to be conducting in his seventies, Copland responded, "I don't feel weighed down by seventy years. Every time I finish conducting, I come off exhilarated, like a boxer after a good ring workout."

Copland was beginning to think about writing an autobiography. He made some notes and an outline, and even considered a title—"The Music Within." Several publishers were interested.[15] Copland promised himself that as soon as the birthday celebrations were over, he would do two things: begin to write his life story and get back to composing.

Copland in London,
1975.

Photograph by Suzie E. Maeder.

372

Breaking New Ground

1971-1979

Verso: Copland in rehearsal, c. 1972.
Opposite: Copland, 1975.

I had a few promises to keep: One was to write a brief salute for the fortieth birthday celebration of the Music Library Association in 1971. I sent off eight measures, a sort of inversion of "Happy Birthday," in fanfare style "for a single brass instrument or several in unison." I see from the markings on my score that it was meant to be played *larghetto pomposo* and *marcatissimo*. After the Music Library Association's conference, Bill Lichtenwanger, head of the reference section of the music division, sent me the program on which my salute was printed, and he wrote (2 February 1971):

> In case the ghost of Joe McCarthy is hovering around, I had better explain that the ink is not pink but ruby. I had hoped to get together a Russian horn band to give the piece its first performance . . . but the meeting was so big and busy and formal that I couldn't get a rehearsal going—so the first performance is still to come.

As far as I know, the first performance is *still* to come.[1]

This commitment fulfilled, I composed a short piece requested by my friend André Kostelanetz—"Estribillo," which when added to my two *Latin-American Sketches* of 1959 make a three-part work. It was played in that form for the first time by the New York Philharmonic, conducted by Kostelanetz (10 June 1972).

In draft stage since 1969 had been a work for flute and piano, commissioned by seventy pupils and friends of William Kincaid, first flutist of the Philadelphia Orchestra from 1921 to 1960.[2] After Kincaid died in 1967, John Solum, a former student, organized the committee, and they offered me the commission.[3] Solum and Elaine Shaffer, also a Kincaid pupil, corresponded with me and were most helpful when it came to preparation of the final score, which is dedicated to the memory of William Kincaid.[4] I composed the slow movement first and sent it off to Elaine Shaffer. When I had the second movement in hand, I asked the two flutists to meet

375

with me—after all, this was my first extensive writing for the flute. In one spot, I had asked the flutist to play with a "thin tone" and was told in no uncertain terms that one never invites a flutist to do that! Instead, Solum recommended some harmonic fingerings that gave just the veiled quality I had in mind.[5]

Duo for Flute and Piano is in three movements, with the following indications: Flowing; Poetic, somewhat mournful; Lively, with bounce. My *Duo* is a lyrical piece, in a somewhat pastoral style. Almost by definition, it would have to be a lyrical piece, for what can you do with a flute in an extended form that would not emphasize its songful nature? Lyricism seems to be built into the flute. Some colleagues and critics expressed surprise at the tonal nature of *Duo,* considering that my recent works had been in a more severe idiom; however, the style was naturally influenced by the fact that I was composing for Kincaid's students, not for future generations (although I hoped younger flutists would play *Duo* eventually). Also, I was using material from earlier sketches in my notebooks, and that may have influenced the style of the piece.[6] For example, the beginning of the first movement, which opens with a solo passage for flute, recalls the first movement of my *Third Symphony.*

The first movement is altogether a rather easygoing pastoral sort of movement, while the second uses harmonic and melodic language more akin to my later works, with the principal idea in the flute projecting a whole-tone sound similar to the opening of the *Piano Quartet.* The second movement has a certain mood that I connect with myself—a rather sad and wistful one, I suppose. The last movement is lively, with a triadic theme in a free form. The whole is a work of comparatively simple harmonic and melodic outline, direct in expression. Being aware that many of the flutists who were responsible for commissioning the piece would want to play it, I tried to make it grateful for the performer, but no amateur could handle the *Duo*—it requires a good player.

The world premiere of *Duo for Flute and Piano* took place in Philadelphia, performed by Elaine Shaffer with Hephzibah Menuhin, pianist (3 October 1971). The concert was a benefit for Philadelphia's Settlement Music School, and I was pleased to attend. *Duo* was played twice: before intermission and again after. The New York premiere followed at the Hunter College Playhouse with the same players (9 October). *Duo* was warmly received in both cities. I wrote to Chávez (25 December 1971), "I have finished a fourteen-minute *Duo for Flute and Piano,* which was premiered in October, but the musical ideas date from the forties, and so, naturally, the piece is not at all 'avant-grade' in sound. *Eh bien, tant pis!* But it *would* be nice to get some '1970' ideas to work on."

After *Duo* was played for the first time in Boston, Michael Steinberg of the *Boston Globe* wrote (25 January):

> Hearing *Duo* was also an occasion for gratefully remembering how extraordinarily and evenly high Copland's standard of achievement has been. He has composed at greater and lesser levels of musical density, but he has never written inattentively nor, for that matter, without huge signs saying "only by Aaron Copland." The *Duo* is lightweight work of a masterful craftsman. It is going to give pleasure to flutists and their audiences for a long time.

When Elaine and I rehearsed for the Columbia recording of *Duo,* I missed several of my own notes, but Elaine just smiled sweetly and missed none at all! I was shocked when I heard later that she was terminally ill at the time. I am told that our recording was the very last time Elaine ever played. Other fine flutists have taken up the piece from time to time, among them Jean-Pierre Rampal, John Solum, Paula Robison, and Doriot Dwyer.[7] After hearing *Duo,* Leo Smit wrote (19 January 1972), "Flute piece simply lovely, Emilyish with tiny touches of *Piano Fantasy.* Happy for all flutists."

The flute part was edited for violin by Bobby (Robert) Mann of the Juilliard Quartet. He played the first performance of *Duo for Violin and Piano* at the Library of Congress with pianist André-Michel Schub (5 April 1978). The new version was well received; in fact, some critics have preferred the violin arrangement to the flute original.

After Doriot Anthony Dwyer (first flutist of the BSO) played *Duo,* she wrote (4 January 1973), "Everyone I know welcomed your *Duo,* because it was the first composition of yours in a long time, and because of its own lovely spirit." Doriot then asked to arrange my early "Vocalise" for flute and piano. We met and I suggested some adjustments. Doriot had been asking me to compose a work for her instrument for years, and even after *Duo,* she spoke to me about a concerto for flute and orchestra or a chamber piece. I composed neither but was pleased to approve Doriot's flute version of "Vocalise." After the first performance, she wrote (9 April 1973), "Well, the 'Vocalise' is launched! I got the right climax to it, and it was all a great deep pleasure to play. I knew everyone would love it and they did!"

There were other memorable occasions in the early seventies that stand out in my mind: One was the opening of the Kennedy Center in Washington. The first concert, in memory of former President Kennedy, featured

63 Stanworth Lane
Princeton, N.J. 08540
Thursday, Feb 8, 1973

My dear Aaron, —

I don't flatter myself unduly that my delinquencies as a letter writer are as notorious as I, alas, deserve! but I can't refrain from writing to tell you how tremendously touched I was to see you last evening & felt afterwards that, simply because I have never quite learned how to behave on such occasions, I might not have made my feelings as clear to you as I would have liked to do.

Believe me, that you took the trouble to come meant more to me than I can possibly say. Although I don't feel in the least as if my life were drawing to a close or anything like that, I have gotten to the point where I have quite a long past to look back at and take a great deal of pleasure and satisfaction in remembering things which have made a very rich life for me, combined with a good deal of somewhat rueful amusement as I remember my own antics at times. The main thing here is how much I value your friendship, and what a delight it is — on levels ranging from Washington Ave., Brooklyn upwards, so to speak — whenever we have a glimpse of each other: all too rarely since, gratias Dei, we are both of us still very busy!

In any case, it was a great joy to see you. Quite apart from the fact that I had a big surprise in the excellent way in which my music was performed, your presence "made" the evening as far as I was concerned. Thank you, my very dear friend — and always, more power to you.

Always yours, in old affection, in which Lisl joins me —

Roger (Sessions)

Letter from Roger Sessions, 8 February 1973.

the premiere of Lenny Bernstein's *Mass*, which caused quite a sensation (8 September 1971). I sat in the box with members of the Kennedy and Bernstein families.

In March 1972, I enjoyed my first visit to Mexico in ten years. It had the pleasant feeling of a homecoming. I conducted the Orquesta Filarmonica de la Universidad, regularly directed by Eduardo Mata. As usual in Mexico, the enthusiasm of the players and audience made up for a certain lack of polished technique. After visiting with Chávez, I returned to enjoy spring in Peekskill until the end of May, when I was off again, this time to London to conduct the LSO for recordings of *The Red Pony*, *Latin-American Sketches*, and *Music for the Movies*. I also conducted a concert in that enormous barn of a Royal Albert Hall, gave a talk for the BBC, and visited with Victor Kraft, who was living in Cambridge.

I was back home when the Composers Committee put on a retrospective concert for Roger Sessions (7 February 1973) and was pleased to be able to attend. Roger and I had not seen each other much in recent years. Since the early years when we had put on the Copland–Sessions Concerts, I had never been sure how Roger felt about me. I was pleasantly surprised to receive a warm and friendly letter from him the day following his concert. Roger wrote (8 February):

> I can't refrain from writing to tell you how tremendously touched I was to see you last evening. I felt afterwards that, simply because I have never learned how to behave on such occasions, I might not have made my feeling as clear to you as I would have liked to do. Believe me, that you took the trouble to come meant more to me than I can possibly say. . . . The main thing here is how much I value your friendship. . . . Thank you, my very dear friend. . . . Always yours, in old affection. . . . Roger

We had another reunion (30 September 1981): Roger, Virgil, and I performed in Stravinsky's *Histoire du Soldat* for a Composers Showcase concert at the Whitney Museum. Virgil took the part of the devil, Roger was the soldier, and I the narrator. Andrew Porter wrote in *The New Yorker* (19 October 1981):

> It was a nostalgic, affectionate runthrough of the piece; it was not without wit, and offered the unusual spectacle of one of America's greatest composers calling another a "lousy, rotten cheat." Mr. Copland was the most coherent speaker and Mr. Thomson the most perky, but Mr. Sessions' soft, bewildered protestations won the heart.

"Composers Showcase" performance of Stravinsky's *Histoire du Soldat,* the Whitney Museum, New York City, 30 September 1981. (Front, left to right): Roger Sessions, Aaron Copland, and Virgil Thomson; (rear): Speculum Musicae musicians and conductor Robert Craft (left of Copland).

It was not my first such appearance: In 1966, Bill Schuman planned a summer series of Stravinsky programs at Lincoln Center in which *Histoire du Soldat* was included (15 July). Lukas Foss conducted, Elliott Carter was the soldier, and John Cage the devil. Cage recalls that Stravinsky was in the audience, and Elliott remembers exactly what Stravinsky said to Cage: "You are the only sensible composer I know—you don't write any notes." Elliott described the occasion:

> Aaron and I had never done this kind of thing, so we rehearsed and practiced at his home. Cage could not be there until the final rehearsal. When he heard us, he said, "What you are doing is so beautiful, it makes me cry. I don't know how I'll ever be able to do this with you." Then he upstaged us terribly and stole the show! We were rather cross with him. The performance was sold out, and I remember Cage calling it, "the history of the sold-out."[8]

After the death of Stravinsky in 1971, Boosey & Hawkes invited sixteen composers to write brief commemorative canons and epitaphs in his memory to be published in two issues of their quarterly, *Tempo.* Each composer was asked to use some or all of the instruments Stravinsky had used for two works in 1959: *Epitaphium* for flute, clarinet, and harp and *Double Canon* for string quartet. I composed *Threnody Igor Stravinsky: In Memoriam,* later called *Threnody I.* It is a two-minute piece for flute and string trio, consisting of a canonic ground in strings over which a flute melody is spun. I used a theme from my notebook of musical ideas dated "February 1942," which was originally intended "for a passacaglia."9 *Threnody I* was first performed on a Radio 3 concert in England conducted by Elgar Howarth (6 April 1972).

Threnody II was composed in 1973 as an elegy to Beatrice Cunningham (Mrs. Robert W. Cunningham), sister of Lawrence Morton and supporter of the Ojai Festival. In this piece, alto flute replaces the C flute of *Threnody I.* It is made up of successions of rich homorhythmic chords, with intermittent solos, brief canonic passages, and various transpositions of a quickly ascending figure. *Threnody II* is somewhat more complex than *Threnody I.* Since both are short, I recommended they be paired. The premiere of *Threnodies I and II* took place at Ojai under Michael Tilson Thomas, director of the twenty-seventh Ojai Festival (2 June 1973). In 1972, between the threnodies, I composed a piano piece for the Van Cliburn piano competition: *Night Thoughts (Homage to Ives).*

I had an exciting five-week conducting tour in the fall of 1973, which included Budapest, Istanbul, Ankara, Prague, and Madrid (23 September–28 October).10 Upon my return, I found in my usual flood of mail an item that caused some consternation. It was from Richard Nixon's office, requesting that some of my music be played at his inaugural concert. I was in a quandary, since I did not admire Mr. Nixon, but I had no desire to take a stand against him by refusing to have my music played. My decision was to allow the performances but not to attend. Afterward, I heard from a few colleagues who thought I should have objected.11 (For Jimmy Carter's inauguration in 1977, I not only attended but conducted the Atlanta Symphony in part of the program.)12

After a quiet seventy-third birthday celebration in New York (lunch with David Del Tredici, dinner with Alvin Ross), I went up to Boston at the end of the month: How could I resist an invitation to participate in a Harvard Law School forum!13

Boulez programmed *Connotations* with the New York Philharmonic the weekend before Christmas, and I spent the week in the city, at rehearsals and performances. My friends asked me to reserve tickets—they

Manuscript, first page of *Night Thoughts, Homage to Ives,* composed in 1972.

© *Copyright 1972 by Aaron Copland. Boosey & Hawkes, Inc., Sole Publishers and Licensees.*

all seemed very interested in hearing Boulez' interpretation of *Connotations.* I had Christmas dinner with Minna and Mel Daniel as usual; this year, Chávez, Victor, and David Walker joined us. One evening, I went to visit Paul Jacobs, taking along my new piano piece, *Night Thoughts,* so I could hear how it sounded played by a really good pianist.

Invitations to conduct were plentiful; the ones that interested me most, after the major orchestras, were those that came from places I wanted to see, such as Scotland (August 1974), Hawaii (November), and El Salvador (1975). Nineteen seventy-four was Koussevitzky's centennial, and I joined in the celebration by conducting the BSO at Tanglewood in *Appalachian Spring* and Prokofiev's *Classical Symphony.* On Koussevitzky's birthday, I shared the program with Lenny (16 July), and while conducting *Quiet City,* I felt the presence of Koussevitzky. As I walked around the grounds, I wished he could have been there to see Tanglewood that day.

Until my seventy-fifth birthday, there had been ten years between major birthdays, but now the celebrations were almost continuous, beginning the spring and summer preceding it and continuing into the following year. To those who mentioned my next birthday in advance, I complained, *"Please* don't rush me!" Gunther Schuller, who had his fiftieth birthday in 1975, expressed my own feelings exactly when he wrote, "I'm about birthday'd out, how about you?" I was not fond of being reminded of my age, but I felt a lot better than I thought I would at seventy-five. I responded to questions from interviewers by saying, "If I had known in advance how well I would be treated, I would not have taken so long to get here!" Donal Henahan of *The New York Times* reported that I was "as old as the century, but in much better shape."

No one wants to be reminded about the passage of time, certainly not me, but when the Bicentennial festivities of 1976 promised to expand the number of performances of American music, we composers managed to bear with it. I detected more interest in American music abroad than there had been in the past. In addition to the Bicentennial, I attributed it to a renewed interest in Charles Ives, which had been sparked by the Ives centennial of October 1974. A Festival-Conference was held in honor of that occasion, with many concerts and presentations, among them a performance by David Barron and myself of the seven Ives songs I had helped introduce at Yaddo in 1932.[14]

Entries in my date books for 1974–1976 piled up beyond feasible listing. I toured Europe in the early fall (31 August–8 October 1975), going first to Copenhagen to conduct American works at the Tivoli, then on to Paris.

Copland's seventy-fifth birthday dinner in New York City: Bernstein, Schuman, and Copland.

In the former, it was Roy Harris' *Third Symphony* that was most admired; in the latter, Gershwin's *Piano Concerto* was preferred. As usual when in Paris, I stayed at the Pont Royal Hotel. Noel Lee gave a party for me and our French friends. Lenny Bernstein was also in Paris, making recordings. He and Harry Kraut were in a studio in the same building where I was rehearsing the Nouvelle Orchestra Philharmonique. When Harry came over to see me, he was shocked at how rude and inattentive the players were. Harry was so furious that he went to get Lenny, who raised hell with the manager of the orchestra.[15] It was not a pleasant experience, and I was relieved to get to London, where I was welcomed warmly by the LSO. I conducted a Proms concert (16 September), and the new director of Boosey & Hawkes, Tony Fell, gave a reception in my honor before I left for conducting dates in Norway.

I wrote to Chávez, "Watch out, here come the birthday fireworks at home!" In October, I played in my *Piano Quartet* with the Juilliard Quartet at the Coolidge Auditorium in Washington, and then went to Cleveland for a celebration called "Mr. Copland Comes to Town." On my birthday, I conducted the first New York concert performance of *Dance Panels* at the Juilliard, sharing the program with Dennis Russell Davies, who led the Juilliard Orchestra in *Statements* and the *Third Symphony*. Concurrently, an exhibit, "Copland and the Theater," was

384

Performance of *Lincoln Portrait*, Marian Anderson speaker, Copland conductor, c. 1975.

Walter Cronkite and Copland in *Lincoln Portrait*, Lincoln, Nebraska, 1977.

being shown in the Music Division of the Lincoln Center Library for the Performing Arts. Two days earlier, a celebration had taken place in Alice Tully Hall, followed by a supper in the Library for the benefit of the MacDowell Colony. At the concert, Bill Schuman, who was chairman of the Colony and of the Norlin Foundation, surprised and delighted everyone when he announced that annual fellowships for composers, marking the occasion of my seventy-fifth birthday, would be made through the Colony by the generosity of the Foundation.

I had the pleasure of conducting the American Symphony Orchestra and the Orpheon Chorale at Carnegie Hall (7 December) in an all-Copland program. During intermission, Daniel P. Moynihan, United States Representative to the United Nations, presented me with a scroll signed by members of the orchestra.

I have not even touched upon the soloists who were kind enough to do me honor, such as Leo Smit and Charles Fierro in all-Copland piano recitals.

The Schwann record catalogue published an all-Copland issue, with articles by Nadia, Clurman, Olga Koussevitzky, Bill Schuman, and Lenny Bernstein. Other writings ranged from the local Croton-on-Hudson weekly, to the powerful *Frankfurter Allgemeine Zeitung,* to a tribute from Tod Perry in the BSO Newsletter, sent on to me with personal messages from Seiji Ozawa, Dan Gustin, and others. Columbia Records released "Aaron Copland: a 75th Birthday Celebration," with the LSO and the New Philharmonia of London, myself conducting. Bill Moyers interviewed me at Aspen for National Public Radio. The BBC's Humphrey Burton put together a special television program and a documentary film was made by Terry Sanders for the USIA. I appreciated all the attention at the time, and now that I stay closer to home and have more time, I take great pleasure in looking at the television programs periodically. I particularly enjoy the conducting segments and the American landscape scenes in the Sanders film.

I accepted a commission for a major Bicentennial work. The plan had been worked out by Tod Perry and others: Composers were each assigned to one of six orchestras—the Philadelphia was to be mine, with a premiere at the Grand Opera House, Wilmington, Delaware, scheduled for May 1976. I heard from Ormandy in the summer of 1974: "I like to learn a work one year before it is to be performed"; later, he said, "Aaron, as an old friend,

I ask you to sit down and make an outline for this commission and give me an idea of its context, the approximate length as well as its orchestration and whether any soloists or chorus will be involved." I was sorry to disappoint Ormandy, but I was not able to come up with fresh ideas; rather than repeat myself, I decided not to compose the work. I was bogged down in terms of composing, but there was always the hope I would bog up again! In the meantime, I had enough conducting dates scheduled to keep me hopping.

The Bicentennial sparked many performances of *Lincoln Portrait,* some under my direction. Among the narrators in performances I conducted were Senator Ted Kennedy and Governor Michael Dukakis of Massachusetts and Senator Eugene McCarthy of Minnesota. While in Minneapolis with the Minnesota Orchestra over the Fourth of July 1976, I received the news that Victor Kraft died while vacationing in Maine a few days earlier. Victor had a history of heart ailment and had had a few serious attacks earlier. Still, it was hard to believe—Victor had been part of my life for so many years! David Diamond wrote to me after Victor died, "He was a beautiful young man. I could never understand what happened to Vic. Please remember Aaron—if there is anything at all I can do, let me know. Anything."

During the Bicentennial, interviewers were asking questions about the state of my career, as well as my views about the musical arts in general. I stated that I was not worried about what I saw in the world of contemporary music, except for so many composers going into academia. They took themselves so far from the larger public! I saw a danger of exclusivity, of composing only for the most knowledgeable audiences. But then, where were our composers to go—except perhaps abroad—in the relatively unreceptive cultural milieu of America in the seventies? I never felt I could criticize those composers with families to support who found academia the only recourse for a steady income.

To questions about my composing, I answered honestly that one tends to slow down in composition after fifty years of it. There seems to be so much more that has to be said at twenty! The creative impulse, the need, was no longer strong with me. That part of creativity is very mysterious. There are people who have every reason in the world to go on, but they just stop writing, while somebody else with no encouragement, no technique, no need—you can't stop him. Very strange. I was thinking of doing a study on the output of composers after the age of seventy. Of course, most earlier composers did not live long enough to have had to face that problem.

As I developed my conducting skills, I always remembered what an elderly Bostonian lady told me years earlier: "Aaron, it is important to engage in an activity when you get older that you didn't do when you were young, so you will not be in competition with yourself as a young man." Aside from that, there is a certain satisfaction in leaving a "document" for the future. For once, I wanted to stand up there and conduct my own music the way I originally thought it should go. It's not that I want to be imitated, and other conductors may reveal something about my music of which I might not have thought, but every composer thinks he knows how a piece he wrote should sound, even if it's not the same every time. (For example, you may change your tempi from one time to the next.)

Any composer, when he hears his work performed under someone else's direction, is curious about how it is going to be read, so to speak. People talk about interpretation as if there were only one correct or really inspired way of reading a piece of music, but if you are free enough in your mind, you can allow that there are more ways than one of producing the baby. An interpreter ought to see a composition from his own angle, must in fact see it that way, and in so doing, he may uncover an aspect of which the composer himself might not have been aware. Occasionally, I have learned about my own music from other conductors. On the other hand, there have been times when I have cringed listening to an interpretation foreign to what I had in mind when composing a work.[16]

If there are advantages for a composer in conducting, it seems to me the opposite also holds true: A conductor can benefit from knowing how to compose. It gives insight into the structure of a piece, the high and low points, and an intimate sense of the formal structure. It is mainly in the overall shaping that being a composer can help a conductor.

I had not suddenly become a conductor, nor did it come about without patience and effort. I don't remember very much about my earliest conducting, probably because it must have been *terrible!* Koussevitzky required all young composers at Tanglewood to do some conducting, like it or not. He was not flattering about mine and soon urged me not to take time away from composing. I recall a turning point in 1946 when conductor Eugene Goossens was taken ill and the manager of the Cincinnati

Symphony asked me to conduct *Appalachian Spring.* I was embarrassed to have to say that I didn't know the piece from the conductor's point of view. I decided then that I would become able to conduct my own works adequately. At about the same time, Stravinsky reinforced my resolve when he told me, "My dear, you *should* conduct your own music, every composer should." But I always felt hesitant to conduct while Koussevitzky was alive. Conducting was a suppressed passion.

I accumulated experience gradually, but it is hard to find an orchestra to practice on. I found a few in Mexico and Latin America in the forties. After conducting my first major orchestra, the Chicago Symphony, at Ravinia in 1956, I began to feel out of the amateur class. It was only when they invited me to return, however, that I knew my conducting had been satisfactory. David Diamond used to ask me whether Lenny was giving me pointers, but Lenny did not think much more of my conducting than Koussevitzky had. He wrote in 1960, "The notion that we're competing is positively quaint!" However, later that year, he wrote again:

> I watched and heard you conduct the BSO for ninety minutes on TV, and it was a joy. Man, you've improved incredibly! Clarity, meaningfulness of beat . . . only problem—die head too much in die score. You must to know die musik better (or at least trust yourself more) . . . want to succeed me at the Phil?

By my sixtieth birthday, I had conducted thirty orchestras in the previous five years; by 1963, the count was up to about one hundred. Of course, I had to go pretty far afield for some of them—Japan and Australia, for example. By June 1972, I had conducted 28 of a possible 30 major American orchestras, in addition to 9 "Metropolitan," 58 foreign, and 17 university groups: a total of 112.[17] Conducting fees improved as I improved. I could make as much as five thousand dollars plus expenses for two appearances with an orchestra. I once said to a friend after receiving a check for conducting the New York Philharmonic, "If only Papa could see me now!" When I was still teaching at Tanglewood in the sixties, I pulled up to the Main Gate one day in my Mercedes, and when Tod Perry saw me, he said, "Aaron, that doesn't look like a composer's car!" I answered jokingly, "Well, it's not! It's a conductor's car."

I admitted to having been bitten by the conducting bug, and once bitten, it gets into your blood and is the very devil to get rid of. I always felt that composing was the really serious business; conducting was for fun. But it has other advantages: It keeps one young, and it pays the bills.

Furthermore, conducting is good for the ego. Nobody can make a move until *you* move your arm!

Conducting was not *all* fun and prosperity. Orchestras in far-off places were not always up to playing some of the music I programmed. While on tour to Hungary and Turkey in 1973, I wrote to Verna Fine, "The orchestras in Turkey—oy! Less said, etc. But it's all plenty exotic. . . ." I wrote in my diary:

> The orchestra in Ankara, alas, is not much better than in Istanbul. Not much interested in their jobs, and only a mild sign of interest in the new music they were reading—Bernstein's *Candide* and *Billy.* I get a kick out of *Billy the Kid* in Turkish—*Billy Tohid.* . . . I talked to the orchestras in German at their request but really had little idea what was understood. I took a certain satisfaction at rehearsal in getting the orchestra to play better than they know how.

A composer has to contend with orchestra players who are potentially the conductor's severest critics. They put up with it when you conduct your own works. It seems like something "authentic"—*you* wrote it, so they assume *you* know best how it goes. But when you tackle works by other composers, watch out! It was my friend Lawrence Morton who first urged me to conduct music by composers other than myself. I developed a core repertoire: My European list included a piece or two by Haydn, Fauré, Roussel, Mahler, Tchaikovsky, Busoni, Mozart, Britten, and Hindemith; of American composers, I included Ives, Schuman, Harris, Diamond, Gershwin, Carter, Sessions, and Del Tredici. I planned three types of programs: all-Copland; all-American; American with standard repertoire.[18] I conducted all of my own works at one time or another, welcoming the opportunity to program those that were not chosen regularly by other conductors.

I was never tempted to accept a regular conducting position. I liked being able to choose from a wide range of offers. Also, I could have some leeway as to what I could conduct. To lead the great orchestras of the world and accompany top performers, such as Isaac Stern and Itzhak Perlman, was one kind of thrill. Another was conducting young performers. It was a challenge to build their confidence while at the same time get them to play better than they thought they could. I tended to look for a clean sound and to avoid the sentimental, overly romantic approach. I may have been influenced by Stravinsky, whose conducting seemed to me dry and precise, and I thought that Hindemith had been admirably businesslike when conducting.

Copland enjoying the informal atmosphere at Interlochen Music Camp, summer 1970.

When I went into universities, in addition to conducting, I would get together with young composers, listen to their music and have a powwow. So it was not just waving a stick. I had that experience, for example, when visiting Yale University in 1977 to receive the Sanford Medal from the School of Music. I was in residence for a few days, ostensibly working, but really enjoying the college atmosphere. I conducted *Appalachian Spring* with the Orchestra of New England in an informal concert in the Morse College dining hall and became an associate fellow of the college (24 January 1977). In the evening, I accompanied my friend Phyllis Curtin in the *Dickinson Songs* and had an opportunity to answer questions from the audience in Yale's recital hall. It was the kind of experience I enjoyed many times over. I found that youngsters in school orchestras could play complicated rhythms as though they had grown up with them—which they had! Seasoned professionals sometimes lost their enthusiasm for the music. I recall conducting Howard Shanet's Columbia University Orchestra (3 December 1973) and the obvious pleasure and enthusiasm the group took in playing *Billy the Kid* under my direction. There was a reception after the concert, and I don't think a single player missed coming up to talk to me.

Of all the orchestras I conducted outside the United States, I most enjoyed the London Symphony Orchestra. They, in turn, treated me with a high degree of respect. Though they are more formal than Americans, they are a great joy to work with, because they are such gentlemen. Part of my success in England is that I have a British publisher who spread the word about my works. The British seem to have special feeling for American music. After all, there is a kind of Anglo-Saxon connection there that a German or a French orchestra wouldn't have in quite the same way.

France was an unrequited love, since they paid little attention to my music in spite of my early connections there. The Italians were not much interested in American composers, either. In Germany and Holland, I felt that it was difficult to communicate our rhythms and our sense of discretion in the expression of emotion. The long impassive line, without crescendo or decrescendo, is difficult to achieve with a foreign orchestra. Audiences are different, too. Americans look for a more glamorous sound, more brilliant, one that is more precise in the jazz-band sense, with more bite. They want to be "wowed."

Another reason I had more success in England than in other countries is due to the fact that many of my recordings were made in London. In fact, the LSO, under my direction, recorded more of my music than any other orchestra anywhere, with the New York Philharmonic holding second place. For me, recording was more nervous-making than live performances. But the advantages to a composer are enormous! Every work of mine has been recorded, except for a complete version of *The Tender Land*. Some pieces have been recorded many times, frequently with my participation as conductor and/or pianist. (*Lincoln Portrait* is the piece that has been most recorded under my baton.)

Each year in London, I would review the tapes made the previous year as well as make fresh recordings. For example, in 1969 I listened to the *Ode* recorded in 1968. I would get so involved with the music, I had to constantly remind myself to pay attention to the sound of the recording! In one day, we recorded fresh the *Orchestral Variations, Rodeo, Letter From Home,* and *John Henry.* About the last, I wrote in my diary, "Was amused at the railroad sounds in the orchestration. I had quite forgotten what the piece sounded like." On another day, we recorded *Lincoln, Fanfare,* and *Down a Country Lane,* which I heard in its orchestral arrangement for the first time while conducting the recording in 1969.

I became aware of a phenomenon at concerts I was conducting, which was corroborated by concert managers, who would speak to me with considerable surprise of the number of high school and college-age youngsters who fill the top balcony seats and respond with unconcertlike enthusiasm to the music. I first noticed it when I was conducting the Houston Symphony, and I was mystified about it. But I hit upon a plausible reason for their presence: Many of these young people are record collectors. In that way, they become familiar with music at home through repeated hearings on their own turntables or cassettes. That is a very different relationship from hearing a new work played once at a concert. I have every reason to be particularly grateful to the creator of the phonograph. We composers owe a profound debt to Thomas Edison!

I had been promising to return to Australia, not having been there since 1961. Australian composer Vincent Plush had interviewed me during the Bicentennial and, at that time, he began making advance arrangements for my visit in 1978. I arrived in March and enjoyed spending some time with Plush and Peter Sculthorpe (both had promoted first performances of some of my works in Australia). I conducted in Sydney and found the new Sydney Opera House on the harbor impressive—the sailboats went right by one's dressing room windows! In Sydney and in Melbourne, I sensed a very warm reception from the audiences.[19]

Whenever I am asked about high points in my conducting career, I mention the National Symphony's concert at the Kennedy Center, which elicited a review by Paul Hume that was reprinted in the *Congressional Record* (5 April 1975). The McDonald's restaurant sponsorship at first struck me as rather odd, but the concert really took off, and I wanted to take that particular audience home in my pocket!

Of them all, it would be difficult to top the experience of Decoration Day [Memorial Day] with the National Symphony in Washington, D.C. (28 May 1979). It was in the open air on the grounds of the Capitol, with admission free to the public. I chose works that were serious but approachable: Ives' *Decoration Day* was an obvious choice; Gershwin's *An American in Paris* supplied the infectious bounce of our popular music; and Samuel Barber's *Overture to the School for Scandal* provided the lively opening. Of my own, I chose *Fanfare for the Common Man*, the *Clarinet Concerto*, and *Lincoln Portrait*, with myself narrating (guest conductor Gerhardt Zimmerman). The usual preconcert suspense was heightened by the rain that threatened to cancel the concert; but luck was with us. By 6 P.M. the heavens began to clear and by 7, the public began to arrive. People seemed to be streaming in from every possible direction. *The Washington Post* the next morning estimated the audience at twenty-two thousand. Imagine standing up to conduct in front of such an audience! As night descended, the lit-up dome of the Capitol spread a soft light on the thousands of music enthusiasts gathered on the lawn below. I could not recall ever before having conducted a concert for so numerous and enthusiastic an audience. The orchestra responded by playing three encores: Sousa marches, of course, and we ended the evening with a bang-up rendition of "Hoe-Down" from *Rodeo*. It was truly a night to be remembered.

I must confess, in all honesty, that I have had more than my share of honors awarded me over the years. I am referring primarily to honorary doctorates from universities. My records show that from 1956 to 1979 I accepted degrees from thirty-two American universities.[20] Also, in 1975 and 1976, I received the American Music Center's Letter of Distinction, the Brandeis Creative Arts Award, the Chancellor's Medal from Syracuse University, the Governor's Medal of the State of New York, and the National Arts Club Award. In 1978, the mayor of New York City, Edward Koch, decided to invite composers to Gracie Mansion after I told him I had never been there. He said, "But you were born in Brooklyn and are one of our great composers. I am *shocked*!" Mayor Koch invited me to be guest of honor at a reception (22 May 1978) at which my music was performed, and a plan to give commissions to young composers was announced by John Duffy, head of Meet the Composer.

I was also guest of honor for a 1979 "State Dinner" given by the Lotos Club of New York City, with Bill Schuman master of ceremonies. I received the Award for Distinguished Achievement in Music from the Third Street Music School Settlement. The gala lunch took place on my seventy-ninth birthday at the grand ballroom of the Plaza Hotel, with Bill Schuman as keynote speaker. I am amazed Bill never seemed to tire of introducing me! The program included the most unusual of the hundreds of performances I have heard of *Appalachian Spring*. It was played by very young students from the Settlement School on various percussion instruments.

A signal honor was to be chosen as the first composer in the field of concert music to receive a Kennedy Center Honor in 1979. These awards were inaugurated the previous year "to give appropriate recognition to individuals who throughout their lifetime have made significant contributions to American culture through the performing arts." It was a special pleasure to receive a Kennedy Center Honor along with Martha Graham,

The Kennedy Center Honors

A National Celebration of the Performing Arts

Aaron Copland

Ella Fitzgerald

Henry Fonda

Martha Graham

Tennessee Williams

At the White House reception during the Kennedy Center Honors, 1979. (Left to right): Copland, Tennessee Williams, First Lady Rosalynn Carter, Ella Fitzgerald, and Henry Fonda.

Courtesy of the White House.

Henry Fonda, Ella Fitzgerald, and Tennessee Williams. The weekend, full of exciting events, included a gala reception in honor of the awardees, which was hosted by Mrs. Carter at the White House.

I stayed at the Watergate Hotel with a few friends who had gone to Washington with me.[21] On the day of the festivities, we were escorted by a female Marine lieutenant who was assigned to drive me in a large black limousine. We soon left all the traffic and drove right up to the front portico of the White House. The spacious rooms and corridors of the executive mansion were packed with people. "Everybody" was there, with the exception of President Carter; he was absent due to the strain of the

397

Iran hostage crisis. The fact that the President was upstairs grappling with an international situation was a dramatic contrast to the festivities.

The White House reception was followed by an evening's entertainment at the Kennedy Center (2 December). The entire program opened with *Fanfare for the Common Man.* Each awardee had a section of the program devoted to a celebration of his or her own artistic production. Bill Schuman wrote a tribute to me in the impressive program book, and Lenny Bernstein hosted "my" segment of the program in typical Lenny fashion. I heard him say things about me that I hope are true—"Copland is a mentor I trust completely as my master, idol, sage, guide, shrink, counselor . . . and beloved friend." Then Lenny conducted "Hoe-Down" from *Rodeo* and Bill Warfield sang "The Dodger" and "The Boatman's Dance" from *Old American Songs I.*

I had the pleasure of being seated in a box between Rosalynn Carter and Ella Fitzgerald. I shall not soon forget the extraordinary contrast between the quiet charm of the President's wife and the unalloyed joy of Ella listening to the singing of songs from her repertoire. We all wore our impressive medals, not designed to be pinned on but to hang around one's neck on a multicolored ribbon. A gala dinner and dance to music by Count Basie and his orchestra followed. I wrote the above description of the Kennedy Center Honors in my journal when I returned home, with a note at the top of the page—"For autobiog."

I had proceeded no further on my autobiography than a few scribbled ideas and part of a beginning chapter about my youth in Brooklyn. When in 1975 Vivian Perlis invited me to participate in the oral history project in American music that she directs at Yale University, I thought it a good idea on its own terms (preservation of material in a composer's own voice) and also as a stimulus toward getting my ideas together.[22] Contrary to music composition, which is best done in solitude, this kind of project benefits from the stimulus of another person asking questions and assisting in organizing one's thoughts. Vivian and I worked together every few weeks through 1976. A year or so later, I was amazed to see the transcripts of the interviews, which in size resembled nothing less than two very large Manhattan telephone books. And the process was absolutely painless! In 1978, we agreed to put our heads together to prepare a coauthored autobiography, using the oral history transcripts and adding to them from my files of correspondence, notebooks, and music manuscripts.

Interlude VII

The winding, heavily wooded driveway is marked with a discreet sign: ROCK HILL. Copland's house is revealed slowly, perched on a ledge looking out toward the Hudson in the distance. The low, long building of natural wood with dark green trim seems almost part of the landscape. There is nothing conspicuous or grand about it, except perhaps the grounds and plantings. Rock Hill is a comfortable place, with a kind of unstudied natural elegance, not unlike Copland himself. Since 1974, I have visited there regularly, first to interview Copland for the Yale oral history project, later to work on his autobiography.[1] During the interviewing, I would drive the distance every few weeks, reviewing in my mind what I planned to cover in each session. I never feared what kind of reception I would receive (except from Sophronus' enormous great dane, Dido). Copland was always the same—the wide grin, a gesture of mock surprise—"What? You came all this way just to see *me*?" He was always gracious and welcoming, never rushed or begrudging of his time.

Interviews were written into the current appointment book and were taken as seriously as other professional commitments. Copland's informal and genial manner can be misleading: He is not an easy person to interview. Never polite for politeness' sake, or chatty to keep things going, he does not embellish what he has to say. If a question is too general or not phrased to his liking, he points it out, tactfully but firmly: "Aren't you taking a rather broad view?" or "Are you asking me or telling me?" If Copland's memory should fail, he might say jokingly, "Do you realize that was almost fifty years ago!" or "Fill me in on that, will you?" It was not long before the similarity between the man and his music became evident: outspoken and straightforward, quick and intelligent, introspective, witty, dependable.

Copland's papers, consisting of correspondence, programs, reviews, lectures, journals, photographs, and some music manuscripts are at Rock Hill,

Copland at Rock Hill, Peekskill, New York.

to be moved to the Library of Congress gradually (most of the manuscripts are already there). The extensive collection, organized through the years by David Walker, proved useful during the interviewing and invaluable for the autobiography. As a composer known for not speaking freely about his music, Copland could be stimulated to comment about various aspects of composition by looking at manuscripts or by reading through a sketch or score at the piano. If asked about a particular piece in a more formal way, his answer was likely to be, "I prefer to leave analysis to those who really know how to do it."

Work sessions were punctuated by cheerful lunches, the most memorable on the terrace overlooking the Hudson when weather allowed. Three, perhaps four or five, would be seated: Copland, David Walker, and myself, or whoever else happened to be there—Sophronus with his delicious food (until he left in 1983 and Victor Basso arrived), or other of Copland's staff: Michael O'Connor, Chris Cole, or later on, Petey Neyland or Ron Caltabiano, or my assistant Janice Fournier. In the seventies, Clurman and Edwin Denby both came to try to recuperate from the illnesses that would claim them. On weekends, Verna Fine, David Del Tredici, or Phillip Ramey might take the train and be picked up at the Croton station. Other friends still visit regularly: David Diamond, Helen and Elliott Carter, Minna Daniel, or Leo Smit and Paul Moor when in New York from out of town. Conversation is always lively. While Copland was still conducting, he would tell about his latest trip, and visitors would relate the latest music news and gossip. Lunch over, his cheerful but inevitable *"au travail"* would send everyone back to work.

When I was a newcomer to Copland's home, Victor Kraft's stormy appearances were puzzling. Who was this odd person who could shatter the peaceful atmosphere by bursting noisily into a conversation or interview in Copland's studio? He was a burly, heavily bearded, barrel-chested man, often carrying a camera; he either talked constantly and noisily or sat morosely and silently before stomping out of the room. Friends explained that Victor had been Copland's intimate friend for many years. Copland had always tried to help Victor and had bailed him out of difficulty more times than he liked to remember. After Victor died, Copland was sad, but he was never gloomy or brooding for long; he has described himself as being "optimistic by nature."

In the long afternoons working through Copland's papers (the files are unpretentiously stored in the basement next to the laundry machines), I occasionally heard him at the piano: one day practicing *Vitebsk* for an upcoming concert in Santa Fe (31 July 1982); another time, the *Dickinson Songs* for a performance with Jan DeGaetani (1978): While playing, Copland sang "Going to Heaven!" with great gusto, laughing out loud at himself as he went along. Occasionally, young performers came to visit, seeking advice or approval for a new instrumentation or arrangement. At such times, David and I would join as audience in the studio, as we did when the Alexander String Quartet arrived to play the movement of an early quartet I had unearthed at the Library of Congress. "Did *I* write *that?*" Copland queried with a chuckle. Then he listened intently and offered suggestions. (*Movement for a String Quartet* was premiered by the Alexander String Quartet and subsequently published.)[2] Copland always enjoyed hearing young people make music. He would say jokingly, "especially *my* music." Youngsters from the Aaron Copland Music and Arts Program in Westchester County have come to see and perform for him every summer, as recently as 1988.

After Copland's oral history interviews were finished, we worked together on a ninetieth birthday tribute to Nadia Boulanger for *The New York Times,*[3] and then progressed naturally to the coauthored autobiography. We chose a literary agent and publisher,[4] and I began to accompany Copland to rehearsals and concerts in order to collect firsthand information. Of these many special occasions in the late seventies and eighties, it is possible to describe only a few.

One involved Copland and Bernstein. After a video interview session with both composers in Washington for the Kennedy Center Honors archive, we all rode together by taxi to the Lincoln Memorial (February 1979). As we drove by the White House, Copland napped and Bernstein talked emotionally about his friendship with the Kennedys and their lost dreams for the arts in America. At the Lincoln Memorial, Copland showed evidence of his patient and even temperament, waiting in the bitter cold, Lenny's white duffle coat over his shoulders, while cameras and lights were set up to film them together in that historic place, the statue and the spirit of Lincoln hovering over all.

Another special occasion was when Copland received an honorary doctorate from Brown University (June 1980). The ritual was extraordinary: the commencement ceremony (which occupied most of a day) parties and dinners, an all-Copland vocal concert conducted by him, an onstage "class" about American music by Copland and me, and finally, a festive dance held outdoors on the campus. Copland was delighted when a vivacious student approached and invited him to dance. They moved at a brisk pace across the dance floor, and he had a wonderful time while other students watched with a mix of pleasure and surprise. During a lively fox-trot, Copland explained to me that he had enjoyed dancing ever since his sister Laurine had taught him when he was a boy in Brooklyn.

Above: Copland receiving Doctor of Music honorary degree from Brown University, 1980.

Below: Copland dancing with a happy student at Brown's commencement party.

Copland rehearsed the Brown Chorus, which included the captain of the football team, for a performance of *In The Beginning* (described by Copland on pages 75–76). Among other things, he told them, "Be tough and not sentimental." After I wrote about that rehearsal in an article for *Keynote* magazine (November 1980), a letter arrived from Robert Reichley, vice-president of Brown University:

> One footnote to the piece. The football captain/chorus member and I were talking about his summer of singing in bars in San Francisco and working out with the Stanford football team to stay in shape for the Brown season. He mentioned that of all the football games he has played in and even the great trip to China with the Brown Chorus, one of his greatest moments at Brown will be the last measure of *In The Beginning*, Aaron Copland conducting.

A memorable occasion in 1980 was the joint celebration of Tanglewood's fortieth anniversary and Copland's eightieth birthday on the Fourth of July weekend. Seiji Ozawa, music director of the BSO, said, "Copland really *made* this place. It is really *his.*" Reviewers of the Saturday evening concert, conducted by Copland (6 July), commented on the fact that the program contained only his accessible music,[5] but as John Rockwell wrote, "The distinction of the evening lay in its symbolic function. What was notable about the program was its reflective cast, its persistently autumnal, lyrical flavor."[6] Copland was concerned about the rainy weather, "and the poor dears out on the lawn." Although the conditions kept attendance down to 8,479, those outside seemed content to huddle under umbrellas. The next day, the kickoff party for Copland's birthday was made official. It took place at Koussevitzky's former home, Seranak. Copland, Bernstein, and Ozawa stood in front of the full-length portrait of Koussevitzky as a large birthday cake arrived. Lenny played "Happy Birthday" and some lively measures from *Rodeo.*

Copland, having given interviews through so many years, was used to dealing with tape recorders and in more recent years, videocameras. Interviews for television productions frequently took place at Copland's home; for example, those made in December 1979 for the documentary "Aaron Copland: A Self Portrait," broadcast by PBS for Copland's eighty-fifth birthday.[7] At such times, the house would be in disarray for days to accommodate wiring and lighting, but Copland took it all in stride. Like a professional actor, he could repeat his favorite stories until the take was just right, yet each telling seemed fresh and spontaneous.

During interviews for television at Copland's home, Mike Wallace and Copland.

Copland enjoyed having a group of close friends and colleagues on hand to help celebrate special occasions. He could depend on Minna Daniel, his oldest friend, to attend those programs she found interesting. Verna Fine was always in a front-row seat. Sylvia Goldstein, Doris and Stuart Pope, Ellis Freedman, Felice Marlin, Roger and Sue Levey (his great-nephew and his wife), David Del Tredici, Phillip Ramey, and Bennett Lerner were often present at concerts, as were Victor Basso, Irene Wiley, and others who helped in various ways at Rock Hill. David Walker, who has worked for Copland longest and knows him best, frequently accompanied him to public festivities and is always with him for the quieter private celebrations.

David Walker[8]

I think possibly the reason that Aaron and I had such a long and workable relationship is that we tended naturally to, so to speak, stay out of each other's way. By that, I mean that we shared whatever work was to be done without any intrusions of a personal nature. We seemed to understand each other without the need of long explanations or any setting down of rules.

Photograph by Terry Flynn

David Walker
and Copland
on the terrace,
with Dido.

(What say you to
this new gimmick
— presented on
arrival!

Aaron Copland
Brown Palace Hotel
Denver, Colorado 80202

Dear David:
This is a birthday
letter — wishing you many more — and
much joy.
But it's also a 20th anniversary
I'm celebrating. It must have been
September '52 that we joined
forces — no? Anyway, I feel like a
very lucky fellow indeed to have had
your help and companionship all these
years. Here's wishing both of us many
more.
With much affection
Aaron

Letter from
Copland to
David Walker,
1972.

I understood instinctively the times he needed privacy and his wish not to discuss any compositional works that were in progress. Sometimes he would play sections of a new piece, asking me to sit in and listen; but usually what I heard when he was at the piano in the evenings was a phrase here, a chord there, realizing silently that these were the makings of a Copland piece that eventually the world would hear and become familiar with.

Aaron was an almost constant worker. There was always a project or two underway—if not composing, he was studying scores, planning programs, working on a lecture, an article, a book, and travel plans. Even on trips to far-off countries, when the musicmaking was over, Aaron was ready to come back home.

There were fun times and serious times, but I never once found him to be "difficult." He knew what he wanted and could make that quite clear. Yet he always had time to listen to others, and in so many, many instances over the years he advised and assisted friends and strangers alike—with a mere phone call, a letter or two, or a series of meetings.

The houses in Ossining and Peekskill were, first of all, places where Aaron lived as privately as possible and worked in as much comfort as possible—which to Aaron meant a good piano, a large desk, ample space, and quiet. The atmosphere was a mixture of an easygoing day-to-day routine interspersed with frequent visits of a business or personal nature. There were times of entertainment with a few guests—drinks and meals, walks in the woods, and, of course, music talk and listening.

Although I work with Aaron on a business basis, we are good friends in the best sense of that word. An ongoing thirty-five years does make a long and fascinating relationship, and I'm happy now to say it was one that worked. On social occasions, instead of being introduced as his assistant, I was "a composer friend." How grateful I will always be for the many dimensions and meanings of this friendship.

The music world and the media were hard put not to repeat themselves as, year after year, one special Copland event followed another, and each tribute seemed more honorific than the last. It would be misleading to focus on these occasions as the fabric of Copland's life. He accepted each degree with pleasure, invitations to the White House with almost boyish wonder (he continued to present his Social Security card, even when he was an honored guest), every black-tie dinner hosted by Bill Schuman or Lenny Bernstein, every celebrity interview (such as the 1978 "Dick Cavett

Show"). They were all special. Copland has a kind of naïve sense of wonder about such things. But life was not held together by major birthdays or the awarding of honors. In fact, Copland usually paid less attention to them than others did. He was always respectful and grateful, but he did not take them so very seriously.

As medals and satin hoods from honorary degrees accumulated, and scrolls and awards were received, Copland would comment on each with appreciation (sometimes amusement). The item would then be displayed for a respectable time before being put away in a drawer or closet with a multitude of similar artifacts. A few presidential medals and photographs have permanent places in Copland's living room and studio, and the famous Oscar always stands on a mirrored shelf in the hallway. For Copland, the real events were the musical ones, when he could face an expectant group of musicians ready to play when he lifted the baton.

Always willing to try a new experience, Copland agreed when pianist and friend the late Paul Jacobs said, "Let's appear at the rock club, the Bottom Line." The owners of the club showed a willingness to experiment by presenting some non-rock acts occasionally. Jacobs and Copland were invited to do a program about the influence of jazz on classical music in the twentieth century (15 December 1979). Jacobs played, and then he and Copland chatted onstage, ending with a performance of *Danzón Cubano* together. Copland confessed to being a little nervous about playing piano in public after a hiatus of several years, but he said, "Paul's an old friend and he talked me into it."

Copland's eightieth birthday began with an official announcement from Washington: "The Congress of the United States joins in honoring this extraordinary American on this occasion with the reading of the following into the *Congressional Record:* 'Aaron Copland, this country's greatest living composer, is the classic American success story: a man from modest beginnings who has reached the top of his profession solely by his own efforts.' " The entry, which continued for several pages, concluded:

> Aaron Copland, always at the frontier of American music, has become its most distinguished elder statesman. He has won every honor in the book, including thirty-three honorary doctorates, the Pulitzer Prize, the Presidential Medal of Freedom and the Kennedy Center Honor. We salute this fine American for his music and for his tireless efforts on behalf of all of American music.

When Copland received notification and a copy of the *Congressional Record* entry, he asked Lawrence Morton, "Has anyone told Roy Cohn?"

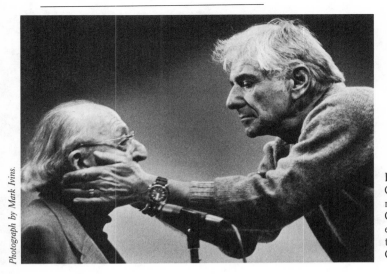

Bernstein and
Copland at
rehearsal for the
Carnegie Hall's
eightieth birthday
tribute to
Copland.

Considering Copland's close relationship with the National Symphony
Orchestra and his friendship with its director, Mstislav Rostropovich, it
is not surprising that the major eightieth birthday celebration was planned
by Rostropovich and took place in Washington.[9] Several spectacular times
were yet to come (such as the eighty-fifth birthday gala in New York), but
Washington 1980 was the last big event in which Copland took an active
role. He has always preferred being involved in the musicmaking to being
a spectator, or as he put it, "merely gracing the occasion." Since it is not
possible to include in detail all of the special events of Copland's eightieth
birthday, or those that followed,[10] perhaps a full account of the Washington festival will convey the quality of excitement and exuberance that
characterized a Copland celebration.

A group of friends and family joined Copland at his favorite Washington hotel, the Watergate. The kickoff event, a National Press Club Symposium, took place between rehearsals for the concert. Leo Smit, who took
part in the symposium, asked Copland whether he had a secret formula
that made him never lose his temper or use harsh words (Smit explained
that one of Copland's most unusual characteristics was an extraordinary
equanimity in face of difficult situations). Copland looked out at the
audience with a serious expression, hesitated for a moment, and said,
"Sounds dull." The audience broke up with laughter, he grinned, and the
symposium continued in the relaxed mood everyone had hoped for.

Behind-the-scenes rehearsals at the Kennedy Center Opera House offered glimpses of private moments as memorable as the glamorous public

Backstage at the Kennedy Center. (Left to right): Sol Linowitz, Rosalynn Carter, President Jimmy Carter, Copland.

ones. When Leo Smit and Copland were rehearsing the *Piano Concerto*, Bernstein came onstage and stood behind Leo, making suggestions. Asked about this afterward, Leo said, "It was fine. It had the feeling of a reunion for the three of us." And there was something touching about the solitary look of Copland as he sat quietly onstage listening to the plaintive trumpet player during the rehearsal of *Quiet City*.

President and Mrs. Carter had not planned to attend the gala evening concert; the presidential box was reserved for Copland's guests. At the last moment, the Carters decided to go after all (Bernstein had something to do with the change). Guests were greeted by President and Mrs. Carter and their guest, Sol Linowitz (a central figure in the Middle East peace negotiations), in the receiving room attached to the presidential box. After conversation and refreshments, the Secret Service seated everyone before the President and First Lady entered. The Carters had not been seen in public since the landslide election of Ronald Reagan eight days earlier. When the audience saw the presidential party, they rose and cheered for several long moments.

The program began with Bernstein leading Copland onstage as the orchestra played *Fanfare for the Common Man,* and it was Bernstein who read a letter to the composer from the President: "Wherever music is played and loved—at home and abroad, among your fellow composers, among musicians and among ordinary listeners—you are justly recognized as America's foremost composer. We are proud to join in this fanfare for

410

Copland and Rostropovich
at the party following the
eightieth birthday concert.

Letter from Rostropovich
to Copland the day after
the birthday concert.

a most uncommon man." Then Rostropovich conducted the audience in "Happy Birthday, dear Aaron!" and enrolled Copland as honorary member of the National Symphony, presenting him with a book of greetings from musicians across the land.[11] Copland took the conductor's stand and led *Appalachian Spring,* which was followed by Rostropovich conducting *El Salón México.* At intermission, more presentations were made.[12] When Copland responded, it was with characteristic simplicity: "I've had some very good evenings in my life, but this is something special—a birthday festival for me. I'm very touched and moved, and I feel like a very lucky fellow."

After intermission, the program continued with Rostropovich conducting *Quiet City,* Copland and Leo Smit performing the *Piano Concerto,* and finally *Lincoln Portrait.* Copland stood tall and erect and his voice was firm as he read the text. *Lincoln Portrait* has been narrated by hundreds of speakers, professional and amateur, political and theatrical, and before presidents and kings, in high school auditoriums, in English and in Spanish, and even once by Rosalynn Carter. Lincoln's words have carried different meanings for each new generation and with every hearing; under the circumstances of 14 November 1980, as spoken by Aaron Copland on his eightieth birthday from the stage of the Kennedy Center, facing the Presidential party, Lincoln's words took on special meaning. "Fellow citizens, we cannot escape history. We hold the power and bear the responsibility. . . ."

Following the concert, Copland's dressing room was filled with people, telegrams, red roses, and colorful balloons, all of which went along to a lavish dinner dance hosted by the orchestra. Copland, a late-night person, was reported to have been at the bar drinking coffee with Slava [Rostropovich] after 2 A.M.

Copland left for New York the following day for a gala Boosey & Hawkes reception at the St. Regis Hotel. New York birthday concerts preceded and followed Washington: Each was extraordinary in its own right.[13] One was "Wall-to-Wall Copland," a ten-hour Copland program (20 November), planned and executed by Allan Miller, artistic director of Symphony Space, with my participation. The program featured many of Copland's friends and colleagues and a great deal of his music, and it had the relaxed atmosphere and quality performances typical of Symphony Space's "Wall-to-Wall" celebrations. Copland's lawyer, Ellis Freedman, commented during the eightieth birthday festivities, "I bet you'll be glad when this is over!" And Copland answered, "Young man, you underestimate my capacity for adulation."

Copland had not been to Europe since 1975. When his agent, Basil Douglas, asked whether he would visit in 1978, Copland responded, "I have no reason to be going to Europe in 1978 or 1979. I'm pleased to say that I've been happily busy with American symphonies in various parts of the country." An invitation followed from the LSO for 1980. Copland accepted and LSO manager Peter Hemmings wrote, "We are delighted to renew our association with you." Copland heard from his old friend John Kenworthy-Browne: "I know what a splendid thing it is to know and to have known you. We met just twenty-two years ago! I hope to see a little of you, as well as coming to your concert. That, too, will be an emotional event."

Copland left for London, Brussels, and Paris (28 November–22 December)[14] accompanied by a young lawyer, William (Bill) Conroy, who spoke French and could assist Copland with arrangements and schedules.

William Conroy[15]

The LSO could not have been more delighted to have Aaron there. At the first rehearsal, the first thing they did was play "Happy Birthday" to Aaron. It was very touching because it was unexpected. It was not a banal gesture; their warmth was clear throughout rehearsals and performances. [16] *Aaron had a terrifically arduous schedule. He just loved it. At the end of the day when everyone else was tuckered, he seemed chipper. One of the musicians commented, "He's not tired at all—only the rest of us!" I think it was the reception in London that did it.*

There was an astounding difference between London and Brussels. The Brussels Philharmonique was only a few years old, but that was no excuse for their impolite and downright rude behavior. Aaron could always take the other side. He said, "Well, how would you feel if you had to play the same things over and over again for years?" Much of the difficulty revolved around the fact that the Short Symphony *had been scheduled for performance, and at rehearsal, it was clear that there was not time for the orchestra to prepare it, particularly since the concert was to be broadcast nationwide on radio and television.* [17] *A compromise was reached—the* Short Symphony *was included in the concert but not the broadcast. One highlight for Aaron in*

Copland
traveling in
Europe, 1981.

*Brussels was seeing his former cook and gardener, Mireille and Gaston,
again. They could not go to the concert but saw the broadcast, and Mireille
said when she saw Aaron at the podium, "Monsieur Copland is in his
element." They came to see us off, and Aaron was absolutely delighted.*

*We arrived in Paris and settled into the Hotel Concorde Lafayette. After
the Brussels experience, I decided not to go to the rehearsals. The concert
was held at the Palais des Congrès (18 December), and it included* Pelléas
et Mélisande *by Fauré, which Aaron had requested to be in memoriam for
Nadia Boulanger. The printed program asked that there be no applause after
it. The silence was touching.*

*Aaron and I went to see some of his old haunts in Paris, including the
Boulevard Raspail, where he had lived with Harold Clurman in the twenties. Aaron said he wished Harold could be there. We went by metro and
had a distance to walk, and Aaron complained that his sore foot (a minor
chronic complaint) was bothering him. After I said, "ne kvetchez pas,"
Aaron laughed and repeated that many times. I was again amazed at his
stamina and energy as he went sightseeing, gave interviews, and went to
rehearsals. Other than his brief remark about Harold Clurman, the only sign
of nostalgia was that Aaron repeatedly asked, "Whatever happened to the
red taxis?"*

As birthday tributes spilled over into 1981,[18] Copland's energy and health remained strong, and for a while after the European trip, travel and conducting continued. In 1981, he conducted the New York Philharmonic and other groups in Las Vegas, Wolf Trap, and Dallas. Copland conducted *Appalachian Spring* for the spring gala of the Graham Company (16 June 1982), explaining, "I never could refuse Martha!"[19] He delighted musicians and audiences as composer-in-residence at the Santa Fe Chamber Music Festival in the summer of 1982. However, conducting was beginning to be a strain, and Copland was limiting the invitations he accepted. As with composing, he made no dramatic decision to stop conducting. It was simply the natural time to do so. Copland's last concert was with the New Haven Symphony Orchestra (7 December 1982), conducting *Outdoor Overture* and the piece that had introduced him to American audiences in 1924, *Symphony for Organ and Orchestra* (organist William Owen).

In 1983 and 1984, Copland attended some of the concerts in his honor,[20] but most of his time was spent at home working on the first volume of his autobiography. He was pleased that his friends and colleagues were contributing interviews and exclaimed, "I can't wait to read what they have to say about me!" While working with Copland, I experienced what others have frequently described: His total confidence that you can do the job makes you do more than what at first seemed possible. Copland would always listen to my ideas with an open mind. He was puzzled when I said his family background and genealogy should be in the book: "Will people be interested? It's not about music!" He also agreed, but without enthusiasm, that his socialist connections in the thirties and the McCarthy hearing in the fifties must be included, but he never wanted to deal with unpleasant situations at great length. He would say, "Agonizing is not my thing!"

Copland read all of the book material carefully and made comments, corrections, and additions. When we drew on writings and speeches from earlier times, as we often had to, it was necessary for me to add missing lines or connective links. Our procedure was for him to read these sections out loud. He never failed to stop at what he had not written and ask, "Did I say that?" I would answer, "No, but how would you say it?" Then Copland would supply in his own words what had been missing.

Copland: 1900 Through 1942 was published in the late summer of 1984. A special book party was given by Minna Daniel. It took place at a country inn at Lake Waramaug, Connecticut, where Minna stayed

Photograph by Suzanne Faulkner Stevens. Courtesy Lincoln Center Archives.

Copland greeting the audience with conductor Zubin Mehta and members of the New York Philharmonic from the stage of Avery Fisher Hall, New York City, 14 November 1985.

summers. The day was sparkling clear, the setting like an old-fashioned lawn party, and Minna saw to it that the guest list was as brilliant as the rest of the event. There were two surprises: a cake that exactly duplicated the cover of the book, and the first copies of the book itself, off the press just in time for the party. When our editor, Richard Marek, first showed us the book, Copland asked, "But when will it actually be in Brentanos?" An official press party for *Copland* was given by St. Martin's Press in New York at the Library at Lincoln Center, attended by the music and publishing world (18 October 1984). The many favorable reviews that followed book publication gave both authors the impetus to work toward completion of the second volume.

Copland could not attend many of the birthday salutes during his eighty-fifth birthday year, but Lenny Bernstein planned a very special one at Tanglewood and convinced his old friend to be there. Copland arrived by limousine at Seranak, where he was greeted by friends and introduced by Bernstein to the composition and conducting students. An all-Copland

416

concert by the Music Center Orchestra included the *Third Symphony*, conducted masterfully by Bernstein (20 July 1985). Performers have described the concert as one of the memorable experiences of a lifetime. When Copland entered the Shed, the entire audience rose and cheered. The reception was extraordinary.

The New York Philharmonic planned to celebrate Copland's eighty-fifth year in the way composers like best: sixteen Copland works performed at twenty-six concerts in the 1985–1986 season by Bernstein, Mehta, James Conlon, Charles Dutoit, and Raymond Leppard. The Philharmonic's plans included the major birthday gala, which Copland attended as guest of honor on his birthday.[21] The event was televised from Avery Fisher Hall and seen by millions on "Live from Lincoln Center." It was announced that a Copland scholarship fund was established by Boosey & Hawkes and ASCAP "to be presented annually to an outstanding composer attending an American high school for the arts."

Among the many tributes of 1985[22] was one that particularly interested Copland: the revival of his opera *The Second Hurricane*, which had a substantial run at the Henry Street Settlement House, where it had first been produced in 1937. Copland attended a matinee performance and was delighted with the new production.[23]

Since Copland was no longer traveling by air, he asked whether I would represent him in Washington on two very impressive occasions in 1986. To receive Copland's awards for him was an honor, but most enjoyable was taking them back to him, along with a full description of the events and greetings from his friends and admirers. The Medal of the Arts was conferred by President Reagan to nine artists and three patrons at a White House luncheon (14 July 1986).[24] It was special—from the dinner for recipients the evening before, to the front entry of the White House and the Marine escorts, to the luncheon itself, with the President and Mrs. Reagan presiding at the two tables reserved for those receiving the honor. A festive State Department reception was held later in the day.

The House of Representatives voted Copland a Congressional Gold Medal, the highest honor that can be awarded a civilian. First given to George Washington, Copland's was the 120th Gold Medal to be approved by Congress. The ceremony (11 November), which preceded Copland's eighty-sixth birthday, was on the stage at the Kennedy Center during a concert conducted by Copland's friend Rostropovich. He conducted *Fanfare for the Common Man* to announce the presentation, made by Representative Vic Fazio. Morton Gould spoke for ASCAP, and I accepted the

A Public Law Bestowing

The Congressional Gold Medal

awarded to

Aaron Copland

accepted on his behalf by

Vivian Perlis

presented by

The Hon. Vic Fazio
Morton Gould

and

Marvin Hamlisch

The Congressional Gold Medal is being awarded to Aaron Copland in recognition
of his special achievement in creating a uniquely American style of composition,
making a vital contribution to American artistic life.

Aaron Copland's

"Fanfare for the Common Man"

National Symphony Orchestra
Mstislav Rostropovich, *Music Director*
Concert Hall
The John F. Kennedy Center for the Performing Arts

November 11, 1986

Courtesy U.S. Mint, Department of the Treasury.

framed bill, signed by members of the House, granting the Gold Medal to Copland.[25] A single gold medal was designed and struck by the Treasury in 1989, with bronze medals to be minted and made available to the public.

Copland's life at Rock Hill continued in its familiar pattern: friends visiting and pleasant lunches the focal point of the day. Copland still wanted to hear talk about music. He would ask, "Who are the new composers?" "What are they writing?" When told about the minimalists, he said, "Well, by definition they can't do much harm!" Copland's composer friends reported about the "new romanticism" (the term introduced by Jacob Druckman in 1983 to denote the return of a more accessible compositional style), and Copland was bemused to think that tonality could be making news.

Copland's career has run parallel to the century. He has seen musical styles come and go. It was no surprise to him that music in the eighties returned to a style that would reach larger audiences. He had seen a similar shift in the thirties, when composers strove for a more accessible kind of music after the exclusiveness of the avant garde in the twenties. Copland had always been affected by the world around him. His music was influenced by current aesthetics, yet the core remained undeniably Copland. By the eighties, he could afford to be philosophical about another swing in musical style, and it interested him to know that young composers were producing a more expressive music, frequently with extramusical connotations, a kind of music that had been scorned for decades.

Copland enjoyed hearing about performances and recordings of his own music. When compact discs arrived, he exclaimed with typical enthusiasm, "What will they think of next!" He was delighted to know that the summer of 1989, as Tanglewood celebrated its fiftieth anniversary, was being dedicated to him with many performances of and lectures about his music.[26] At the conclusion of the festival, Leonard Bernstein saluted his friend by conducting *Music for the Theatre* and the *Music for Movies* at a most appropriate occasion—Tanglewood's annual Serge and Olga Koussevitsky Memorial Concert.

Copland has been part of the world of music for over seventy years, most of the time in the public eye. Those who have become acquainted with him only recently might be reminded that within the familiar genial, avuncular figure is a fighter for American music, a strong leader, one who has done more for composers and for American music than any other one person in this century. By now, it is rare to find anyone connected to twentieth-century music who has not had a Copland experience. William Schuman wrote in the Kennedy Center Honors program book, "This erudite man of music with the hearty laugh is asked everywhere, and he accepts. He is a peripatetic conductor of America's symphonies large and small, not to mention those abroad, and he is a familiar figure on college campuses. Everywhere he goes, the visit ends with the same question, 'When can you return?' "

Each of the many places Copland visited treasures its own set of Copland memories and anecdotes, ready to be told as though unique. It was a Copland talent to face each occasion with anticipation, fresh spirit, and genuine pleasure. He has shared himself with so many musicians and listeners that he has become part of the American consciousness. The media helped to make familiar the tall, lanky figure with the spectacles and quick grin, but the enduring affection of the public for Copland has more to do with the vast accumulation of his sharing of himself, the continuous sound of his music in the collective ear, and the successful transference of his own pleasure in making music. The American people are fond of Aaron Copland, and when he says, "I'm a lucky guy to have lived my life in music," they believe it and like him all the more.

Reflections on a
Life in Music

It has been my good fortune to spend my life with the art of music.* As I see it, being a composer is a great privilege. I find a profound satisfaction in the fact that the works I composed in my own home have found a response in the outside world. To compose an extended composition, and to evoke those sounds from an orchestra of a hundred men playing many different instruments, can certainly be considered one of the grander experiences of mankind.

An artist can take his personal sadness or his fear or his anger or his joy and crystallize it, giving it a life of its own. Thus he is released from his emotion as others cannot be. The arts offer the opportunity to do something that cannot be done anywhere else. It is the only place one can express in public the feelings ordinarily regarded as private. It is the place where a man or woman can be completely honest, where we can say whatever is in our hearts or minds, where we never need to hide from ourselves or from others.

Early in life, I set myself certain standards. I studied works of the great masters and found common denominators; one is the ability of the truly great work of art not to look tired. To keep my ideas fresh, I was able to lend myself to different occasions and to different kinds of musical materials that suggested themselves to me. I consider myself fortunate; some composers are stuck with the style they adopt in the first place and go on writing in that style. But I had the feeling that I was living in a continuing state of self-discovery. I wished others could share in that adventure. I always wanted to take the average man in the street by the arm and say,

*These reflections are drawn from various Copland sources: an unpublished typescript for a lecture, "The Composer's Experience," presented during the late fifties and sixties at eleven universities; an article, "The Pleasures of Music," first published in *The Saturday Evening Post,* reprinted in *The Adventures of the Mind* (New York: Alfred A. Knopf, 1959); an unpublished lecture written for NBC's "Comment" program, Edwin Newman host; and interviews with Bill Moyers and Vivian Perlis.

"Look, here is a wonderful living art," and let him know that without it, he's missing something worthwhile.

Some people are more ear-minded than others. We must seem mesmerized to our less musically inclined friends! All of us, however, can understand and feel the joy of being carried forward by the flow of music. It is one of the great beauties of the world, and those people who react to music and enjoy it are privileged people.

Part of the pleasure of involving oneself with the arts is the excitement of venturing out among its contemporary manifestations. But a strange thing happens in this connection in the field of music. The same people who find it quite natural that modern books, plays, or paintings are likely to be controversial seem to want to escape being challenged and troubled when they turn to music. Composers don't write music to console their audiences as though they were composing lullabies. They write music to stir people up, to make them think about the varieties of human experience depicted in their work. But audiences crave that which is familiar. Moreover, the American public suffers from what might be called a masterpiece complex. You would think that nothing but the best music was good enough! They are willing to concern themselves only with music that is perfect, but not music in the process of becoming so.

No composer worthy of the name has ever written anything merely to be as great as or better than some other composer. He writes in order to say something of his own—to put down some expression of his own private personality. If he succeeds, the results should be listened to by his countrymen, even though they may not be as great or better than the music of the immortals. At any rate, it is the only way we shall ever have a music of our own.

One hears a great deal of pessimism expressed not only about the arts today but about the world in which we live. I think that in music we are not doing so badly. I do not subscribe to the notion that the symphony orchestra will soon disappear or that opera is dead. True, orchestras are having a difficult time with escalated production costs, and recent American operas have not fared well. However, in composition, I see a trend toward something that has been missing in music for a long time. It worried me that one did not meet up with the kind of composer we used to think of as being "musical." Years ago, if you said of someone, "He or she is terribly musical," that was the highest compliment you could pay. More recently, to stress "musicality" would seem to be pinning a bad name on a composer or making him or her look not so interesting. I am pleased to see that in young composers today "musicality" seems to be making a comeback.

Artists have also become skeptical about *inspiration*. Perhaps the word has become meaningless through being used loosely. But the composer *has* to believe in inspiration. It means being well disposed for the thing you're doing—it is the time when the theme comes clearly, when the path opens up, when the process almost does itself.

I have often been asked, "Why become a composer?" It is a question to which there is really no answer—composers have no choice. It is a peculiar thing to be born a composer. It doesn't happen to everyone, and it comes as rather a surprise to those to whom it does happen. The rewards are likely to be small from a practical point of view. No money in the bank. No good reviews in the papers the next day. You really have to be strong. By that I mean in the sense that you must be sure that what you are doing is absolutely what you mean to do. You can't worry about whether audiences will love you right away—that has never been the story with new music.

Composing is a lonely occupation, and perhaps there is some advantage in the fact that many composers must add other more sociable activities to their schedules in order to make a living. I was able to devote myself almost exclusively to composition during most of my career, although there were some difficult years before I became financially secure. The fact is that the creative artist is a kind of gambler, since there are no guarantees of success. Yet, every true artist has a sense of the importance of his or her own contribution, if only because the artist knows in his deepest innards that only the individual can conceive what he or she alone can create. Look at Charles Ives—the courage he had to compose without hearing his music played! But he knew within himself what he was. I think it is for this reason that I have given so much time and energy to advancing the interests of my fellow composers by doing what I could to help get their music performed.

Some people have a sense of where they are in the world more than others. They absorb it better, feel it more. Something is inside them that makes them want to reflect the sense of the life that they live. And that, I think, is essential for those who create works of art. The world badly needs its artists, if only because the artist's life affirms the individual and the importance of the individual. Such artists symbolize the free man, the man who must decide for himself what is right, who must be free to make his own mistakes.

425

Music is a world of the emotions, feelings, reactions. It can be very strong, it can be very heroic. It can reflect deep religious feeling. But it cannot write out programs for the future. The language of music exists to say something—not something that can be translated into words necessarily, but something that constitutes essential emotions that are seized and shaped into meaningful forms. I wouldn't want to translate it into so many words because that would be limiting it. The feelings are like feelings *are*—emotional, and sometimes sort of vague. It shouldn't always be possible to put them into words. If it was, you wouldn't need poems or paintings or all the media where people express themselves.

I think that my music, even when it sounds tragic, is a confirmation of life, of the importance of life. If there is a unifying core in it all, it is a sense of affirmation. I would also like to think that my music enlarges the listener's sphere of reference, just as when I listen to a great work by Bach or Palestrina, I have a *larger* sense of what it means to be alive than if I didn't hear that work. That is one of the great things about art, of course, that it does enlarge the sense of who you are and what life is all about.

Perhaps the answer to why a man such as myself composes is that art summarizes the most basic feelings about being alive. Just as we look to eighteenth-century works to try to experience that time, our arts mirror the whole atmosphere of the present. By reflecting the time in which one lives, the creative artist gives substance and meaning to life as we live it. Life seems so transitory! It is very attractive to set down some sort of permanent statement about the way we feel, so that when it's all gone, people will be able to go to our art works to see what it was like to be alive in *our* time and place—twentieth-century America.

Aaron Copland

Notes

The notes were prepared by Vivian Perlis.
The manuscripts and papers referred to as being in Copland's files will be permanently housed in the Music Division, Library of Congress.

INTRODUCTION
MUSIC IN WARTIME AMERICA

1. See Louis Worth, *Community Life in a Democracy*, ed. Florence C. Bingham (Chicago: National Congress of Parents and Teachers, 1942).

2. Warren I. Susman, "Culture and Commitment," in *Culture as History* (New York: Pantheon Books, 1984), p. 201.

3. Susman, *Culture as History*, p. 209.

4. See interviews, Henry and John Steinway, Steinway Project, Oral History, American Music, Yale University.

5. Edmund Wilson, *The Forties* (New York: Farrar Straus Giroux, 1983), p. 43.

6. For a prototypical study of the émigré composer, see the Hindemith Project, Oral History, American Music, Yale University.

7. The program for "An Aaron Copland Evening" (17 February 1943) included *Divertimento for String Orchestra* (Mozart), *Music for the Theatre*, *Piano Sonata* (first U.S. performance), *Music for Movies* (premiere). Performers were the Saidenberg Little Symphony, Daniel Saidenberg conductor; Copland pianist.

8. Other composers represented were Henry Cowell, Douglas Moore, Nicolai Berezowsky, Norman Dello Joio, Howard Hanson, Roy Harris, Bernard Herrmann, Werner Josten, Darius Milhaud, Walter Piston, Quincy Porter, Bernard Rogers, and Roger Sessions. See Claire R. Reis, *Composers Conductors and Critics* (New York: Oxford University Press, 1955; Detroit Reprints in Music, 1974), pp. 163–66.

9. Otto Friedrich, *The City of Nets* (New York: Harper & Row, 1986), pp. 46–47.

10. Pauline Kael in Studs Terkel, *The Good War* (New York: Pantheon Books, 1984), p.123.

11. See Clayton R. Koppes and Gregory D. Black, *Hollywood Goes to War* (New York: The Free Press, 1987).

12. Mel Powell, interview with Vincent Plush, Oral History, American Music, Yale University, 13 May 1983, Van Nuys, California.

13. See Steve Metcalf, "Previn, the maestro, looks back at Hollywood roots," in *The Berkshire Eagle*, Sunday, 19 June 1988, E 6.

14. See Copland's files for his lecture notes on film music.

15. See Copland's files and the Library of Congress for the correspondence between Copland and Harold Spivacke and G. Howland Shaw, Assistant Secretary of the Department of State.

16. See Copland's files for lecture notes.

Notes

1. Copland derived his Russian tunes from *Russische Volkslieder* (Leipzig: J.H. Zimmermann [19—?]. From Copland's conducting score in his files: "Going to School" was from Zimmermann, no. 2, arranged by Copland for two accordians; "Song of the Fatherland" was composed by I. Dunayevsky, transcribed by Copland, lyrics adapted by I. Gershwin; "Younger Generation" and "Collective Loading Time Song" were adapted from traditional Russian melodies; "Death of Little Boy" and "Scorched Earth" were composed by Copland.

2. "Younger Generation," "Song of the Guerrillas," and "No Village Like Mine" were published individually as sheet music for voice and piano by Chappell & Co., Inc. (no longer available) and in piano-vocal and choral SATB, arranged by Frederick Fay Swift, by Boosey & Hawkes.

3. A score copy with autograph corrections is at the Music Division, The New York Public Library at Lincoln Center, donated by Elliott Carter.

4. Interview, Robert Lewis with William Owen for Perlis, 12 May 1981, Irvington, New York. For excerpts from this interview, see *Copland: 1900 Through 1942* (New York: St. Martin's/Marek, 1984) p. 220.

5. The unpublished Bernstein score is in Copland's files.

6. Hans Heinsheimer, representing the newly formed Boosey & Hawkes Artists' Bureau, wrote to Copland (26 May 1943) to arrange a contract between Copland and the New York Philharmonic for the world premiere of a Copland piano concerto to be played by the composer on 10 February 1944, with a provision for cancellation. A letter requesting the cancellation (unsigned carbon, 12 October 1943) from Boosey & Hawkes to Bruno Zirato of the Philharmonic is in Copland's files.

7. At the Library of Congress: pencil copy of the first two movements; first pencil sketch; ink score (36 pages); ink score for "Lento" movement and ink violin part.

8. Copland's description of the *Violin Sonata* is derived from his early program notes.

9. Copland's lectures in 1943–1944 included Mt. Holyoke College (2 December 1943) and the University of Chicago (April 1944).

10. Lesser known American composers performed by Koussevitzky included Mabel Daniels, Arcady Dubensky, Henry Eichheim, Blair Fairchild, and Alexander Steinert. For a complete list, see Aaron Copland, "Serge Koussevitzky and the American Composer," *Musical Quarterly*, XXX:3 (July 1944), pp. 261–64. At the testimonial dinner Randall Thompson's "Alleluia" and Schuman's "Holiday Song" were performed by the Collegiate Chorale under Robert Shaw. Howard Hanson and Copland made tributes; Koussevitzky responded.

11. The autograph score of the original version was in the Paul Whiteman Collection at Williams College. It was loaned out and not returned; a search is in progress. A recording of the radio broadcast is in the Whiteman Collection. The original instrumentation of *Letter From Home* (with Copland's suggestions for alternatives) was: flute, oboe, 1st alto saxophone (bass clarinet, 2nd clarinet), 2nd saxophone (1st clarinet), 1st tenor saxophone (clarinet, flute, bassoon), baritone saxophone (clarinet, bass clarinet, flute, oboe, English horn), 1 horn, 3 trumpets, 3 trombones, tuba, guitar, piano, harp, percussion, strings. Pencil sketches and a piano reduction with instructions for instrumentation are in Copland's files.

12. For the performances conducted by Szell, Copland suggested an augmented version of his alternate instrumentation. Szell used 3 flutes, piccolo, 2 oboes, English horn, 2 clarinets, bass clarinet, 2 bassoons, 2 contrabassoons, 4 horns, 3 trumpets, 3 trombones, 1 tuba, timpani, percussion, harp, and strings.

13. The instrumentation of the 1962 revised version of *Letter From Home* is 2 flutes, 2 oboes, 2 clarinets, bass clarinet, 2 bassoons, 2 horns, 2 trumpets, 2 trombones, timpani, percussion, harp or piano (score marked "ad lib"), and strings. A recent performance was at Copland's eighty-fifth birthday concert at Avery Fisher Hall, the New York Philharmonic, Zubin Mehta conductor (14 November 1985). *Letter From Home* is also published in an arrangement for school orchestra (with piano conductor).

14. For *Dithyrambic*, see *Copland: 1900 Through 1942*, p. 183.

15. After Copland turned down the script, *Daughter of Colchis,* Graham sent it to Carlos Chávez, who composed a score Graham considered incompatible with the script. (Chávez eventually composed music for a Graham ballet with a different script, *Dark Meadow.*)

16. For a thorough description of the commissioning of the ballet, see Wayne Shirley, "Ballet for Martha, the Commissioning of *Appalachian Spring,*" *Performing Arts Annual 1987* (Library of Congress), pp. 102–23.

17. See Erick Hawkins to Elizabeth Sprague Coolidge (16 June 1942), Hawkins and Coolidge Collections, Library of Congress.

18. All quotations from Copland to Mrs. Coolidge and Harold Spivacke are from the Coolidge Collection, Library of Congress.

19. Two Graham scripts are in Copland's files: the rejected *Daughter of Colchis* and *House of Victory* (later *Appalachian Spring*). The script Copland presented to Mrs. Coolidge is in the Coolidge Collection, Library of Congress. It is untitled and bears the inscription "Name?".

20. The book of Shaker songs was compiled by Edward Deming Andrews. Elder Joseph Brackett, Jr., composed "Simple Gifts" in 1848 for dancing during Shaker worship. See Edward Deming Andrews, *The Gift to Be Simple: Songs, Dances and Rituals of the American Shakers* (New York: J.J. Augustin, 1940; New York: Dover Publications, 1962).

21. In the script Graham sent to Copland (and in Mrs. Coolidge's script at the Library), she described a segment of the leading dancer's role, then called "The Daughter": "She begins to dance in some simple way something like a song, any kind of song."

22. See Roger L. Hall, *The Story of "Simple Gifts"* (Holland, Michigan: The World of Shaker, 1987).

23. The *Daughter of Colchis* script finally settled with Samuel Barber. It became one of Graham's most successful ballets, *Cave of the Heart.*

24. The recordings are at the Recorded Sound Reference Center, Library of Congress. (A tape duplicate available to the public is missing the ending.)

25. The early scripts approximated a dramatization of "The Dance," a poem by Hart Crane. For further explanation, see Perlis, Interlude I, p. 53

26. Martha Graham sent the material quoted here, 22 November 1988.

27. Interview, Erick Hawkins with Perlis, 19 December 1985, New York City.

28. Martha Graham's fee for the choreography was covered by a Guggenheim Fellowship. Costs for the costumes were $425 and for curtains, $150. See Hawkins correspondence, Library of Congress.

29. For the third ballet, Graham used Milhaud's *Jeux de Printemps*. Reports from the dancers confirm that *Imagined Wing* was put together at the last minute and was not successful.

30. See interview, Isamu Noguchi with Tobi Tobias, Dance Collection, The New York Public Library at Lincoln Center, January–February 1979. Noguchi had previously designed sets for Graham in a similar style for *American Frontier.*

31. The recording of the second Washington performance is at the Recorded Sound Reference Center, Library of Congress.

32. Cunningham sent this description to Perlis, 9 April 1989.

33. Interview, Pearl Lang with Perlis, 19 December 1985, New York City.

34. See discussion of Copland's seventy-fifth birthday celebrations, pp. 385–86.

35. Interview, May O'Donnell with Perlis, 23 January 1986, New York City.

36. In New York, *Appalachian Spring* was programmed with *Salem Shore,* music by Paul Nordhoff, and *Death and Entrances,* music by Hunter Johnson.

37. Virgil Thomson, "Two Ballets," New York *Herald Tribune,* 20 May 1945, reprinted in *The Art of Judging Music* (New York: Alfred A. Knopf, 1948)pp. 161–64.

38. For correspondence about the Monteux recording, see Copland's files.

39. The first performance of the thirteen-instrument version was at the Leo S. Bing Theater (14 November 1970); first European performance was at Queen Elizabeth Hall, London, with the English Chamber Orchestra, Lawrence Forster conducting (13 October 1971).

40. The 1974 Columbia Records' release of *Appalachian Spring Suite,* original thirteen-instrument version, conducted by Copland, includes a rehearsal recording. A tape of this docu-

ment, an excellent demonstration of Copland's conducting language and style, is at the Recorded Sound Reference Center, Library of Congress. For another example of Copland rehearsing

41. Copland's comments here are taken from the 1974 rehearsal recording, see note 39.

INTERLUDE I

1. The leading roles were danced by Yuriko Kimura, Bride; Tim Wengerd, Husbandman; Janet Eilber, Pioneering Woman; Larry White, Preacher. Stanley Sussman conducted.

2. The other two Followers, Marjorie Mazur and Nina Fonoroff, also have had long and successful careers; Jean Rosenthal became a leading theatrical lighting designer, and Edythe Gilfond, a highly acclaimed costume designer.

3. For more about the "affirm America" movement, the Group Theatre, and other American influences, see Interlude III, *Copland: 1900 Through 1942,* pp. 217–30.

4. Interview, Isamu Noguchi.

5. Hart Crane, *The Collected Poems of Hart Crane* (New York: Liveright, 1933). See pp. 19–23 for "The Dance," a part of the long poem *The Bridge.* The stanza ending with "O Appalachian Spring" appears on p. 20.

6. See Coolidge Collection, Library of Congress, for manuscripts: bound ink score with dedication "To Elizabeth Sprague Coolidge" (Copland wrote simply "Ballet" on the first of 84 pages); first rough sketches and 84 miscellaneous pages showing various instrumentations, cues from Graham's scenario, such as "Fear of the Night" and "Day of Wrath," and dates "5 Ju 43, 20 Ju 43" (p. 47 shows the theme and 5 variations with the title "Shaker Melody: 'It's the gift to be simple' "). See also ink score for piano (copies in Copland's files and at Boosey & Hawkes). The piano score differs considerably from the instrumental versions, particularly in the variations section.

7. See Marta Robertson, "Aaron Copland's *Appalachian Spring:* Music and Dance Interactions," presentation at the Sonneck Society Annual Meeting (14 April 1988).

8. The program opened with *Fanfare for the Common Man,* conducted by Copland, followed by a Martha Graham talk and dances; *Diversion of Angels,* music by Norman Dello Joio; *Letter to the World,* music by Hunter Johnson; and *Appalachian Spring.*

9. Anecdote recounted to Perlis by David Walker, who was at the rehearsal. Also in the cast were Yuriko Kimura, Bride; Ross Parkes, Husbandman, and Janet Eilber, Pioneering Woman.

10. Stanley Sussman met Copland during the summer of 1959 when he was a student in Leon Kirchner's composition class at Tanglewood. In addition to an active conducting career (principally for the dance), Sussman has continued to compose.

11. Scores include: (1) original ballet for thirteen instruments; (2) augmented instrumentation used by the Graham Company; (3) full orchestra ballet score; (4) *Appalachian Spring Suite* for full orchestra; (5) *Suite* for thirteen instruments; (6) expanded *Suite* for thirteen instruments; (7) *Variations on Shaker Melody* for youth orchestra, band, and in an arrangement for one piano, four-hands by Bennett Lerner.

12. An example is the ten measures at the start of the Bride's solo that do not appear in other scores. The Graham Company uses the original thirteen-instrument score and parts with augmented strings (woodwinds and piano remain as were). According to Sussman, the orchestra is usually about thirty in number.

13. Nureyev spoke briefly to Perlis following the rehearsal.

14. See Anna Kisselgoff, "Dance View," *The New York Times,* 18 October 1987, C 26, 40.

15. David Walker and Vivian Perlis attended the dress rehearsal; Perlis and composer Ron Caltabiano (Copland's assistant from 1985 to 1989) were present for the performance.

ACROSS THE AMERICAS/1945–1949

1. Copy of the ink score of Goossens' *Jubilee Variations* was located by Sylvia Goldstein of Boosey & Hawkes in 1986 among Goossens' papers in London, which are privately owned. The 1987 recording by Telarc of Copland's variation by the Cincinnati Pops Orchestra with Kunzel conducting includes *Lincoln Portrait,* narration by Katharine Hepburn.

2. Rough sketches for *The Cummington Story* score in Copland's files include dates: "Begun June 12; composition finished June 28/ orchestration–1945 June 19/ Recorded July 24." The original score consists of fourteen sections.

3. The credits read: "United Films/ The American Scene; A Series # 14/ *The Cummington Story*/ Music Composed by Aaron Copland." No other credits are cited. The script was written by Howard Smith Southgate, produced by Frank Beckwith, and directed by Helen Grayson. Larry Madison was director of photography. See Richard Dyer MacCann, *The People's Films* (New York: Hastings House, 1973), pp. 143–44, and Richard Meran Barsam, *Nonfiction Film* (New York: E.P. Dutton, 1973), p. 217. Barsam writes: "Viewing these films, a foreign audience would get these impressions: America is a country of small towns, quiet churchgoing citizens, and lazy leisure-time activities. . . . *The Cummington Story* (1945), a beautiful and moving evocation of the American Dream captures all that is best in a small New England town, and, by implication, the country." Barsam's Appendix (p. 301) lists the film as twenty minutes in length and gives the producer, editor, and narrator as Sidney Meyers for the USIS. Prints at the Museum of Modern Art, New York, and at Library of Congress.

4. For *In Evening Air*, see Interlude IV, p. 59.

5. See interview, Harold Shapero with Perlis, 9 October 1980, Natick, Massachusetts: "I loved the first and second themes, but I didn't like one theme and told him that he ought to take it out: 'That's awful. All this other stuff's so pure and that heavy thing comes in.' Aaron sort of smiled. What amazed me was when the *Symphony* got completed, that theme, which I still don't like in the first movement, comes in in a minimal form in the third movement, and it's very interesting. I didn't like it or think it was necessary at the time, but it *was* necessary. Aaron knew it and left it there. I don't remember his ever changing anything for anybody."

6. See also interview, Paul Moor with Perlis, 1 June 1980, Peekskill, New York.

7. The orchestral score is in the Koussevitzky Foundation Collection, Library of Congress, with the dedication: "To the memory of my dear friend/ Natalie Koussevitzky/ *Third Symphony*/ Composed by Aaron Copland/ Commissioned by the Koussevitzky Music Foundation." On the last page (255) Copland inscribed the date of completion: "Sept 19, 1946."

8. Copland's analysis of the *Third Symphony* here is derived from his program notes for the first performance.

9. At the Library of Congress: miscellaneous rough sketches not in order; a rough pencil sketch with many datings and other markings; a separate folder marked "Movt IV" with detailed indications for "last movt plan"; pages of corrections; piano ink-sketch copy; bound ink-orchestral-score copy with large markings in blue crayon (perhaps Koussevitzky's conducting score).

10. Copland discounts what seems to be quotation of the cowboy tune, "So long, Old Paint."

11. "Copland's Third," *Time* magazine (28 October 1946), p. 55.

12. Virgil Thomson, "Copland as Great Man," New York *Herald Tribune*, 24 November 1946, p. 6.

13. Arthur Berger, "The *Third Symphony* of Aaron Copland," *Tempo* no. 9 (Autumn 1948), pp. 20–27.

14. Arthur Berger, *Aaron Copland* (New York: Oxford University Press, 1953; reprinted Westport, Connecticut: Greenwood Press, 1980).

15. For a summation of Copland's *Third Symphony,* including the cut in the final movement, see William Malloch, "Copland's Triumph," *Opus* (February 1988), pp. 22–25.

16. For Bernstein on the *Third Symphony,* see interview, Bernstein with Perlis, *Copland: 1900 Through 1942,* p. 341.

17. The pages showing the cut for the final version are in Copland's files.

18. Helen Carter also described to Perlis the visit to rent the tuxedo and the dance-hall experience (August 1988).

19. Copland made recordings of the *Third Symphony* with the London Symphony Orchestra and the Philharmonia Orchestra.

20. Bernstein conducted the New York Philharmonic in a weekend of subscription concerts

for Copland's seventy-fifth birthday, with Roy Harris' *Third Symphony* and David Diamond's *Violin Concerto No. 3* (premiere); for the eightieth and eighty-fifth birthdays, Bernstein conducted Copland's *Third Symphony* with the Tanglewood Music Center orchestra; also for the eighty-fifth, the New York Philharmonic, with the Harris and Schuman *Third* symphonies.

21. As is Bernstein's preference, the 1985 concerts were recorded live and the Copland *Third Symphony* was released with *Quiet City* in a digital recording by Deutsche Grammophon.

22. See Copland's files for ink score with corrections in red pencil dated "April 5, 1947." See also Library of Congress for pencil manuscript with directions for mezzo-soprano: "in a story-telling manner," "freely and naïve (in a gentle and narrative manner) like reading of a familiar oft-told story," and ink manuscript marked "Chap I:1–II:7" dated "April 1, 1947."

23. Participants in the symposium included E. M. Forster, Roger Sessions, Archibald T. Davison, Alfred Frankenstein, Olga Samaroff, Virgil Thomson, Otto Kinkeldey, Olin Downes, and Paul Henry Lang.

24. The Graham Company performed *Dark Meadow*, music by Chávez, and *Night Journey*, music by Schuman.

25. During a visit in 1983, Copland's friend Paul Moor played and sang "Alone at Night" from memory; in 1984, he transcribed the song and sent it to Copland. No other manuscript exists.

26. Materials relating to *Tragic Ground* are in Copland's files. Copland drew on some of them later when preparing his arrangements of *Old American Songs* and when composing his opera *The Tender Land*.

27. See Abe Meyer correspondence in Copland's files about *Earth and High Heaven*.

28. See interview, Robert Fizdale with William Owen for Perlis, 15 February 1982, New York City.

29. For a description of this performance of *Lincoln Portrait*, see *Copland: 1900 Through 1942*, p. 346.

30. See travel diary #3 for 1947 Latin American tour. Also pertaining to the tour, in Copland's files are scripts, lecture notes, drafts and final typescripts, bills and receipts for expenses, fan mail, invitations, calling cards, and programs. See also Donald Fuller, "A Symphonist Goes to Folk Sources," *Musical America*, LXVIII:3 (February 1948), pp. 29, 256.

31. Copland, "Composer's Report on Music in South America," *The New York Times*, 21 December 1947, X 9.

32. The diary formed the basis of the 1948 lecture course "Music of Latin America." See also *Tanglewood Newsletter* (1948).

33. See interview, Hans Heinsheimer with Perlis, 21 May 1981, New York City.

34. See Copland's files for Boosey & Hawkes correspondence.

35. Richard Franko Goldman became executive director; various committee chairmen completed the board. An office was secured at Steinway Hall and concert manager David Rubin and assistant Claire Rosenstein were drawn into the organization. A concert to honor Edwin Franko Goldman took place as planned.

36. Copland's income in 1947 was $17,473—up slightly from 1946.

37. Composer and political activist Hanns Eisler (brother of communist Gerhart Eisler) was active in the Composers' Collective in the thirties. See *Copland: 1900 Through 1942*, pp. 218, 224, 227.

38. Bernard Herrmann conducted the LSO in the first performance in England, a BBC broadcast in 1956. For materials relating to *The Red Pony*, see Library of Congress: film "open score," pencil with cues written in, such as "He let him die" and "dissolve to stable," measures numbered in red pencil, dated "Jan 29–March 26, 1948"; ink score for *Suite from the Red Pony* ("Childrens' " crossed out on title page). For onionskin masters of conductor's score and parts, see Brigham Young University, Republic Pictures Collection.

39. Andor Foldes wrote to Copland asking permission to make a piano arrangement from *The Red Pony*, but it was never realized. A band suite was arranged by Copland from the last four movements of the orchestral version. The first performance was by the U.S. Navy Band,

Anthony A. Mitchell conducting at the Midwest Band Clinic, Chicago (December 1968).

40. For a television presentation, narrations were arranged by Katherine Rosen (18 March 1973).

41. Ink transparencies are at the Library of Congress. A cover page indicates in pencil a tentative title—"In the American Grain/Pieces for Piano." Pencil sketches include *Three Blues*. One page contains the title *Five Sentimental Melodies* (1926), and sketch pages for "III" are dated in two places: "22 Jan 47" and "4 Jan 48."

42. *Blues No. 1* (1947) is dedicated to Leo Smit; *Blues No. 2* (1934), to Andor Foldes; *Blues No. 3* (1948), to William Kapell; *Blues No. 4* (1926), to John Kirkpatrick.

43. The first version of the "coda" cadenza is at the Library of Congress, with a memo by Copland: "too difficult for Benny Goodman." Faint pencil jottings can be seen toward a second version, which became the published version. See also pencil sketch score of 57 pages showing first movement (almost complete) and second with changes and deletions, dated "Dec 1945/Feb 1946." Also see a rough pencil sketch score dated "Feb 20 46/Aug" with the first-movement title "Pas de deux." This score is paginated 58–87, with some pages blank and others of solo clarinet writing.

44. Interview, Benny Goodman with Perlis (telephone), 24 March 1984.

45. See interview, Harold Shapero with Perlis: "It was terrific. He played his head off. I remember telling Benny when he got to the interlude, 'You're supposed to swing it. It's written for you, you know.' So he said, 'Yeah? You think so?' Benny was very resistant to criticism of any kind. He did loosen it up. When we got done with the performance, he said, 'Okay, kid, now tell me how to play jazz.'"

46. The class session was taped, see miscellaneous tapes, Oral History, American Music, Yale University.

47. Interview, Jerome Robbins with Perlis, 10 August 1981, New York City.

48. The principal dancers were Jerome Robbins, Diana Adams, Nicholas Magallanes, Jiliana and Roy Tobias, Melissa Hayden, Herbert Bliss, and Tanaquil LeClerq.

49. See Copland's files for pencil draft of Copland's letter to Wyler.

50. Martini (1741–1816) was the pen name for Johann Schwartzendorf. "Plaisirs d'Amour" was composed by Martini and Jean Florian.

51. See Copland's files for photocopies of two-piano score with markings toward the orchestration by Copland, orchestrator Nathan Van Cleave. It includes the following sections: "Prelude"; "Cherry Red Dress"; "Virginia Reel," featuring "Galop de Bravura by Jules Schulhoff"; "Mazurka No. 1," incorporating "Gaetana" and "First Love Mazurka" by E. Ketterer, arranged by Van Cleave and George Parrish; "Polka No. 1," using "Coquette Polka" by Charles D'Albert; "Gavotte" by F. Joseph Gossec, arranged by Copland; "Waltz No. 2," using "Queen of the Flowers" by Ketterer; "Fortune Hunting," based on the folk song "Ching-a-Ring Chaw," arranged by Copland; "Dream Gavotte," composed by Gossec, arranged by Copland; "Early Morning Visitor"; "Morris Suggests Love," using "Plaisirs d'Amour," arranged by Copland. Additional cues: "Proposal," "Catherine's Engagement," "The Appointment," "The Departure," "Paris," "Reunion with Morris—Parts I and II," "A Plan to Elope—Parts I and II," "Anticipation," "Love Not Consoled," "A Defeated Catherine," "new Intro: To Love," "Doctor's Examination," "A Sick Doctor," "Intro: A Sick Doctor," "A New Catherine," "Washington Square," "Five Years Later," "Morris Returns," "Morris Unmasked," "Catherine's Triumph," "The Bolted Door," "Cast," "Three Irish Reels (Fiddlin Silas, Miss McCloud's Reel, The Pioneer)," "My Love Loves Me," adapted from "Plaisirs d'Amour." See Library of Congress for bound scrapbook engraved with gold lettering: "Presented to LC by Paramount Pictures Corp., Hollywood, Ca.," dated 30 November 1948; also: Wyler's revision dated 20 January 1949; timings; script.

52. Copland wrote his own mazurka, waltz, and polka. The polka was played by hand organ.

53. See Copland's files, "curiosity" folder, for correspondence from Joseph C. Keeley, editor, *The American Legion Magazine*, questioning why Copland, rather than Martini, was credited with the music in *The Heiress*. See also responses by Mort Nathanson, Copland, and Louis Lipstone.

54. See score (photocopy) in Copland's files for two versions of the "Prelude": Copland's original, dated "30 Nov 1948"; and one marked in pencil, "after my departure from Hollywood," with Copland's name crossed out and dated "22 January 1949." In fact, the version arranged after Copland left Hollywood segues to bar 26 of the original version, so both were used.

55. Copland, "Tip to Moviegoers: Take Off Those Ear-Muffs," *The New York Times Magazine*, 6 November 1949, pp. 28–32. See also Frederick W. Sternfeld, "Copland as Film Composer," *Musical Quarterly*, XXXVII:2 (April 1951), pp.161–75.

INTERLUDE II

1. See video interview, Jacob Druckman with Vivian Perlis, 16 July 1985, New York City. Segments of this interview can be seen on the documentary television production *Aaron Copland: A Self Portrait*, produced by Allan Miller, Ruth Leon, and Vivian Perlis, 1985).

2. For Copland at Tanglewood from 1940 through 1942, see *Copland: 1900 Through 1942*, Interlude IV, pp. 305–320, and pages 340, 364. For a history of Tanglewood, see Herbert Kupferberg. *Tanglewood* (New York: McGraw Hill, 1976).

3. During the war, the trustees of the Boston Symphony Orchestra and the Berkshire Music Festival board argued over control of Tanglewood; the Orchestra won. See Koussevitzky Collection, Library of Congress. In 1944, the festival consisted of a two-weekend, four-concert Mozart Festival with thirty members of the BSO, Dorothy Maynor soloist; in 1945, a three-weekend Bach and Mozart Festival with forty orchestra members, duo-pianists Abram Chasins and Constance Keene, pianists Alexander Brailowky, Alexander Borovsky, Robert Casadesus, and Lukas Foss.

4. See Copland's files for complete lists of students and faculty of the composition department from 1940–1965, with Copland's comments on his students, and lists of programs and activities. See Koussevitzky Collection, Library of Congress, and the Music Center files at Tanglewood for bound yearly reports.

5. Tuition in 1946 was $120 (up $20 since 1942).

6. Regulars at Tanglewood included Tod Perry (assistant to Boston Symphony manager George E. Judd and Koussevitzky's executive secretary, succeeding Margaret Grant), Leonard Burkat (librarian), Robert Shaw and Hugh Ross (choral music), Gregor Piatigorsky (chamber music with Ralph Berkowitz, accompanist), Irving Fine (harmonic analysis), and Olin Downes (lecturer on music criticism). Faculty for individual instrumental teaching were members of the BSO. Copland said, "Titles didn't mean too much. Everybody took care of his own classes and his own work."

7. Professional singers in the production were William Horne, Joseph Laderoute, Florence Manning, Frances Yeend. Two students, Mildred Miller and Phyllis Smith (later Curtin), later made impressive professional careers. *Peter Grimes*, commissioned by the Koussevitzky Music Foundation, had had its world premiere in London in 1945. (According to Leonard Burkat, Koussevitzky referred to Britten's opera as "Peter und Grimes.") Britten and stage director Eric Crozier came to assist director Max Graf at Tanglewood. Graf withdrew close to performance time to go to Hollywood, and Koussevitzky never invited him back. Graf's assistant, Boris Goldovsky, became director. Among Goldovsky's many successes at Tanglewood was the first American performance of Mozart's *Idomeneo, Re Di Creta* (1947). See Boris Goldovsky, *My Road to Opera* (Boston: Houghton Mifflin Company, 1979).

8. The Martinů–Lopatnikoff students were Sarah Cunningham, Earl George, George Hurst, Louis Lane, Hugh Mullins, Grace Schneck, Howard Shanet, and Vladimir Ussachevsky.

9. In addition to Orbón and Ginastera, Latin Americans at Tanglewood in 1946 included Roque Cordero (Panama), Jeanette Herzog (Argentina), Claudio Spies (Chile), Juan Orrego-Salas (Chile), and Hector Tosar (Uruguay).

10. Interview, Julián Orbón with William Owen for Perlis, 1 July 1981, New York City.

11. Interview, Alberto Ginastera (Aurora Ginastera translating) with William Owen for Perlis, 23 November 1981, New York City.

12. Administration: Copland, Perry, Burkat; Chapple was dean of students with Berkowitz assisting; Koussevitzky's conducting assistants were Bernstein, Carvalho, Burgin, and Chapple;

Primrose headed the chamber music program while Piatigorsky was on leave; Ross and Shaw supervised choral conducting and singing; Fine, harmonic analysis; Herford and Wolff, solfège.

13. Barber's students were Gordon Playman, Daniel Pinkham, Leon Ricklis, Ruth Wylie, Jack Fitzer, Samuel Beversdof, Jean Miller, and Howard Shanet.

14. Each of the three faculty lectured once a week for five weeks, ending with a panel discussion. See Copland's files for course outline.

15. The five departments of the Center were: I. Conducting (orchestral, choral and operatic); II. Orchestra and Chamber Music (including song repertoire); III. Composition; IV. Opera; V. Ensemble Playing and Choral Singing (including the Festival Chorus, Madrigal Group, and Small Choir).

16. In Copland's files is a manila folder, "Tanglewood Forums," with a typewritten list of topics through 1956 and handwritten outlines of each forum Copland moderated.

17. In 1947, total operating expenses were $24,548 for the Music Center; $137,780 for the Festival; $62,786 for building and maintenance; and $17,036 for cafeteria expenditures.

18. Interview, Leonard Burkat with Perlis, 11 May 1986, Danbury, Connecticut.

19. Interview, Tod Perry with Perlis, 4 August 1987, West Stockbridge, Massachusetts.

20. For descriptions of other Koussevitzky birthday presentations at Tanglewood, see interviews: Leonard Burkat, Lukas Foss and Howard Shanet.

21. Interview, Olga Koussevitzky with Perlis, Oral History, American Music, Yale University, 31 May 1977, New York City.

22. Interview, Ned Rorem with Perlis, 20 January 1987, New Haven, Connecticut. Revised by Rorem, August 1988.

23. When a gold watch was presented to Koussevitzky in Carnegie Hall at the end of the orchestra's spring tour (16 April 1949), he addressed the audience: "I know that all of you have not liked the new music I have played. But it was necessary to play it, for the good of the art and of the young new artists, the composers." A work had been commissioned from Copland for chorus and orchestra with text by Walt Whitman, but Copland could not compose it in time, and he wrote his apologies to Koussevitzky. A dinner was held at Symphony Hall with the orchestra players as guests; the program featured a "Cantata" composed by six Tanglewood alumni living in Boston. The dedication on the score reads: "For Serge Koussevitzky. 'In grato Jubilo, an Occasional Cantata' by Irving Fine, Daniel Pinkham, Gardner Read, Alan Sapp, Herbert Fromm [Paul Fromm's brother], Lukas Foss. The text by David McCord. Musical offering from the Boston Chapter of the Tanglewood Alumni Association composed for Dr. Koussevitzky and performed for the first time at the Testimonial Dinner in his honor upon the completion of his 25th season as conductor of the Boston Symphony Orchestra, Symphony Hall, 2 May." Phyllis Curtin was soprano soloist. Leonard Burkat organized the creation and performance of this work. A copy of the "Cantata" is in Verna Fine's collection of Irving Fine's papers. For Koussevitzky's response at the banquet, see Koussevitzky Collection, Library of Congress. The League of Composers gave a banquet at the Waldorf-Astoria, New York (10 May 1949). Claire Reis put together an album of composers' letters for presentation to Koussevitzky. Copland was host, Schuman spoke, and Koussevitzky conducted the Tanglewood Alumni String Orchestra. See Copland's files for list of invitees, the invitation, speech texts, program, and letters. See also Koussevitzky Collection, Library of Congress, for correspondence between Reis and Koussevitzky, typescript of Schuman talk, Blitzstein about excerpts from *Regina* (sung at the dinner), and seating list.

24. See Koussevitzky Collection, Library of Congress.

25. Ralph Berkowitz became Koussevitzky's executive assistant; Sarah Caldwell joined Goldovsky's staff as opera coach.

26. Darius Milhaud, *Notes sans musique* (Paris: Renée Juilliard, 1949).

27. In 1948, Milhaud's students were Olga Gratch, Robert Kurka, Hector Tosar, John Freeman, Bruce Howden, Lester Trimble, Arthur Frackenpohl, and Eugene Kurtz. Copland's students were Sidney Cox, Edward Lewis, Charles Strouse, Pia Sebastiani, William Flanagan, Robert Nagel, Herbert Brün, and Edino Krieger.

28. See video interview, Jacob Druckman with Perlis, July 1985, New York City.

29. See Koussevitzky Collection for letter from Messiaen (19 February 1949) agreeing to an interpreter, $1,000 fee and $360 expenses.

30. In 1949, Messiaen's students were Easley Blackwood, Harry Freedman, Sidney Palmer, Irving Mopper, Jean Catoire, Jack Fitzer, Lockrem Johnson, Carlos Riesco, Robert Turner, and Herman Berlinski.

31. The International Motion Picture Division (MPO), Hamilton McFadden, chief of the Department of State, made the arrangements with George Judd and Koussevitzky for a film for foreign distribution. It was directed by Larry Madison. Included are segments of Koussevitzky conducting the BSO and the Festival Chorus in a commissioned work by Randall Thompson, and Copland conducting the Department II (student) orchestra.

32. Interview, Arthur Berger with Perlis, 13 November 1981, Cambridge, Massachusetts.

33. Interview, Verna Fine with Perlis, 8 November 1987, New York City.

34. See Abram L. Sachar, "A Host at Last," *Atlantic Monthly Book Press* (XIII, 1976), pp. 145–49.

35. Considered for visiting composer had been Malipiero, Poulenc, Walton, Ibert, Kodály, Dallapiccola, and Boulanger (Boulez' name came up every year; he never accepted). Boulanger refused and Walton cabled Copland (6 January): SORRY IMPOSSIBLE WRITING. Ibert's students were F. Cook, Stanley Kregs, Kaljo Raid, Charles Schwartz, Forrest Suycott, Raymond Wilding-White, Robert Cantrick. Copland's students were Georgia Akst, Martin Boykan, Theodore Snyder, Gerald Kechley, Henrich Gandelman, Joseph Harnell, and Jacob Druckman.

36. Koussevitzky was greatly disturbed when the board of the Symphony invited Victor De Sabata as guest conductor without consulting him. See Koussevitzky Collection, Library of Congress, uncatalogued materials.

37. Copland's talk on Sessions can be found in Copland's files of lecture notes, #3. Other lectures on various subjects were given by Peter Gradenwitz, Arthur Mendel, Hans David, Lukas Foss, Julius Herford and Irving Fine.

38. Interview, Howard Shanet with Perlis.

39. For Copland's opening addresses in full, see Berkshire Music Center yearly reports.

40. Dallapiccola's students were James Francis Brown, Pierre Mercure, Raymond Wilding-White, Robert Pitton, Arnold Freed, Julia Perry, and Mimi Sandbank. Copland's students were Noel Farrand, Robert Parris, Bryan Dority, Norman Grossman, and Charles Schwartz.

41. See interview with Tod Perry.

42. For recordings of Koussevitzky's voice and for Copland about Koussevitzky, see Recorded Sound Research Center, Library of Congress.

AROUND THE WORLD/1949–1953

1. See travel diary #4.

2. Composers of the " 'new' Boulangerie" were Noel Lee, Bob Middleton, Lawrence Rosenthal, and Sarah Cunningham.

3. See interview, Alexei Haieff with Perlis, 8 October 1984, New York City.

4. For preparation of the organ arrangement, Carl Weinrich assisted Copland with the registrations.

5. The members of the New York String Quartet were Alexander Schneider, violin; Milton Katims, viola; Hermann Busch, violoncello; and Mieczyslaw Horszowski, piano.

6. For Copland on serialism, see Edward T. Cone, "Conversation with Aaron Copland," *Perspectives of New Music*, vol 6, no. 2 (Spring–Summer 1968), pp. 57–72.

7. See sketches of the *Quartet for Piano and Strings*, Copland Collection, Library of Congress. Also: ink score, 43 pp. signed at end: "Oct 20, 1950/Sneden's Landing, N.Y."; miscellaneous sketches and complete pencil sketch.

8. Copland's analysis here was written for the program notes of the Ojai Festival, May 1951.

9. See Recorded Sound Research Center, Library of Congress, for interview by Pierson Underwood with Copland the day following the premiere of the *Piano Quartet* during the Eleventh Coolidge Festival.

10. Arthur Berger, *Aaron Copland* (New York: Oxford University Press, 1953), pp. 83–85, and David Joseph Conté, "Aaron Copland's *Piano Quartet*—an Analysis," Master of Fine Arts thesis, Cornell University.

11. Virgil Thomson, "Music in Review," New York *Herald Tribune*, 11 September 1949, V 5.

12. The League of Composers program in honor of Copland featured the Juilliard and New York quartets, the Schola Cantorum, with Hugh Ross conducting and soloists Sara Carter, Winifred Cecil, Katharine Hansel, Julius Baker, Leonid Hambro, and David Oppenheim. The program included "As It Fell Upon a Day," *Sextet, Seven Songs from Twelve Poems of Emily Dickinson, Piano Quartet,* and *In The Beginning.* Program notes were by Arthur Berger.

13. Other programs in which Lawrence Morton programmed the *Piano Quartet:* 1956–1957 season, American Chamber Players with Ingolf Dahl; 1978 Monday Evening Concerts, the Sequoia Quartet with Charles Fierro.

14. Olin Downes, "Copland at 50," *The New York Times,* 29 October 1950, X 7; "Trailblazer from Brooklyn," *Time* magazine (20 November), pp.50–52; Robert Sabin, "Aaron Copland Reaches the Half Century Mark," *Musical America* LXX:13 (15 November 1950).

15. Lectures in late fall 1950 included Toronto Conservatory, Canadian Broadcasting Corporation, Brandeis University, and the New England Conservatory.

16. Copland, "The New 'School' of American Composers," *The New York Times Magazine,* 14 March 1949, pp. 18, 51–52; reprinted in *Copland on Music* (New York: Doubleday & Company, Inc. 1944), pp. 164–74.

17. In Copland's library is a copy of *Emily Dickinson Poems, First & Second Series,* edited by Mabel Loomis Todd and T. W. Higginson (Cleveland: The Living Library, The World Publishing Company, 1948). This is a reissue of the publication of the 1890s. Other of Copland's sources (Bianchi/Hampson primarily) are not among his books. In her thesis for a Master's degree, "Strange Company," from New York University (1988), p. 39, n.19, Helen Didriksen discusses Copland's text sources for the *Songs.*

18. For Emily Dickinson, see Richard B. Sewall, ed., *Emily Dickinson: A Collection of Critical Essays* (Englewood Cliffs: Prentice Hall, Inc., 1963).

19. Pencil sketches at the Library of Congress indicate various alternate orderings of the songs.

20. The first edition by Mabel Loomis Todd and Thomas Wentworth Higginson (1890) attempted to correct the unconventional aspects of Emily Dickinson's poetry. *The Dickinson Songs* predated a more reliable variorum edition by Thomas H. Johnson (1955). Copland used an edition by Martha Dickinson Bianchi and Alfred Leete Hampson (1914–1930), which did not change Dickinson's intentions as much as Todd and Wentworth; however, scholars maintain that it also contained errors and misreadings. In a symposium in Columbus, Ohio (5 May 1988), Dickinson scholar Daniel R. Barnes pointed out that Copland made minor changes in Dickinson's texts (for example, in "The Chariot," a stanza is missing and a line is changed).

21. See Copland, Library of Congress: other poems considered and rejected, among them "A Bird Came Down the Walk" and "Only a Shrine, but Mine"; five different prefinal versions of the piano introduction to the first song; pencil sketches; ink transparencies dated "April 10, 1949" with a list of the final ordering of the *Songs* and another showing their order of composition; a bound copy of the holograph of *Eight Poems.*

22. For musical analysis, see Robert Michael Daugherty, doctoral dissertation, part I, Ohio State University (1980).

23. Copland worked out transpositions for the traditional soprano voice. See Copland to Leo Smit (13 October 1960): "#3 up minor third; #4 up minor second; #7 up major second; #10 up minor third; #11 up major second; #12 up minor second."

24. Interview, Alice Howland with Perlis, 6 December 1988, New York City.

25. Ross Parmenter, "Columbia Begins Sixth Music Fete," *The New York Times,* 19 May 1950, p.31.

26. No specific reasons have been discovered for Copland's choices concerning the dedications. When asked, he said, "At the time, something about each song felt right for each person."

The dedicatees themselves had no further information when questioned by Didriksen.

27. William Flanagan, "American Songs: A Thin Crop," *Musical America*, LXXII:2 (February 1952), pp. 23, 130. See also Flanagan liner notes for Columbia Records.

28. Henry Cowell, "Current Chronicle," *Musical Quarterly*, XXXVI (July 1950), p.453.

29. Irving Fine, "Solo Songs," *Notes*, XI (December 1953), pp.159–60.

30. Robert Tear and Philip Ledger recorded the *Songs* for Argo. Other recordings were Adele Addison with Copland, re-release on Columbia Records with *Old American Songs* by William Warfield; also for Columbia, Martha Lipton (as a mezzo, she found it necessary to transcribe some of the songs); Mildred Miller for Columbia Records.

31. The eight orchestrated songs are "Nature," "Wind Like a Bugle," "The World Feels Dusty," "Heart We Will Forget Him," "Dear March, Come In," "Sleep Is Supposed to Be," "Going to Heaven!," and "The Chariot." The setting is for flute (piccolo), oboe, two clarinets, bassoon, horn, trumpet, trombone, harp, and strings.

32. Other singers associated with the *Dickinson Songs* are Nell Tangeman, Martha Lipton, and Meriel Dickinson.

33. Allan Miller, producer, "Lincoln Center Presents," WNDT Channel 13, New York City, 1964.

34. Interview, Phyllis Curtin with Perlis, 5 August 1986, Lenox, Massachusetts.

35. "Long Time Ago" was an anonymous blackface tune. The words were adapted by George Pope in 1837 and set to music by Charles Edward Horn.

36. See Paul Moor to Perlis, 29 December 1984, Peekskill, New York: "Aaron set 'I Bought Me a Cat' with Agnes de Mille's *Tragic Ground* in mind. His clapping obviously was connected in his mind with what he had expected the dancers to do in the show. The surprise came with the very last stanza when Aaron clapped three times, accenting the last clap to heighten the effect. I've always wished some singer would interpolate the hand claps."

37. The Pears/Britten recording was reissued by EMI in 1980.

38. "Ching-a-Ring Chaw" is number 17 in the Harris Collection of American Poetry and Players, Series of Old American Songs (1833). The title reads: "Ching-a-Ring Chaw or Sambo's 'Dress to He' Bred'rin." The description reads: "The hope that the republic [*sic*] of Haiti (1822–43) might prove the solution of the negro [*sic*] problem inspired this song, which combines jocularity and pathos in its appeal for emigration to the black paradise."

39. *Old American Songs I:* "The Boatsmen's Song," SATB and TTBB with baritone solo (Fine); "The Dodger," TTBB with baritone solo (Fine); "Long Time Ago," SSA (Straker), SATB (Fine); "Simple Gifts," SA or TB (Fine); "I Bought Me a Cat," SSA (Straker), SATB with tenor or soprano solos (Fine), TBB with TBB solo (Fine). *Old American Songs II:* "The Little Horses," SA, SA, TTBB (Wilding-White); "At the River," SA, SSA, SATB, TTBB (Wilding-White); "Ching-a-Ring Chaw," TTBB (Copland), SSAA, SATB (Fine).

40. Interview, William Warfield with Perlis (telephone), 8 February 1989.

41. Copland's income was $20,092 in 1949; $15,431 in 1950.

42. See interview with Robert Fizdale.

43. See interview, Leo Smit with Perlis, 29 January 1981, New York City.

44. See travel diary #7.

45. See lecture notes in Copland's files.

46. For a complete list of the performers and the works presented following each Norton Lecture, see Copland, *Music and Imagination*, "Programs," pp. 112–14.

47. Copland, *Music and Imagination* (Cambridge: Harvard University Press, 1952; paper, 9th printing, 1979).

48. One review was by Virgil Thomson, "A Composer's Universe," in the column "Music and Musicians," *Herald Tribune*, 12 October 1952, Section 4, p. 5.

49. The official appointment letter continued: "For your services the Boston Symphony Orchestra will pay you a salary of $1500. In addition the Orchestra will pay you an allowance of $360 for your living expenses in the Berkshires."

50. Copland, "Tanglewood's Future," *The New York Times*, 24 February 1952; reprinted in *Tempo*, no. 24 (Summer 1952), pp. 22–23.

51. Copland's students in 1952 were Edward Chudakoff, Halim El-Dabh, Roger Hollinrake, Yehoshua Lakner, Ben-Zion Orgad, Arno Safran, and Raymond Wilding-White; Dallapiccola's other students were Marshall Bialosky, Arnold Freed, Mimi Sandbank Maazel, Mayer Mandelbaum, Robert Pitton, and Ilhan Usmanbas.

52. Copland's three lectures were: "Variation Form"; "Functional Music I: Music for Films"; "Functional Music II: Music for Ballet, Radio and Theatre."

53. Ralph Berkowitz's title was changed to Dean of the Music Center; Piatigorsky was on leave due to illness, so for the first time, there was no separate chamber-music head.

INTERLUDE III

1. Irving Howe, *A Margin of Hope* (San Diego: Harcourt Brace Jovanovich, 1982), pp. 206, 213. See also Victor Navasky, *Naming Names* (New York: Penguin Books, 1981); Fred J. Cook, *The Nightmare Decade* (New York: Random House, 1971); Lillian Hellman, *Scoundrel Time* (Boston: Little, Brown and Co, 1976).

2. See interview, Harold Clurman with Perlis, 20 May 1979, New York City.

3. William Alexander, *Film on the Left: American Documentary Film from 1931 to 1941* (Princeton: Princeton University Press, 1981), p. 15.

4. See interview with Harold Clurman.

5. Koussevitzky was chairman of the American-Soviet Music Society; Betty Bean was executive secretary. Among the members were composers Bernstein, Blitzstein, Copland, Cowell, Gould, and Siegmeister. In 1947, Copland became chairman. See Eric A. Gordon, *Mark the Music: The Life and Work of Marc Blitzstein* (New York: St. Martin's Press, 1989).

6. See Claire R. Reis, *Composers, Conductors and Critics* (Detroit: Detroit Reprints in Music, 1974), pp. 143–46.

7. See interviews, Claire R. Reis with Perlis, Oral History, American Music, Yale University.

8. *Proceedings and Debates of the Eighty-third Congress, First Session*, Appendix, volume 99, part 9 (3 January 1953–23 March 1953), pp. 169–71.

9. Under the heading "Copland and Inaugural Concert, extension of remarks of Hon. Fred E. Busbey of Illinois in the House of Representatives, Friday, January 16, 1953." Also in *Daily Record*, vol. 99, part 9, pp. A 169–171.

10. See "To a Reader" (29 January 1953) and "To Ernst Bacon" (24 February 1953) in *Selected Letters of Virgil Thomson*, ed. Tim Page and Vanessa Weeks Page (New York: Summit Books, 1988), pp. 262, 266.

11. See Copland's files for pencil draft and typescript.

12. Telephone requests in October 1988 to the Eisenhower Archive in Abilene, Kansas, revealed no trace of Copland's letter to Eisenhower: The entire documentation of the inaugural ceremonies has disappeared or been removed. The Archive has no explanation. A draft copy of Copland's letter to Eisenhower is in Copland's files.

13. Vivian Perlis accepted the signed bill granting the Congressional Gold Medal to Copland at the Kennedy Center. It was presented by The Honorable Vic Fazio and Morton Gould, president of ASCAP.

14. See House of Representatives, Select Committee to Investigate Tax-exempt Foundations and Comparable Organizations, 11 December 1952. Transcript, pp. 17, 18.

15. In 1958, Oscar Cox drafted a bill, "The National Music Act." Its purpose was "to encourage the creation and understanding of serious music."

16. See stenographic transcript of *Hearings*, volume 88, which includes *Proceedings of the Committee on Government Operations*, U.S. Senate, Testimony of Aaron Copland, pp. 47–98.

17. See Clurman interview.

18. See Fred J. Cook, *The Nightmare Decade* (New York: Random House, 1971), particularly Chapter 18, "The Witch Hunt Continues," pp. 393–424.

19. See diary #3, Copland's files.

20. Correspondence between Cox and Copland and all materials relating to the hearing and its aftermath are in Copland's files.

21. See Harold Clurman, *All People Are Famous* (New York: Harcourt Brace Jovanovich, 1974), p. 133, for description of McCarthy's questions concerning Hanns Eisler.

22. See interview with Arthur Berger.

23. The correspondence between Copland and Kennedy, and Dean Marten ten Hoor and Dean J. H. Newman was sent to Perlis by Mrs. Gurney Kennedy, March 1988, along with a program of the 1967 festival and the degree citation.

24. See interview with Lukas Foss.

25. The Gold Medal from the American Academy and Institute of Arts and Letters was presented to Copland by Virgil Thomson.

26. See Andrew Porter's mention of "Copland's hilarious account" in *The New Yorker* (2 December 1985), p. 132.

THE TENDER LAND/1953–1954

1. Ingolf Dahl returned to direct the Tanglewood Study Group; Lukas Foss taught the analysis classes, and Irving Fine taught the third group of composition students.

2. In addition to Ichiyanagi, Copland's students were John (Jack) Brodbin Kennedy, Robert Cogan, Sarah Cunningham, Alvin Epstein, Norman Grossman, Arno Safran, and Joseph Weiss.

3. Arthur Berger, *Aaron Copland.*

4. Interview, Arthur Berger with Perlis, 13 November 1981, Cambridge, Massachusetts.

5. For a description of the Young Composers Group of 1932 of which Berger was an active member, see *Copland: 1900 Through 1942*, pp. 192–94.

6. See Copland, "La Forme Fatale," *Copland on Music*, p. 129.

7. For scripts and notes, see folder, "Opera Ideas," in Copland's files, which includes a copy of Robert Lowell's play *Benito Cereno*, sent by Lowell when he heard Copland was interested. The play was originally intended as an opera libretto.

8. Jerome Moross was second choice for the commission; Foss and Bernstein tied for third. Rodgers and Hammerstein had given similar awards to Leon Kirchner in 1950 and Irving Fine in 1951.

9. See Perlis for Claire Reis' copy of the piano-vocal score of *The Tender Land* autographed by Copland: "For Claire, the 'Prime Mover' of the opera/ Gratefully and Affectionately, Aaron/ March 1956."

10. Interview, Erik Johns with William Owen for Perlis, 3 November 1981, Mt. Carmel, New York. See also Erik Johns, *Center: A Magazine of the Performing Arts* (March 1954), pp. 14–26.

11. This information is derived from librettos belonging to Erik Johns. Also, see Library of Congress for a pencil sketch with the title *Picket Fence Horizon*, the dates "1952–54," and timings of each act at the end. Rough sketches contain various memoranda: p.14, "murder music," with "murder" crossed out and "rape" written above; p. 42, "opera ideas" listed; p. 47, a memo, "no. 198 Cecil Sharp"; p.275, "Way Down the Ohio" from *English Folk Songs from the Southern Appalachia."* Other rough sketches contain additional scenes that were added to the original after the first production. A piano-vocal score in the collection is dated "1952–53."

12. The recording of excerpts by Columbia Records is no longer available. The entire opera has not been recorded.

13. See Copland's *Old American Songs II* for arrangements of "Zion's Walls" and "Ching-a-Ring Chaw" that are closer to the original folk songs.

14. Copland found "I was Goin' Acourtin'" in *English Folk Songs from the Southern Appalachia*, collected by Cecil J. Sharp and Olive Dame Campbell, ed. Maud Karpeles (New York: Oxford University Press, 1932).

15. See also interviews, Harold Churman and Jerome Robbins with Perlis.

16. Arthur Berger, "On First Hearing Copland's 'Tender Land,'" *Center*, vol. I, no. 3 (April–May 1954), pp. 6–8.

17. The arrangement of the *Suite* for chorus and orchestra was first performed at "Tanglewood on Parade" (8 August 1957).

18. In 1958, the opera was produced at Northwestern School of Music and at the University of Minnesota, Copland directing; in 1962, the first British production took place in Cambridge, England, Philip Ledger conducting, Copland supervising.

19. Another television production was planned in 1969. According to the script in Copland's files, it was to involve Gower Champion, and the New York Philharmonic or the Chicago Symphony, perhaps with Frank Corsaro as director. Use of the music from the *Suite* (slightly changed) was made by Eugene Loring for a ballet by the Oakland Ballet in California in October 1978. It was conducted by Copland at the Paramount Theatre, Oakland.

20. See Vivian Perlis, "A New Chance for *The Tender Land,*" *The New York Times,* 26 April 1987, pp. 21, 32; and Perlis, "Aaron Copland and Opera," *Program Book,* Long Wharf Theatre (24 April–7 June 1987), pp. 30–35.

21. See interviews, Murry Sidlin and Arvin Brown with Perlis, April 1987, New Haven, Connecticut.

22. Leading performers in the Long Wharf production were Kristen Hurst-Hyde (Ma Moss), Jamie Louise Baer (Laurie), Bruce Kramer (Grandpa Moss), Craig Schulman (Martin), James Javore (Top), Rebecca Hanson and April Armstrong (Beth). David Bell was choreographer; Michael H. Yeargan set designer.

23. Copland was seated between Johns and Perlis (30 May 1987). The conversation reported here took place at that time.

NEW HORIZONS, NEW SOUNDS/1954–1957

1. The original manuscript of "Dirge in Woods" and two photocopies are at the Library of Congress, sent from the estate of Nadia Boulanger (June 1980). The title page reads "Words by G. Meredith/ music by Aaron Copland/ written especially in honor of Nadia Boulanger's fiftieth year of teaching."

2. In 1954, Jean Morel was acting head of the orchestral-conducting program assisted by Seymour Lipkin; Boris Goldovsky and Sara Caldwell were absent (Frederic Cohen was acting head of the opera department); George Judd retired at the end of the season and Tod Perry became Manager of the BSO. The concerts in the Shed formerly presented in the last three weeks of the Festival were spread out over six weeks, expanding these concerts from nine to twelve. The Bach-Mozart chamber-music concerts, formerly presented in the first three weeks of the season, were shifted to Friday evenings.

3. Other Copland students in 1954 were George Green, Stefan Grove, and Richard Maxfield.

4. "Let us now praise famous men, and our fathers that begat us" is from Ecclesiasticus 44:1. The words were used in a fourteenth-century poem, "Freedom," from "The Bruce" by John Barbour (1320–1395). In Copland's files are typed pages of the poem and one copy in Copland's hand (pencil), four verses in ink, pencil sketches for a choral work (1949) marked "incomplete," and the chorale from *Canticle* signed "Aaron Copland 1955."

5. For the revised *Canticle,* see pencil sketches, pencil score (reproduction), and final score in David Walker's hand, Library of Congress. The manuscript for the revised *Canticle of Freedom* bears the memo: "original version *not to be played,*" and "original pp. 1–77; rev. new pp. 1–20; then 33–70 of original."

6. See *The New York Times Magazine,* 13 March 1955, Pleasants, pp. 14, 57, 59; Copland, pp. 15, 60, 62.

7. See travel diary #5.

8. The judges were Frank Martin (Switzerland), Lennox Berkeley and Arthur Benjamin (England), Georges Auric (France), Andrze Panufnik (Poland), Necil Aknes (Turkey), Niles Viggo Bentzon (Denmark), Rodolfo Halffter (Spain), and Alexander Spitzmueller (Austria).

9. For a full description of the original *Symphonic Ode* and the revised version, see *Copland: 1900 Through 1942,* pp. 165–71.

10. For Virgil Thomson's presentation speech, see *Proceedings,* Second Series, no.7, American Academy and Institute of Arts and Letters.

11. Copland, "Our Music Isn't Obscure; Most of Its Curators Are," *The Washington Post,* 15 July 1956; Copland, "The Dilemma of Our Symphony Orchestras," *Musical Courier,* 1 November 1956, pp. 6, 39; Copland, "Report on American Music, 1956," the Associated Press.

12. According to David Walker, Copland decided to make all final copies of his scores himself when the Library of Congress informed him that appraisals would be lower for works copied by others.

13. Eleazar de Carvalho took Bernstein's place as head of orchestral conducting and the Department I orchestra, assisted by Lipkin; chamber music became a separate program again under Burgin and Kroll; High Ross was in charge of choral music, assisted by James Aliferis and Lorna Cooke de Varon; Goldovsky and twelve others ran the opera program, and Ingolf Dahl was back and in charge of the Tanglewood Study Group.

14. Copland's students in 1956 were Hector Campos-Parsi, Carlos Farinas, Thomas Putsche, Jr., Eino Juhani Rautavaara, Michael Sahl, José Serebrier, and Ramon Zupko.

15. The Fromm composers were Ben Weber, Alvin Epstein, Leland Smith, and Julián Orbón (the Epstein and Smith pieces were premieres). Other composers represented were Stravinsky, Britten, Schoenberg, Webern, de Falla, Petrassi, Barber, Milhaud, and Copland (*Vitebsk* was played by Burgin, Mayes, and Copland). Leonard Burkat handled the Fromm concert arrangements and David Walker assisted.

16. Pencil sketches for a choral work with a Whitman text, "Come, Heavenly Death," are in Copland's files.

17. This letter from Copland to Kapell was printed in the program book of the William Kapell Memorial Concert (26 October 1983, which took place at The Symphony Space, New York City), pp. 9, 10.

18. Copland, *"Fantasy for Piano,* Composer explains its particular problems," *The New York Times,* 20 October 1957, X 9, reprinted in *Tempo,* no. 46 (Winter 1958), pp. 13, 14. See also Arthur Berger, *"Piano Fantasy," Juilliard Review* (Winter, 1957–1958) and Merilyn Kae Hutchinson, *A Stylistic and Pianistic Evaluation of Aaron Copland's Piano Fantasy,* Master's Thesis, North Texas State University, Denton, 1968.

19. See the Library of Congress for holograph pencil score; ink score; 113 pages of rough pencil sketches with the title page inscribed "P. F. Piano Fantasy (1951–56 rough sketches)" and various dates on other pages (one dated "Nov 23 '49 for slow section"); a page marked "Plan (Elements) July '55," with the title "Fantasy: The Music Within (La Musica por dentr)"; 74 pages of a second pencil score that is sketchy at the end but inscribed "Apr 29 '56"; an ink score in a separate envelope with the title page inscribed "Piano Fantasy/Aaron Copland/(1955–57)" and on page two, "Commissioned by the Juilliard School of Music/William Schuman, President on the occasion of its fiftieth anniversary celebration/ and/ dedicated to the memory of William Kapell/finished Jan 19 '57/ duration 30 min."

20. Interview, William Masselos with Perlis, 3 November 1978, New York City, for the Steinway Project, Oral History, American Music, Yale University.

21. A recording of the Juilliard premiere is in Copland's files. It can be heard on tape at the Recorded Sound Research Center, Library of Congress.

22. See interview, Ned Rorem: "Morton Feldman booed from the balcony. That is a fact . . ." Rorem also described Masselos' performance of the *Piano Fantasy* at the 1983 tribute to Kapell:

Masselos was so nervous that he had a student who knew the piece in the wings. All these famous pianists came out and then Masselos made it out. You know how the *Fantasy* begins with an E flat? Masselos took his finger of his right hand and aimed it with the aid of his left hand and hit the note. Once he hit that note, I knew everything was going to be okay. He missed some notes, but I have never heard such piano playing in my life. He is no second Kapell, but he is a major pianist, eccentric as hell, but very big time.

23. Interview, Leo Smit with Perlis, 29 January 1981, New York City.

24. See the liner notes for *Complete Works for Solo Piano,* in which Leo Smit reads all of Copland's markings in the *Piano Fantasy.*

25. When the *Saturday Review of Literature* asked Copland for a list of books he particularly admired, Copland sent the following: *An Anthology of Contemporary American Poetry,* ed. Dudley Fitts; Christopher Isherwood, *Lions and Shadows; Journals of André Gide,* ed. Julian Huxley; Paul Collaer, *Darius Milhaud;* Truman Capote, *Other Voices, Other Rooms; Don Quixote de La Mancha* (Mexican edition: Editorial Seneca); Alfred Kinsey, *Sexual Behavior in the Human Male;* James Agee, *Let Us Now Praise Famous Men;* and Donald Friede, *The Mechanical Angel.*

INTERLUDE IV

1. Quoted from Virgil Thomson, "Copland as Great Man," *New York Herald Tribune,* 24 November 1946, p. 6.

2. The ink score of the early *Piano Sonata* is in Copland's "Juvenilia" file, Library of Congress.

3. One example of Copland's unusual use of piano in an orchestral score is in *Connotations* (1962), where big percussive chords, normally orchestrated for timpani or percussion instruments, are left to the piano.

4. John Kirkpatrick to Perlis, 3 September 1986, New Haven, Connecticut.

5. See Douglas Young, "The Piano Music," *Tempo* no. 95 (Winter 1970–1971), pp.15–22.

6. See interview with Harold Clurman.

7. Copland's *Piano Album* includes *Petit Portrait, Down a Country Lane, Midsummer Nocturne, In Evening Air, Piano Blues No. 1* and *No. 4, Saturday Night Waltz, Sentimental Melody, The Resting-Place on the Hill, The Young Pioneers,* and *Sunday Afternoon Music.*

8. See Copland's files for ink score copied by David Walker, xeroxed copies of original score (with the addition later of the title *Midsummer Nocturne*), and corrected proofs.

9. *In Evening Air* and *Night Thoughts* were recorded by Meriel and Peter Dickinson in *An American Anthology* (Unicorn).

10. See Copland's files for rough sketches, pencil version, ink score, and photocopies.

RUSSIA AND THE FAR EAST/1957–1960

1. For more on the 1957 performance of *Lincoln Portrait* in Venezuela, see *Copland: 1900 Through 1942,* p. 346.

2. Howard Taubman, "Composers of 9 Lands Aid Colleague," *The New York Times,* 26 March 1957, p. 35, and Taubman, "Lavish Festival," *The New York Times,* 24 March 1957, Section II, p. 7.

3. Copland conducted Purcell, *Three Fantasias;* Diamond, *Rounds;* Britten, *Serenade;* Grieg, *From Holberg's Time;* Haydn, *Symphony No. 95;* Fauré, *Pelléas & Mélisande Suite;* Stravinsky, *Suite No. 2;* Copland, *Clarinet Concerto* and *The Tender Land* (the dance, Act II and the finale, Act I).

4. The Brandeis Festival program included Copland's *Music for the Theatre, Appalachian Spring* (complete ballet), and *The Tender Land* (the dance, Act II and the finale, Act I).

5. The autograph full score for "The World of Nick Adams" is in the Music Division, the New York Public Library at Lincoln Center; photocopy in Copland's files. Also in Copland's files are a conducting score and pencil sketches of a piano version dated "10 Nov 1957."

6. For a full description of the *Orchestral Variations,* see *Copland: 1900 Through 1942,* pp. 183–84.

7. Copland's listings of monthly and yearly income are in his diaries. In 1957 his income was $53,799; in 1958 $63,000.

8. For Copland's memoir of this trip, see travel diary #6.

9. Copland, "Performers and New Music," *London Sunday Times,* 12 October 1958, p. 20, reprinted in *Copland on Music* as "Interpreters and New Music," pp. 261–65.

10. The lecture was adapted as an article: Copland, "The Pleasures of Music," *The Saturday Evening Post*, 4 July 1959, reprinted in *Adventures of the Mind*, ed. Richard Thruelsen and John Kobler (New York: Alfred A. Knopf, 1959), pp.190–205; translated German, 1961, reprinted in *Copland on Music*, pp. 23–51.

11. From interview, Jerome Robbins with Perlis. Approved by Robbins for publication in "Critics Mailbag," a response by Perlis to Jack Anderson, *The New York Times*, 19 November 1987, p. C 29.

12. See Copland's files for score, pencil sketches with indications for orchestration, photocopy of first version, photocopy of uncorrected copy (38 pages), and pencil revisions dated "Oct '62 new plan."

13. Copland's description here is drawn from his liner notes for the Columbia Records recording, LSO, Copland conducting.

14. The ballet's full title was *Dance Panels: Ballet in Seven Verses;* libretto and Epitaphs by Scott Burton, direction by Robert Mulligan; designed by John Braden. The ballet was first announced under the title "Greenwood." In Copland's files is a page indicating "New Plan for Ballet/TV version—18 min;" the television version was not realized.

15. For the recording, measures 8–14 were cut and slight changes made in the percussion ending of the fifth section.

16. See Arthur Berger, "What Mozart Didn't Have/ The Story of the Fromm Music Foundation," *Hi Fidelity*, vol. 9, no. 2 (February 1959), pp. 41–43, 126, 128. For description and list of commissioned works from 1952–1972, see Paul Fromm, *The Fromm Music Foundation, 20th Anniversary*, published by The Fromm Foundation. (The Foundation also supported the establishment of a new publication, *Perspectives of New Music;* the first issue was Fall 1962.)

17. Copland's students in 1957 were Egil Hovland, Pohlman Mallalieu, Joel Mandelbaum, Malcolm Peyton, José Serebrier, Gordon Sherwood, and Ramon Zupko. In 1958: Bruce Archibald, Asher Ben-Yohanan, Mario Davidovsky, Michael Kassler, Robert Lombardo, Joseph Lukewitzk, Thea Musgrave, and Rolv Berger Yttrehus. In 1959: Grant Beglarian, Wilson Coker, James Anderson, and Karl Korte.

18. Interview, Mario Davidovsky with William Owen for Perlis, 22 September 1981, New York City.

19. Eleazar de Carvalho and Seymour Lipkin, orchestra; Burgin and Kroll, chamber music; Ross and deVaron, choral music; Ludwig Zirner, followed by Jacob Avshalomov, the Tanglewood Study Group; Roger Voisin, solfège.

20. See Copland's files for minutes of full faculty meeting (6 July), and planning committee (20 July).

21. Interview, Lukas Foss with Perlis, 4 November 1986, New Haven. Also derived in part from a video interview for the television documentary, *Aaron Copland: A Self Portrait*, August 1985.

22. Bernstein conducted the New York Philharmonic in 1959 in Moscow, Leningrad, and Kiev. It was the first visit by a major American musical organization after the signing of the United States–Soviet Cultural Exchange Agreement of 1958. Bernstein visited Pasternak in Peredelkino and invited Mr. and Mrs. Pasternak to his concert the next evening. Surprisingly, they were allowed to attend and to speak to Bernstein backstage. See Hans N. Tuch, "A 'Nonperson' Named Boris Pasternak," *The New York Times*, 14 March 1987, p. 27.

23. See also article by Copland headed "Copland Finds Composers in Russia Cooperate," *New York Herald Tribune*, 8 May 1960, Section 4, p. 5, reprinted in *BSO Program Book* (October 1961).

24. For the trip to Russia and Japan, see Copland travel diary #6.

25. Copland conducted the London Symphony Orchestra in the Royal Festival Hall (19 April 1960): *Statements for Orchestra, Piano Concerto* (Julius Katchen, pianist), *First Symphony*, and *El Salón México.* He conducted the BBC Symphony in a broadcast of *Quiet City* and *Tender Land Suite* (23 April 1960).

26. Copland's students in 1960 were Nicholas Cappabianca, John Duffy, Karl Korte, David Loev, Robert McMahan, Ezra Sims, Timothy Thompson, and Cesar Tort.

27. Electronic equipment, consisting of an Ampex 300 stereo tape recorder and four groups of speakers (supplied by East Coast Company and the Concert Network, Boston) was placed, along with the necessary transformers and amplifiers, in trees on the lawn and adjoining the Main House. Berio manipulated the console from the Main House. The audience was encouraged to move about the lawns in order to hear the 360-degree perimeter of sound. Composers represented were Berio, Maderna, Boucourchliev, Varèse, Ussachevsky, Ligeti, and Stockhausen.

28. The Tanglewood Study Group was abandoned in favor of a "Listening and Analysis" program directed by G. Wallace Woodworth and Florence Dunn. Goldovsky produced one-act operas.

29. David Walker to Vivian Perlis.

30. Copies of the Fromm radio series tapes are at Oral History, American Music, Yale University.

31. Aaron Copland, *Copland on Music* (New York: Doubleday, 1963; paperback, New York: W. W. Norton & Company, 1963); in England (London: André Deutsch, 1962); reprinted in U.S. (New York: Da Capo Press, 1976).

32. Copland, "Nadia Boulanger: An Affectionate Portrait" was written for *Copland on Music* and appeared in advance in *Harper's Magazine* (October 1960), p. 49.

33. Performing were the Juilliard String Quartet, Jan DeGaetani, Stanley Drucker, Leonid Hambro, and Juilliard students.

34. Copland birthday concerts were held in Washington (Library of Congress), St. Louis, Rochester, and Los Angeles, where a Copland evening was organized at U.S.C. by West Coast friends Leo Smit, Lukas Foss, and Ingolf Dahl.

35. Eric Salzman, "Dean of Our Composers at Sixty," *The New York Times Magazine*, 13 November 1960, pp. 51, 61, 63–64, 66, 68.

36. Copland's description of *Nonet* is from his program notes written at the time of the work's premiere.

37. A recording of Copland rehearsing *Nonet* is at the Library of Congress, Recorded Sound Reference Center. It was taped before a concert in honor of Nadia Boulanger in 1977.

38. Eric Salzman and Paul Des Marais, "Aaron Copland's *Nonet*: Two Views," *Perspectives in New Music*, Fall 1962, pp. 172–179.

39. Stephen Plaistow, "Some Notes on Copland's *Nonet,*" *Tempo*, no. 64; (Spring 1963), pp. 6–11.

INTERLUDE V

1. John Kenneth Galbraith, *The Affluent Society* (New York: New American Library, 1958).

2. Eric F. Goldman, *The Tragedy of Lyndon Johnson* (New York: Alfred A. Knopf, 1969), Chapter Sixteen, "The President and the Intellectuals," pp. 418–75.

3. For family letters and photographs, some with Copland, see the Verna and Irving Fine archive at the Library of Congress. For tributes to Fine, including Copland's "A Composer's Praise," see Brandeis University newspaper, *The Justice*, 30 October 1962. Copland helped organize a committee to endow a studio at the MacDowell Colony, the "Fine Studio," in Irving Fine's memory.

4. Copland, "In Memory of Marc Blitzstein (1905–1964)," *Perspectives of New Music* (Spring/Summer 1964), pp. 6–7, reprinted in Blitzstein Memorial Program Book, see Copland's files.

5. Hans Heinsheimer, followed briefly by Betty Bean, was in charge early on. David Adams was president of Boosey & Hawkes in the United States until Stuart Pope replaced him in 1964, when Adams returned to London. Robert Holton was also associated with Copland's music at Boosey, as has been Robert Wharton, David Huntley (since 1976), and James M. Kendrick, president of the U.S. branch (since 1984).

6. Interview, Sylvia Goldstein with Perlis, 5 January 1989, New York City.

7. Interview, Stuart Pope with Perlis, 6 July 1988, New York City.

8. From a taped dialogue between Copland and Piston at the Recorded Sound Reference Center, Library of Congress.

9. See interview with Paul Moor.

10. See travel diary #6.

11. See travel diary #7.

12. See travel diary #8.

13. In 1961, the composition faculty included Roberto Gerhard, Wolfgang Fortner, and Lukas Foss. Copland had three students: Enrique Diaz, Michael Horvit, and Ben-Zion Orgad. In 1962, Iain Hamilton and Witold Lutoslawski taught composition. Ralph Berkowitz filled in as acting chairman of the faculty. For listings of yearly activities, faculty and students, see bound reports, Director's Office, Main House, Tanglewood, prepared at various times by Ralph Berkowitz, Leonard Burkat, Viola Aliferis, and Dan Gustin.

14. Interview, Harry Kraut with Perlis, 26 July 1987, New York City.

15. Fromm support was withdrawn for the Fromm Week at Tanglewood in 1983 and given to the Aspen Festival in 1985; the Fromm Foundation continued to support the Fellowship program at the Tanglewood Music Center.

16. Video interview, David Del Tredici with Perlis, August 1985 for *Aaron Copland: A Self Portrait:* also, interview with Mark Carrington, December 1981, for Oral History, American Music, Yale University.

17. Copland works performed in 1962: *Violin Sonata, Outdoor Overture* (students), *Quiet City* (BSO under Munch); 1963: *El Salón México, Music for the Theatre, Sextet* (Fromm Players), *Two Pieces for String Quartet* (Juilliard Quartet); 1964: "As It Fell Upon a Day," four *Dickinson Songs, Music for the Theatre* (students); 1965: *Music for a Great City* (BSO under Leinsdorf).

18. Eric Salzman, "Music," *Herald Tribune,* 23 August 1964, p.23.

19. The five pieces were "As It Fell Upon a Day," *Vitebsk, Sextet, In The Beginning,* and *The Piano Fantasy.*

20. See interview with Leonard Burkat. Among the composers present were Babbitt, Bernstein, Carter, Diamond, and Mennin.

21. Degrees received by Copland in the sixties were Harvard (1961); Syracuse, Michigan, Rhode Island (1964); Kalamazoo College (1965); Utah (1966); Jacksonville, Rutgers (1967); Fairfield (1968); Peabody Institute (1969).

22. Arnold Dobrin, *Aaron Copland: His Life and Times* (New York: Thomas Y. Crowell, 1967); and Catherine Owens Peare, *Aaron Copland: His Life* (New York: Holt, Rhinehart and Winston, 1969).

23. See interview with Paul Moor.

24. Bernstein to Perlis, 6 February 1989.

THE MUSIC WITHIN/1961–1969

1. The Copland text on *Something Wild* here is adapted from an unpublished article of December 1961, "Composing for *Something Wild.*" Also in Copland's files is a page with two measures marked "Violent/Apr 21 '47/ used in 'Something Wild'" and miscellaneous sketch pages. Materials at the Library of Congress include a reproduction of the conducting score with autograph pencil markings, complete piano score marked "short version" and dated "Apr–Sept 10, 1961," and cue sheets with timings.

2. "Notes on Making a Movie Score" in Copland journal #6 (March 1961) includes a listing of various scenes and a script with inserts of musical ideas and remarks about the score and film.

3. David Walker to Perlis.

4. Interview, Jack Garfein with Perlis, 7 May 1987, New York City.

5. Interview, Carroll Baker with Perlis (telephone), 10 June 1987.

6. See Copland's files for rough pencil sketches identified as "concert suite from *Something Wild.*"

7. Copland's description here of *Music for a Great City* derives from his program notes of 1964.

8. At the Library of Congress: rough pencil sketches dated "1961–62" that include a theme labeled "violent" and dated "Feb 10/60"; sketches of tone rows; a page marked "10/20/61 for

end/sudden entrance piano allegretto/violent"; and an open score sketch (complete) with titles on the verso dated "Sept 11, '62."

9. Other titles considered were *Chaconne for Orchestra* (on 3 four-voiced chords); *Connotations and Distillations; Pregnancies; Composition 'No. 80'; Chaconne on 3 four-voiced Chords; Symphonic Connotations;* and *Orchestral Connotations.*

10. The description here is quoted from Copland's program notes for the premiere. See also Peter Evans, "Copland on the Serial Road, An Analysis of *Connotations," Perspectives of New Music* ii/2 (Spring–Summer 1964), pp. 141–149, and Evans, "Copland's *Connotations,* a Review of the First Performance," *Tempo*, no. 64 (Spring 1963), pp. 30–33.

11. "Opening Night at Lincoln Center," broadcast from 9 to 11 P.M., produced by Robert Saudek and hosted by Alistair Cooke; intermission featured interviews with Governor Nelson Rockefeller and William Schuman, president of Lincoln Center.

12. For Copland letters to Virgil Thomson, see Beinecke Rare Book and Manuscript Library, Yale University.

13. See Copland's files: "rough sketches" dating in part from 1946 with pages that include marginalia and comments such as "firm, somewhat drugged," and working titles, *Composition for Band, Band Piece;* complete pencil score with orchestral markings signed "Aaron Copland/ Nov 1964" and title page, *"Chant/Emblems for Band";* original ink manuscript. See also uncatalogued materials at the Library of Congress: 42-page pencil score with title page, *"Piece for Band/Emblems for Band/* begun 8/24/64."

14. The Medal of Freedom had been initiated in wartime. In 1952, its scope was broadened to include civilian contributions to national security.

15. Copies of the television tapes are at WNET, Channel 13, New York City; audio tapes and transcripts are in Copland's files.

16. See Copland Collection for tape recording of the CBS "signature music."

17. Gerard Manley Hopkins, *The Letters of Gerard Manley Hopkins to Robert Bridges,* ed. Claude Colleer Abott (London: Oxford University Press, 1935, rev. 1955), p. 66.

18. See Copland's files: rough sketches (1963–1967); first complete sketch (1967); piano reduction (1967); final sketch with orchestral indications (1967). For analysis and description of source materials, see David Joseph Conté, "A Study of Aaron Copland's Sketches for *Inscape,"* dissertation, Cornell University, Ithaca, N.Y., 1983.

19. Other programs on which *Inscape* was included under Copland's direction: Musica Viva Concert by the San Francisco Symphony (15 June 1968); The National Symphony at Lincoln Center, New York City (16 February 1969); the New York Philharmonic in honor of Copland's seventieth birthday. The first performance in France was part of an all-Copland concert, the Orchestre National, Jean Martinon conducting. Chávez conducted *Inscape* at Cabrillo (1970), and Mehta conducted it during the Philharmonic's 1983–1984 season.

20. Interview, Phillip Ramey with Perlis, 10 November 1987, New York City.

21. Copland's agents in Europe were Robert Paterson as sole representative for Great Britain and Europe and Thea Dispeker for the choice of local managers in Europe.

22. See Copland's files for sketches toward the string quartet: two pages of tone rows dated "June '48"; a page from *The Tender Land,* Act III; two pages from "The World of Nick Adams"; a page titled "Folk Trilogy."

23. Copland, *The New Music: 1900–1960* (New York: W. W. Norton & Company [paperback], 1968). See *Copland: 1900 Through 1942* for comparison of *Our New Music* and the revision, pp. 315–17.

24. See travel diary #11. See also "Aaron Copland: A Visit to Israel," in *Boosey & Hawkes Newsletter,* vol. III, no. 2 (Spring 1969), p. 1.

25. The commission of $1,000 was offered by letter (19 May 1969).

26. See Copland's files for the original pencil score with indications for orchestration. The envelope is marked, in Copland's hand, "not to be published as is."

27. See Copland's files for pencil sketches, original full-orchestra pencil score, photocopy ink score.

28. See Copland's files for original piano manuscript, sketches dating from 1942 and 1944, and a photocopy of the orchestral score, marked "unedited copy."

INTERLUDE VI

1. See Paul Johnson, *Modern Times* (New York: Harper & Row, 1983), Chapter Eighteen, "America's Suicide Attempt," pp. 613–58.

2. See H. Wiley Hitchcock, *Music in the United States,* Third Edition (New Jersey: Prentice Hall, 1988), Chapter Twelve, "Our Pluralistic Post-Modern Era: Since the Mid-1970s," pp. 312–46.

3. See interview with Ned Rorem.

4. See interviews, Claire Reis with Perlis, Oral History, American Music, Yale University, 1976–1977, New York City.

5. Ned Rorem, "Copland's Birthday (at Seventy)," *Settling the Score* (New York: Harcourt Brace Jovanovich, 1988), pp. 21–24.

6. See Copland's files for seventieth birthday tribute book.

7. Copland's letters to Claire Reis are at the Music Division, the New York Public Library at Lincoln Center.

8. Orchestras conducted by Copland in 1970 were: Minneapolis, Toledo, Columbus, Chicago, St. Louis, Rochester, Interlochen, BSO, BMC, Cleveland, Los Angeles Philharmonic, Los Angeles Chamber Orchestra, BBC, Berlin, Bamberg, New York Philharmonic, and LSO.

9. Copland conducted the BSO (24 July): Busoni *(Rondo Arlechinesco);* Copland *(Dance Panels, Clarinet Concerto);* Schubert *(Symphony No. 5);* he conducted the BSO at "Tanglewood on Parade" (28 July): Bernstein *(Overture to Candide);* Tchaikovsky *(Romeo and Juliet);* and he led the Music Center Orchestra: Hindemith *(Metamorphosis on Weber);* Copland *(The Tender Land Suite).*

10. A sampling of seventieth birthday tributes: "The Kid from Brooklyn," *Newsweek* (23 November 1970); Donal Henahan, "He Made Composing Respectable Here," *The New York Times,* 8 November 1970; articles by Wilfred Mellers, Hugo Cole, and Norman Kay in a Copland birthday issue of *Tempo,* no. 95 (Winter 1970–71); Phillip Ramey in Boosey & Hawkes Newsletter (November 1970).

11. See travel diary #11.

12. Organizations Copland was actively working with in the early seventies included The American Academy of Arts and Letters (Copland was president from 1971–1974); The Pulitzer Prize Committee (chairman); The MacDowell Colony (president); and board member of American Music Center, Koussevitzky Music Foundation, Brandeis Committee, Naumburg Foundation (until 1973), Ives Society (1973–1978), American branch of the Aldeburgh Festival, and ASCAP.

13. See Harold Lawrence in *The LSO Diary* (October–November 1972).

14. Ellis Freedman to Perlis, 16 February 1989.

15. See Copland's files for notes toward an autobiography and letters from publishers Knopf, Harcourt Brace Jovanovich, and Braziller.

BREAKING NEW GROUND/1971–1979

1. The Institute for Studies in American Music, Brooklyn College, printed the salute on the cover of the *ISAM Newsletter,* Vol. X, no. 1 (November 1980) as a tribute to Copland on his eightieth birthday.

2. See *Duo* folder, Copland's files, for the list of supporters.

3. Also on the committee were John Knell and Kenton Terry.

4. See Edward Blakeman and John Solum, "William Kincaid (1895–1967) a Tribute," *Pan* (December 1987), pp. 4, 5.

5. For details on changes and suggestions, see *Duo* folder, Copland's files.

6. Several sketch pages, from which segments of *Duo* derive, are dated December 1943 and

are for a trio of clarinet, flute, and bassoon. Other pages dated 1944 and 1945 are for flute and piano.

7. Some other notable performances of *Duo* were by Jean-Pierre Rampal and Robert Veyron-Lacroix, Library of Congress (25 Feb 1972); Louise Ditullio and Ralph Grierson, West Coast premiere, Los Angeles Monday Evening Concerts (20 March 1972); Jayne Rosenfeld and Cheryl Selzer, Copland Retrospective, Performers' Committee for Twentieth Century Music (1974); John Solum and Ann Schein, Copland seventy-fifth birthday program, Library of Congress; Doriot Dwyer and Gilbert Kalish, fiftieth anniversary of Copland-Sessions Concerts, Tanglewood. Others who have performed *Duo:* Harvey Sollberger and Charles Wuorinen; Karl Kraber and Paul Jacobs; Paula Robison and Charles Wadsworth. The first movement of *Duo* was played at the Memorial Service for Harold Clurman (18 September 1980), Shubert Theatre, New York City, with Samuel Barron flutist.

8. From a telephone conversation, Elliott Carter to Perlis, 1 June 1989.

9. Copland noted on the manuscript, "A Spanish tune from Schindler." He was probably referring to Kurt Schindler, *Folk Music and Poetry of Spain and Portugal* (New York: Hispanic Institute in the United States, 1941).

10. For programs and schedules, see "Trips" and "Programs" in Copland's notebook (compiled by David Walker).

11. See letter from John Vinton in Copland Collection (14 January 1973): "I was very much disturbed to read that a piece of yours would be played . . . honoring Richard Nixon. Nothing I have ever read about you would lead me to believe that you want to support this man's actions."

12. Copland conducted the first half of the Carter inaugural concert; Robert Shaw the second half. Copland was responsible for "The Star Spangled Banner," *Fanfare for the Common Man,* Bernstein's *Overture to Candide,* Barber's *Essay No.1,* and *Rodeo.*

13. The Harvard Law School Forum was cosponsored by the music department; panel members were chosen by Arthur Berger.

14. The Ives Festival-Conference was coproduced by H. Wiley Hitchcock and Vivian Perlis and held in Brooklyn, New York City, and New Haven (17–21 October 1974). Barron and Copland performed at the opening event at the National Institute of Arts and Letters, New York City. Copland also appeared on a panel moderated by Gilbert Chase (18 October). See *An Ives Celebration,* edited by Hitchcock and Perlis (Urbana: University of Illinois Press, 1977), pp. 16–28.

15. See interview with Harry Kraut.

16. This paragraph and some other material in Copland's discussion of his conducting career are drawn from Aaron Copland and Leon Kirchner, "The Composer as Conductor and Performer," *The American Symphony Orchestra,* ed. Henry Swoboda (New York: Basic Books, 1967), pp. 75–89.

17. See conducting folders in Copland's files.

18. In Copland's files are lists of typical programs, such as: "Type A: *Statements, Our Town, El Salón México, Music for the Theatre, Appalachian Spring.* Or *Third Symphony, Quiet City, Old American Songs.*"

19. See correspondence of Vincent Plush to Perlis for description of Copland's visit to Australia. The concerts were not totally successful from a musical standpoint, but Copland's presence was greatly appreciated by musicians and audiences. See also Jill Sykes, "Exchanges with Aaron Copland," *The Sydney Morning Herald,* 18 March 1978, p. 16.

20. During Copland's seventy-fifth birthday and Bicentennial years, honorary degrees were received from Brooklyn College, Tulane, and Rochester universities; in 1979, from Catholic University; in 1976 and 1979, respectively, from two British schools, University of Leeds and York University.

21. Joining Copland at the Kennedy Center Honors were Verna Fine, David Del Tredici, Vivian and Sandy Perlis, and Copland's niece, Felice Copland Marlin.

22. An arrangement between Oral History, American Music, Yale University and the Oral History Research Office at Columbia University allows for transcripts of Copland's oral history to be available through both collections.

1. For Copland oral history interviews (1974–1976) and video interviews (1978) by Perlis, see Oral History, American Music, Yale University.

2. *Movement for String Quartet* was performed by the Alexander String Quartet at the press party for *Copland: 1900 Through 1942*, Amsterdam Gallery, the New York Public Library at Lincoln Center (18 October 1984); the public premiere was at Merkin Concert Hall in New York City (19 December 1985). The work is dedicated to Vivian Perlis.

3. Copland and Perlis, "Boulanger—20th Century Music Was Born in Her Classroom," and "Copland Salutes Boulanger," *The New York Times*, 22 September 1977, D 25–26.

4. Literary agent for Copland's autobiography is Robert Lantz and his associate Joy Harris; publisher for *Copland: 1900 Through 1942* was St. Martin's/Marek.

5. The Tanglewood program included: *Fanfare, El Salón México, Clarinet Concerto* (Harold Wright, soloist), *Suite from The Tender Land*, and *Four Dance Episodes from Rodeo*.

6. John Rockwell, "Music: Copland Conducts Copland at Tanglewood," *The New York Times*, 7 July 1980, C 11.

7. *Aaron Copland: A Self Portrait* was coproduced by Ruth Leon Productions, Music Project for Television (Allan Miller), and Vivian Perlis; Leon and Miller, directors; Perlis, writer and interviewer. Released by PBS as the first in the series "American Masters" (16 October 1985), as a Copland eighty-fifth birthday tribute.

8. Interview, David Walker with Vivian Perlis, October 1988, Weston, Connecticut.

9. The eightieth birthday celebration at Kennedy Center was edited for public television as "A Copland Celebration" and broadcast in the series, "Kennedy Center Tonight" (1 April 1981); Stephen Dick, writer; Hal Holbrook, narrator; Rodney Greenberg, director.

10. Events were co-ordinated by Toni Greenberg for Boosey & Hawkes.

11. The book of tributes is in Copland's files.

12. Leonard Silverstein, president of the National Symphony Orchestra board also spoke.

13. Among the many tributes in 1980: the New York Philharmonic performed *Symphonic Ode*, Copland conducting (18 January); The National Orchestral Association presented *Clarinet Concerto* and *Music for a Great City*, Copland conducting, Michael Webster clarinetist (5 February); The Chamber Music Society of Lincoln Center performed two concerts of *Nonet* and six choral works (31 October, 2 November); Brooklyn College featured The American Symphony Orchestra, Copland conducting the Oratorio Society of New York with soprano Linda Wall (9 November); The American Symphony at Carnegie Hall, Bernstein conducting all-Copland (9 November), with a festive party afterward at the Hampshire House; piano concerts by John Kozar in London and Leo Smit in New York (18 November); American Composers Orchestra played *Orchestral Variations*, Jorge Mester conducting (24 November).

14. See folder, "Europe, 1980," Copland's files.

15. Interview, William Conroy with Perlis, 26 March 1981, New York City.

16. The London program included *Fanfare, Appalachian Spring, Three Latin American Sketches, Clarinet Concerto*, and *Suite from The Tender Land*.

17. The Brussels program also included: *Quiet City, El Salón México, Clarinet Concerto*, and *Billy the Kid*.

18. Some special tributes to Copland in 1981: The New York Philharmonic, Bernstein conducting (*Appalachian Spring, Clarinet Concerto*, and *Dance Symphony* (29, 30, 31, January, 3 February); a Doctor of Humane Letters degree from Queens College and the renaming of the school as "The Aaron Copland School of Music" (2 June); *Stereo Review*'s 1981 Award of Merit (15 January); Century Association, "Musical evening honoring Copland, Luening and Schuman" (17 February); Da Capo Chamber Players, "Aaron Copland and His Friends," Carnegie Hall, included works by Del Tredici, Schuman, Carter, Berger, Thomson, and Fauré (16 March); Library of Congress, "A Copland Celebration," Coolidge Auditorium (14 November).

19. For Copland's conducting of *Appalachian Spring* in 1982, see Interlude I, pp. 57–58.

20. Among the Copland concerts and tributes of 1983 and 1984: American Chamber Orchestra, Charles Baker conducting an all-Copland program, Carnegie Hall (28 November 1983); Mayor Koch presentation of the New York City Seal of Recognition (15 November 1983);

Jan DeGaetani and Gilbert Kalish, premiere of an early Copland song, "Alone," at Carnegie Hall (4 December 1984).

21. The eighty-fifth birthday program by The New York Philharmonic included *Fanfare for the Common Man, Letter From Home, John Henry, Piano Concerto* (Bennett Lerner), *Proclamation for Orchestra* (orchestrated by Phillip Ramey), *Prairie Journal,* and *Symphony No. 1.*

22. Some highlights of the 1985 Copland year: Chicago Symphony performances of the *Third Symphony,* Leinsdorf conducting (March); "Meet the Moderns," Brooklyn Philharmonic in "Music by, for and about Aaron Copland," Foss conducting, Smit soloist in *Piano Concerto* (14 May); concerts by the Philadelphia, Atlanta, St. Louis symphonies; The National Chorale, Merkin Concert Hall (13 November); The American Symphony Orchestra in an all-Copland program, Gould conducting, Walter Cronkite narrating *Lincoln Portrait,* Madison Square Garden (13 November); the First Annual Paul Jacobs Memorial Lecture, Avery Fisher Hall, delivered by Perlis (6 November 1985).

23. *The Second Hurricane* ran from 13 November–1 December, Tazewell Thompson, director and choreographer; Charles Barker, conductor; David Walker, consultant; artist contributors to the sets: Willem de Kooning, Louise Nevelson, John Cage, Elaine de Kooning, Red Grooms, David Katz, Larry Rivers, and Rudy Burckhardt.

24. The six artists who could not attend the awards ceremony due to age or ill health were Marian Anderson, Frank Capra, Copland, Willem de Kooning, Eva Le Gallienne, and Lewis Mumford. Attending were Agnes de Mille, John Lomax, and Eudora Welty. The patrons honored were Dominique de Menil, Seymour H. Knox, and the Exxon Corporation.

25. A reception was hosted by the Equitable Life Assurance Society.

26. The season-long Copland tribute was planned and organized by Daniel Gustin, Richard Ortner, Costa Pilavachi, Oliver Knussen, and Vivian Perlis. In addition to the many performances of a wide range of Copland's music by the BSO and the faculty and fellows of the Music Center were some unusual events: the presentation of the score for the early ballet *Hear Ye! Hear Ye!* and "Skyline" from *Music for a Great City* by the Music Center orchestra under Knussen; and songs from the film *The North Star* (lyrics by Ira Gershwin) sung by Lisa Saffer. Highlights of this summer included the *Piano Variations* played by Gilbert Kalish, the *Piano Quartet* by Kalish and the Juilliard Quartet, and *Sextet* by members of the Boston Symphony Chamber Players. A lecture series presented by Steven Ledbetter and Vivian Perlis concluded with a panel discussion moderated by Ledbetter with Perlis, Lukas Foss, and Tod Perry.

Index

References in boldface indicate illustrative material.